Writings of Nichiren Shōnin

EDITORIAL ADVISOR
Dr. Hōyō Watanabe
Former President, Risshō University

PROJECT INITIATOR
Rev. Bungyō Yoshida
President, NOPPA

ENGLISH TRANSLATION COMMITTEE
Dr. Kyōtsū Hori
Former Professor, Tokyo Risshō Junior College for Women
Rev. Zenchō Kitagawa
Professor, Risshō University
Rev. Taikyō Yajima
Kōkokuji Temple, Tokyo
Rev. Keiryū Shima
Jikōji Temple, Tokyo
Rev. Chikō Ichikawa
Myōanji Temple, Tokyo
Rev. Ryōkō Mochizuki
Daikyōji Temple, Tokyo
Rev. Hōyū Maruyama
Sempukuji Temple, Kanagawa-ken
Rev. Kenryū Asai
Jōsen'in Temple, Tokyo
Rev. Shinkai Oikawa
Secretary-General, NOPPA
Rev. Gen'ichi Oikawa
Honryūji Temple, Hachiōji-shi, Tokyo

Writings of Nichiren Shōnin
VOLUME ONE

DOCTRINE I

Translated by Kyōtsū Hori
Edited by Jay Sakashita and Shinkyo Warner

Eighteen writings of Nichiren
included in the *Nichiren Shōnin Zenshū*
Complete Writings of Nichiren Shōnin
Volume I: Theology I
by Hōshō Komatsu
Tokyo, Shunjū-sha, 1992

Nichiren Shu Overseas Propagation Promotion Association
7–12–5 Nishishinjuku, Shinjuku-ku, Tokyo, Japan

日蓮宗
Nichiren Shu

© Copyright 2003, 2021
Nichiren Shu Overseas Propagation Promotion Association.
All rights reserved.
Printed in the United States of America.

ISBN 978-0-9719645-9-4

Art Direction and Design by Alan Rowe

Contents

Translator's Note *vii*

1. **Shugo Kokka-ron (ST 15)** *1*
   Treatise on Protecting the Nation
2. **Sainan Kōki Yurai (ST 20)** *75*
   The Cause of Misfortunes
3. **Sainan Taiji-shō (ST 21)** *82*
   Treatise on the Elimination of Calamities
4. **Risshō Ankoku-ron (ST 24)** *96*
   Treatise on Spreading Peace Throughout the Country by Establishing the True Dharma
5. **Ankoku-ron Soejō (ST 48)** *132*
   Covering Letter to the "Risshō Ankoku-ron"
6. **Ankoku-ron Gokanyurai (ST 49)** *134*
   The Reason for Submitting the "Risshō Ankoku-ron"
7. **Yadoya Nyūdō Sai-gojō (ST 51)** *139*
   Second Letter to Lay Priest Yadoya
8. **Ankoku-ron Okugaki (ST 69)** *141*
   Postscript to the "Risshō Ankoku-ron"
9. **Ko Saimyōji Nyūdō Kenzan Gosho (ST 71)** *143*
   Letter about Meeting the Late Lay Priest Saimyōji
10. **Kingo-dono Gohenji (ST 73)** *144*
    A Reply to Lord Ōta Jōmyō
11. **Ankoku-ron Sōjō (ST 108)** *147*
    A Letter Requesting the "Risshō Ankoku-ron"
12. **Musō Gosho (ST 111)** *148*
    Record of a Dream
13. **Kassen Zai-Genzen Gosho (ST 155)** *149*
    A War Right Under Your Nose
14. **Ken Risshō-i Shō (ST 156)** *150*
    A Tract Revealing the Gist of the "Risshō Ankoku-ron"

15. **Shinkoku-ō Gosho (ST 168)**   *154*
   Sovereigns of Our Divine Land
16. **Senji-shō (ST 181)**   *171*
   Selecting the Right Time
17. **Gōnin-jō Gohenji (ST 200)**   *229*
   Response to Gōnin's Letter
18. **Kangyō Hachiman-shō (ST 395)**   *232*
   Admonition of Bodhisattva Hachiman

    Glossary   *253*
    Japanese Equivalents   *319*
    Index   *327*

Translator's Note

This volume, the 10th project of the English Translation Committee of the Nichiren Shu Overseas Propagation Promotion Association (NOPPA), constitutes all 18 writings of Nichiren included in the *Nichiren Shōnin Zenshū, Complete Writings of Nichiren Shōnin*, Volume I: Theology 1 by Professor Hōshō Komatsu, published by Tokyo Shunjū-sha in 1992. Despite its all-inclusive title, the *Zenshū* includes only writings considered bibliographically authentic in light of modern scholarship. Among the printed texts, the most authoritative are considered those included in the *Shōwa Teihon Nichiren Shōnin Ibun, Writings of Nichiren Shōnin Standardized in the Shōwa Period*, compiled by the Risshō Daigaku Nichiren Kyōgaku Kenkyū-jo, Center for the Study of Nichiren Buddhism, in four volumes and published by the Kuonji Temple in 1952–59. In this collection of documents, abbreviated as ST, each writing is referred to by the title. However, occasionally two or more documents have exactly the same title, making it necessary for us to use the document numbers to identify them.

Most of the writings included in this volume have previously been published by NOPPA, but they were extensively rewritten for this edition to conform to the style of writing and the translator's interpretation of the modern Japanese text in the *Zenshū*.

The English Translation Committee of NOPPA made the following "Guidelines" for translators to follow:

(1) Translate more or less freely rather than word-by-word, making it easy for laymen to read.
(2) In transliterating foreign terms, the pronunciations of the language of its origin be used—those from Japan in Japanese pronunciation, those from China in Chinese pronunciation using the Wade-Giles System, and those from India in Sanskrit. Foreign terms not found in a collegiate dictionary are to be italicized and accompanied by macrons.
(3) Titles of sutras and names of Buddhas, bodhisattvas, etc. be translated into English as much as possible except those widely used.
(4) Footnotes be kept at a minimum.

(5) Mark words and phrases found in the glossary with asterisks.
(6) The introductory remarks for each writing be placed in front of each writing.
(7) Book titles, including titles of sutras be italicized.

We are grateful to have the help of Dr. Jay Sakashita, Instructor of Religion at the University of Hawaii, in editing and improving my writing. Finally but not least I am grateful to NOPPA members for continuing to support our project. We hope that this book will be helpful to those interested in Buddhism.

>With *gasshō*,
>Kyōtsū Hori
>September 2002

Shugo Kokka-ron (ST 15)

Introduction

Nichiren Shōnin (1222-1282) wrote the *Shugo Kokka-ron* in the first year of the Shōgen Period (1259) when he was 37 years old. The original manuscript, kept in the Kuonji Temple on Mt. Minobu, was destroyed in a fire in 1875.

Nichiren's purpose in writing this treatise was to criticize extensively the Pure Land teaching advocated by Hōnen (1133-1212) and make it clear that only the teaching of the *Lotus Sutra* offers salvation and ensures peace during the Latter Age of Degeneration, or *mappō*. Organizing the treatise into 16 parts over seven sections, Nichiren denounced Hōnen's *Collection of Passages on the Nembutsu* as an evil work that destroyed the True Dharma, and led people into hell while bringing calamities to the country. The *Shugo Kokka-ron* is Nichiren's only work with an introduction by Nichiren himself and discussion organized in sections and parts.

In the opening section, Nichiren explains that the teachings of the Buddha expounded in the sutras can be divided into two types, the provisional and the true, and that all sutras except the *Lotus Sutra* are expedient and provisional. The *Lotus Sutra* alone is the true and supreme sutra. In Section Two, Nichiren describes the rise and fall of Buddhism through the three ages after the death of Śākyamuni Buddha. These are the Age of the True Dharma, the Age of the Semblance Dharma, and the Latter Age of Degeneration. He maintains that the teaching of the *Lotus Sutra* is the most appropriate teaching for the Latter Age of Degeneration. In Section Three, Nichiren explains why the *Collection of Passages on the Nembutsu* is an evil work that abuses the True Dharma of Śākyamuni Buddha, citing passages from the work as evidence. Nichiren then cites a number of sutras in Section Four including the *Sutra of the Benevolent King*, the *Sutra of the Great Assembly*, the *Sutra of the Golden Splendor*, and the *Nirvana Sutra*, as proof that slanderers of the True Dharma must be dealt with appropriately. Nichiren argues that the king of a land must take responsibility for chastising slanderers of the True Dharma. Section Five explains the difficulty for those born in the Latter Age of Degeneration as human beings to meet both a "good friend," namely a dependable religious leader, and the True Dharma. In Section Six, Nichiren argues that those who believe in the *Lotus Sutra* and chant its title will attain the merit of not falling into the three evil realms: hell, the realm of hungry spirits, and that of beasts. Nichiren further explains that Japan is a land of Mahayana Buddhism and shares karmic ties to the *Lotus Sutra*. As such this *Sahā* World inhabited by believers of the *Lotus Sutra* is the true Pure Land. Section Seven describes the criticisms and accusations leveled by other Buddhist sects against believers in the *Lotus Sutra* and instructs believers how to deal with such accusations.

Compared to the Nichiren Lotus theology produced after Nichiren's exile to Sado, ideas and doctrinal positions stated in the *Shugo Kokka-ron* are not as developed. Examples include defining the True Dharma as the establishment of the "Lotus-Shingon," or claiming that the merit accrued by chanting the *Odaimoku* is "not falling into the three evil realms." Nevertheless, the *Treatise on Protecting the Nation* is an important writing representing early doctrines of Nichiren.

Treatise on Protecting the Nation

Prologue

Upon reflection, I consider myself fortunate to have been born in the *Sahā*, human World* in Japan and to have unexpectedly escaped the three evil realms.* For our chances of being born in the evil realms are as numerous as the number of dust particles in all the worlds of the universe while our chances of being born in the human realm are as small as the amount of soil on a fingernail.* This being said, there is no doubt that in my future lives I will forfeit the rare opportunity of being born a human in Japan to be reborn in the three evil realms.

The causes for human beings falling into evil realms after death vary. They go to evil realms, such as hell, for sinful acts committed for the sake of family and relatives. They go for the grave crime of killing living beings and other brutal acts. They go as national rulers for the sin of neglecting the sorrows of the people. They go for taking refuge in depraved teachings without knowing the right or wrong of the various Buddha Dharmas. Or they go for being encouraged by wicked teachers. Of those mentioned, even the uninformed are able to discriminate right from wrong when it comes to the morals of daily affairs. It is not easy, however, even for enlightened sages, to distinguish true from false dharmas and teachers. How much more difficult it is for us, ordinary men* in the Latter Age!

Ever since Śākyamuni Buddha passed away in India and His teaching spread to China, the light of wisdom exalted by commentators who guided people as Four Reliances* in India, daily lost its luster and the stream of Buddhism in China transmitted by *tripiṭaka* masters* grew polluted month by month. Commentators* in India, who misinterpreted the true sutra,* covered the moon of truth with clouds of illusion. All the while translators, who attached themselves to provisional sutras,* changed the jade of the true sutras into the worthless rocks of provisional sutras. How can there then be no errors in the sectarian doctrines established by Chinese teachers* who depended on those misinterpreted sutras? How much more so in the remote land of Japan, where Buddhist scholars have been guided by the Chinese! There must be more mistakes and less truth in the Buddhist schools of Japan than in China. Accordingly those who study such schools are as numerous as the number of dragon scales, while those who attain Buddhahood are as scarce as those who gain the giraffe's horns. This is because most either practice provisional teachings, or seek refuge in teachings unsuitable to the time and capacity of people in the Latter Age of Degeneration, or blindly practice a teaching without knowing whether it is taught by an ignorant teacher or a sage. Many also practice both provisional and true teachings at the same time without knowing the difference between the two. Or they practice only the provisional teaching, misinterpreting it for the true teaching. Or with conceit they consider themselves to have reached higher stages of practice. As a result ignorant people routinely study and practice Buddhism in order to be free of the chain of birth and death but instead they are accumulating karma causing themselves to be stuck in the chain.

About 50 years ago a crafty monk wrote a book entitled the *Collection of Passages on the Nembutsu and the Original Vow*,* in which he maligned the doctrines of all Buddhist schools by advocating, for ignorant people in the Latter Age, only the practice of the *nembutsu*, the calling of the name of the Buddha of Infinite Life. In the name of the three Chinese masters, T'an-luan, Tao-ch'o, and Shan-tao, he divided all the Buddhist scriptures into two parts: the Holy Way Gate and Pure Land Gate. As a result, provisional sutras were substituted for the true ones, thereby closing the direct road to Buddhahood of Lotus-Shingon Buddhism* leading to Buddhahood and opening instead the narrow and steep way of the triple Pure Land sutras.*

However, since provisional sutras were in fact preached to prepare people for the true sutras, to choose the former and discard the latter is also against the true intent of the triple Pure Land sutras. This is an act of slandering* both the true as well as provisional sutras. It is an evil teaching that will forever prevent people from reaching the level of the four holy ones:* Buddhas, bodhisattvas, *pratyekabuddha* and *śrāvaka*. It will also cause all of them to fall to the depth of the Hell of Incessant Suffering. Nevertheless, the public at large follows this teaching just like twigs are swayed by strong winds, and his disciples revere this crafty monk just as gods revere Indra.*

Many books have been written with the aim of refuting this evil doctrine, such as *Deciding the Meaning of the Pure Land*,* *Denouncing the Collection of Passages on the Nembutsu*,* and *Refuting the Evil Dharma*.* Although the authors of these books are all well-known Buddhist monks of high virtue, they have not thoroughly revealed the fundamental reason why the *Collection of Passages on the Nembutsu* discredits the True Dharma. Contrary to their intention, therefore, they only helped to propagate the book. They are like a light drizzle during a severe drought, that helps to kill trees and grasses instead of reviving them, or like cowardly soldiers placed in the front line of a battle, who only serve to encourage a powerful enemy.

This was so disturbing to me that I wrote this work entitled *Treatise on Protecting the Nation* to clearly explain why the *Collection of Passages on the Nembutsu* denigrates the True Dharma. I hope that all people, clergy and laity alike, will make use of this work, ignoring the mundane to plant the seedling of merit for aeons to come. Now I would like to examine whether the dharma expounded in the *Collection of Passages on the Nembutsu* is true or false according to the Buddha's sutras and their interpretations by bodhisattvas. I will leave it entirely up to the Buddha whether those who read this treatise will put faith in it or call it slander. I will not insist on my own opinion.

I will divide this treatise into seven sections. In the first section, I will try to make it clear that the teachings of the Buddha should be divided into two: the true and the provisional. The second section will cover the rise and fall of Buddhism in the Ages of the True, Semblance and Latter Dharmas* after the death of Śākyamuni Buddha. The third section will expound on why it is correct to characterize the *Collection of Passages on the Nembutsu* as maligning the True Dharma. In the fourth section, we will see what the sutras say about slanderers of the True Dharma and how they should be dealt with. In the fifth section, I will show how difficult it is to encounter a "good friend"* and the True Dharma, while in the sixth section I will discuss the cautions that those who practice the *Lotus* and *Nirvana Sutras* should bear in mind. In the seventh section, I will answer questions that pertain to the above.

SECTION I
True and Provisional Teachings

In this first section, I shall try to explain why the teachings of the Buddha should be divided into the true and provisional teachings. This section will be subdivided into four parts: the first part will clarify the order in which major sutras and their branch sutras were preached. The second part will show the comparative depth in doctrine among various sutras. The third part will distinguish Mahayana from Hinayana teachings. And finally the fourth part will explain why the provisional teachings should be discarded in favor of the true teachings.

Part 1: The Preaching Order of Major Sutras

To start, I shall make clear the order in which major sutras and their branch sutras were preached.

Question: Which sutra was first preached by the Buddha?

Answer: The *Flower Garland Sutra.**

Question: Is there proof for this?

Answer: Yes, there certainly is. The Seken Jōgen chapter of the 60-fascicle *Flower Garland Sutra* states, "This is what I heard. At the time the Buddha attained Perfect Enlightenment for the first time at the Hall of Enlightenment* in the Magadha Kingdom.*" This statement proves that this sutra was preached under the *bodhi* tree where Śākyamuni Buddha had attained Buddhahood.

Moreover, it is stated in the first Introductory chapter* of the *Lotus Sutra* that when the Buddha showed a potent omen of emitting a ray of light* from the white curls between His eyebrows, Bodhisattva Maitreya* saw Buddhas of the numerous worlds in the universe expound major sutras in five periods.* He then asked Bodhisattva Mañjuśrī* what this all meant: "The Buddhas, Saintly Masters, the Lion-like Ones, expounded the most wonderful sutra. I also saw them teaching many billions of bodhisattvas with pure and gentle voices." This indicates that the first preaching of the Buddha was the *Flower Garland Sutra* for bodhisattvas.[1] Also, in the Expedients chapter* of the *Lotus Sutra* the Buddha refers to His experience upon attaining enlightenment stating, "Sitting under a *bodhi* tree for the first time, I meditated on the tree, strolled about…then various heavenly beings such as the King of the Brahma Heaven,* Indra, the Four Heavenly Kings* who protect the world, Great Freedom God* and billions of their retainers respectfully held their hands in *gasshō*, bowed and requested Me to preach.*" This passage from the *Lotus Sutra* indicates when the *Flower Garland Sutra* was preached. Hence the first fascicle of the *Flower Garland Sutra* includes such names as Vaiśravaṇa,* moon god, sun god, Indra, King of the Brahma Heaven, and Great Freedom God, all of whom attended the assembly of the *Flower Garland Sutra*.[2]

Regarding when the *Flower Garland Sutra* was preached, fascicle 27 of the *Nirvana Sutra** states:

"Upon attainment of Buddhahood by the Buddha, the King of the Brahma Heaven requested Him to preach saying, 'Buddha, please open wide for the people the gate to the dharma, which is as delicious as nectar....' The King of the Brahma Heaven pleaded with the Buddha again, 'All the people can be divided into three groups—the wise, mediocre, and slow. Of the three, the wise will be able to understand Your teaching. Please preach the dharma for them.' The Buddha then declared, 'Listen carefully, King of the Brahma Heaven! I now will open the gate to the Buddha Dharma for all people.'"

Considering when the *Flower Garland Sutra* was preached, fascicle 33 of the *Nirvana Sutra*, also states, "It was the same as what I had already expounded in detail for the various bodhisattvas in the past regarding the meanings and reasons of all Mahayana sutras among the twelve kinds of scriptures.*" These statements prove that when Buddhas appeared in the world to preach all the scriptures of Buddhism, they necessarily began with the *Flower Garland Sutra*.[3]

Question: The *Sutra of Infinite Meaning* declares, "The Four Noble Truths* in the Hinayana sutras were preached at the beginning...which were followed by Hōdō sutras, the *Wisdom Sutra*, and the ocean-imprint meditation of the *Flower Garland Sutra*.*" According to this, the *Flower Garland Sutra* was expounded after the *Wisdom Sutra*.

How do you respond to this discrepancy?

Answer: I believe the above list of teachings was preached not in chronological order but according to the order of profundity in doctrine. On the other hand, if it was preached in chronological order, placing the *Flower Garland Sutra* after the *Wisdom Sutra* may be due to the latter part of the *Flower Garland Sutra* that was expounded after the first part of the sutra was preached by the Buddha during the first three weeks upon attaining Buddhahood. The Expedients chapter of the *Lotus Sutra* lists the lifetime teachings of the Buddha according to the profundity in doctrine, "There is no other teaching except the *Lotus Sutra*, neither the *Flower Garland Sutra* nor the *Wisdom Sutra* and the Hōdō sutras."

Question: What sutras were preached following the *Flower Garland Sutra*?

Answer: Āgama, that is Hinayana sutras* were preached following the *Flower Garland Sutra*.

Question: How do you know this?

Answer: Regarding what sutras were preached after the *Flower Garland Sutra*, the Introductory chapter of the *Lotus Sutra* states, "To those who suffer, and hate old age, sickness and death, the Buddha preaches the teaching of Nirvana,* showing ignorant people the way to tranquility and extinction of worldly passions." In the Expedients chapter of the same sutra, it states, "The Buddha went to Deer Park in Bārāṇasī Kingdom*... and preached the dharma to five monks."* It is also stated in the *Nirvana Sutra,* "The Buddha preached on the Middle Way in the Deer Park of the Bārāṇasī Kingdom." This indicates what sutras were preached after the *Flower Garland Sutra.* According to these scriptural statements, it seems clear that the Āgama sutras for *śrāvaka* disciples were expounded after the *Flower Garland Sutra* for great bodhisattvas.

Question: What sutras were expounded following the Āgama sutras?

Answer: The Hōdō sutras.*

Question: How do you know this?

Answer: It is stated in the *Sutra of Infinite Meaning,* "At the beginning, the teaching of the Four Noble Truths was preached in Āgama sutras ... the Hōdō sutras were preached next." The *Nirvana Sutra* also states, "The Hōdō sutras were preached after the Āgama sutras."

Question: Mahayana is an Indian term meaning Hōdō in Chinese and Japanese. The *Flower Garland, Wisdom, Lotus* and *Nirvana Sutras* all belong to the Mahayana Hōdō sutras. Why do you then call only those sutras preached in the Hōdō period[3a] the Hōdō sutras?

Answer: In fact, not just sutras of the Hōdō period are considered Hōdō sutras. Such Mahayana sutras as the *Flower Garland, Wisdom,* and *Lotus* also belong to this category. Nevertheless, there are clear reasons why only those teachings preached during the Hōdō period are called Hōdō sutras. Precedents for this can clearly be found in the *Sutra of Infinite Meaning* and the *Nirvana Sutra.* The enlightenment preached in the Āgama sutras is strictly of the Hinayana teaching. The Buddha then preached the Mahayana teachings beginning with the Hōdō sutras. The teachings from the Hōdō sutras onward then are all considered Mahayana. However, since the teachings in the Hōdō sutras are the beginning of the Mahayana teachings, they are called Hōdō to distinguish these teachings from those preached afterwards. For instance, when the *Verses on the Treasury of Abhidharma* analyzes cognition into 18 elements,* although only 10 and a half of the 18 are of matter, while the remaining seven and a half elements are of mind, they are called realms of matter because they begin with matter.

Question: Which sutra was preached following the Hōdō sutras?

Answer: The *Wisdom Sutra.**

Question: How do you know this?

Answer: The *Nirvana Sutra* states that the *Wisdom Sutra* was preached after the Hōdō sutras.

Question: Which sutra was preached after the *Wisdom Sutra*?

Answer: The *Sutra of Infinite Meaning.**

Question: What evidence do you have to support this?

Answer: The conclusion of the *Wisdom Sutra*, the *Sutra of the Benevolent King*,* states that this teaching was preached "in the 29th year" since the Buddha began preaching the *Wisdom Sutra*. As the Buddha had spent 12 years preaching the Āgama sutras, it was in the 42nd year of His preaching when He finished preaching the *Wisdom Sutra*. And the *Sutra of Infinite Meaning* declares, "The truth had not been revealed for 40 years or so* since His attainment of Buddhahood."

Question: According to the statement in the *Sutra of Infinite Meaning* cited earlier, the *Wisdom Sutra* was followed by the *Flower Garland Sutra*. Yet according to the *Nirvana Sutra*, the *Wisdom Sutra* was followed by the *Nirvana Sutra*. However, you now state that the *Wisdom Sutra* was followed by the *Sutra of Infinite Meaning*. How can these discrepancies be explained?

Answer: The 14th fascicle of the *Nirvana Sutra* enumerates sutras that were expounded before the *Nirvana Sutra* in order to make doctrinal comparisons with them. However, the *Lotus Sutra* is omitted from this list since it includes only those up to the *Wisdom Sutra*. Yet the ninth fascicle of the *Nirvana Sutra* makes it clear that the *Lotus Sutra* was preached before the *Nirvana Sutra* as it mentions the "800 śrāvaka in the *Lotus Sutra*." According to the Introductory chapter of the *Lotus Sutra*, moreover, the *Sutra of Infinite Meaning* is the preface* to the *Lotus Sutra*. Namely, it is stated in this first chapter that Mañjuśrī, in answering Maitreya, said that Sun-Moon-Light Buddha in the past had preached the *Lotus Sutra* following the *Sutra of Infinite Meaning*, and that it would be the same this time. Although the *Sutra of Infinite Meaning* enumerates the *Flower Garland Sutra* after the *Wisdom Sutra*, as stated earlier, the *Flower Garland Sutra* was preached first of all. Therefore, that which was preached after the *Wisdom Sutra* is the *Sutra of Infinite Meaning*.

Question: What sutra was preached after the *Sutra of Infinite Meaning*?

Answer: That was the *Lotus Sutra.**

Question: What proof do you have to support this?

Answer: The Introductory chapter of the *Lotus Sutra* states, "The Buddha preached a Mahayana sutra entitled Infinite Meaning, the dharma to instruct bodhisattvas, which had been upheld by the Buddhas. When He had finished preaching the sutra, He sat crosslegged and began meditating on the ultimate reality of all phenomena in order to preach the *Lotus Sutra.*"

Question: Which sutra was preached right after the *Lotus Sutra?*

Answer: The *Sutra of Meditation on Universal-Sage Bodhisattva.**

Question: How do you know this?

Answer: Defining when it was preached, the Buddha declared in the sutra,"I shall enter Nirvana in three months time.... I have already preached extensively the One Vehicle True Way on Mt. Sacred Eagle and in other places. I will now preach it here in the Great Forest Monastery."

Question: Which sutra was preached after the *Sutra of Meditation on Universal-Sage Bodhisattva?*

Answer: The *Nirvana Sutra.*

Question: How do you know this?

Answer: It is stated in the *Sutra of Meditation on Universal-Sage Bodhisattva,* "I, the Buddha, shall enter Nirvana in three months time."[4] Also found in fascicle 30 of the *Nirvana Sutra* are the passages "Why will the Buddha enter Nirvana in the second month?" and "The Buddha's dates of birth, renouncement of His family, attaining enlightenment and His first preaching were all on the eighth day. Why will His day for entering Nirvana alone be the 15th?"

Generally speaking major sutras of Buddhist scriptures were preached in the order stated above. However, various sutras beside these, Mahayana as well as Hinayana, do not agree regarding the time when they were preached. Some maintain that the *Flower Garland Sutra* was preached after the Āgama sutras were, while others insist that the Hōdō and Hannya sutras were expounded after the *Lotus Sutra* was. These sutras, though not known when they were preached, should be put in one of the five periods according to the similarity in doctrine.

Part 2: Comparative Profundity in Doctrine

Secondly, I shall make clear the comparative profundity in doctrine among various sutras. It is stated in the *Sutra of Infinite Meaning*: "At the beginning, the teaching of the Four Noble Truths was preached in the Āgama sutras. Next, doctrines of roundabout ways to Buddhahood* requiring long term practice for attainment of enlightenment were explained through preaching of the Hōdō sutras, the *Great Wisdom Sutra* and the ocean-imprint meditation of the *Flower Garland Sutra.*" The sutra also states: "The truth has not been revealed for 40 years or so" and "The *Sutra of Infinite Meaning* is supreme of all the sutras." According to these statements there is no doubt that those sutras expounded during the 40 years or so before the *Sutra of Infinite Meaning* are inferior.

Question: The *Sutra of the Pure Land of Mystic Glorification* states that it is "supreme of all the Buddhist scriptures." The *Great Cloud Sutra* claims to be the Wheel-turning Noble King* of sutras whereas the *Sutra of the Golden Splendor** says of itself to be the king of sutras. From these statements we can see that it is customary for Mahayana sutras to claim they are supreme. How can you then say from only one passage in the *Sutra of Infinite Meaning* that it is superior to all those sutras preached in the 40 years or so before it?

Answer: When Lord Śākyamuni Buddha preaches in each sutra that it is the supreme sutra, we cannot distinguish between Mahayana and Hinayana sutras or between provisional and true sutras. If sectarian people merely talk about the differences among the various sutras and compare the profundity of their doctrines when no actual differences exist, it will be not only the source of controversy but also cause the evil karma of slandering the True Dharma.

When those sutras preached during the 42 years of the pre-*Lotus* period* claim that they are the prime sutras, however, they are not comparing themselves with the definitive sutra. Some sutras claim to be supreme in comparison to Hinayana sutras. Others claim to be first because their Buddhas have the Reward Body, enjoying eternal longevity instead of 80 years of life. Still others say that theirs are first merely because they explain completely the triple truth:* the truth of the temporal, the void, and the middle. They do not claim to be first of all the Buddhist scriptures. On the contrary, this *Sutra of Infinite Meaning* states that it is the prime sutra of all the sutras preached in 40 years or so before it was preached.

Question: Which is superior, the *Lotus Sutra* or the *Sutra of Infinite Meaning*?

Answer: The *Lotus Sutra*.

Question: How do you know this?

Answer: The *Sutra of Infinite Meaning* reveals neither the possibility of obtaining Buddhahood by Two Vehicles*, the two categories of Hinayana saints, *śrāvaka* and *pratyekabuddha*, nor the attaining of Enlightenment by Śākyamuni Buddha in the eternal past. Therefore, in The Teacher of the Dharma chapter of the *Lotus Sutra*, when it is claimed that the *Lotus Sutra* is superior to all the sutras, those already preached, now being preached and yet to be preached,* the *Sutra of Infinite Meaning* is included among those being now preached.* This makes it clear and so easy both to understand and to have faith that it actually is less truthful than the *Lotus Sutra*.

Question: Which is superior, the *Lotus Sutra* or the *Nirvana Sutra*?

Answer: The *Lotus Sutra*.

Question: Why do you say that?

Answer: In the *Nirvana Sutra*, the Buddha Himself declared, "8,000 śrāvaka were guaranteed to be future Buddhas in the *Lotus Sutra*. It is as though a great harvest was reaped in autumn and stored in the warehouse for winter, leaving nothing else to be done in the *Nirvana Sutra*." Again it is said in The Teacher of the Dharma chapter in the *Lotus Sutra* that the sutras to be preached,* like the *Nirvana Sutra*, are not as difficult to believe and understand as the *Lotus Sutra*. This means that the *Nirvana Sutra* is not as truthful as the *Lotus Sutra*.

Question: According to the *Nirvana Sutra*, the sutras preached before it all contain false views. What do you think of that?

Answer: The Buddha's purpose of appearing in the world was to preach the *Lotus Sutra*, in which He proclaims in the second chapter, Expedients, "My old wish has already been fulfilled. It is indeed the time now to expound the Mahayana teaching definitively." In the 16th chapter, The Duration of the Life of the Tathāgata, he declares, "actually, Good Men, I have been the Buddha since the eternal past." Nevertheless, regarding the comparative superiority in doctrine, the Buddha Himself declares in the 10th chapter, The Teacher of the Dharma, that although He has expounded numerous, thousands, tens of thousands and hundreds of millions of sutras, the *Lotus Sutra* is superior to all the sutras which have been preached, are being preached, and will be preached. Then, in the 11th chapter, Beholding the Stupa of Treasures, the Buddha of Many Treasures appeared from underground testifying: "What has been said by Śākyamuni Buddha is all true," while various Buddhas, the manifestations* of Śākyamuni Buddha in the worlds all over the universe, stretched out their tongues to reach the Brahma Heaven attesting the words of Śākyamuni to be true.

Thus, the comparative superiority between the *Lotus Sutra* and all other sutras has been resolved by Śākyamuni Buddha, the Buddha of Many Treasures,* and Buddhas manifested in worlds all over the universe. No further comparison between the *Lotus Sutra* and sutras preached before and after it is necessary because they are all preached by the one Śākyamuni Buddha.

Therefore, when the *Nirvana Sutra* rejects sutras preached before it, the *Lotus Sutra* is not included, because the *Nirvana Sutra*, too, is trying to say that the *Lotus Sutra* is superior to others. However, the phrase "those of the false view" in the *Nirvana Sutra* refers to Kāśyapa Bodhisattva and his followers who could not attain Buddhahood by listening to the *Lotus Sutra*, but attained it through the *Nirvana Sutra*. That is, Kāśyapa Bodhisattva and his followers confessed themselves to have been "of false view before the *Nirvana Sutra*." This has nothing to do with the comparative superiority of sutras.

Part 3: Distinction Between Mahayana and Hinayana Teachings

In the third place, I would like to distinguish between Mahayana and Hinayana teachings.

Question: What are the differences between Mahayana and Hinayana teachings?

Answer: Generally speaking, the sutras preached in the Agon period are Hinayana, while those preached in the Kegon, Hōdō, Hannya and Hokke-Nehan periods are Mahayana. In addition, those sutras which expound the six unenlightened realms of hell, hungry spirits, beasts and birds, *asura*, human beings, and heavenly beings without expounding the four enlightened realms of *śrāvaka*, *pratyekabuddha*, bodhisattvas, and Buddhas, are Hinayana while those which expound all 10 realms are Mahayana. Other than these two main distinctions, comparing the truthfulness in doctrine between the *Lotus Sutra* and other sutras, those sutras preached in the 40 years or so before the *Lotus Sutra* are in reality Hinayana although they are commonly called Mahayana sutras. Only the *Lotus Sutra* is Mahayana.

Question: It is customary for each Buddhist sect to claim that only its basic sutras are the real Mahayana while those of other sects are merely the provisional Mahayana. It is impossible for us, later students, to decide whether or not claims made by various sects are true. Besides, I have never heard of a scriptural statement to prove that various Mahayana sutras are "Hinayana" in comparison to the *Lotus Sutra*. Do you have any scriptural proof for your claim?

Answer: The doctrines upon which various sects were established conflict with one another. Especially in the Latter Age of Degeneration,* when error takes precedence over the truth in worldly matters as well as within Buddhism, it is regrettable that we, the ignorant, cannot tell what is right and what is wrong. Nevertheless, even with my low intelligence, when I come across a clear statement in the *Sutra of Infinite Meaning* stating, "The truth has not been revealed for 40 years or so," I cannot trust judgements of right or wrong by masters of various sects unless they are based on scriptural passages superior to this one.

Besides, in answering your question I should not say categorically that compared to the *Lotus Sutra* various Mahayana sutras are Hinayana. So let me quote scriptural proofs. It is stated in the Expedients chapter of the *Lotus Sutra*, "The Buddha Himself resides in the Mahayana teachings.... Enlightened with the Mahayana dharma, a great wisdom of equality, if He guides the people with Hinayana dharma, even just one, He would be committing the sin of greed. He certainly would not do it."

This passage means that various Mahayana sutras, other than the *Lotus Sutra*, are all Hinayana. The 16th chapter of the *Lotus Sutra*, The Duration of the Life of the Tathāgata, also refers to "those with less virtue and much delusion who are satisfied with small dharma, Hinayana teachings." These are examples of statements in sutras designating all the sutras other than the *Lotus Sutra* preached by Śākyamuni Buddha during 40 years or so as Hinayana. Annotations by Grand Masters T'ien-t'ai* and Miao-lê* also regard those sutras of 40 years or so to be Hinayana teachings, which would probably be unacceptable to teachers of other sects. Therefore, I have cited passages only from these sutras.

Part 4: Reasons for Discarding Provisional Sutras

In the fourth place, let me explain why we should discard provisional sutras, and instead put faith in the true sutras.

Question: What scriptural statements support your contention?

Answer: Ten scriptural statements support my contention. First, it is stated in the *Lotus Sutra*, chapter three, A Parable, "You should try to uphold only Mahayana sutras... without putting faith in even a verse of other sutras."

Secondly, the *Nirvana Sutra* states, "We should depend on sutras which thoroughly reveal the truth* and not on those which do not." Sutras which do not thoroughly reveal the truth refer to those sutras expounded in the 40 years or so before the *Lotus Sutra*.

Thirdly, it is stated in the *Lotus Sutra*, chapter 11, Beholding the Stupa of Treasures, "It is difficult to uphold this sutra. If anyone upholds it even for a moment, I, as well as the other Buddhas, will rejoice and praise him. He is a man of valor and endeavor. He is observing the precepts and practicing the rules of frugal living."* In the Latter Age of Degeneration, we might not observe various precepts defined in the sutras expounded during 40 years or so before the *Lotus Sutra*. Upholding the *Lotus Sutra* single-mindedly may be called observing the precepts and rules of frugal living.*

Fourthly, the *Nirvana Sutra* states, "Those who do not exhort themselves to uphold the dharma may be called indolent, but those who do not exhort themselves to observe the precepts may not be. Bodhisattvas, if you are not lax in putting faith in this Mahayana dharma, you deserve to be called the upholders of the precepts. In order to uphold that True Dharma, you bathe in the water of Mahayana. Therefore, even when bodhisattvas break the precepts, they may not be called indolent." This scriptural passage elaborates the spirit of observing the precepts in the *Lotus Sutra*.

For the fifth, it is stated in the *Lotus Sutra*, fascicle four, chapter 11, Beholding the Stupa of Treasures, "The *Lotus Sutra*... is entirely true." This is the attestation by the Buddha of Many Treasures.

For the sixth, in the *Lotus Sutra,* fascicle eight, chapter 28, The Encouragement of Universal-Sage Bodhisattva,* Universal-Sage Bodhisattva, swearing to Śākyamuni Buddha, declares, "I will make sure that this sutra will be spread all over the world, the Jambudvīpa,* and not be destroyed, after the extinction of the Buddha."

For the seventh, it is stated in the *Lotus Sutra,* fascicle seven, chapter 23, The Previous Life of Medicine-King Bodhisattva, "I will not let this sutra perish in the world, the Jambudvīpa,* during the fifth 500-year period after My extinction." This is an oath from Śākyamuni Buddha Himself.

For the eighth, explaining why the Buddha of Many Treasures and various Buddhas manifested in many worlds all over the universe gathered together around Śākyamuni Buddha, the *Lotus Sutra,* fascicle four, chapter 11, Beholding the Stupa of Treasures, declares, "They have come together in order to perpetuate the dharma in this world."

For the ninth, regarding the place where those who practice the *Lotus Sutra* reside, the sutra, fascicle seven, chapter 21, The Supernatural Powers of the Tathāgata, preaches:

> "After the extinction of the Buddha, you should single-mindedly uphold, read, recite, expound, copy this sutra and act according to its teachings.... Wherever a copy of this sutra is, regardless where it may be, in a garden, in a forest, under a tree, in a monastery, in the house of a layman, in a hall, in a mountain, in a valley or in a wilderness, a stupa should be erected and offerings be made to it. Why is that? It is because this is the place of enlightenment. It was here that Buddhas attained Buddhahood."

And for the 10th, it is stated in fascicle nine of the *Nirvana Sutra,* a sutra preached for amplification of the *Lotus Sutra:*

> "During the last 80 years when the True Dharma will be about to expire after My death, this sutra will spread widely in this world, the Jambudvīpa. Then, however, evil monks will steal this sutra, cutting it up into pieces to kill its original color, fragrance and flavor. In reading this sutra, unable to understand the essence of the Buddha's profound enlightenment, they will insert flowery phrases and meaningless sentences just to save appearances. They might put a beginning sentence at the end, an ending sentence at the beginning, a beginning or ending sentence in the middle, or a middle sentence at the beginning or at the end. You should know that these evil monks are not the Buddha's disciples but the Devil's companions.... Those evil monks are like a dairymaid who dilutes cow's milk with much water to make a quick profit. Likewise, they will mix the Buddha's words in this sutra with worldly words, making it misleading. Many people will

not be able to talk about, copy and comprehend this sutra correctly, or be able to praise, make offerings to and revere it. Guided solely by self-interest, those wicked monks will be unable to spread this sutra widely. It will spread so slightly that it will not be worth mentioning. It is just like a poor dairymaid selling cow's milk, which was resold and repurchased many times.... When, finally, milk gruel is made of it, it will have no taste of milk. Likewise, this great *Nirvana Sutra*, a Mahayana sutra, while being transmitted from person to person, will lose its flavor until in the end it will be tasteless. Nevertheless, it is still 1,000 times superior to other sutras just as the taste of milk, no matter how much diluted, is 1,000 times better than the taste of bitterness. It is because this great *Nirvana Sutra*, a Mahayana sutra, is supreme of all the sutras transmitted by the direct disciples of Śākyamuni Buddha."

Question: Suppose we should discard the *furyōgi-kyō*, sutras not thoroughly revealing the truth, putting faith in the *ryōgi-kyō*, sutras thoroughly revealing the truth. Should we depend on such Mahayana sutras as the *Daiengaku Shutara Ryōgi-kyō, Perfect Enlightenment Sutra*. and the *Daibutchō Nyorai Mitsuin Shushō Ryōgi-kyō, Crown of the Buddha's Top Sutra*, because they claim to be *ryōgi-kyō* in their titles?

Answer: The designation of *ryōgi-kyō* and the *furyōgi-kyō* differs comparatively. Compared to the teachings preached by Buddha's disciples such as the Two Vehicles,* i.e. *śrāvaka* and *pratyekabuddha*, and by bodhisattvas, which do not reveal the intent of the Buddha completely, the teachings expounded by the Buddha in His lifetime all reveal the truth completely. Regarding the teachings of the Buddha, Hinayana sutras are the *furyōgi-kyō* while Mahayana sutras are *ryōgi-kyō*. Of Mahayana sutras, those preached in 40 years or so are *furyōgi-kyō* whereas such sutras as the *Lotus Sutra, Nirvana Sutra* and *Great Sun Buddha Sutra* are *ryōgi-kyō*. Such sutras as the *Perfect Enlightenment Sutra* and the *Crown of the Buddha's Top Sutra* are *ryōgi-kyō* compared to Hinayana sutras and those Mahayana *furyōgi-kyō* which require aeons of practices for attaining Buddhahood. However, they are not the *ryōgi-kyō* as the *Lotus Sutra* is compared to all other sutras.

Question: Founders of sects, other than the Tendai and Shingon, such as the Kegon (Flower Garland), Hossō and Sanron, each believed to have thoroughly mastered the profound doctrines of their respective canonical sutras. What do you think of this?

Answer: According to the *Flower Garland Sutra*, the Kegon sect* considers the other sutras expediencies to preach the True Dharma of the *Flower Garland Sutra*. The Hossō sect* regards such sutras as the Āgama sutras and *Wisdom Sutra* with contempt but equates the *Flower Garland Sutra, Lotus Sutra,* and *Nirvana*

Sutra to the *Revealing the Profound and Secret Sutra** as preachings of the Middle Way. Nevertheless, the sect maintains that both the *Lotus* and *Nirvana Sutras* are *furyōgi,* not really revealing the true intent of the Buddha as they preach the One Vehicle teaching leading to Buddhahood for one group of people, whereas the *Revealing the Profound and Secret Sutra* is *ryōgi,* completely revealing the truth because it preaches the "five mutually distinctive natures,"* approving attainment of Buddhahood by some but not by all people.

The Sanron sect* divides all the scriptures of Buddhism into two storehouses* of *śrāvaka* storehouse, Hinayana, and bodhisattva storehouse, Mahayana. Based on the *Wisdom Sutra,* they do not discuss the comparative profundity among Mahayana, bodhisattva scriptures. These founders of various sects might have been the Four Reliances, bodhisattvas relied upon by Buddhists as great teachers. They probably had profound reasons for establishing such classifications, which I dare not attempt to criticize.

However, in order to dispel my own doubt, setting aside their various opinions for now, let us examine those basic sutras on which they established their sects. The *Flower Garland Sutra* consists of either 50 or 60 fascicles in the old translation,* and 80 or 40 fascicles in the new translation.* In neither of them is it clearly declared, as in the *Lotus* and *Nirvana Sutras,* that all the holy teachings of the Buddha's lifetime* are expedient. Although it preaches four kinds of teaching applicable to *śrāvaka, pratyekabuddha,* bodhisattvas and Buddhas, in explaining the teaching leading to Buddhahood, it does not reveal either the "mutual possession of the 10 realms"* doctrine nor Śākyamuni Buddha's attainment of Perfect Enlightenment in the eternal past.* These two doctrines of the *Lotus Sutra,* are the profoundest of all Buddhist doctrines. Therefore, the *Lotus Sutra* is incomparable to the *Flower Garland Sutra.* Nevertheless, Chinese patriarchs of Flower Garland Buddhism established the doctrine of five teachings* including various sutras all in the first four teachings, which they called expedient to the fifth teaching, the *Flower Garland Sutra.*

Establishing the doctrine of the "three-period teaching,*" the Hossō sect equates such sutras as the *Lotus* to the *Revealing the Profound and Secret Sutra* as sutras preaching the Middle Way. Nowhere in the five-fascicled *Revealing the Profound and Secret Sutra,* however, is it clearly stated that such sutras as the Lotus be included in the Middle Way teaching.

Instituting the two-storehouse doctrine, the Sanron sect includes such sutras as the *Flower Garland* and *Lotus* in the bodhisattva storehouse, equating them to the *Wisdom Sutra.* Going through the new translation of the 600 fascicled *Great Wisdom Sutra,* however, there is no passage whatsoever that equates the *Great Wisdom* to the *Lotus* and *Nirvana Sutras.*

Some claim that the *Flower Garland Sutra* is an abrupt teaching* whereas the *Lotus Sutra* is a gradual teaching,* but this is an arbitrary classification established by Chinese teachers not based on the Buddha's words.

In the case of the *Lotus Sutra*, on the contrary, its preface,* the *Sutra of Infinite Meaning*, clearly defines the years of preaching as "40 years or so" and names the titles of representative sutras as the Flower Garland, Hōdō sutras, Wisdom and others. It definitely states that "the truth has not yet been revealed" in them. In determining the comparative superiority of all sutras preached during His lifetime in the main discourse* of the *Lotus Sutra* proper, Śākyamuni Buddha uttered these golden words in the 10th chapter, The Teacher of the Dharma, "The sutras I have preached number immeasurable thousands, tens of thousands, and hundreds of millions. Of the sutras I have preached, am now preaching, and will preach, this *Lotus Sutra* is the most difficult to believe and the most difficult to understand." Just then the Buddha of Many Treasures emerged from underground in the 11th chapter, Beholding the Stupa of Treasures, to testify, "What is said in the *Lotus Sutra* is all true," while Buddhas manifested* in the numerous worlds all over the universe came together in the 21st chapter, The Supernatural Powers of the Tathāgata, to attest it to be the truth by touching the Brahma Heaven with their tongues.

Taking these into consideration, I guess it is in my own hands to compare the superiority and profundity in doctrine or difficulty in practice among sutras as numerous as the number of dust particles in the whole universe, including those transmitted to China and Japan, more than 5,000 fascicles in old translations and more than 7,000 fascicles in new translations, those which have not been transmitted but existed in India, the Dragon's Palace and the Four-king Heavens,* and finally those preached by the Past Seven Buddhas* and left out of Ānanda's* collection.

How can the "immeasurable thousands, tens of thousands, and hundreds of millions of sutras" referred to in The Teacher of the Dharma chapter of the *Lotus Sutra* not include every sutra preached by Śākyamuni Buddha? Is there any sutra that does not fall into the time-span of the Buddha's preaching when He "has preached, now preaches, and will preach" them?

I pray that people in the Latter Age may somehow discard the meaningless doctrines established by founders of various sects on feeble scriptural bases, putting faith in the significant teaching supported by Śākyamuni and the Buddha of Many Treasures as well as numerous Buddhas manifested in the worlds all over the universe with strong evidence in sutras. How much less should they rely on latter scholars of various sects pre-occupied with sectarian prejudices, and the ignorant people of the Latter Age who discard sutras and commentaries according to such latter sectarian scholars?

Therefore, it is stated in the *Nirvana Sutra*, the postscript of the *Lotus Sutra*, which was preached last in the *śāla* forest,* and that the Buddha bequeathed to Kāśyapa Bodhisattva: "Rely upon the dharma preached by the Buddha, not upon the words of the man. Rely upon the true meaning of the Buddha, not upon the words and letters. Rely upon wisdom, not upon knowledge. And rely upon the sutras completely revealing the true meaning, not upon sutras that do not completely reveal the true meaning."

As I observe the world today, people praise a teacher of their own sect as enlightened and the first in wisdom. However, he is actually unenlightened without the virtue of converting people to the dharma through the true sutras. Instead, insisting that such sutras as the *Sutra of Meditation on the Buddha of Infinite Life*, which do not reveal the truth completely, are appropriate to the time and capacity of the people, he discards the *Lotus* and *Nirvana Sutras*, which thoroughly reveal the truth, despising them as too exquisite* in doctrine for people in the Latter Age to understand. Is this not against the Buddha's will? Telling people to rely upon the man, not upon the dharma? Telling people to reply upon the words and letters, not upon the true meaning? Telling people to rely upon knowledge, not upon wisdom? And telling people to rely upon sutras not revealing the true meaning, not upon sutras revealing the true meaning? I pray that those with right minds may think of this carefully.

It has already been more than 2,200 years since the Buddha passed away. During these years, Bodhisattva Mañjuśrī,* Mahā-kāśyapa,* and Ānanda* collected the sutras, and after that many bodhisattvas of high virtue, called the Four Reliances, appeared in this world to write commentaries to explain the meaning of the sutras. However, later commentators in India began to misunderstand, while some translators into Chinese were not well versed in both Sanskrit and Chinese or adhered to provisional teachings, forcibly interpreting the meanings of the true sutras and commentaries to be those of the provisional. Besides, because of their associations with provisional teachings in the past, Chinese monks began to prefer provisional to true sutras and commentaries. Moreover, if they found a passage which did not suit them even a little, they forcibly interpreted it in such a way to agree with their opinions. Even when they realized their mistake, they did not discard the provisional teaching and convert themselves to the true teaching. Rather they preferred to keep their honor and profit, or keep from losing the patronage of their followers.

Being uninformed, all people, laymen as well as clergy, are unable to distinguish between right and wrong. They just depend on the man, not upon the dharma. They follow the evil dharma in which many people put faith, even if they know it is an evil one, and they do not believe in the True Dharma advocated by one person without followers. It is sad that most people remain wandering in the world of illusion. Even in seeking freedom from the chain of birth and death, they most likely depend on provisional sutras. It is regrettable that these sinful people, regardless of how good or bad they behave, are unable to escape the chain of birth and death.

Nevertheless, all ignorant people in the world today, even if they might be persecuted in this life, should believe in the passages cited earlier[5] from the *Nirvana Sutra*, fascicle nine, supporting the Lotus to be the prime sutra, and should try putting faith in the *Lotus* and *Nirvana Sutras*. The reason is that the truth of even trivial matters in the world is lost, and mistakes about them increase when transmitted many times by word of mouth. How much more so with the profound doctrines of Buddhism! In more than 2,000 years after the death of the Buddha, so many false doctrines may have been added to Buddhism that not even one out of 10,000 may be the true teaching.

Many Buddhist scriptures, therefore, may have errors. For instance the doctrine of the "inherent seed of natural emancipation from delusions" preached in the *Meditation on the Mind-base Sutra* denies Buddhahood for such as men of *śrāvaka* and *pratyekabuddha*. The Transmission chapter in the *Lotus Sutra* is placed at the end in Dharmarakṣa's translation instead of the 22nd chapter as in Kumārajīva's translation. The *Great Commentary on the Abhidharma* translated by Hsüan-chuang arbitrarily adds 16 characters not found in the Sanskrit original. The consciousness expounded in the *Collection of Mahayana Essentials* by Asaṅga is divided into eight parts in one translation by Hsüan-chuang but nine in another by Paramārtha. Discrepancies exist between Vasubandhu's *Commentary on the Lotus Sutra* and the *Lotus Sutra* in Chinese. The *Treatise on the Nirvana Sutra* by Vasubandhu states that the *Lotus Sutra* is smeared by evil passions. The Hossō sect insists that those with fixed nature of *śrāvaka* and *pratyekabuddha* and *icchantika* without Buddha-nature will never attain Buddhahood. And the She-lun (Shōron) sect maintains that the *Lotus Sutra's* claim of attainment of Buddhahood by those who chant, "Homage to the Buddha!" just once is merely an expedient means of encouraging idlers.*

These are all mistakes rendered by translators of sutras and commentaries and teachers of various sects. There may be many more errors beside these in sutras preached in the 40 years or so before the *Lotus* and *Nirvana Sutras*. Although there might be, or might not be mistakes in the *Lotus* and *Nirvana Sutras*, those sutras preached in the 40 years or so should be discarded and the *Lotus* and *Nirvana Sutras* followed. The reason was made clear earlier in the citation from the *Nirvana Sutra*, fascicle nine. How can those who put faith in sutras with many mistakes preached before the *Lotus* and *Nirvana Sutras*, free themselves from the cycle of birth and death?

SECTION II
Rise and Fall of Buddhism in the Three Ages after the Death of the Buddha

In the second section, I would like to explain the rise and fall of Buddhism during the three ages after the death of Śākyamuni Buddha: the Age of the True Dharma, the Age of the Semblance Dharma, and the Latter Age of Degeneration. This section consists of two parts. In the first part, I shall determine which sutras will be responsive to people for longer in the Latter Age of Degeneration: the sutras preached during 40 years or so before the *Lotus Sutra* or the triple Pure Land sutras. In the second part, I shall determine whether the *Lotus* and *Nirvana Sutras* or the triple Pure Land sutras will be responsive to people for longer.

Part 1: The Pre-Lotus Sutras or the Triple Pure Land Sutras?

In this first part, I shall determine whether the sutras preached during 40 years or so before the *Lotus Sutra* or the triple Pure Land sutras will be responsive for longer to people living in the Latter Age of Degeneration.

Question: It is useless to discuss the difference between Mahayana and Hinayana dharmas, profound and shallow teachings, or supreme and inferior doctrines. They should be responsive to our prayers only if we choose one suitable to our time and to our capacity for understanding. However, it is stated in such sutras as the *Kalpa of Continuance Sutra*, the *Sutra of the Great Plan* and the *Sutra of the Great Assembly* that beyond 2,000 years after the death of the Buddha, the Buddha's teachings will all become worthless, that is to say, His teachings will remain but nobody will put them into practice or attain Buddhahood by practicing them.

Accordingly, when we open the *Treatise on the Light for the Latter Age of Degeneration* by Grand Master Dengyō, we find it states, "The twentieth year of the Enryaku Period (801) is the 1750th year after the death of the Buddha according to one view." It has been more than 450 years since the twentieth year of the Enryaku Period, so we are already in the Latter Age of Degeneration. Therefore, even if we have the teaching of the Buddha, none of us can put it into practice or attain Buddhahood. If this is the case, not even one out of 10,000 of those who practice Buddhism would be able to attain Buddhahood.

However, it is stated in the *Two Fascicle Sutra*,* the *Sutra of the Buddha of Infinite Life*, "Buddhism will become extinct in the future, but with compassion and pity I shall have just this one sutra remain in this world for 100 years. Those who encounter this sutra then will all be saved as they wish." According to this passage, it is clear that in the Latter Age of Degeneration, after the complete destruction of the holy teaching of Śākyamuni Buddha preached in His lifetime, the teaching of the *nembutsu* of the *Sutra of the Buddha of Infinite Life* alone will remain responding to prayers of the people."

Skimming through commentaries by the Pure Land masters, we find that they sound alike because their commentaries all are based on this passage. In China, for instance, Zen master Tao-ch'o* declared, "The current Latter Age of Degeneration is the evil of five defilements,* when only the teaching of Pure Land Buddhism is the way to enlightenment." Venerable Shan-tao* wrote, "During the 10,000 year period of the Latter Age of Degeneration the three treasures of the Buddha, the Dharma and the *Saṃgha* will all disappear while only this sutra will remain for 100 years." And Grand Master Tz'ŭ-ên* explained, "Other sutras will all disappear in 10,000 years of the Latter Age. Only the teaching of the Buddha of Infinite Life will prosper and respond to prayers of the people."

In Japan, Venerable Eshin* (Genshin), a now deceased monk of virtue on Mt. Hiei, wrote the *Essential Collection Concerning Rebirth in the Pure Land,** in which he collected the essence of the holy teaching preached during the lifetime of the Buddha as a guide for people in the Latter Age. In its preface Venerable Eshin declared, "The teaching and practice for rebirth in the Pure Land of Bliss are the eyes and legs for people in the Latter Age of defilement and corruption. Among monks and lay persons, high and low, who does not believe in this? However, the exoteric and esoteric teachings* are not a few in number, with many ways of practicing them. It may be possible for men of wisdom and perseverance to practice these teachings. Nevertheless, how can it be possible for an ignorant person like myself?" Following this, he also declared, "Especially the teaching of the *nembutsu* will help people only in the Latter Age of defilement and corruption, after the extinction of the teaching of the Buddha." Thus, scholars of various Buddhist sects generally agree with this idea of the *Sutra of the Buddha of Infinite Life*. Scholars of the Tendai sect following Venerable Eshin especially should not disagree with this, should they?

Answer: Each of those sutras, preached during 40 years or so before the *Lotus Sutra*, prospers and declines depending on the times and capacity of the people, so most of them would disappear before the triple Pure Land sutras. Most of those sutras preach attainment of Buddhahood by the three vehicles,* *śrāvaka*, *pratyekabuddha* and bodhisattvas, within one life. Yet, it is very rare for people in the Latter Age to attain Buddhahood within the present life because of their inferior capacity. Rebirth in Pure Lands all over the universe is, therefore, preached mostly to help people of low caliber in the Latter Age.

Regarding this, most sutras recommend the Pure Land of Bliss to the west because it is near the *Sahā* World, because it is the lowest of Pure Lands which is thought to be open even for ignorant people, and because the sun rises in the east and sets in the west, making the west appear as a natural place to be after death. Therefore, it was not only the founders of Pure Land Buddhism that preached rebirth in the Western Pure Land. Expounding the pre-*Lotus* sutras, T'ien-t'ai and Miao-lê also preached this occasionally. It was also not only Chinese monk-teachers but also Nāgārjuna and Vasubandhu of India who believed in such rebirth. The view that the Pure Land teaching would last longer than any other pre-*Lotus* teachings is merely one of many. For instance, the *Sutra of the Benevolent King* claims to last longer than the triple Pure Land sutras, namely, for 8,000 years beyond the 10,000 year period of the Latter Age of Degeneration. It is, therefore, impossible to decide which of the pre-*Lotus* sutras will last the longest.

Part 2: The Lotus and Nirvana Sutras or the Triple Pure Land Sutras?

In this second part, I shall determine whether the *Lotus* and *Nirvana Sutras* or the triple Pure Land sutras will be responsive to people for longer.

Question: Which will disappear first, the *Lotus* and *Nirvana Sutras* or the triple Pure Land sutras?

Answer: The triple Pure Land sutras will disappear before the *Lotus* and *Nirvana Sutras*.

Question: How do you know this?

Answer: Referring to the representative sutras preached during the 40 years or so of the pre-*Lotus* period, the *Sutra of Infinite Meaning* declares, "The truth has not been revealed in them." This means that words and letters in the *Sutra of the Buddha of Infinite Life* such as "I shall leave just this one sutra in this world for 100 years" are all expedient and false.

Judging from the truth preached in the *Sutra of Infinite Meaning*, the teachings of rebirth in the Pure Land* or the attainment of Buddhahood* preached in sutras such as the *Flower Garland Sutra*, Hōdō sutras, the *Wisdom Sutra* and *Sutra of Meditation on the Buddha of Infinite Life*,* whether occurring suddenly or after *kalpa*, that is aeons, of practice, "will not in the end be able to lead us to supreme Buddhahood even after practicing them for an infinite, unlimited, inconceivable number of *kalpa*... because practicing them is like walking up a steep path encountering many obstacles." Both rebirth in the Pure Land and the attainment of Buddhahood preached in those sutras are merely expedient to encourage idlers.*

The *Sutra of the Great Assembly, Sutra of the Buddha of Infinite Life,* and others explain which sutras will or will not disappear and in what order, but these opinions are all expedient. Expedient sutras preached before the *Lotus Sutra* are the same as non-Buddhist teachings,* in which no one can be reborn in the

Pure Land or attain Buddhahood. For instance rivers which do not flow into the ocean cannot become one, and people and subjects who do not follow their great king cannot be united. No matter how hard we practice such teachings, there will not be any merit at all unless we reach the *Lotus* and *Nirvana Sutras*. It will be the same as practicing non-Buddhist teachings in which Buddhahood is not attainable. They are the teachings nobody practices and no one can attain Buddhahood by practicing them either in the Latter Age of Degeneration or during and after the lifetime of the Buddha.

In winter, however, trees appear dead, but pine and oak trees do not wither. Grasses die, but chrysanthemums and bamboo remain unchanged. The same is true with the *Lotus Sutra*, which will remain forever helping people even after other sutras all disappear. Śākyamuni Buddha declared in the 10th chapter of the *Lotus Sutra*, The Teacher of the Dharma, that the *Lotus Sutra* was supreme of all the sutras He had preached, was preaching, and would be preaching. Moreover, in the 11th chapter, Beholding the Stupa of Treasures, the Buddha of Many Treasures attested the *Lotus Sutra* to be true. And in the 21st chapter, The Supernatural Powers of the Tathāgata, Buddhas manifested in various worlds all over the universe also verified the truth of the *Lotus Sutra* by touching the Brahma Heaven with their tongues. Their sole purpose was to have the dharma of the *Lotus Sutra* last forever* in this world.

Question: Do you have any scriptural passages proving that the *Lotus Sutra* alone will remain even after other sutras all disappear?

Answer: In the 10th chapter of the *Lotus Sutra*, The Teacher of the Dharma, Śākyamuni Buddha declared in order to spread the sutra, "The sutras I have preached number immeasurable thousands, tens of thousands, and hundreds of millions. Of the sutras I have preached, am now preaching, and will preach, this *Lotus Sutra* is the most difficult to believe and to understand." This means that of all the sutras which the Buddha has preached, is now preaching, and will preach* during 50 years of His lifetime, the *Lotus Sutra* is the supreme sutra. Of the 80,000 holy teachings, it was preached especially to be retained for people in the future.

Therefore, in the following chapter, Beholding the Stupa of Treasures, the Buddha of Many Treasures emerged from the great earth, and Buddhas in manifestation from the worlds all over the universe gathered. Through these Buddhas in manifestation as His messengers, Śākyamuni Buddha made this declaration to bodhisattvas, *śrāvaka*, *pratyekabuddha*, heavenly beings, human beings, and eight kinds of supernatural beings* who filled the innumerable, 400 trillion *nayuta* worlds in eight directions:

> "The purpose of the emergence of the Buddha of Many Treasures and the gathering of Buddhas in manifestation all over the universe is solely

for the *Lotus Sutra* to last forever. Each of you should vow that you will certainly spread this *Lotus Sutra* in the future worlds of five defilements* after the sutras which have been preached, are being preached, and will be preached, will have all disappeared when it will be difficult to believe in the True Dharma."

Then 20,000 bodhisattvas and 80 trillion *nayuta* of bodhisattvas each made a vow in the 13th chapter, Encouragement for Keeping This Sutra, "We will not spare even our lives, but treasure the Unsurpassed Way." Bodhisattvas emerged from the great earth, as numerous as dust particles of the entire world, as well as such bodhisattvas as Mañjuśrī, and in the 22nd chapter, Transmission, they all also vowed, "After the death of the Buddha...we will widely spread this sutra." After that, in the 23rd chapter, The Previous Life of Medicine-King Bodhisattva, the Buddha used 10 similes* to explain the superiority of the *Lotus Sutra* over other sutras. In the first simile, the pre-*Lotus* sutras are likened to river-water and the *Lotus Sutra*, to a great ocean. Just as ocean water will not decrease even when river-water dries up in a severe drought, the *Lotus Sutra* will remain unchanged even when the pre-*Lotus* sutras with four tastes[6] all disappear in the Latter Age of defilement and shameless corruption. Having preached this, the Buddha clearly expressed His true intent as follows, "After I have entered Nirvana, during the last 500-year period you must spread this sutra widely throughout the world lest it should be lost."

Contemplating the meaning of this passage, I believe that the character "after" following "after I have entered Nirvana" is meant to be "after the extinction of those sutras preached in 40 years or so." It is, therefore, stated in the *Nirvana Sutra*, the postscript of the *Lotus Sutra*, "I shall entrust the propagation of this supreme dharma to bodhisattvas who are skillful in debate. Such a dharma will be able to last forever, continue to prosper for incalculable generations, profiting and pacifying the people."

According to these scriptural passages the *Lotus* and *Nirvana Sutras* will not become extinct for immeasurable centuries. Nevertheless, not knowing this, scholars in the world consider "the extinction of Buddhism in the last, fifth 500-year period"* predicted in the *Sutra of the Great Assembly*, which is a provisional sutra, applicable to the *Lotus* and *Nirvana Sutras*, insisting that they will be extinct before the triple Pure Land sutras. Theirs is a misinterpretation which has forgotten the significance of the whole *Lotus Sutra* from the beginning to end.

Question: As said earlier, such monks as T'an-luan, Tao-ch'o, Shan-tao and Venerable Eshin (Genshin) all regarded the Lotus-Shingon sutras to be unsuitable for the Latter Age. Accordingly, Genkū (Hōnen Shōnin)* and his disciples called the Lotus-Shingon teachings "miscellaneous practices" unnecessary for rebirth in the Pure Land, rejected them as difficult to practice, and slandered those who practice these teachings as bandits, villains or heretics. Shōkō-bō likened them to Grandfather's shoes too big to be useful, and Namu-bō said that they were less worthy than string music, which comforts people. In short these opinions held that the Lotus-Shingon teachings did not suit the times and the capacity of people to understand. What do you think of their contention?

Answer: Dividing the preachings of 50 years in His lifetime into two, provisional and true, Śākyamuni Buddha Himself clearly declared that we should discard provisional sutras and seek refuge in the true sutras. Thus it is stated in the second chapter of the *Lotus Sutra,* Expedients, that the Buddha preached provisional sutras during 40 years or so because He was afraid that "the people would be unable to understand and sink in pain if He praised only the way to Buddhahood." He, nevertheless, was also concerned that "if I guide people merely with Hinayana dharma, even just one person, I would be committing the sin of greed." Therefore, in order to avoid committing such a sin and upholding "His basic purpose of leading people into Mahayana teaching," the Buddha expounded the *Lotus Sutra,* achieving His purpose.

Then in preaching the *Nirvana Sutra,* the Buddha promised, "After My death I will entrust Four Reliances, leading masters people can rely upon, to spread both provisional and true teachings." Accordingly Bodhisattva Nāgārjuna, appearing in this world 800 years after the death of the Buddha, wrote such provisional commentaries as those in which he expounded such Mahayana sutras as the *Flower Garland Sutra,* Hōdō sutras, and the *Wisdom Sutra.* He also authored the *Great Wisdom Discourse,** distinguishing between the *Lotus* and *Wisdom Sutras,* claiming the former to be the true Mahayana and superior to the latter.

Bodhisattva Vasubandhu, who was born to this world 900 years after the death of the Buddha, explained Hinayana sutras in his *Verses on the Treasury of Abhidharma,* expounded the Hōdō sutras in his *Treatise on the Theory of Consciousness-Only,* and finally wrote the *Treatise on Buddha-nature,* in which he explained the *Lotus* and *Nirvana Sutras,* distinguishing between sutras revealing the whole truth, and those not revealing the whole truth. Thus, both Bodhisattvas Nāgārjuna and Vasubandhu did not defy the will of the Buddha when they expounded provisional sutras first and the teachings of the *Lotus* and *Nirvana Sutras* in the end. Later commentators and translators, however, adhered to provisional sutras, and forcibly embedded words and phrases of true sutras into provisional sutras, causing a mixture of true and provisional sutras without distinction. Then, in the time of Chinese masters *(ninshi*),* each sect was based on its own canonical sutras, forcibly despising other sutras as provisional. Thus commentators, translators, and Chinese masters all became more and more against the intent of the Buddha.

However, two of the three Pure Land masters, T'an-luan and Tao-ch'o, divided all the scriptures of Buddhism into two groups: "difficult to practice" and "easy to practice," or Holy Way Gate and Pure Land Gate, according to the *Commentary on the Ten Stages*. Had they, contrary to the *Commentary*, included the Lotus-Shingon sutras in their grouping, they would not be considered reliable. Examining the *Commentary on the Discourse on the Pure Land* by T'an-luan and the *Collection of Passages Concerning Rebirth in the Pure Land* by Tao-ch'o, I find they generally follow the opinions of the *Commentary on the Ten Stages*.

Venerable Shan-tao also advocated the single practice of chanting the name of the Buddha of Infinite Life and sole vow of rebirth in the Pure Land according to the teaching of the triple Pure Land sutras. But She-lun (Shōron) masters during the four dynasties of Liang, Chen, Sui, and T'ang in China categorized all the scriptures of Buddhism and denigrated the single practice of Pure Land Buddhism as mere encouragement for idlers. This contradicted the views of Venerable Shan-tao, who rebuffed the She-lun masters likening them to bandits because they spoiled the merit of the *nembutsu* for rebirth in the Pure Land, without fail, upon death.

Shan-tao also labeled the practices of She-lun masters "miscellaneous practices," because they insisted that various practices could lead to rebirth in the Pure Land. He rejected She-lun masters saying, "Even one out of 1,000 of them would not be reborn in the Pure Land" because it was they who began preaching various practices for the purpose of rebirth in the Pure Land. Thus, the term "miscellaneous practices" as used by Shan-tao does not refer to masters of the Lotus-Shingon, but to She-lun masters.

Venerable Eshin, that is Genshin,* of Japan was a disciple of Grand Master Jie, the 18th Chief Abbot of the Enryakuji Temple on Mt. Hiei. He wrote many books entirely for the purpose of spreading the *Lotus Sutra*. His purpose for writing the *Essential Collection Concerning Rebirth in the Pure Land* was not an exception. Of those sutras preached in 40 years or so before the *Lotus Sutra*, there are two kinds: those preaching rebirth in other lands and those preaching the attainment of Buddhahood in this *Sahā* World. Discarding the attainment of Buddhahood* which is the way difficult to practice, Genshin chose rebirth in the Pure Land,* a way easy to practice. Of the practices for rebirth in the Pure Land, he regarded, as the most important, meditation, that is, *nembutsu*, on the Pure Land of the Buddha of Infinite Life to nurture aspiration for Buddhahood.

In the seventh item of the 10th chapter, Questions and Answers, in his *Essential Collection*, Genshin discussed the comparative superiority in merit of various practices and considered the *nembutsu* the most reliable for rebirth in the Pure Land. Immediately after this, he compared the *nembutsu*, the supreme practice in sutras preached before the *Lotus Sutra*, to the merit of having a moment of true faith* as preached in the *Lotus Sutra* , decisively stating that the merit of having a moment of true faith is hundreds, thousands, tens of thousands times greater than that of concentrated practice of the *nembutsu*.

Thus, you should know that the true purpose of Genshin in writing the *Essential Collection* was to convert people to faith in the *Lotus Sutra* by comparing the merit of the *nembutsu*, supreme of all pre-*Lotus* sutras, to the least merit of the *Lotus Sutra* showing the superiority of the latter. Therefore, when Genshin wrote the *Essentials of the One Vehicle Teaching** after the *Essential Collection* to reveal his own beliefs, he based it on the *Lotus Sutra*. That is to say, Genshin never preached that the *Lotus Sutra* should be discarded and to put faith in the *nembutsu* instead.

Not knowing this, Genkū (Hōnen Shōnin) and his disciples put the Lotus-Shingon teachings into the categories of difficult to practice, Holy Way Gate, or miscellaneous practices, which the three Pure Land masters had rejected, and the exoteric and esoteric teachings which Genshin had rejected in the preface to his *Essential Collection*. Thus, they caused the three masters and Genshin to indirectly slander the Lotus-Shingon teachings.

They, moreover, taught all people in Japan, priests as well as lay people, that the Lotus-Shingon teachings were too profound to be suitable for the times and the capacity of the people in the Latter Age so that Japanese people would not have any connection with Lotus-Shingon Buddhism. Are they not those whom the Buddha predicted in the 13th chapter of the *Lotus Sutra*, Encouragement for Keeping This Sutra, which states, "In the evil age, some monks will be cunning and crooked?" How can they escape what is stated in the third chapter of the *Lotus Sutra*, A Parable, the punishment of "immediately destroying all the seeds of becoming a Buddha in this world and falling into the Hell of Incessant Suffering upon death"?

Moreover, Genkū (Hōnen) likened the schools of Mt. Hiei and the Miidera Temple, esotericism of the Tōji Temple, Tendai esotericism, and those who study Lotus-Shingon Buddhism all over Japan to bandits, villains and heretics. In what life would Genkū be able to finish paying the penalty for this grave sin?

Preaching the sin of abusing upholders of the *Lotus Sutra*,* The Teacher of the Dharma chapter of the *Lotus Sutra* states, "Suppose a person with evil intent keeps speaking ill of the Buddha in His presence for as long as a *kalpa*, aeons. His sin is rather light. Suppose a person utters a word to curse lay persons or monks who read and recite the *Lotus Sutra*. His sin is extremely grave."

The sin of cursing just one upholder of the *Lotus Sutra* is this serious. How much more serious is the sin of writing books, causing people all over Japan to curse the upholders of the *Lotus Sutra!* How much more serious is the sin of discouraging those who practice the *Lotus Sutra* by designating this sutra the teaching through which not even one out of 1,000 persons would be able to attain Buddhahood! How much graver is the sin of slandering the True Dharma, causing people to desert this true sutra for such provisional sutras as the *Sutra of Meditation on the Buddha of Infinite Life!* May all followers of Genkū, disciples and lay persons, promptly abandon the evil dharma of his *Collection of Passages on the Nembutsu* and seek refuge in the *Lotus Sutra* immediately in order to escape the Hell of Incessant Suffering.

Question: Do you have clear scriptural evidence to show that Genkū slandered the *Lotus Sutra*?

Answer: It is stated in the *Lotus Sutra*, fascicle two, chapter three, A Parable, "If a person does not believe in but slanders this sutra, he will immediately destroy all the seeds for attaining Buddhahood in this world." It is because one aspect of having no faith in this sutra, is that it causes others to abandon the *Lotus Sutra*. Interpreting this, Bodhisattva Vasubandhu, therefore, states in the first fascicle of his *Treatise on Buddha-nature*, "He who hates and contradicts Mahayana becomes an *icchantika*,* one who has no goodness in his nature and therefore, no possibility of attaining Buddhahood, because such a person causes people to abandon this dharma." Causing people to abandon this dharma is an aspect of slandering the True Dharma. Is not the *Collection of Passages on the Nembutsu* a book causing others to abandon the *Lotus Sutra*? Are not the two characters of "put aside" and "throw away" in the *Collection of Passages on the Nembutsu* the same as the two characters of "hate" and "contradict" in the *Treatise on Buddha-nature*?

Another example of slandering the *Lotus Sutra* is treating the *Lotus Sutra* as equal to the pre-*Lotus* sutras and regarding the doctrine of "achieving Buddhahood through a minor act of merit"* preached in the *Lotus Sutra*, chapter two, Expedients, as a mere expedient means of encouraging idlers. Therefore, Grand Master T'ien-t'ai declares in his *Words and Phrases of the Lotus Sutra*, fascicle five, "If a person does not believe in the attainment of Buddhahood through a minor act of merit, he immediately destroys all the seeds for attaining Buddhahood in this world." Grand Master Miao-lê explains further in his *Annotations on the Words and Phrases of the Lotus Sutra*, fascicle five, "This *Lotus Sutra* elucidates that all those in the six realms of the unenlightened possess the seeds for becoming a Buddha. One who slanders this sutra, therefore, destroys all the seeds for attaining Buddhahood."

Thus, according to the opinions of Śākyamuni Buddha, the Buddha of Many Treasures, Buddhas manifested in the worlds throughout the universe, Vasubandhu, T'ien-t'ai and Miao-lê, Genkū slanders the True Dharma. In sum, the *Collection of Passages on the Nembutsu* was written with the firm intention of causing people to discard the Lotus-Shingon teachings. There is no doubt that it is a work which denigrates the True Dharma.

SECTION III
Reasons Why the Collection of Passages on the Nembutsu Slanders the True Dharma

In this section, I should like to explain the reasons why the *Collection of Passages on the Nembutsu* is said to slander the True Dharma.

Question: What is your proof for accusing Genkū of slandering the True Dharma?

Answer: Reading through the *Collection of Passages on the Nembutsu*, we see that it slanders the True Dharma. It divides all the holy teachings of the Buddha's lifetime* into two: one group called the gate to the Holy Way,* difficult-to-practice way* or miscellaneous practices, and another group termed the gate to the Pure Land, easy-to-practice way, or correct practice.* The first holy-difficult-miscellaneous group includes the *Flower Garland Sutra*, Āgama sutras, Hōdō sutras, *Wisdom Sutra*, *Lotus Sutra*, *Nirvana Sutra* and *Great Sun Buddha Sutra*, whereas the second pure-easy-correct group refers to such teachings as the *nembutsu*, or chanting the name of the Buddha of Infinite Life, preached in the triple Pure Land sutras.

Criticizing the shortcomings of the holy-difficult-miscellaneous category, Genkū insinuated in the *Collection of Passages on the Nembutsu* that of the ignorant people in the Latter Age practicing sutras in this category, merely one or two of 100 of those who practice, or three or five of 1,000 who practice might be able to be reborn in the Pure Land at the most. Maybe not even one out of 1,000 might be reborn there. He also definitely considered those who practice these sutras to be bandits, villains, heretics, or men of evil opinions, and evil outcasts.

Stating the advantages of the pure-easy-correct group, Genkū declared that of all those ignorant people in the Latter Age who practice sutras in this category, 10 out of 10, 100 out of 100 will be reborn in the Pure Land. This is the evil doctrine that slanders the True Dharma!

Question: Dividing the holy teachings preached during the Buddha's lifetime into two groups of the Holy Way and Pure Land, the difficult-to-practice and easy-to-practice or the miscellaneous and correct practices, insisting that of the two the holy-difficult-miscellaneous group of teachings is unsuitable to the time and capacity of the people, is not a new doctrine established by Genkū alone. This is the same doctrine also preached by the three Chinese masters: T'an-luan, Tao-ch'o and Shan-tao. Again, it was not an arbitrary idea of these Chinese masters. It stemmed from Bodhisattva Nāgārjuna's *Commentary on the Ten Stages*. If you call Genkū a slanderer of the True Dharma, are you not indirectly accusing Bodhisattva Nāgārjuna as well as the three Chinese masters of being slanderers?

Answer: Bodhisattva Nāgārjuna and the three Chinese masters divided the sutras preached in the 40 years or so before the *Lotus Sutra* with criteria such as difficulty in putting into practice, but their division did not include the Lotus-Shingon sutras. However, beginning with the publication of the *Collection of Passages on the Nembutsu* by Genkū, such terms as "difficult-to-practice way" employed by Nāgārjuna and the three Chinese masters were used in a different sense, putting the Lotus-Shingon sutras in the group of difficult-to-practice or miscellaneous practices. Not knowing this error made by their teacher, Genkū's disciples believed his false doctrine to be correct and propagated it all over Japan. Consequently the Japanese people were all convinced that the Lotus-Shingon sutras were unsuitable to the time and capacity of the people.

Furthermore, Tendai and Shingon scholars, who desired worldly honors and profit, spoke ill of their own Lotus-Shingon sutras as unsuitable to the time and capacity of people in order to cater to the whims of the public, reinforcing in effect the evil doctrine of the *Collection of Passages on the Nembutsu*. Guided by fleeting self-interest, these so-called scholars broke the vow sworn in the assembly of Śākyamuni Buddha, the Buddha of Many Treasures, and Buddhas manifested in the worlds all over the universe, stating that they would "ensure that the True Dharma endures forever in this world" as stated in the 11th chapter, Beholding the Stupa of Treasures, and "be spread widely in this world" as stated in the 23rd chapter, The Previous Life of Medicine-King Bodhisattva. These scholars motivated all living beings to commit the sin of cutting off the tongues of numerous Buddhas manifested in the worlds all over the universe throughout the past, present and future, with which these Buddhas touched the Brahma Heaven to attest the vow to be true. As stated in the 13th chapter, Encouragement for Keeping This Sutra, this sin solely originates from, "monks in the evil world being cunning, crooked and thinking that they have attained what they actually have not.... Possessed by evil demons, they fail to understand the Buddha's expedient means to preach the dharma in accordance with what is appropriate."

Question: You say that Bodhisattva Nāgārjuna and the three Chinese masters did not include the Lotus-Shingon sutras in the difficult-holy-miscellaneous category, but Genkū arbitrarily included them. How do you know this?

Answer: We don't have to look far for the answer. It is found in the *Collection of Passages on the Nembutsu*.

Question: What did you find?

Answer: In Book One of the *Collection of Passages on the Nembutsu*, Genkū quotes from the *Collection of Passages Concerning Rebirth in the Pure Land* by Tao-ch'o, under the heading of "the statement by Zen Master Tao-ch'o establishing gates for the Holy Way and Pure Land, encouraging people to discard the Holy Way and put faith in the Pure Land." It is followed by Genkū's opinion:

> "First, regarding the gates to the Holy Way, there are two: Mahayana and Hinayana. Within Mahayana, differences exist between the exoteric and esoteric teachings or provisional and true teachings. Now this *Collection of Passages Concerning Rebirth in the Pure Land* includes only exoteric Mahayana and provisional Mahayana as the gates to the Holy Way. That is to say, Tao-ch'o rejected these as being roundabout practices needing an immeasurably long period of time to attain Buddhahood. In the same manner, I believe, esoteric Mahayana and true Mahayana should also be included as gates to the Holy Way."

Thus is written in the *Collection of Passages on the Nembutsu*. Although Zen Master Tao-ch'o's *Collection of Passages Concerning Rebirth in the Pure Land* divided only the pre-*Lotus* sutras into two gates for the Holy Way and the Pure Land, Genkū himself thought it appropriate that the Lotus-Shingon sutras, the true Mahayana and esoteric Mahayana, should also be included in the Holy Way just as those provisional Mahayana sutras preached in 40 or so pre-*Lotus* years. This is an arbitrary opinion of Genkū. The four characters meaning "in the same manner, I believe" show this.

Accordingly, citing T'an-luan's difficult-to-practice and easy-to-practice ways, Genkū again by his own preference included the Lotus-Shingon in the difficult-to-practice way. Then, dividing the correct and miscellaneous practices according to Shan-tao, Genkū again placed the Lotus-Shingon in the miscellaneous practices. His numerous sins in defaming the True Dharma throughout the 16 chapters of the *Collection of Passages on the Nembutsu* originated from these four characters. He is wrong. How terrible it is!

Genkū's Disciples Defended Their Teacher's Evil Doctrine

It is customary for Buddhist sects to put similar doctrines into one group without definite scriptural proof. Moreover, although the *Collection of Passages on the Nembutsu* puts the Lotus-Shingon sutras together with the miscellaneous practices and rejected all of them as inferior to the correct practice of the *nembutsu*, it does not at all deny the doctrines expounded in those sutras. Concluding that uneducated people in the Latter Age are ignorant and always suffering in the sea of birth and death, it maintains that the easy-to-practice way is better than other teachings merely because the *nembutsu* practice of calling the name of the Buddha of Infinite Life seems to be suited to people of such caliber, who need an easy-to-practice teaching. It does not consider whether the teaching is provisional or true, or whether or not it is profound.

Also, the use of the term "miscellaneous" practices does not mean rejection. "Miscellaneous" means "impure." Besides, similar opinions have been expressed by various sutras, commentaries and masters. For instance we can find identical opinions in the *Essential Collection Concerning Rebirth in the Pure Land* by Venerable Eshin, that is Genshin, a man of virtue on Mt. Hiei in the past. His preface to the *Essential Collection Concerning Rebirth in the Pure Land* declares, "Exoteric and esoteric teachings are not just a few. Many kinds of meditation on the phenomenal aspects and the nominal principle exist. They may not be too difficult for wise and diligent people to study and practice, but they are perplexing for the ignorant like myself. This is the reason I rely on the teaching of the *nembutsu*."

According to this preface Venerable Eshin, a man of virtue in the past, also did not reject the Lotus-Shingon doctrines. He just avoided them because he just thought that they were too arduous for uneducated people like himself to comprehend and put into practice. It was because he thought that he was not intelligent enough that he avoided the Lotus-Shingon doctrines.

Furthermore, it is stated in the eighth of the 10-chaptered main discourse following the preface, "Now, encouraging the practice of the *nembutsu* does not intend to deny various other effective practices. It is only because the *nembutsu* is easy for anyone to practice, regardless whether the person is a man or woman, high or low, is walking, staying still, sitting or lying down, whenever, wherever and under whatever circumstances.... And in the last moments of life, this *nembutsu* is the most convenient for anyone to pray for rebirth in the land of bliss to the west."

Looking at these passages, we see that although Genkū's *Collection of Passages on the Nembutsu* and Genshin's (Venerable Eshin's) *Essential Collection* differ in the number of fascicles, one and three respectively, their purpose is the same, in that they chose the easy-to-practice way of all the scriptures of Buddhism in order to save ignorant people in the Latter Age. If Genkū Shōnin should fall into evil realms just because he called the Lotus-Shingon sutras the difficult-to-practice way, Venerable Eshin, a man of virtue in the past, would also not be able to escape this punishment. What do you say about this?

Answer: You seem to be trying to save your teacher from his sin of slandering the True Dharma by referring to Genshin's *Essential Collection,* but on the contrary, you are doubling his sin. Let me explain. Defining the significance of the first 42 years of His 50 years of preaching, the Buddha declared in the *Sutra of Infinite Meaning* that it was "like walking on a steep road with many obstacles." Then He defined the meaning of His preachings after the *Sutra of Infinite Meaning* as being "like traveling on a straight, broad road without an obstacle."

These are the Buddha's words of division between the two ways, the difficult and easy ways, or the superior and the inferior. Suppose anyone, except the Buddha, from the top-ranking bodhisattvas down to the ignorant masters in the Latter Age, would arbitrarily make a division between difficult and easy ways, contrary to the Buddha's words in the *Sutra of Infinite Meaning*. Wouldn't such a person be like a heretic or a King of Devils who preaches to deceive the people? Bodhisattva Nāgārjuna, one of the Four Reliances, four ranks of Buddhist leaders after the death of the Buddha, divided the pre-*Lotus* sutras into difficult-to-practice and the easy-to-practice in his *Commentary on the Ten Stages*, but he did not name the sutras preached after 40 years or so such as the *Lotus Sutra* as difficult-to-practice.

Moreover, suppose the definition of "easy-to-practice" is "what is easy to put into practice." The 50th person who with joy hears the *Lotus Sutra* transmitted from one person to the next as expounded in the *Lotus Sutra*, chapter 18, The Merits of a Person Who Rejoices at Hearing This Sutra, finds the sutra a hundred, a thousand, ten thousand, a hundred million times easier to practice than calling the name of the Buddha of Infinite Life in the *nembutsu*.

Or, suppose we define "easy-to-practice" as having "greater merit." Chapter 17 of the *Lotus Sutra*, The Variety of Merits, compares the merit of practicing for 80 trillion *kalpa*, that is aeons, charity, observing precepts, perseverance, efforts and *nembutsu* meditation, the first five of the six *pāramitā*, through which a bodhisattva attains Buddhahood as preached in the pre-*Lotus* sutras of 40 years or so, to the merit of having true faith for a moment in the *Lotus Sutra*. It declares that the merit of having true faith for a moment is a hundred, a thousand, ten thousand, a hundred million times superior to the merit of the five practices such as *nembutsu* meditation. In terms of both ease of practice and greatness in merit, *nembutsu* meditation, in comparison to the *Lotus Sutra* is the most difficult of the difficult and the most inferior of the inferior.

Besides, saving the evil and ignorant depends on the profundity of the teaching. It does not matter whether or not the teaching is easy to practice. The more grievous a sin is, the more profound the teaching must be to save the sinner. The precepts in the Āgama sutras, preached in the twelve-year period, do not permit those who committed the four major sins, killing, stealing, adultery and lying, or the five rebellious sins* to attain Buddhahood in this life. Such Mahayana sutras as the *Flower Garland Sutra*, Hōdō sutras, the *Wisdom Sutra*, and the *Sutra of the Buddha of Infinite Life*, however, are more profound than the Hinayana Āgama sutras are, so they save those grievous sinners when preaching wisdom. Yet, in preaching the Buddhist precepts, they do not allow violators of the seven rebellious sins* even to accept precepts in this life. Nevertheless, they deny both the attainment of Buddhahood and acceptance of precepts to men of *śrāvaka* and *pratyekabuddha* with "fixed nature"* and *icchantika*, those without Buddha-nature.*

On the contrary, such sutras as the *Lotus* and *Nirvana*, not only save those who committed the five rebellious sins, seven rebellious sins and slandered the True Dharma, but also men of *śrāvaka* and *pratyekabuddha* with "fixed nature" and *icchantika* without Buddha-nature. Especially in the Latter Age of Degeneration, many *icchantika* are drowned in the sea of birth and death. How can they be saved by provisional sutras such as the *Sutra of Meditation on the Buddha of Infinite Life* preached 40 years or so before the *Lotus Sutra*? *Icchantika* without Buddha-nature and men of *śrāvaka* and *pratyekabuddha* with "fixed nature" can only be saved by the *Lotus* and *Nirvana Sutras*. Masters who rely on the pre-*Lotus* sutras cater to those who could be saved by such provisional sutras. Such masters err because they do not realize the importance of comparative study of Buddhist doctrines.*

Just from skimming the preface of the *Essential Collection Concerning Rebirth in the Pure Land*, it may seem that the Lotus-Shingon sutras are included in the exoteric and esoteric teachings, which are too profound for people in the Latter Age to understand. Examining the main discussions of the *Essential Collection*, however, in three fascicles, we can find a discussion on the comparative superiority in merit among various practices in the seventh item of the 10th chapter on "Questions and Answers." Citing such pre-*Lotus* sutras and commentaries as the *Meditation on the Buddha Sutra*, the *Sutra of Meditation to Behold Buddhas*, the *Commentary on the Ten Stages*, the *Accumulated-Treasure Sutra*, and the *Sutra of the Great Assembly*, Venerable Eshin holds that the practice of the *nembutsu* is supreme of all practices.

Then, in the last set of questions and answers Eshin states that the merit of practicing the *nembutsu*, supreme of all the pre-*Lotus* teachings, is a hundred, a thousand, ten thousand and a hundred million times inferior to the merit of having true faith in the *Lotus Sutra* for a moment. In the answer following this, it is declared that the *nembutsu* is designated supreme of all practices within the limit of provisional pre-*Lotus* sutras. Thus, you should know that Venerable Eshin's purpose for writing the *Essential Collection* was to educate ignorant people in the Latter Age to understand and believe in the *Lotus Sutra*. It was the same as the Buddha preaching provisional sutras for 40-odd years to prepare the people to have faith with understanding in the *Lotus Sutra*.

Therefore, Venerable Eshin, in the end, wrote the *Essentials of the One Vehicle Teaching* to propagate the *Lotus Sutra*. In the preface, he wrote:

> "It has long been disputed among various teachings concerning which is true and which is expedient. Based on their own canons, each sect has contended to be the true teaching. I lamented this during the winter of the 10th month of the third year in the Kankō Period (1006), when I was

sick, saying, 'I have been fortunate to be able to encounter Buddhism but I have been unable to thoroughly understand the intent of the Buddha. Should I end this life without understanding anything, I would never be able to grieve enough.' So I had other people investigate the meanings of sutras and commentaries, as well as annotations on them written by sages and I myself studied them in search of the basis of the Buddha's wisdom, both provisional and true, without sectarian prejudice. Finally, I became convinced that the One Vehicle teaching leading to Buddhahood is true while the five-vehicle teaching differentiating human beings, heavenly beings, śrāvaka, pratyekabuddha and bodhisattvas is expedient. Having dispelled all the illusions of this life, I have nothing to regret even if I die this evening."

This preface represents the true intention of Venerable Eshin. When he cast away his sectarian prejudice, he must have also abandoned the Pure Land teaching. Convinced that the One Vehicle teaching led to Buddhahood, he believed solely in the *Lotus Sutra*.

Venerable Eshin wrote the *Essential Collection* in the winter of the 11th month in the second year of the Yōgan Period (984) and the *Essentials of the One Vehicle Teaching* in the winter of the 10th month in the third year of the Kankō Period (1006), after a lapse of some 20 years. He preached the expedient teaching first and the true teaching later just as the Buddha did, and just as Nāgārjuna, Vasubandhu, and T'ien-t'ai had done. You may be trying to redeem your teacher's sin of slandering the True Dharma by referring to the *Essential Collection*, which is not at all similar to Hōnen's *Collection of Passages on the Nembutsu*.

You say that sutras of similar doctrines are gathered in one group, but where is the similarity? The "mutual possession of the 10 realms" doctrine expounded in the *Lotus Sutra* is not preached in any of the pre-*Lotus* sutras. The *Flower Garland Sutra*, which discriminates against two categories of people, śrāvaka and pratyekabuddha, not allowing them to attain Buddhahood, does not have the "mutual possession of the 10 realms" doctrine. The Hōdō sutras and the *Wisdom Sutra* also do not preach the doctrine. Without the "mutual possession of the 10 realms" doctrine, the teaching of rebirth in the Pure Land preached in the *Sutra of Meditation on the Buddha of Infinite Life* is merely expedient. The attainment of Buddhahood and rebirth in the Pure Land preached in the pre-*Lotus* sutras are unlike those preached in the *Lotus Sutra*. They were preached simply for the purpose of bolstering idlers.

Besides, if Venerable Genshin called the *nembutsu* easy practice and the *Lotus Sutra* difficult practice on the grounds that the *nembutsu* is easy to practice, whereas the *Lotus Sutra* is difficult to practice in daily life, he, a Tendai monk, was against the interpretations of T'ien-t'ai and Miao-lê, founding fathers of the

T'ien-t'ai (Tendai) sect. This is because Grand Master Miao-lê, in explaining the practice of the Lotus teaching in his *Annotations on the Great Concentration and Insight*, declared that the *Lotus Sutra* would be easy to practice for ignorant and slow people in the Latter Age because they would be able to meet Universal-Sage Bodhisattva, the Buddha of Many Treasures and Buddhas manifested in various worlds throughout the universe, by simply practicing the teaching of the sutra. In addition Miao-lê declared, "You may recite the *Lotus Sutra* inattentively. You don't have to meditate or concentrate. With your whole heart pray to characters of the *Lotus Sutra* all the time whether sitting, standing or walking."

The aim of this interpretation is solely to save the ignorant in the Latter Age. Miao-lê contrasts the "inattentive mind," meaning the mind of an ordinary person engaged in daily routines, with "concentrated mind." By "reciting the Lotus Sutra" he means to recite either the whole eight fascicles or just one fascicle, one character, one phrase, one verse or the *Odaimoku*. It means also to rejoice upon hearing the *Lotus Sutra* even for a moment, or the joy of the 50th person who hears the sutra transmitted from one person to the next. "Whether sitting, standing or walking" means regardless of what you are doing in daily life. "Whole heart" means neither spiritual concentration nor the rational faculty of the mind. It is the ordinary inattentive mind. "Praying to characters of the *Lotus Sutra*" means that each character of the *Lotus Sutra*, unlike that of other sutras, contains all the characters of all the Buddhist scriptures and the merit of all Buddhas.

Grand Master T'ien-t'ai, therefore, states in his *Profound Meaning of the Lotus Sutra*,* fascicle eight, "Without opening this sutra he who believes in the *Lotus Sutra* reads it all the time. Without uttering a word, he recites various sutras widely. Without the Buddha preaching, he always listens to the resounding voice of the Buddha. And without contemplating, he shines over the entire dharma world." The meaning of this statement is that those who believe in the *Lotus Sutra* are upholders of this sutra* 24 hours a day, even if a person does not hold the eight fascicles. It means that those who believe in the *Lotus Sutra* are the same as those who continuously read all the Buddhist scriptures every day, hour and second even if they do not raise their voices in reciting the sutras. It means that it has already been more than 2,000 years since the passing of the Buddha, whose voice remains in the ears of those who believe in the *Lotus Sutra*, reminding them every hour and minute that the Buddha has always been in this *Sahā* World. And it means that without contemplating the doctrine of the "3,000 existences contained in one thought,"* those who believe in the *Lotus Sutra* observe all the worlds throughout the universe.

These merits are endowed solely to those who practice the *Lotus Sutra*. Therefore, those who believe in the *Lotus Sutra* have the virtue of shining over the dharma world without intention, reciting all the scriptures of Buddhism without voice, and upholding the eight-fascicled *Lotus Sutra* without touching it, although they do not pray to the Buddha at the moment of death, do not recite sutras by voice or enter a practice hall. Is this not a hundred, a thousand, and ten thousand times easier than chanting the *nembutsu* 10 times by followers of Pure Land Buddhism, a provisional teaching, expecting tranquility of mind at the moment of death?*

Grand Master T'ien-t'ai thus wrote in his *Words and Phrases of the Lotus Sutra*, fascicle 10, "The 18th chapter of the *Lotus Sutra* is entitled The Merits of a Person Who Rejoices at Hearing This Sutra, because the sutra's merit is superior to all other sutras in every respect." The *Lotus Sutra*, more than any other sutra, enlightens those whose capacity to understand is limited. Unaware of this, teachers of other sects maintain that only those with superior capacity in understanding can have faith in the *Lotus Sutra*. Rebutting this, Grand Master Miao-lê stated in his *Annotations on the Words and Phrases of the Lotus Sutra*, fascicle 10, "Those erroneous teachers probably did not realize that even those just beginning to practice can have great merit. They insisted that the *Lotus Sutra* can be practiced only by those with advanced training, slighting those with little training. Thus, the 18th chapter shows the great merit of those who begin to practice, revealing the excellent merit of this sutra."

"Revealing the excellent merit of this sutra" in this annotation shows that the *Lotus Sutra* is superior to such provisional sutras as the *Sutra of Meditation on the Buddha of Infinite Life* and has more merit with less practice. It purports to save those with little capacity for understanding. If Venerable Eshin had said that the *Lotus Sutra* is more difficult than the *nembutsu* and has no power to save the ignorant and the stubborn, he would have committed the sin of a heretic rebellious to T'ien-t'ai and Miao-lê, patriarchs of the Tendai sect. Or he may have been one of "those erroneous teachers" referred to above by Miao-lê.

According to the three great works of T'ien-t'ai, *Profound Meaning of the Lotus Sutra, Words and Phrases of the Lotus Sutra,* and *Great Concentration and Insight,* and Miao-lê's annotations on them, the *Lotus Sutra* is to save those who are ignorant, those who are evil, and women, whom other sutras are unable to save, as well as *icchantika*, who are eternally drowned in the sea of birth and death. Yet, teachers of other sects, who do not know this aim of the Buddha, consider the *Lotus Sutra* either equal to other sutras, good only for much-practiced bodhisattvas above the stages of *shoji* and *shojū*,* or promising Buddhahood to the ignorant merely as a means of encouragement.

T'ien-t'ai and Miao-lê refuted these erroneous doctrines, declaring that those wandering in the six realms of illusions are exactly whom the *Lotus Sutra* aims to address. They preached the two doctrines of *jurui* seed and *sōtai* seed,* recognizing both merits and demerits of the past as the seed of Buddhahood. They also declared that those born into the realms of heavenly beings or human beings must have accumulated in the past the merit of keeping the five precepts or the 10 virtuous acts[7] enabling them to become Buddhas. If Venerable Eshin was opposed to this doctrine of T'ien-t'ai and Miao-lê and considered the *Lotus Sutra* unsuitable for people in the Latter Age, he must have been ignorant of his own Tendai sect.

However, Genkū, who was much confused about this, misunderstood the *Essential Collection Concerning Rebirth in the Pure Land,* influencing others as well. Due to his good karma accumulated in the past, Genkū was fortunate enough to study the true teaching of the Lotus, but he persuaded people into believing in the expedient *nembutsu*. Moreover, he caused them to abandon the true teaching. Is he not an evil teacher?

The reason why those who had received the seed of Buddhahood in the eternal past have been transmigrating the six realms, lower states of existence, since as long as "500 dust-particle *kalpa*,"[8] without attaining Buddhahood, and those who had heard the *Lotus Sutra* at the time of Great Universal Wisdom Buddha have been undergoing transmigration in the six realms since "3,000 dust-particle *kalpa*"[9] was because they abandoned the great teaching of the *Lotus,* seeking refuge instead in expedient and Hinayana sutras preached 40 years or so before the *Lotus Sutra*. Later they also gave up faith in those expedient sutras, and thus have continued to transmigrate through the six realms.

Those who slighted and persecuted Never-Despising Bodhisattva had to suffer in the Hell of Incessant Suffering for as long as 1,000 *kalpa*. This was from the sin of believing in evil propagators of expedient teachings and slandering the propagator of the true teaching. Genkū not only discarded the true teaching and sought refuge in an expedient teaching, but also persuaded others to forsake the true sutra putting faith in expedient sutras, and then dissuaded followers of expedient sutras from switching to the true sutra. Moreover, Genkū despised those who practiced the true sutra. Is not his sin of slandering the True Dharma serious enough to drown him in the Hell of Incessant Suffering forever?

Question: The *Commentary on the Ten Stages* by Nāgārjuna is a general commentary on all the Buddha's teachings during His lifetime dividing them into hard-to-practice and easy-to-practice ways. Why do you say that the Shingon sutras, *Lotus Sutra,* and the *Nirvana Sutra* are not included in one of these ways?

Answer: Of Mahayana sutras preached during Śākyamuni Buddha's lifetime, the *Flower Garland Sutra* consists of two parts: the initial, sudden part preached during the first three weeks after His enlightenment, and a part added later. The initial, sudden part of the *Flower Garland Sutra* does not preach the attainment of

Buddhahood by the Two Vehicles, two groups of Hinayana sages called *śrāvaka* and *pratyekabuddha*. Those sutras preached in the Hōdō period positively deny the attainment of Buddhahood by the Two Vehicles as well as the *icchantika*, who do not possess Buddha-nature. Sutras belonging to the Hannya period preached the same. In sum, those Mahayana sutras preached before the *Lotus Sutra* during the period of 40 years or so, unlike the *Lotus, Nirvana* and *Great Sun Buddha Sutras*, do not recognize the attainment of Buddhahood by the Two Vehicles or the *icchantika*. From this viewpoint, the difference between the *Lotus Sutra* and those sutras preached before it is as clear as water and fire.

Of the commentators in India after the death of Śākyamuni Buddha, both Nāgārjuna and Vasaubandhu wrote 1,000 commentaries each. Their commentaries are of two kinds: general and special. Their general commentaries in turn can be divided into two groups: commentaries on the pre-*Lotus* sutras and those on all sutras preached during 50 years of the Buddha's lifetime. The criterion used for separating the two groups is whether or not they recognize the attainment of Buddhahood by the Two Vehicles, whose inherent nature is fixed, and the *icchantika*, who have no Buddha-nature. With this standard it is judged whether those commentaries are expedient, covering only the pre-*Lotus* sutras, or true, covering all the sutras including the *Lotus* and other sutras.

Now, the *Great Wisdom Discourse*, written by Bodhisattva Nāgārjuna and translated into Chinese by *Tripiṭaka* Master Kumārajīva,* sometimes does not allow the Two Vehicles to become Buddhas according to the *Wisdom Sutra*, and at other times does allow them to attain Buddhahood based on the *Lotus Sutra*. It shows that the *Great Wisdom Discourse* is the true general commentary covering both provisional and true sutras. On the other hand, the *Commentary on the Ten Stages*, also written by Nāgārjuna and translated by Kumārajīva, does not allow the attainment of Buddhahood by the Two Vehicles at all. Therefore, it is known that this commentary is a general work, covering only the pre-*Lotus* Mahayana sutras.

Question: Where in the *Commentary on the Ten Stages* is it stated that the Two Vehicles will never attain Buddhahood?

Answer: The *Commentary on the Ten Stages*, written by Bodhisattva Nāgārjuna and translated by *Tripiṭaka* Master Kumārajīva, fascicle five, states, "Falling into the realms of *śrāvaka* and *pratyekabuddha* means death to a bodhisattva. In other words, such a bodhisattva has lost the aspiration to save himself and others. One should not be afraid of falling into hell as much as falling into the realms of Two Vehicles. Even if one should fall into hell, he still has a chance of eventually attaining Buddhaood, but if he should fall into the realms of the Two Vehicles, he will never be able to become a Buddha." This passage is a distinct verification that the *Commentary on the Ten Stages* does not allow *śrāvaka* and *pratyekabuddha* to become Buddhas. It is similar to a statement in the *Vimalakīrti Sutra* and others that men of the Two Vehicles are like spoiled seeds that will never germinate in Buddhism.

Question: Do you have scriptural evidence to say that the *Great Wisdom Discourse* sometimes does not permit the Two Vehicles to attain Buddhahood according to the *Wisdom Sutra* but at other times does allow the attainment of Buddhahood by the Two Vehicles according to the *Lotus Sutra*?

Answer: The *Great Wisdom Discourse*, fascicle 100, written by Nāgārjuna and translated by Kumārajīva, says:

> "The question is asked whether there is any dharma superior to the *Wisdom Sutra* and why You entrust Ānanda, a *śrāvaka*, with the *Wisdom Sutra* while that other sutra is to be entrusted to a bodhisattva. It is answered that the *Wisdom Sutra* is not what the Buddha has secretly treasured in His heart, that such sutras as the *Lotus* promise the attainment of Buddhahood in the future even to those *śrāvaka* with fixed nature who have attained arhatship. Therefore only great bodhisattvas can uphold and make use of the sutra just as only excellent physicians can make use of poison as medicine."

The *Great Wisdom Discourse* also states in fascicle 93, "The attainment of Buddhahood by those *śrāvaka*, whose inherent nature is fixed and who have won arhatship is incomprehensible to commentators. Only the Buddha knows this." According to these passages, commentators in India, just as the Buddha did, preached the expedient teachings first and the true teachings later.

Nevertheless, later masters who relied on expedient sutras at their own discretion equated such sutras as the *Lotus* to such expedient sutras as the *Sutra of Meditation on the Buddha of Infinite Life*, using the doctrines of such sutras as the *Lotus* and *Nirvana* to be the virtue of the triple Pure Land sutras, and promising rebirth in the Pure Land to the Two Vehicles with fixed nature, to *icchantika* who lack Buddha-nature, and to the ignorant drowned eternally in the sea of birth and death. These later masters cannot escape from the sin of taking the expedient for the true. They are, for instance, similar to those Chinese Confucian scholars who study non-Buddhist scriptures* stealing Buddhist doctrines to embellish their own classics. They cannot escape from the sin of slandering the True Dharma, can they?

The Buddha Himself distinguished expedient from true teachings. His criterion for making this division was whether or not the attainment of Buddhahood was allowed for the Two Vehicles, who had been considered incapable of becoming Buddhas, and those who do not have Buddha-nature. Yet, those translators who did not know this, translated the pre-*Lotus* sutras into Chinese in such a way to enable the Two Vehicles as well as those without Buddha-nature to attain Buddhahood through those expedient sutras. Only those translators, who were aware of this, translated the pre-*Lotus* sutras in such a way as not to allow the Two Vehicles and those without Buddha-nature to attain Buddhahood.

Therefore, Buddhist masters who did not understand the true aim of the Buddha, thinking that the pre-*Lotus* sutras also preach attainment of Buddhahood by both the Two Vehicles and those without Buddha-nature, equated those pre-*Lotus* sutras to the *Lotus Sutra*. Seeing passages in the pre-*Lotus* sutras denying the attainment of Buddhahood to the Two Vehicles and those without Buddha-nature, others believed that these pre-*Lotus* sutras revealed the true intent of the Buddha while the *Lotus* and *Nirvana Sutras*, preaching the attainment of Buddhahood by all sentient beings did not. Neither of these masters knew the intent of the Buddha and were lost in the difference between expedient and true sutras.

This misunderstanding is not limited to Genkū alone. Some commentators and translators in India and Buddhist masters in China made similar mistakes. For instance, the *betsuji ishu* doctrine, expedient means of encouraging idlers, by the Jiron (Ti-lun) and Shōron (She-lun) sect, and also Shan-tao and his disciple Huai-kan's opinion that the *Lotus Sutra's* claim of the attainment of Buddhahood by those who chanted "Homage to the Buddha!" just once is merely an expedient means of encouraging idlers — these mistakes all stemmed from ignorance of the difference between expedient and true sutras. Even those bodhisattvas in India who wrote commentaries on the sutras, translators who translated the sutras into Chinese, and Buddhist teachers in China who attained enlightenment by practicing *samādhi*, that is mental concentration, they all made these mistakes. How much more so with the ignorant teachers in the Latter Age!

Question: How can you, a latter student of Buddhism in Japan, refute those commentators and translators of the sutras of India and ministers of China?

Answer: I don't think I deserve such criticism. The interpretations of Shan-tao and the She-lun ministers failed to distinguish between expedient and true teachings. They arbitrarily decided that the attainment of Buddhahood promised in the *Lotus Sutra* is merely an expedient means to encourage idle people. Their interpretation diametrically opposed T'ien-t'ai and Miao-lê as fire and water. Setting aside different opinions of the Chinese scholar-ministers, I, therefore studied the sutras and commentaries to determine whether or not their interpretations are correct. Thus, I found that this distinction between expedient and true teachings was plainly explained by the Buddha, and that both Vasubandhu and Nāgārjuna redefined it. Therefore, I revere those scholar-ministers who follow the doctrine defined by the Buddha and bodhisattvas, not accepting opinions of those who contradict it. I have never judged right and wrong at my own discretion. I have just pointed out the differences between their opinions and that of the Buddha.

SECTION IV
Scriptural Statements to Show Why Slanderers of the True Dharma Should Be Punished

In this fourth section, statements will be cited from sutras to show that slanderers of the True Dharma should be punished. This section is divided into two parts. The first explains that the Buddha entrusted His dharma to the king, his ministers and four categories of Buddhists: monks, nuns, laymen and laywomen. The second part will present scriptural statements that slanderers of the True Dharma within the royal domain should be punished.

Part 1: Entrusting the Dharma to Kings, Ministers, and the Four Categories of Buddhists

First, I would like to explain how the dharma is entrusted to the kings, ministers, monks, nuns, laymen and laywomen. The *Sutra of the Benevolent King* states: "The Buddha told King Prasenajit…, therefore, I entrust the dharma to the kings of various states. I did not entrust it to monks, nuns, laymen or laywomen because they did not have the authority of the king…. Now I entrust the three treasures of this sutra to the kings of various states, monks, nuns, laymen and laywomen."

The *Sutra of the Great Assembly*, fascicle 28, states: "Suppose the king of a state does not try to save My dharma which is on the verge of destruction. Even if he practices charity, observes precepts, and nourishes wisdom for the duration of innumerable lives, his merit would all disappear and the three calamities of warfare, epidemics and famine would befall his state…. He would fall into the great hell upon death."

According to the *Sutra of the Benevolent King*, the Buddha entrusted the dharma first to the king of a state, then to the four categories of Buddhists. Therefore, the ruling king and his ministers who govern the state should do so in accordance with the Buddha's dharma.

The *Sutra of the Great Assembly* states that it is not enough for the king of a state and his ministers try to master Buddhism for the duration of incalculable *kalpa*, that is aeons, by practicing the charity of giving away their head and eyes, observing 80,000 precepts, and studying numerous teachings of the Buddha. Unless they rectified the dharma prevalent in their country, their land would be overcome by the three calamities of strong winds, severe droughts and heavy rain, people would flee the country, and both the king and his ministers would certainly fall into the three wretched realms: hell, the realm of hungry spirits and that of beasts.

Also, it is stated in fascicle three of the *Nirvana Sutra*, preached before Śākyamuni Buddha passed away under the twin *sala* trees: "I now entrust this True Dharma to the kings, ministers, prime ministers, monks, nuns, laymen and laywomen.... I call those who do not protect the dharma 'shaved-headed' monks in appearance only." The sutra also says: "Gentlemen, those who protect the True Dharma should neither adhere only to the five precepts nor behave only in a dignified manner. Arm yourselves with swords, bows and arrows, and spears." Again: "Even without observing the five precepts, those who protect the True Dharma can be said to be Mahayana Buddhists. Those who protect the True Dharma should arm themselves with swords and sticks."

According to the precepts of the *Brahma-net Sutra* preached during the pre-*Lotus* period of 40 years or so, neither kings and ministers nor others may keep any kind of weapon such as swords, sticks, bows and arrows, halberds and axes. Anyone who violated this prohibition would certainly lose his throne or his status of a monk or a nun in this life and would fall without fail into the three wretched realms of hell, the world of hungry spirits and the world of beasts. As both clergy and laity today all carry bows and arrows, swords and sticks, they all will undoubtedly fall into these three evil realms as stated in the *Brahma-net Sutra*. How can we save them without relying on those passages of the *Nirvana Sutra* cited above?

According to the two statements in the *Nirvana Sutra* cited above, it is promised that those who arm themselves with bows and arrows, swords and sticks to chastise monks of the evil dharma and protect monks of the True Dharma would extinguish their four major sins and five rebellious sins committed in previous lives and attain the Supreme Way without fail.

Also, the *Sutra of the Golden Splendor*, fascicle six, states:

"Suppose the king of a state, aware of this sutra, does not try to propagate it in his domain, dislikes getting close to the sutra, does not wish to give offerings to, revere and praise the sutra, nor reveres and gives offerings to the four categories of Buddhist clergy and laity who believe in this sutra. As a result we, the Four Heavenly Kings, and our servants and numerous heavenly beings, unable to listen to this profoundly wonderful dharma, to taste the nectar and to bathe in the stream of the True Dharma, would all lose authority and power. Evil spirits of the four evil realms, hell, realms of hungry spirits, beasts and *asura*, would grow rampant while virtuous spirits of the human and heavenly realms would grow weaker in the king's domain, and people all would go astray from the way of Nirvana, falling into the river of delusion of birth and death.

"World Honored One! Upon seeing this state of the king's domain, we, the Four Heavenly Kings, our servants and such demigods as *yakṣa* would abandon this land, having lost our desire to protect it. Not only we, but also numerous protective gods and deities of this land would all forsake it. If we all gave up and deserted this land, it would be overtaken by all kinds of calamities and disasters and its king would be dethroned. People would all lose their virtue, arresting, killing, fighting, slandering, flattering one another and even punishing the innocent. Epidemics would be rampant. Comets would often appear. Two suns would rise at the same time. The eclipse of the sun and moon would occur irregularly. Two rainbows, black and white, would predict bad omens. Meteors would appear. The earth would quake. Sounds would come out of wells. Storms would occur out of season. Crops would not bear fruit and famine would continue. Many places would be invaded by foreign bandits causing much hardship to people, who would not have a place to live in peace."

We must know that, according to this scriptural passage, the reason why the three calamities* continue, despite prayers for peace and tranquility of the land, is the prevalence of the evil dharma. Recently many prayers have been said in Buddhist temples and Shinto shrines for peace and tranquility of the land. Yet in the first year of the Shōka Era (1257) we had a severe earthquake, and in the following year strong winds and torrential rains destroyed crops. I am certain that it was due to the dissemination of evil dharmas in Japan causing national destruction.

In the second chapter of the *Collection of Passages on the Nembutsu*, it states: "First of all, believing, reading or reciting any of the sutras, Mahayana or Hinayana or exoteric or esoteric, other than such as the *Sutra of Meditation on the Buddha of Infinite Life*, which preaches rebirth in the Pure Land, are all called miscellaneous practices in reading and reciting." It also says: "Next, if I compare the relative merits of correct practice and miscellaneous practices, practicing teachings such as the Lotus-Shingon miscellaneously is useless while practicing the triple Pure Land sutras is useful."

Then a passage is cited from Venerable Shan-tao's *Hymns of Praise Concerning Rebirth in the Pure Land*, "All who practice it correctly will be reborn in the Pure Land, 10 out of 10 or 100 out of 100. And of the 1,000 who practice miscellaneous teachings, not even one will be able to be reborn in the Pure Land." Following this citation Genkū declares: "In my opinion, this passage clarifies that we should discard miscellaneous practices and concentrate on the sole practice of the *nembutsu*. Why should we give up the sole practice of the *nembutsu*, which guarantees 100 out of 100 to be reborn in the Pure Land, and stick to miscellaneous practices, in which not even one out of 1,000 will be able to be reborn in the Pure Land? Those who practice should contemplate this thoroughly."

Reading these sentences, how can people in the world, clergy as well as laity, believe in any sutras other than the triple Pure Land sutras? Later in chapter three, defining the comparative superiority and difficulty in the miscellaneous practices of such as the *Lotus Sutra* and the correct practice of the *nembutsu*, Genkū also declares: "There are two means of comparing the two — first, superiority, second, how easy it is to put them into practice. First, as for comparative superiority, the *nembutsu* is superior to any other practice. Next, as for comparative ease of practice, the *nembutsu* is easier to practice than any other practice."

Additionally, in chapter 12, Genkū defines the ineffectiveness of teachings such as the Lotus-Shingon stating: "Therefore, miscellaneous practices are unsuitable to the capacity of comprehension of the people and the times: ignorant people in the Latter Age. Rebirth in the Pure Land by means of the *nembutsu* alone is the practice suitable to the capacity of the people and times." Closing the gate to the miscellaneous practices of teachings such as the Lotus-Shingon, Genkū further states: "Preaching the expedient dharma according to the caliber of those who listened to Him, the Buddha temporarily opened the gate to two ways of practicing meritorious deeds, one with a concentrated mind and another with a scattered mind (*jōsan*).* However, in preaching the True Dharma in accordance with His true intent without considering the capacity of the listeners, the Buddha closed the gate to the two ways of practicing meritorious deeds. Opening the gate which, once opened, will never be closed forever, is done solely by calling the name of the Buddha of Infinite Life."

Expressing his true intent, Genkū advocates the sole practice of the *nembutsu* in the last, 16th chapter: "Should you wish to leave the chain of birth and death immediately, of the two excellent teachings, you should at once choose to enter the gate for the Pure Land, setting aside the gate for the Holy Way. Should you wish to enter the gate for the Pure Land with correct and miscellaneous practices, you should choose without delay to seek refuge in correct practice, discarding various miscellaneous practices."

Genkū's disciples disseminated the *Collection of Passages on the Nembutsu* all over Japan spreading the rumor among ignorant people that the priest who wrote this book, Genkū or Hōnen Shōnin, was the wisest person, who decided that the *nembutsu* is the true teaching. They claimed that there is no scriptural statement allowing us to reopen the gate to the Lotus-Shingon teachings once it was closed or to revitalize those teachings again after discarding them. Consequently, people in Japan, both clergy and lay people, all bowed and believed in Hōnen Shōnin (Genkū). For those who have questions concerning his teaching, the gist of the *Collection of Passages on the Nembutsu* was rewritten in kana and biographical tales of Hōnen Shōnin were written. So people began condemning the Lotus-Shingon teachings as being worthless as last year's calendar or grandfather's shoes. Some claimed that reading the *Lotus Sutra* was less worthy than listening to music.

Evil books such as this disseminated all over Japan, and nobody wanted to listen to the preaching of teachings such as the Lotus-Shingon although they existed in this country. If by chance, people came across those who practiced the Lotus-Shingon teachings, people did not revere them. Those who practiced the *nembutsu* alone were warned that any association with the *Lotus Sutra* would hinder their chances of rebirth in the Pure Land, so they felt like staying away from any association with the *Lotus Sutra*. As a result, heavenly beings, unable to hear and to taste the wonderful True Dharma, lost their power and authority. Thus, the Four Heavenly Kings and their followers abandoned this land and the protective deities of Japan left.

This is the reason we had severe earthquakes in the first year of the Shōka Period (1257). Then in the following year torrential rains washed away seedlings in spring, bad drought killed plants and trees in summer, fruit was knocked down by strong winds in autumn, causing famine, with the people all fleeing the land. This is exactly what is predicted in the *Sutra of the Golden Splendor*. Is this not entirely due to the sin of the *Collection of Passages on the Nembutsu*? The words of the Buddha are true. As evil dharma spread, three calamities have ravaged the country. Should we not deal with this evil dharma? How can all the people in Japan be saved from falling into the three evil realms as stated by the Buddha?

As a matter of fact, impressed by the passage in the 13th chapter of the *Lotus Sutra*, "We do not spare even our lives. We treasure only the Supreme Way," I have recently had a desire for seeking the dharma just as Young Ascetic in the Snow Mountains* and Ever-Weeping Bodhisattva,* determined to propagate the *Lotus Sutra* at the cost of their lives, and loudly warned that those who believe in the *Collection of Passages on the Nembutsu* praying to be reborn in the Pure Land would all fall into the Hell of Incessant Suffering.

Thereupon, disciples of Hōnen Shōnin tried to conceal the evil teachings of *Collection of Passages on the Nembutsu* as pointed out above by insisting that rebirth in the Pure Land is attainable through miscellaneous practices,* and that the *Collection of Passages on the Nembutsu* does not refute the Lotus-Shingon teachings. They also spread a rumor, in order to hide the evil of the *Collection of Passages on the Nembutsu*, to the effect that Nichiren is merely intimidating those who chant the *nembutsu* by saying that they would all fall into the three evil realms: hell, the worlds of hungry spirits and beasts.

Question: Is there anything wrong with disciples of Hōnen Shōnin stating that rebirth in the Pure Land is possible through miscellaneous practices?

Answer: Insisting that rebirth in the Pure Land is possible through miscellaneous practices while claiming to be a disciple of Hōnen Shōnin is heresy for Hōnen Shōnin. Those who insist that rebirth is possible through miscellaneous practices today secretly believe that rebirth in the Pure Land is not possible except through chanting of the *nembutsu* solely. Yet they outwardly state that they do not slander other practices. Are they not aware of the *Collection of Passages on the Nembutsu* urging to "abandon, close, set aside, cast away"* the Lotus-Shingon teachings, likening those who believe in them to "groups of bandits, of heretics, of evil opinions, or of evil outcasts" and insisting that "not even one out of 1,000 believers of them will be able to be reborn in the Pure Land"?

Part 2: Scriptural Statements to Show Why Slanderers of the True Dharma Must Be Dealt With

Here, I would like to present passages in sutras stating that slanderers in the royal domain should be dealt with. It is stated in the *Nirvana Sutra*, fascicle three: "The Buddha asked, 'The king and ministers of a state and four categories of Buddhists, monks, nuns, laymen, and laywomen, should severely deal with those who are idle in practicing Buddhism, break Buddhist precepts, and slander the True Dharma.

"'Gentlemen, do you think this king and others who punish such people are committing a sin?' 'No, World Honored One, we do not think so,' answered Kāśyapa and others. The Buddha stated, 'Gentlemen, such a king and the four categories of Buddhists are innocent of any sin.'"

The sutra also states in fascicle 12: "In a past life I was born to this *Sahā* World as King Sen'yo*, leader of a great state. I cherished and revered Mahayana sutras, having a pure and virtuous mind without a bad temper and jealousy.... Gentlemen, as I firmly believed in Mahayana, as soon as I heard Brahmans slander Mahayana sutras, I killed them. Gentlemen, because of this merit of protecting the True Dharma, I have never again fallen into hell."

Question: According to the *Brahma-net Sutra*, slandering the four categories of Buddhists such as monks is a major sin for which one is expelled from his order. Therefore, is it not an act of inviting the Hell of Incessant Suffering to accuse Genkū (Hōnen Shōnin) of slandering the True Dharma?

Answer: The *Nirvana Sutra*, fascicle 33, states, "Kāśyapa Bodhisattva asked the World Honored One why He predicted that Sunakṣatra (Zenshō Biku) would fall into the Hell of Incessant Suffering. The Buddha replied: 'Gentlemen, Sunakṣatra had many followers, who all considered him an arhat, a sage who attained enlightenment. In order to crush such erroneous thinking, I predicted that Sunakṣatra would fall into hell due to his licentiousness.'"

"Licentiousness" in this passage designates "slandering the True Dharma." Just as Sunakṣatra did, Genkū, who slandered the True Dharma, will also fall into the Hell of Incessant Suffering. Without knowing the evil of the *Collection of Passages on the Nembutsu*, Genkū's disciples, nevertheless, call Genkū a man of wisdom mastering all teachings, regarding him as an avatar of Great-Power-Obtainer Bodhisattva (Mahāsthāmaprāpta), or that of Shan-tao. In order to refute such erroneous thinking, I pointed out Genkū's sin of slandering the True Dharma at its root. This is exactly what is preached in the *Nirvana Sutra* already cited.

What is preached in the *Brahma-net Sutra* cited above means that those who slander the four categories of Buddhists, except for slanderers of the True Dharma, will fall into hell. This does not contradict what is preached in the *Nirvana Sutra*. Therefore, the Buddha warned His disciples, "Those who do not reprimand slanderers of the True Dharma are not His disciples." Thus it is stated in the *Nirvana Sutra*, fascicle three: "Suppose after My extinction there will be a monk who strictly observes Buddhist precepts, acts with dignity, and believes in the True Dharma. Upon seeing those who destroy the True Dharma, he should at once chase, chastise and punish them. Then he will gain immeasurable happiness." The sutra says also, "Suppose there is a virtuous monk who, upon seeing slanderers of the True Dharma, leaves them alone without reprimanding, chasing, and punishing them, you should know that he is an enemy of Buddhism. If he chases, reprimands, and punishes them, he is My disciple and a true *śrāvaka*."

Hoping to be counted a disciple of the Buddha, I wrote this treatise to define the sin of slandering the True Dharma and propagate it among the people. May Buddhas in all the worlds in the universe help me disseminate this treatise and stop the worst dharma spreading further in order to save all people from the sin of slandering the True Dharma!

SECTION V
Difficulty of Meeting "Good Friends" and the True Dharma

In this fifth section, which is divided into three parts, I would like to explain how difficult it is to meet a "good friend,"* meaning a reliable teacher, and the True Dharma. In the first part, I will explain how difficult it is to be born a human being and to encounter Buddhism. In the second part, I will illustrate that even if one is born a human being and encounters Buddhism, difficult as it is, he may fall into the three evil realms if he associates with "evil friends"* meaning evil teachers. In the third part, I will elucidate about a "good friend" for the unenlightened in the Latter Age.

Part 1: The Difficulty of Being Born a Human Being and Encountering the Buddha Dharma

In explaining the difficulty to be born a human being and to encounter the teaching of the Buddha, the *Nirvana Sutra*, fascicle 33, states:

> "The Buddha then picked up a small portion of soil placing it on a fingernail and asked Kāśyapa whether or not this was more than the soil in the worlds all over the universe. Kāśyapa Bodhisattva answered the Buddha, 'World Honored One, the amount of soil on a fingernail cannot be compared to that in the worlds all over the universe.'
>
> "With this simile in mind, the Buddha preached to Kāśyapa, 'Gentlemen, it is as rare as the amount of soil on a fingernail for a man to be reborn as a man or for those in the three evil realms to be reborn in the human realm equipped with all six organs in the central land of Buddhism, and furthermore to have the correct faith, study the way of the Buddha, attain freedom by practicing the correct way, and then to enter Nirvana. On the contrary, it is as vast as an occurrence as the soil in the worlds throughout the universe for human beings to fall into the three evil realms after death, for those in the evil realms to be reborn in those evil realms again, and for those who were born to the human realm without having six organs properly functioning, to be reborn in remote corners where Buddhism is unknown, to believe in evil ideologies or to practice evil ways without ever attaining freedom or Nirvana.'"

Many teachings are condensed in this passage, so some words of explanation are needed. The number of human beings who will be reborn in the human realm after death is as small as the amount of the soil on a fingernail while those who will fall into the three evil realms are as vast as the soil in the worlds all over the universe. The number of those in the three evil realms who will be born after death in the human realm is as little as the amount of soil on a fingernail while those who will be reborn in the three evil realms after death are as immeasurable as the soil in all the worlds of the universe. Those who will be born human beings are as numerous as the soil in the worlds of the universe, but those who will be born human beings with six senses functioning properly are as small in number as the soil on a fingernail. Of those born human with six senses properly functioning, those born in remote areas are as numerous as the soil in the worlds all over the universe but those born in the center of the land are as small in number as the soil on a fingernail. Even though those born in the center of the land are as numerous as the soil in the worlds all over the universe, those who encounter Buddhism are as minute as the soil on a fingernail.

The *Nirvana Sutra* states also: "Those who do not become *icchantika*, those without Buddha-nature, who do not sever the root of virtue, and believe in this *Nirvana Sutra* are as minute as the soil on a fingernail.... Those who become *icchantika*, who cut off the root of virtue and do not believe in this sutra, are as numerous as the soil in the worlds all over the universe." According to this passage those who do not believe in the *Lotus* and *Nirvana Sutras*, becoming *icchantika*, are as many as the soil in the worlds throughout the universe while those who believe in the *Lotus* and *Nirvana Sutras* are as meager as the soil on a fingernail. Seeing this passage and thinking of my fortune in encountering the precious True Dharma, I feel so moved that I cannot suppress my tears.

From what I observe of people today in Japan, most of them are practicing expedient teachings. Although they appear to be practicing the true teaching in "body and mouth," they still believe in expedient teachings deep in their hearts. Therefore, Grand Master T'ien-t'ai says of these people in his *Great Concentration and Insight*,* fascicle five:

> "Ignorant people, heavily dosed with poison, having lost their minds, cannot believe in efficacious medicine. Since they cannot believe in it, it does not help them at all.... They are sinful people.... Those who dislike the world seeking the way of the Buddha by clinging to expedient teachings are like those who try to cut a tree by trimming the leaves and branches instead of chopping the trunk. They are similar to a dog who befriends a servant instead of its master, and to those who revere a monkey as Indra, or take pieces of tile or pebbles for gems. They are unreasonable. How can we discuss the Buddhist way with them?"

Reflecting on this passage, it can be seen that Genkū and his disciples have been heavily intoxicated with the three poisons of greed, anger, and stupidity. They have lost their true minds, with which they had listened to Great Universal Wisdom Buddha preach the *Lotus Sutra*. Suspicious of the *Lotus* and *Nirvana Sutras*, they have become *icchantika* and believe in such inferior teachings as the *Sutra of Meditation on the Buddha of Infinite Life*, adhering to the expedient teaching of calling the name of the Buddha of Infinite Life that is worthless as rubble. They have revered Priest Hōnen, who is as ignorant as a monkey, taking him for Indra, the wisest, and have abandoned the *Lotus* and *Nirvana Sutras*, which are as precious as the wish-fulfilling gem, slandering the holy teachings of the Buddha. This is because they are unable to distinguish the expedient from the true teachings.

Therefore, the *Annotations on the Great Concentration and Insight*,* fascicle one, states: "Those who listen without revering the perfect and sudden true teaching are influenced by the recent academic tradition of 'mixing up' expedient and true teachings among those who study Mahayana Buddhism." Those who do not know the difference between the expedient and true teachings of the Mahayana are referred to as "mixed up." As a result those who believe in the *Lotus Sutra*, the true Mahayana teaching, are as rare as the soil on a fingernail while those who do not believe in the sutra and are diverted to expedient teachings are as immeasurable as the dust in the worlds throughout the universe.

Regretting this, Grand Master Miao-lê laments in his *Annotations on the Great Concentration and Insight,* fascicle one: "In the Age of the Semblance Dharma and the Latter Age of Degeneration, people are so heartless and impious that they don't even try to contemplate the perfect and sudden true teaching to the very end, scriptures of which are overflowing libraries and chests. They are born and die in vain. How pathetic their lives are!" I believe this remark in the *Annotations* by Grand Master Miao-lê, an avatar of a bodhisattva, is his long-range prediction* on the state of Japan today, in the Latter Age of Degeneration.

Question: Some disciples of Priest Hōnen revere all the Buddhist scriptures and practice the *Lotus Sutra*. Why do you refer to them all as slanderers of the True Dharma?

Answer: They open all the Buddhist scriptures and read the *Lotus Sutra* only to make certain that these scriptures preach the "difficult-to-practice way" and then promote the evil teachings of the *Collection of Passages on the Nembutsu*. The more they read sutras and commentaries, the more grievous is their sin of slandering the True Dharma. They are like Monk Sunakṣatra, who read all the scriptures of Buddhism but nonetheless fell into the Hell of Incessant Suffering, and Devadatta,* who mastered 60,000 Buddhist teachings and rebelled against Śākyamuni Buddha. They call themselves wise in order to appear respectable and to help spread the evil dharma of the *Collection of Passages on the Nembutsu*.

Part 2: Falling into the Three Evil Realms Led by Evil Teachers

Here, I would like to illustrate that even if one was born a human being and encountered Buddhism, as difficult it is, he may fall into the three evil realms because of his encounter with an "evil friend." It is stated in the *Buddha Repository Sutra:*

> "After the extinction of Great Adornment Buddha in the remote past there lived five monks, one of whom, Monk Fuji, learned the True Dharma and saved millions of people. The remaining four, however, adhered to evil dharmas, falling into the Hell of Incessant Suffering after death. Lying

on their backs, on their stomachs, on their left sides and right sides, they rolled about in agony for 900 trillion years.... Those who befriended the four, clergy as well as laymen, and their followers, totaled 604 trillion. They were born, died and then burned and boiled in the worst hell together with those four monks. After suffering incalculable years in this Hell of Incessant Suffering, the four monks and their 604 trillion disciples and followers were reborn again in the same hell in another world to be tormented for aeons."

It is also declared in the *Nirvana Sutra*, fascicle 33:

"Once there lived a Jain named Kutoku in the town of Rājagṛha.... Upon death he became a hungry ghost, living near his own corpse. Monk Sunakṣatra, a disciple of the Buddha, asked the ghost of Kutoku who he was. 'I was born to the realm of hungry spirits because of my hostility toward the Buddha. Heed this carefully, Sunakṣatra,' answered Kutoku.... Sunakṣatra then returned to the Buddha falsely saying, 'World Honored One, Jain Kutoku after death was reborn to the heaven of 33 gods....' The Buddha, together with Kāśyapa, later visited Sunakṣatra to reprimand him for lying. Seeing the Buddha approaching, Sunakṣatra had an evil thought, for which he fell into the Hell of Incessant Suffering alive."

Monk Sunakṣatra, a son of the Buddha, was born while the Buddha was practicing the way of the bodhisattva. Following the example of the Buddha, he renounced family ties, studied all the Buddhist scriptures, extinguished evil passions in the realm of desires,[10] and mastered the four stages of meditation.* Having encountered an "evil friend" Kutoku, a heretic, and having doubted the true teaching of Buddhism, Sunakṣatra lost the merit of renouncing family ties, receiving Buddhist precepts and studying all the Buddhist scriptures, and fell into the Hell of Incessant Suffering alive. Those 604 trillion people who befriended those four monks such as Kugan had to undergo suffering, together with the four monks, in the Hells of Incessant Suffering throughout the universe.

Buddhists today, clergy as well as lay followers, revere the *Collection of Passages on the Nembutsu* so much that they show respect to the portrait and statue of Genkū and accept the evil teaching insisting that all the scriptures of Buddhism are impossible to practice. They are similar to those disciples of Monk Kutoku, a Jain, paying respect to the ashes of their Jain master and falling into the three evil realms, hell, the realm of hungry spirits and that of beasts. I pray that people today, both clergy and lay followers, will make offerings or pay respect to the *Collection of Passages on the Nembutsu* only after ascertaining whether or not it preaches the correct teaching. Otherwise, they will certainly suffer remorse. Therefore, it is stated in the *Nirvana Sutra*:

"Bodhisattvas, do not be afraid of such things as wild elephants, but fear 'evil friends.' Why? Because a wild elephant may destroy our bodies but not our minds, while an 'evil friend' can destroy both. A wild elephant may crush merely one person, but an 'evil friend' can crush both bodies and minds of innumerable persons. An elephant may crush merely an impure, stinking body, but an 'evil friend' can destroy both pure body and mind. A wild elephant may merely ruin our flesh and blood, while an 'evil friend' can corrupt our Buddha-nature. Killed by a wild elephant, we may not fall into the three evil realms. However it seems inevitable for us to fall there when we die because of an 'evil friend.' This wild elephant is only a physical enemy, while this 'evil friend' is the enemy of the True Dharma. You, Bodhisattvas, therefore, should always be careful to stay away from 'evil friends.'"

I hope that people today, clergy and lay persons, will set aside for a moment the thought that this writing of Nichiren may preach an erroneous doctrine, and open the *Commentary on the Ten Stages* by Bodhisattva Nāgārjuna to ascertain whether the *Lotus Sutra* is included in the difficult-to-practice way. I hope that they will then think thoroughly whether or not the four character phrase meaning "in the same manner, I believe" in the *Collection of Passages on the Nembutsu* is an arbitrary interpretation of Genkū before deciding which is correct. I hope they will not waste precious life by mistakenly putting faith in an evil teacher and learning an erroneous dharma.

Part 3: A Teacher Helpful for the Ignorant in the Latter Age

In this third part, I would like to define a "good friend," a reliable teacher, for the ignorant in the Latter Age of Degeneration.

Question: According to the *Flower Garland Sutra*, Bodhisattva Good Treasures* met some 50 "good friends," in search of the way. Among his "good friends" were such distinguished bodhisattvas as Universal-Sage, Mañjuśrī, Avalokiteśvara, Kannon, and Maitreya. Ever-Weeping Bodhisattva, King Spotted-Feet,* King Wonderful-Adornment,* and King Ajātaśatru* were led to emancipation from the illusion of birth and death respectively by Bodhisattva T'an Wu-chieh, King Fumyō, King Wonderful-Adornment's wife and two sons, and Minister Jīvaka.

These teachers were, however, great sages, and difficult to encounter after the passing of the Buddha. After the extinction of the Buddha there lived such great teachers as Nāgārjuna and Vasubandhu in India, but they died, and such teachers as Nan-yüeh, T'ien-t'ai's teacher, and T'ien-t'ai of China are no longer here. How can we then sever the chain of birth and death?

Answer: "Good friends," reliable teachers, exist even in the Latter Age. They are the *Lotus Sutra* and *Nirvana Sutra*.

Question: Commonly speaking, "good friend" refers to a person.
Do you have any evidence for saying the dharma is a "good friend?"

Answer: Usually "good friends" are persons. However, true "good friends" do not exist in the Latter Age. So there is much evidence for regarding dharmas as "good friends." For instance it is stated in the *Great Concentration and Insight*, fascicle one, "Following either 'good friends' or sutras, we will be able to listen to the truth of the Buddhahood of the One Vehicle, the *Lotus Sutra*, as preached above." This passage regards sutras as "good friends."

It is stated in the *Lotus Sutra*, chapter 28, The Encouragement of Universal-Sage Bodhisattva, "If there is anyone who can practice and uphold the *Lotus Sutra* in this world, he had better think that it is all due to the divine help of Universal-Sage Bodhisattva." It means that it is with the help of the "good friend," Universal-Sage Bodhisattva, that the ignorant in the Latter Age can have faith in the *Lotus Sutra*.

The sutra in the same chapter claims also, "Anyone who keeps faith in, recites, memorizes correctly, practices and copies this *Lotus Sutra* should know that he is like thóse who see Śākyamuni Buddha in person and listen to Him preach this sutra. You should know that he is making offerings to Śākyamuni Buddha." According to this passage, the *Lotus Sutra* is identical to Śākyamuni Buddha, who would enter Nirvana and never appear in front of those who do not believe in the *Lotus Sutra*, but would always appear in front of those who believe in the *Lotus Sutra* as if he were alive in this world even after death.

It is also stated in the *Lotus Sutra*, chapter 11, Beholding the Stupa of Treasures, that when the Buddha of Many Treasures was practicing the bodhisattva way, he made a great vow, declaring, "If the *Lotus Sutra* is preached anywhere in the worlds all over the universe after I have attained Buddhahood and passed away, my mausoleum stupa will spring up on the spot so that I may listen to the sutra and testify to it." It means that when we, the ignorant in the Latter Age, chant the title of the *Lotus Sutra*, the Buddha of Many Treasures will inevitably appear in order to carry out his original vow.

The sutra also states in the same chapter, "The Buddha called together all the Buddhas preaching the dharma in the worlds throughout the universe in a single spot." Thus, Śākyamuni Buddha, the Buddha of Many Treasures, all the Buddhas manifested in the worlds throughout the universe, Universal-Sage Bodhisattva and others are all our "good friends." So long as we believe in the *Lotus Sutra*, we are guided by these great teachers personally. In this sense, our merits accumulated from our previous lives are more than those of Bodhisattvas

Good-Treasures, Ever-Weeping and King Spotted-Feet so that we are able to meet better teachers than they were. This is because they met teachers of expedient sutras while we met teachers of true sutras. They met bodhisattvas of expedient sutras and we met Buddhas and bodhisattvas of true sutras.

The *Nirvana Sutra* declares, "Rely on the dharma, not on the man. Rely on wisdom, not on knowledge." In this passage, "rely on the dharma" means to rely on the eternal dharma preached in the *Lotus* and *Nirvana Sutras*. "Rely not on the man" means not to rely on those who do not believe in the *Lotus* and *Nirvana Sutras*. Those who do not have faith in the *Lotus Sutra*, even Buddhas and bodhisattvas, are not "good friends," reliable teachers for us in the Latter Age, not to mention commentators, translators and teachers after the extinction of the Buddha who do not believe in the *Lotus* and *Nirvana Sutras*. "Rely on wisdom" means to rely on the wisdom of the Buddha. "Rely not on knowledge" means not to rely on the opinions of bodhisattvas in the highest stage and below.

Today in the Latter Age, people in the world, both clergy and lay persons, spread the false report that Genkū, a man of high virtue, is an avatar of Mahāsthāmaprāpta, Great-Power-Obtainer Bodhisattva, in order to conceal his sin of slandering the True Dharma. You should not believe such a rumor. Non-Buddhists in India who have mastered five superhuman powers* may move a mountain and dry up an ocean, but they are inferior to ignorant believers of Hinayana-Āgama sutras without superhuman power. Men of Two Vehicles, *śrāvaka* and *pratyekabuddha,* who have attained arhatship through Hinayana sutras and six superhuman powers* are inferior to ignorant people who believe in expedient Mahayana sutras of the Kegon, Hōdō and Hannya periods. Even bodhisattvas in the highest stage in the expedient Mahayana sutras of the Kegon, Hōdō and Hannya periods are inferior to ignorant people who are in the initial *myōji-kangyō** stages of practicing the *Lotus Sutra,* the true Mahayana sutra. You should not trust anyone who believes in expedient sutras as your "good friend" even if he is equipped with superhuman powers and wide knowledge.

We, ignorant *icchantika* of the Latter Age, always drowning in the sea of birth and death, want to believe the *Lotus Sutra*. It forecasts our inherent Buddha-nature being revealed. Grand Master Miao-lê explains this in his *Annotations on the Great Concentration and Insight,* fascicle four, "Unless the Buddha-nature in each of us develops gradually to fill our minds, how can we attain Buddhahood? It is this wonderful power of the Buddha-nature in each of our minds that enlightens us. Therefore, we call this wonderful power of Buddha-nature our teacher-protector."

The doctrine of the "mutual possession of the 10 realms"* is not explained in any sutras expounded during 40 years or so of the Buddha's preaching other than the *Lotus Sutra*. Since the "mutual possession of the 10 realms" doctrine is not preached, believers of those sutras do not know about the realm of Buddhas inherent in their minds.

Unaware of the realm of Buddhas in their minds, they do not know of other Buddhas outside of their minds either. Namely, those who practice expedient sutras preached in the pre-*Lotus* period of 40 years or so do not know of Buddhas. Even if they see Buddhas, they merely see Buddhas in other worlds, not real Buddhas.

Those who practice the two teachings, *śrāvaka* and *pratyekabuddha,* are unaware of the Buddha within their own minds, so they cannot become Buddhas. Bodhisattvas of the pre-*Lotus* sutras, unaware of the "mutual possession of the 10 realms," themselves deny the attainment of Buddhahood to those who practice *śrāvaka* and *pratyekabuddha* teachings. Thus, they are unable to fulfill their vow of saving all people. These bodhisattvas do not see the Buddha. Likewise ignorant people do not know the "mutual possession of the 10 realms," so the Buddha realm inherent in them is not revealed. As a result, the Buddha of Infinite Life will not come to welcome them at the last moment of life, and Buddhas will not come to help them upon request. They are like the blind who cannot see their own shadow.

Now in the *Lotus Sutra,* it was clarified that the Buddha realm is inherently possessed by even those in the unenlightened nine realms, enabling those who had listened to the expedient pre-*Lotus* sutras — bodhisattvas, Two Vehicles, *śrāvaka* and *pratyekabuddha,* and those in the six realms of illusion — all to see for the first time the Buddha realm in themselves. It was the first time that those people were able to become true Buddhas, true bodhisattvas and true *śrāvaka* and *pratyekabuddha.* It was the first time that bodhisattvas, *śrāvaka* and *pratyekabuddha* attained Buddhahood and ignorant people were able to be reborn in the Pure Land. Regardless, during or after the lifetime of the Buddha, the true, trustworthy teacher, the "good friend" of all the people is the *Lotus Sutra.* Tendai scholars in general assert that one can achieve enlightenment through pre-*Lotus* sutras, but I, Nichiren, do not accept it. Having no time to discuss this thoroughly in this treatise, I merely mention it here briefly. I hope to discuss it in detail someday.

SECTION VI
Precautions that Those Who Practice the Lotus and Nirvana Sutras Should Keep in Mind

In this sixth section, I would like to introduce the precautions which those who practice the *Lotus* and *Nirvana Sutras* should keep in mind. I have already discussed in the previous sections the comparative superiority, profundity and

Shugo Kokka-ron (ST 15) 57

difficulty of the teachings the Buddha preached during His lifetime. Here I would like to expound on the teachings for the sake of those difficult to save and ignorant people, such as sinners of the five rebellious sins,* slanderers of the True Dharma or *icchantika* of the Latter Age, who are thinking only about the next life and are constantly drowned in the sea of birth and death.

I divided this section into three parts. In the first, I shall explain how lay believers can escape from the sufferings of birth and death by upholding the True Dharma, but will fall into the three evil realms of hell, hungry spirits, and beasts and birds if they believe in evil dharmas. In the second, I shall expound how ignorant lay believers can be saved from the three evil realms only by chanting the title of the *Lotus Sutra*. And in the third, I shall explain how the purpose of the *Nirvana Sutra* is the amplification of the *Lotus Sutra*.

Part 1: Upholding the True Dharma by Lay Believers

First of all, I would like to state that lay believers will be able to escape the sufferings of birth and death if they uphold the True Dharma, but will fall into the three evil realms if they believe in evil dharmas.

The *Nirvana Sutra*, fascicle three, declares: "Answering Kāśyapa's question, the Buddha preached that it was due to His upholding the True Dharma in previous lives that He gained a body like an eternally indestructible piece of diamond." It continues: "Once there was a king called Virtuous* (Utoku).... Defending the True Dharma...the king engaged in fierce battles against evil monks who violated Buddhist precepts.... Mortally wounded, King Virtuous greatly rejoiced to hear Monk Virtue Consciousness,* Kakutoku, preach the dharma. Upon death he was reborn in the land of Immovable, Akṣobya Buddha* to the east." According to the passage, lay followers of Buddhism, without special wisdom or training, can liberate themselves from sufferings of birth and death if they chastise slanderers of the True Dharma.

Question: How should lay followers of Buddhism uphold the dharma?

Answer: It is stated in the *Nirvana Sutra*:

> "To those who desire to have property, I would first give it to them, and then encourage them to read this *Sutra of the Great Nirvana*.... To those aristocratic people, I would first please them with gentle words, and gradually encourage them to read this *Mahayana Sutra of the Great Nirvana*. To those ignorant people, I would force them to read this sutra. To those self-conceited people, I would serve them as a servant, catering to and flattering them before trying to teach and guide them with the *Sutra of the Great Nirvana*. If there are those who slander Mahayana sutras, I would

compel them to admit their error, encouraging them to read the *Sutra of the Great Nirvana*. To those who believe in Mahayana sutras, I would personally visit and pay my respects, give offerings, revere and praise them."

Question: As people today, both clergy and lay persons, having attached themselves solely to the *Collection of Passages on the Nembutsu,* believe the *Lotus* and *Nirvana Sutras* to be unsuitable for them, they have no intention of saving these sutras from extinction by helping to promote them. If someone happens to speak up against the erroneous doctrine of the *Collection of Passages on the Nembutsu,* they will accuse him all over the country of slandering the *nembutsu*. What do you think of such people?

Answer: This is too grave a question for me to answer in my own words. The Buddha, Himself, speaks about such people in the *Sutra of the Benevolent King:*

> "Great King, after My death, those who should believe and protect the three treasures, Buddha, Dharma, and Buddhist order, namely monks, nuns, laymen and laywomen followers, and the king, crown prince and princes of various petty kingdoms, these people will instead destroy the three treasures. They are no different than parasites in the intestines of a lion eating it up. Those who destroy Buddhism are not usually non-Buddhists. They are mostly Buddhists eradicating their own Buddha Dharma, committing a terrible sin.
>
> "As the True Dharma declines, virtuous conduct disappears, evil multiplies, and the life span of people shortens day by day, so none will live more than 100 years. People will eradicate Buddhism while filial children will vanish, with quarrels prevailing in families. But divine help will not be forthcoming. Instead epidemics will spread, evil and devils will threaten people day after day, calamities will occur consecutively, and upon death people will fall into hell and to the realm of hungry spirits and that of beasts and birds."

Following this, the sutra also states: "Great King, in the future kings of petty kingdoms, monks, nuns, lay Buddhists, both men and women, will commit this sin of mistakenly believing in erroneous dharma causing their kingdoms to perish.... For the sake of their own honor and profit, many wicked monks will preach false dharma to the king, crown prince and princes, causing destruction of Buddhism and downfall of the kingdom. When the king, unable to distinguish the true from the false, believes and listens to their words...the True Dharma will soon be eradicated."

Looking at the *Collection of Passages on the Nembutsu*, I, Nichiren, see that this prediction* made in the *Sutra of the Benevolent King* has turned out to be completely true. The *Collection of Passages on the Nembutsu* defines the True Dharmas of the Lotus-Shingon sutras as miscellaneous and difficult to practice, unsuitable for us in the Latter Age in terms of both time and capacity of comprehension, insisting that not even one out of 1,000 of those who practice them will be able to be reborn in the Pure Land.

Despite the fact that the Buddha preached such sutras as the Lotus last, invalidating expedient sutras, Genkū closes the gate to the Lotus-Shingon teachings leaving open the sole gate to the *nembutsu*. Branding those who practice the Lotus-Shingon teachings in the Latter Age as bandits, Genkū converts people today, clergy and laity, all to his *Collection of Passages on the Nembutsu*, convincing them that it represents the true words of the Buddha. As a result people today, both clergy and laity, no longer aspire to promote Buddhism, the fountainhead of the Lotus-Shingon. True Dharma will soon dry up, and the gods and upright deities decrease in number while evil in the three evil realms multiplies daily. This is solely due to the false teaching of the *Collection of Passages on the Nembutsu*.

The term "after My extinction" among the words of the Buddha in the *Sutra of the Benevolent King* cited above means the last 80 years in the Age of the True Dharma, the last 800 years in the Age of the Semblance Dharma and the last 8,000 years in the Latter Age of Degeneration. The *Collection of Passages on the Nembutsu* was published toward the end of the Age of the Semblance Dharma, in the beginning of the Latter Age of Degeneration, namely, within the last 800 years in the Age of the Semblance Dharma. It was exactly the time predicted in the *Sutra of the Benevolent King*. "The king of various petty kingdoms" means the king of Japan. It is said in the *Sutra of the Benevolent King* that those who had practiced the "ten virtuous acts" in past lives with a mediocre or inferior mind would be born kings of petty states as tiny as scattered grains of millet.

"Intestinal parasite in a lion" refers to Genkū, a disciple of the Buddha. "Many evil monks" mean disciples of Genkū. "Preaching false dharma causing the destruction of Buddhism and downfall of the kingdoms" is in reference to the *Collection of Passages on the Nembutsu* cited above. "The king, unable to distinguish the true from the false, believes and listens to their words" refers to Buddhist clergy and lay followers today, unable to tell virtue from iniquity, indiscriminately believing in the wicked dharma. May the people, both clergy and lay persons, carefully distinguish the true from the false, put faith in the True Dharma, and pray for peace in the next life! It is hard to be born a human, but unless the human listens to the True Dharma, he will lose the chance to be reborn in the human realm, falling into the three evil realms: hell, the realm of hungry spirits, and that of beasts and birds. Then it will be too late to repent.

Part 2: The Odaimoku, the Way Out of the Three Evil Realms

Here, I would like to elucidate the merits of the *Odaimoku*, the title of the *Lotus Sutra*, for saving those who chant only it from the three evil realms. It is stated in the *Lotus Sutra*, fascicle five, chapter 14, Peaceful Practices, "Mañjuśrī, this *Lotus Sutra* is so difficult to encounter that its name has never been heard in innumerable countries." The sutra also preaches in the eighth fascicle, chapter 26, Dhāraṇīs, "You will gain incalculable good fortune by simply protecting those who believe in chanting the title of the *Lotus Sutra*." Again in chapter 12 of the *Lotus Sutra*, the Devadatta chapter,* it is stated: "Upon listening to the Devadatta chapter of the *Lotus Sutra*, those who believe in it wholeheartedly with a pure mind will not fall into hell and realms of hungry spirits and beasts." The Myōjikudoku chapter, The Merit of the Title of the Nirvana Sutra, asserts: "There is no reason for virtuous people, men or women, hearing the title of this sutra, to fall into evil realms." The *Nirvana Sutra* is specially cited here because it was preached to amplify the merits of the *Lotus Sutra*.

Question: How can anyone escape the three evil realms just by hearing the *Odaimoku*, the title of the *Lotus Sutra*, without understanding its meaning?

Answer: It is due to the meritorious acts of past lives that anyone happens to be born in a land where the *Lotus Sutra* is known, hears the title of the sutra and has faith in it. Even though he is ignorant and wicked in this life, because of the meritorious acts in previous lives, he can believe in this sutra upon hearing its name. As a result he will not fall into evil realms.

Question: Is there evidence of meritorious acts in past lives?

Answer: The *Lotus Sutra*, fascicle two, chapter three, A Parable, states, "He who believes in this sutra in this life must have seen the Buddha, shown respect to Him, given offerings and listened to Him preach this sutra." The sutra also suggests in the 10th chapter, The Teacher of the Dharma, "Suppose there are those who, upon listening to even a verse or a phrase of the *Lotus Sutra*, will rejoice even for a moment of thought after the extinction of the Buddha.... You should know that such persons made offerings to 10 trillion Buddhas in previous lives."

The *Nirvana Sutra*, amplifying the *Lotus Sutra*, preaches: "Those who received guidance from Buddhas as numerous as the sands of the Hiraṇyavatī River,[11] aspiring for Buddhahood in previous lives, will be able to believe in this sutra without slandering it in this debased world. Gentlemen, those who received guidance from Buddhas as numerous as the sands of the Ganges River, aspiring for Buddhahood in past lives, will not slander this dharma and endear and revere this sutra in this corrupt world."

According to these sutras, it is due to the great merit of his virtuous acts in past lives that anyone listens to the *Lotus Sutra* without slandering it, though unable to understand it. The chances of our being born in the three evil realms are more numerous than particles of dust on earth, while chances of our being born in the human realm are as scarce as the specks of dirt on a fingernail. The chances of our encountering expedient sutras preached in the 40-odd years before the *Lotus Sutra* are more numerous than the particles of dust on earth, while encountering the *Lotus* and *Nirvana Sutras* is as scarce as specks of dirt on a fingernail. It is just as the passage cited above[12] from the *Nirvana Sutra*, fascicle 33 stated. To be able to believe in this *Lotus Sutra,* even one character or one phrase, is due to the profound association with it from previous lives, which is a great blessing.

Question: If anyone associates with a false teacher, despite his faith in the *Lotus Sutra,* he will fall into the three evil realms, won't he?

Answer: If anyone without comprehension of the *Lotus Sutra,* meets with "evil friends" of expedient teachings and retreats from the true teaching, he will without fail fall into the three evil realms because of his sin of putting faith in the wicked teacher. Those who despised and persecuted Bodhisattva Never-Despising, for instance, fell into the Hell of Incessant Suffering, though faithful to expedient teachings. Those who had associated with the *Lotus Sutra* at the time of Great Universal Wisdom Buddha have been unenlightened for as long as 3,000 dust-particle *kalpa* because they had retreated from the *Lotus Sutra,* believing in expedient teachings.

Those who believe in the *Lotus Sutra,* however, except for abandoning their faith in the *Lotus Sutra* and following the teacher of expedient teachings, will never fall into the three evil realms for committing sins in worldly matters. It is because such sins are not grave enough to upset the merits of the *Lotus Sutra.*

Question: How is Japan concerned with the *Lotus* and *Nirvana Sutras?*

Answer: The *Lotus Sutra,* fascicle eight, chapter 28 on the "Encouragement of Universal-Sage Bodhisattva" declares, "I will have this sutra spread throughout this world and not be eradicated after the extinction of the Buddha." It also states in the seventh fascicle, chapter 23, The Previous Life of Medicine-King Bodhisattva, "You must propagate this chapter widely in this world and never let it be destroyed." The *Nirvana Sutra,* fascicle nine, states, "Likewise, this *Nirvana Sutra,* a Mahayana sutra, should be widely propagated for bodhisattvas in the South." In the vast universe, the Buddha Himself has chosen the South to be where the *Lotus* and *Nirvana Sutras* should be spread. Of the lands in the South, Japan especially is the land where the *Lotus Sutra* should be disseminated.

Question: Do you have any evidence for that?

Answer: Seng-chao, disciple of Kumārajīva, writes in his postscript to *Translating the Lotus Sutra*: "Meeting *Tripiṭaka* Master Śūryasoma and receiving a copy of the *Lotus Sutra* from him, *Tripiṭaka* Master Kumārajīva was told that just as the sun has set over the western mountains, the Buddha has passed away in India, but the residual of His teachings continue to shine in the northeast, and that as this sutra is closely related to the lands to the northeast, you should respectfully transmit and spread it there."

The northeast in this passage refers to Japan, which is northeast of India, which is to the southwest of Japan. The passage thus points to Japan. Venerable Eshin, therefore, stated in his *Essentials of the One Vehicle Teaching*: "The entire land of Japan seems ready to believe solely in the perfect teaching. "Those in the capital as well as in the country, those nearby as well as afar, will all seek refuge in the One Vehicle teaching. Both clergy as well as laity and the high as well as the low aspire to attain Buddhahood." I pray that both the clergy and laity of Japan in this life are ready to cast away their long-standing habit of putting faith in the *Collection of Passages on the Nembutsu,* and believe in the lucid statements in the *Lotus* and *Nirvana Sutras,* relying on what was said of Japan by Seng-chao and Eshin, and trying to gain peace of mind by practicing the *Lotus Sutra.*

Question: Which "Pure Land" should those who practice the *Lotus Sutra* pray to be reborn in?

Answer: It is stated in the 16th chapter, The Duration of the Life of the Tathāgata, the essence of the *Lotus Sutra* consisting of 28 chapters, "I will always stay in this *Sahā* World," "I reside here always," and "This world of Mine is at peace." According to these statements, the Eternal True Buddha, the origin of all Buddhas in manifestation, is always in this *Sahā* World. Then why should we wish to be anywhere other than this *Sahā* World? You should know that there is no Pure Land other than the very place where the one who practices the *Lotus Sutra* resides. Why should we concern ourselves seeking a Pure Land in any other place?

It is, therefore, stated in the 21st chapter of the *Lotus Sutra,* The Supernatural Powers of the Tathāgata, "Wherever scrolls of the sutra are placed, whether it may be in a garden, a forest, under a tree, in a monastery, a layman's house, a palace, a mountain, a valley or a wilderness ..., you should know that it is the very place to practice Buddhism." The *Nirvana Sutra* states: "You should know, Gentlemen, that wherever this *Nirvana Sutra* spreads becomes the Pure Land as indestructible as a diamond, inhabited by people with bodies as imperishable as a diamond." Those who believe in and practice the *Lotus* and *Nirvana Sutras,* thus should not seek the Pure Land anywhere other than the very place where they themselves, believers of this sutra, reside.

Question: Sutras such as the *Flower Garland Sutra,* Hōdō sutras, *Wisdom Sutra,* Āgama sutras, and the *Sutra of Meditation on the Buddha of Infinite Life* recommend being reborn in the Tuṣita Heaven of Bodhisattva Maitreya, the Pure Land of the Buddha of Infinite Life to the west, and Pure Lands all over the universe. The *Lotus Sutra,* too, recommends being reborn in the Tuṣita Heaven, Pure Land to the west, and Pure Lands throughout the universe. Why do you contradict these sutras and recommend this impure land filled with tiles, stones, and thorny shrubs?

Answer: The Pure Lands preached in the pre-*Lotus* expedient sutras are mere substitutes tentatively shown by replicas of Śākyamuni Buddha, the Eternal True Buddha. In fact they all are lands of impurity. Therefore, when the true Pure Land was described in The Duration of the Life of the Tathāgata chapter of the *Lotus Sutra,* the essence of which consists of the Expedients chapter and The Duration of the Life of the Tathāgata chapter, it was declared that this *Sahā* World is the true Pure Land of Tranquil Light.

As for the question why the *Lotus Sutra* also recommends the Tuṣita Heaven, the Realm of Peace and Sustenance, that is the Pure Land of the Buddha of Infinite Life, and Pure Lands all over the universe, it is merely that designations of the Pure Lands, such as Tuṣita Heaven and Realm of Peace and Sustenance, preached in the pre-*Lotus* sutras are used without modification to name the Pure Lands to be established in this world. It is like names of the three vehicles, *śrāvaka, pratyekabuddha,* and bodhisattva, mentioned in the *Lotus Sutra,* which does not actually preach three different teachings. It preaches the sole teaching leading to Buddhahood. It is stated in the *Lotus Sutra,* chapter 23, that those who practice this sutra "will immediately be reborn in the World of Happiness." In the *Annotations on the Words and Phrases of the Lotus Sutra,* fascicle 10, Grand Master Miao-lê interprets: "This does not mean the Pure Land of the Buddha of Infinite Life preached in the *Sutra of Meditation on the Buddha of Infinite Life."* His interpretation is the same as stated above.

People today without karmic relations with the *Lotus Sutra,* wishing to be reborn in the Pure Land to the west, are in fact praying for rebirth in the land of rubble, giving up the *Sahā* World, which is the true Pure Land. People who do not believe in the *Lotus Sutra* will not be able to be reborn even in such lands as the Tuṣita Heaven and the Realm of Peace and Sustenance, which are in reality the Pure Lands in this *Sahā* World given such temporary names.

Part 3: the Nirvana Sutra for Amplifying the Lotus Sutra

In this third part, I would like to state that the *Nirvana Sutra* was preached to elaborate the *Lotus Sutra.*

Question: Such virtuous Chinese priests as Fa-yün of the Kuangchê-ssu Temple and Hui-kuan of the Tao-ch'ang-ssu Temple, regarded the *Lotus Sutra* as having been preached in the fourth period of the Buddha's lifetime of preaching, and they held that compared to the *Nirvana Sutra* preached in the fifth period it is merely a teaching of transiency, like the tasting of *jukuso*, butter, which does not taste quite as satisfactorily as *daigo*, ghee.[13] Grand Master T'ien-t'ai criticized this in his *Profound Meaning of the Lotus Sutra*, fascicle 10, maintaining that although the *Lotus* and *Nirvana Sutras* are of the same *daigo* flavors, the *Lotus Sutra* is like the harvest in autumn while the *Nirvana Sutra* is like the gleaning. Both Fa-yün and T'ien-t'ai are avatars of the great sage. Both are virtuous monks. Whose opinion is correct to dispel our doubts?

Answer: You should suspect anyone, even among commentators and translators of India, who does not comply with the commandment of the Buddha to distinguish expedient from true teachings. How much more so with commentaries written by such Chinese masters as T'ien-t'ai, Nan-yüeh (Hui-ssu), Fa-yün, Hui-kuan, Chih-yen, Chia-hsiang or Chi-ts'ang, and Shan-tao! You can trust even scholars of the Latter Age if they keep the teaching of the Buddha in the *Nirvana Sutra*, "Rely on the dharma, not on persons," and if they do not contradict basic sutras and commentaries.

Question: The *Nirvana Sutra*, fascicle 14, likens all Mahayana sutras expounded during the Buddha's 50 years of preaching to the first four of the five flavors,* comparing the *Nirvana Sutra* to the fifth and supreme taste of *daigo*, and decisively states that all Mahayana sutras are a billion times inferior to the *Nirvana Sutra*. Moreover, Bodhisattva Kāśyapa revealed to the Buddha, "I gained the right view today for the first time. Until today we have all had a mistaken view." It means that sutras, such as the *Lotus Sutra*, preached before the *Nirvana Sutra* are all of mistaken views. You should know that the *Lotus Sutra* is of a false view, neglecting the right view, the eternal presence of Buddha-nature. Deciding on the comparative superiority of the *Nirvana Sutra* and other sutras in his *Treatise on the Nirvana Sutra*, Bodhisattva Vasubandhu placed the *Lotus Sutra* and the *Wisdom Sutra* equally in the fourth period. How can you consider the *Nirvana Sutra* of the right view as being an amplifier of the *Lotus Sutra* of the false view? What do you think of this?

Answer: It is clearly stated in the *Lotus Sutra* that the true intent of the Buddha has completely been preached in it. The second chapter, Expedients, declares, "Now is the time to expound the wisdom of the Buddha." The 16th chapter, The Duration of the Life of the Tathāgata, states, "I have always been contemplating how I should lead all people into the Supreme Way, enabling them to become Buddhas promptly." The 21st chapter, The Supernatural Powers of the Tathāgata, states, "In sum, the teachings of the Buddha ... are all revealed and clearly expounded in this sutra."

These statements of the Buddha clearly show that the enlightenment of Śākyamuni Buddha is revealed in this sutra without reservation. Moreover, the Buddha of Many Treasures and Buddhas in manifestation in the worlds all over the universe gathered together in the courtyard on Mt. Sacred Eagle to validate the words of Śākyamuni Buddha: "Of all the Buddhist scriptures, which have been preached, are being preached and will be preached in the future...," deciding that no sutras are as difficult to understand and put faith in as the *Lotus Sutra*, supreme of all scriptures. Nevertheless, suppose Śākyamuni Buddha alone changed His mind, after the Buddha of Many Treasures and Buddhas in manifestation throughout the universe returned to their respective worlds as preached in the 22nd chapter, Transmission, and preached the *Nirvana Sutra* declaring that the *Lotus Sutra* is inferior to the *Nirvana Sutra*, who would believe this?

With this deeply in mind, I perused the ninth fascicle of the *Nirvana Sutra*. It preaches amplification of the *Lotus Sutra*, "Just as fruit will profit all living beings and bring about much comfort in life to them, the appearance of this *Nirvana Sutra* will reveal the Buddha-nature inherent in people. Just as the guarantee of future Buddhahood granted to 8,000 *śrāvaka* in the *Lotus Sutra* is like the huge bearing of fruit, after the harvest in autumn and stockpiling for winter, the *Nirvana Sutra* has nothing to do except gleaning." According to this passage, if the *Lotus Sutra* is a false teaching, is not the *Nirvana Sutra* also false? It is clearly stated here that the *Lotus Sutra* is like a great harvest while the *Nirvana Sutra* is a gleaning. Thus, the *Nirvana Sutra* declares itself to be inferior to the *Lotus Sutra*. There is no mistake about the words of the *Lotus Sutra*, chapter 10, The Teacher of the Dharma, stating that it is superior even to the sutras yet to be expounded, including the *Nirvana Sutra*.

Bodhisattva Kāśyapa's words of understanding and the passage in the 14th fascicle of the *Nirvana Sutra*, comparing Mahayana sutras to five flavors, do not intend to slight the *Lotus Sutra*. As Kāśyapa himself and his disciples then for the first time upon listening to the *Nirvana Sutra* were able to understand the meaning of the "eternal presence of Buddha-nature" and "attainment of Perfect Enlightenment by Śākyamuni Buddha in the eternal past" expounded in the *Lotus Sutra*, they simply stated that their understanding had not been correct up until then. It is not that they were comparing the superiority of doctrines. As for the simile of five flavors, it denied, again in the *Nirvana Sutra*, the pre-*Lotus* sutras, which had been invalidated in the *Sutra of Infinite Meaning*. It was not to negate the *Lotus Sutra*.

Regarding the *Treatise on the Nirvana Sutra,* as is mentioned in the note beneath the title, it was a work of Bodhisattva Vasubandhu and was translated by Bodhiruchi. The *Commentary on the Lotus Sutra,* likewise, was written by Bodhisattva Vasubandhu and translated by Bodhiruchi, which has many discrepancies as compared to the *Lotus Sutra.* The *Treatise on the Nirvana Sutra,* too, has discrepancies as compared to the *Nirvana Sutra.* I believe these discrepancies stemmed from mistakes on the part of the translator. You should not trust his translations.

Question: Suppose a sutra that tries to save those who had not been saved by preaching of previous sutras is called a sutra of amplification, are Āgama sutras amplifiers of the *Flower Garland Sutra?* Does the *Lotus Sutra* amplify the pre-*Lotus* sutras with the first four flavors preached during the first four periods of the Buddha's lifetime of preaching?

Answer: Those pre-*Lotus* sutras with the first four flavors will enable bodhisattvas, human beings and heavenly beings to attain Buddhahood. However, they will not allow the Two Vehicles or *śrāvaka* and *pratyekabuddha,* whose natures are fixed, and *icchantika,* who do not have Buddha-nature, to attain Buddhahood.[14] Moreover, if we delve into the heart of the Buddha, the attainment of Buddhahood by bodhisattvas, human beings and heavenly beings preached in these sutras actually has no substance. It is because those sutras have not preached the doctrines of "mutual possession of the 10 realms"* and "attainment of Perfect Enlightenment by Śākyamuni Buddha in the eternal past."*

Question: Do you have any proof to say that sutras with the first four flavors, preached during the first four periods, will not enable anyone to attain Buddhahood?

Answer: The Expedients chapter of the *Lotus Sutra* states, "If I use the Hinayana teaching to convert even one person, I will be accused of being greedy. So it is impossible to do so." I will omit the meaning of this passage for now because my main purpose at present is to refute the false teaching of the *Collection of Passages on the Nembutsu* and I have not had time to describe anything else. Therefore, I will not discuss here whether or not the pre-*Lotus* sutras will enable us to attain Buddhahood, which will be discussed in detail later.

However, as sutras preached during the period of 40 years or so before the *Lotus Sutra* do not save ignorant people, the *Lotus Sutra* was not preached to explain those sutras. As the doctrines of "mutual possession of the 10 realms" and "attainment of Perfect Enlightenment by Śākyamuni Buddha in the eternal past" were preached in the *Lotus Sutra* saving all people, the *Nirvana Sutra* was preached to amplify the *Lotus Sutra.*

SECTION VII
Questions and Answers

In this seventh section, I would like to answer further questions. Suppose even one out of 10,000 ignorant people in the Latter Age are converted to the *Lotus Sutra* by the explanations in the previous six sections of this treatise. Followers of other sects having faith in expedient sutras, because of either their doubts about the *Lotus Sutra* or bigotry coming from their own sects, will try to corrupt believers of the *Lotus Sutra* criticizing them with citations from the pre-*Lotus* sutras and the *Nirvana Sutra*. Moreover, as there are many believers of expedient sutras, they may either threaten the true followers by their sheer numbers, induce others with worldly goods, or harshly condemn the true followers and make a living by catering to the whims of the multitude. Or, as there are many scholars among believers of the expedient teachings and merely a few wise persons among followers of the true teaching, not even one out of 10,000 believers of the true teaching would survive the criticism and attack of other sects. I wrote this section to fend off false attacks by followers of expedient teachings.

Question: Scholars of other sects would criticize the *Lotus Sutra* as follows. The Kegon (Flower Garland) sect would say:

> "The *Flower Garland Sutra* was preached by 'reward-bodied'[15] Vairocana Buddha, at seven places in eight assemblies and it represents the true intent of the Buddha, promptly leading to Buddhahood. Whereas the *Lotus Sutra* was preached by 'accommodative-bodied' Śākyamuni Buddha. The lords of these two sutras are not equally the same. How can there be no difference in depth of their preachings? While the congregation who listened to the preaching of the *Flower Garland Sutra* was only of great bodhisattvas such as Fa-hui, Kung-te-lin and Chin-kang-chui, exclusive of *śrāvaka* and *pratyekabuddha*, the congregation for the *Lotus Sutra* was of *śrāvaka* and *pratyekabuddha* such as Sāriputra."

Based on the *Revealing the Profound and Secret Sutra*, the Hossō (Dharma Characteristics) sect would criticize:

> "The *Revealing the Profound and Secret Sutra* was preached to such great bodhisattvas as Mañjuśrī and Avalokiteśvara, and it is, therefore, more profound than the *Lotus Sutra*, which was preached for *śrāvaka* and *pratyekabuddha*. According to the understanding of Shōgishō Bodhisattva, all the Buddhist scriptures are divided into three: temporal, void and the middle way.[16] Of the three teachings the middle way teaching is supreme,

which consists of such sutras as the *Flower Garland, Lotus, Nirvana* and *Revealing the Profound and Secret Sutra*. That is to say, the *Lotus Sutra* is about equal to the *Revealing the Profound and Secret Sutra* in profundity of teaching. On the contrary, confirmation of Grand Master T'ien-t'ai's 'five-period* doctrine' in the Understanding by Faith chapter of the *Lotus Sutra* is expressed through the understanding by four great śrāvaka. As we compare the two sutras, the *Revealing the Profound and Secret Sutra* and the *Lotus Sutra*, although both preach the same middle way, as the former was understood by a bodhisattva while the latter by śrāvaka, there must be as great a difference in superiority between them as heaven and earth."

The Jōdo (Pure Land) sect would quibble:

"We do not slander sutras such as the *Lotus Sutra*, which were preached chiefly for those great people like bodhisattvas and only secondarily for us, the ignorant. They preach profound doctrines to eliminate evil passions and attain enlightenment. Even if we, the ignorant in the Latter Age, would practice them, not even one out of 1,000 would have the capacity to be able to understand those doctrines. Besides, many lay persons are illiterate, having never even heard of 'Flower Garland' and 'Dharma Characteristics,' not to mention their teachings. Under the circumstances, the Pure Land sect maintains that if only we, the ignorant, chant the six-character title of the Buddha of Infinite Life, the *nembutsu*, the Buddha will dispatch 25 bodhisattvas to this *Sahā* World to protect us who practice, surrounding us thick and fast as the shadow follows the body.

"Therefore, so long as we chant the *nembutsu*, we will be free of the seven calamities and have seven happinesses in this world.... At the last moment of life the Buddha of Infinite Life will never fail to welcome us, taking us upon the lotus pedestal of Bodhisattva Avalokiteśvara promptly to the Pure Land, where lotus flowers bloom according to our karma while we listen to the *Lotus Sutra* and become enlightened to the truth of all phenomena. Why should we bother with ways difficult to practice in this impure world? Is there anything good about it? Instead, we should concentrate on calling the name of the Buddha of Infinite Life, putting aside everything else."

Zen people would say:

"All the scriptures of Buddhism are like a finger pointing to the moon, which is useless after seeing the moon. Such things as heaven, earth, the sun and moon all stem from illusions of your mind. Pure Lands throughout the universe are shadows of your greedy mind. Śākyamuni Buddha and His replicas manifested in the worlds throughout the universe are variations of your enlightened mind. Those who attach themselves to letters are as ignorant as a hunter who keeps on guarding a stump with which a hare once collided and died. Our Grand Master Bodhidharma, without using letters or other expedient means, transmitted this dharma of Zen, which the Buddha had entrusted directly to Kāśyapa, in addition to the holy teaching of His lifetime. Sutras such as the *Lotus Sutra* do not reveal the true intent of the Buddha."

These are some criticisms by other schools of Buddhism against the *Lotus Sutra*. How can we defend faith in the *Lotus Sutra* against these accusations?

Answer: Those who practice the *Lotus Sutra* should keep deeply in mind such scriptural statements as the following: "The truth has not been revealed in sutras preached during the pre-*Lotus*, 40 years or so" from the *Sutra of Infinite Meaning*. "Of all the sutras which have been preached, are being preached and will be preached, this sutra is the most difficult to believe and understand" from the 10th chapter of the *Lotus Sutra*. "What is preached by Śākyamuni Buddha is all true" from the 11th chapter of the *Lotus Sutra*. And "Rely upon the dharma, not the word of persons" from the *Nirvana Sutra*. However, these passages should not be mentioned.

When criticized by followers of other sects, you should conversely ask, on what sutras are their teachings based? If they answer your question by citing sutras, you should ask them when, during the Buddha's 50-year lifetime of preaching, their sutras were preached — whether it was before, after or at the same time as the *Lotus Sutra*, or undetermined.

If their answer is before the *Lotus Sutra*, you should then challenge them with the passage, "The truth has not been revealed in sutras preached during the pre-*Lotus*, 40 years or so." You need not ask about the content of their sutras. If their answer is after, you should confront them with the statement, "Of all the sutras which will be preached...." If they answer at the same time as the *Lotus Sutra*, you may confront them with the statement, "Of all the sutras which are now being preached...." If they answer they don't know when their sutras were preached, you should know that those which are not known when preached are unimportant expedient sutras preached on particular occasions for particular persons. They are not worthy of discussion.

Besides, even those sutras without a particular date must have been preached either before, after or at the same time as the *Lotus Sutra*. Even if those sutras expounded hundreds, thousands, and tens of thousands of doctrines, unless it is stated in them that the "during 40 years or so" in the *Sutra of Infinite Meaning* is untrue, you should not believe in them. This is because the Buddha bequeathed to us, "Do not rely on sutras which do not thoroughly reveal the truth." Even if followers of other sects accuse you by citing words of such Chinese patriarchs as Chih-yen of the Flower Garland sect, Chia-hsiang of the Sun-lun sect, Tz'ŭ-ên (K'wei-chi) of the Fa-hsiang (Hossō) sect, and Shan-tao of the Pure Land sect, lauding their high virtue, you must not trust those Buddhist monks who contradict the teaching of the *Lotus* and *Nirvana Sutras*. It is because you must stay firm with the words of the Buddha, "Rely on the dharma, not the word of persons."

Question: For ignorant believers of the *Lotus Sutra* I shall also explain two kinds of faith: first, faith through the Buddhas and second, faith through the sutras. First, I shall explain the establishment of faith by Buddhas. Suppose scholars of other sects believing in expedient sutras came to challenge us saying, "Venerable Shan-tao, who attained enlightenment by concentration of thought on the *nembutsu*, is an avatar of the Buddha of Infinite Life. Grand Master Tz'ŭ-ên, an avatar of the 11-faced Bodhisattva Avalokiteśvara, is said to have poured out ashes of the Buddha from the tip of his writing brush. They both have established their teachings based on scriptural passages in respective sutras. Why do you not believe in their sutras and opinions?"

Answer: Listen carefully. Suppose grand masters and late monks of virtue of all other sects, Śāriputra and Maudgalyāyana, such bodhisattvas as Universal-Sage, Mañjuśrī and Avalokiteśvara, and such Buddhas as Infinite Life, Medicine Master and Śākyamuni would come together in front of us declaring, "The *Lotus Sutra* is unsuitable to our capacity, and therefore it would be better for us to practice such expedient teachings as the *nembutsu* to be reborn in the Pure Land, where we should be awakened to the truth of the *Lotus Sutra*." Even if they should preach thus to us, we should never listen to them. The reason is that the title of the *Lotus Sutra* was never mentioned in sutras preached during 40 years or so before the *Lotus Sutra*. How can there be any of those pre-*Lotus* sutras discussing their suitability to the capacity of the people, in comparison to the *Lotus Sutra*?

In the *Lotus Sutra*, however, Śākyamuni and the Buddha of Many Treasures and replica Buddhas from various worlds in the universe gathered together to make a choice, declaring, "We will ensure that this dharma of the *Lotus Sutra* lasts forever," and "will see to it that after the death of the Buddha it will spread widely in this world without being destroyed." Suppose a new Buddha besides these "three" appeared and decided that the *Lotus Sutra* is unsuitable to the Latter Age, it would contradict the decision made by the "three Buddhas" in the *Lotus Sutra*. This new Buddha would be no other than a demon in the shape of a Buddha, as predicted in the *Nirvana Sutra* to appear after the death of the Buddha in order to destroy Buddhism. We should not believe in such Buddhas, much less those below them, such as bodhisattvas, *śrāvaka* and monks. No doubt, they are demons in the shape of bodhisattvas after the demise of the Buddha as predicted in the *Nirvana Sutra*.

The reason I say this is that the place for preaching the *Lotus Sutra* is not limited just to Mt. Sacred Eagle, but expands beyond this world to innumerable other worlds. Filling this vast world, bodhisattvas, *śrāvaka* and *pratyekabuddha*, human and heavenly beings, and eight kinds of gods and demi-gods, who protect Buddhism, vowed at the request of the Buddha to spread the *Lotus Sutra* in their respective lands of residence. If such as Shan-tao were avatars of Buddhas or bodhisattvas, why did they not propagate the *Lotus Sutra* after spreading expedient teachings first as Nāgārjuna and Vasubandhu had done?

Why were they not among those who were requested by the Buddha to spread the *Lotus Sutra*? Why did they not propagate the *Lotus Sutra* after spreading expedient sutras first, as the Buddha had done? Unless this order of preaching is followed, we should not believe in even a Buddha. As I explained here why we should believe in Buddhas of the *Lotus Sutra* exclusively, I entitled this section the establishment of faith by Buddhas.

Question: If you call what was preached by Śākyamuni Buddha the true teaching because it was attested to as the truth by other Buddhas, why do you not believe in the *Pure Land Sutra*?

Answer: I do not believe in the *Pure Land Sutra* because it was not attested to as the truth by other Buddhas, as the *Lotus Sutra* was.

Question: In reading the *Pure Land Sutra*, we can see that when Śākyamuni Buddha preached the chanting of the *nembutsu* for a day or seven days, Buddhas in the worlds in six directions (east, west, south, north, above and below, attested to it by stretching their tongues, each covering the whole world. Why do you say that the *Pure Land Sutra* has no validity?

Answer: The *Pure Land Sutra* was not at all validated by other Buddhas as the *Lotus Sutra* was. In the *Pure Land Sutra*, Śākyamuni Buddha alone preached to Śāriputra, "It is not only I who preach the *Pure Land Sutra* but also Buddhas in the worlds in six directions stretch their tongues to cover the whole world preaching the sutra." However, this is what was said by Śākyamuni Buddha alone. Buddhas in the worlds in six directions did not come to verify it.

Besides, this is a statement in an expedient sutra. During the 40-odd years of the pre-*Lotus* period, the Lord Buddha was also the expedient Buddha, an accommodative Buddha who attained Buddhahood for the first time under the *bodhi* tree near Buddhagaya. Since the Lord Buddha was an expedient Buddha, what was preached by Him must have been expedient. Therefore, what was preached by an expedient Buddha during the 40 years or so must not be believed.

Contrary to this, the *Lotus* and *Nirvana Sutras* are the accurate teaching of the perfect Buddha who attained true enlightenment in the eternal past, trustworthy words revealing the principle of the "mutual possession of the 10 realms."* Moreover, the Buddha of Many Treasures and Buddhas manifested in the worlds throughout the universe came to attest their truth. Therefore, we must put faith in them. The teaching of the *Pure Land Sutra* on the other hand is completely invalidated by the statement in the *Sutra of Infinite Meaning*, "The truth has not been revealed during the 40 years or so." Besides, its validation was made by Śākyamuni Buddha alone, not by other Buddhas themselves.

Secondly, let me explain the establishment of faith by sutras. Referring to the sutras preached during the 40-odd years, the *Sutra of Infinite Meaning* states, "The truth has not been revealed." The *Nirvana Sutra* declares, "The Buddha would not purposely lie, but He may preach expedient teachings as necessary when He is convinced that it would benefit people more." The sutra also states, "Rely on the sutra that reveals the whole truth. Do not rely on the sutras that do not thoroughly reveal the truth." Many more of these kinds of scriptural statements can be found, declaring that those sutras preached by the Buddha Himself during 40 years or so without exception are falsehoods, expedients, sutras not revealing the whole truth, and teachings of devils. This is solely for the purpose of guiding people to abandon their expedient sutras and enter into faith in the *Lotus* and *Nirvana Sutras*.

For what reason do people, however, adhere to their expedient sutras, practice them and attempt to attain Buddhahood? In this section I explained that we should get rid of our adherence to expedient teachings, putting sole faith in the true teaching. Therefore, I call this section the establishment of faith by sutras.

Question: Venerable Shan-tao also mentions the establishment of faith by persons and by practices. What is the difference between his contention and yours?"

Answer: Shan-tao's faith is based on the triple Pure Land sutras such as the *Pure Land Sutra* without making distinction between the sutras "thoroughly revealing the truth" and those "not revealing the truth thoroughly" among all the scriptures preached during His lifetime.

Therefore, Shan-tao's doctrine based on sutras not revealing the truth thoroughly would be defeated in debate by my doctrine based on the *Lotus* and *Nirvana Sutras*, sutras which are revealing the whole truth.

Notes

1. According to T'ien-t'ai's classification, the *Flower Garland Sutra* was preached for bodhisattvas.
2. Those who listened to the Buddha preach the *Flower Garland Sutra* are claimed to have been identical to those who asked the Buddha to preach in the Expedients chapter of the *Lotus Sutra*, cited immediately above.
3. Nichiren seems to claim that the *Flower Garland Sutra* was preached for bodhisattvas at the request of the King of the Brahma Heaven and other heavenly beings. See notes 1 and 2.
3a. See "Five periods" *(goji)* in the glossary.
4. The *Nirvana Sutra* is believed to have been expounded immediately before the death of the Buddha.
5. Section 1, Part 4, the paragraph beginning with "And for the 10th...." (on page 14 in this book)
6. According to Tendai doctrine, sutras preached in the five periods, Kegon-ji, Agon-ji, Hōdō-ji, Hannya-ji and Hokke-Nehan-ji, are likened to the taste of five milk products: (1) *nyū*, milk, (2) *raku*, cream, (3) *shōso*, curdled milk, (4) *jukuso*, butter, and (5) *daigo*, ghee.
7. The five precepts, or *gokai* for lay Buddhists: (1) not to kill, (2) not to steal, (3) not to commit adultery, (4) not to lie, and (5) not to drink intoxicants. The 10 virtuous acts, or *juzen*: 1 through 4 are the same as the first four above, (5) not to speak harsh words, (6) not to say words causing enmity between two or more persons, (7) not to engage in idle talk, (8) not to be greedy, (9) not to be angry, and (10) not to have wrong views.
8. The term "500 dust-particle *kalpa*" means an inconceivably long period of time described in the 16th chapter of the *Lotus Sutra* indicating how much time has elapsed since Śākyamuni's original enlightenment: "Suppose someone smashes 500 billion *nayuta, asaṃkhya* worlds into dust, and then takes them all east, dropping one particle each time he passes 500 billion *nayuta, asaṃkhya* worlds. Suppose he continues traveling eastward in this way until he finishes dropping all the particles. Suppose all these worlds passed by him, whether they received a particle or not, are once more reduced to dust. Let one particle of this dust represent one *kalpa*. The time which has passed since I attained Buddhahood surpasses this by 100 billion *nayuta, asaṃkhya kalpa*."
9. The "3,000 dust-particle *kalpa*" is the immeasurably long period of time described in the seventh chapter of the *Lotus Sutra* indicating how much time has elapsed since Śākyamuni preached the *Lotus Sutra* as the 16th son of Great Universal Wisdom Buddha: "Suppose someone crushed a major world system, consisting of 1,000 x 1,000 x 1,000 worlds, into ink-powder. Then he traveled eastward making a dot as he passed 1,000 worlds until the ink-powder was exhausted. Then all the worlds he went through were crushed into dust. The number of *kalpa* which have elapsed since Great Universal Wisdom Buddha passed away is infinitely larger than the number of dust particles thus produced."

10. The realm of desire is the lowest of the three realms of transmigration. The *sangai*, or triple world, consisting of hell, the realm of hungry spirits or *gaki*, the realm of beasts and birds, the realm of fighting spirits or *asura*, the realm of human beings and the lower part of the heavenly realm.
11. Hiraṇyavatī River, a tributary of the Ganges, also known as the Ajiravatī, is called the Gandak River today. The Buddha is said to have passed away in a forest of *sala* trees on the west bank of this river near Kuśinagara.
12. Section 5, Part 1 (page 49).
13. See note 6.
14. According to the Hossō doctrine of the "five mutually distinctive natures."
15. A Buddha is said to have three bodies, or *sanshin*. The first is *hosshin* or Dharma Body, the body of the ultimate reality. The second is *hōjin* or Reward Body, received as the reward for meritorious practices. The third is *ōjin* or Accommodative Body, a body of a Buddha manifested to meet different needs of living beings.
16. See "Triple truth" *(santai)* in the glossary.

Sainan Kōki Yurai (ST 20)

Introduction

Nichiren Shōnin wrote the *Sainan Kōki Yurai* in the first 10 days of the second month in the second year of the Shōgen Period (1260), when he was 38 years old. The beginning portion of this work is missing. However, 10 pages of the original manuscript have been kept in the Hokekyōji Temple in Ichikawa City, near Tokyo, and are designated as an important cultural asset of Japan.

Citing various sutras, Nichiren demonstrates in this document that the cause of the successive calamities affecting Japan is the prevalence of evil teachings slandering the True Dharma, and that in order to prevent these calamities, slanderers of the True Dharma must be eradicated so that the True Dharma can be established. This treatise is regarded as a trial essay for the *Risshō Ankoku-ron, Treatise on Spreading Peace Throughout the Country by Establishing the True Dharma*, both because it was written only five months prior to Nichiren's submission of the latter essay to Hōjō Tokiyori, *de facto* ruler of the Kamakura military regime, and because the treatises make the same argument.

The Cause of Misfortunes

(hitherto missing)

Answer: Yes, you are right. That is what happened in the reigns of such ancient Chinese rulers as King Chieh of the Hsia, King Chou Hsin of the Yin and King Yu of the Chou dynasties.

Question: As Buddhism had not been introduced in China during their reigns, slanderers of the True Dharma* wouldn't have existed. How did they destroy their own kingdoms?

Answer: Such leaders as the Yellow Emperor and Confucius established the five virtues as a means of governing the country. These virtues were: benevolence, justice, courtesy, wisdom and fidelity. However, ignorant kings violated the teaching of courtesy preached by such sages as Confucius causing calamities that destroyed their kingdoms.

Question: If that is so, and calamities in this world are caused by violating the five virtues, how can we say that those calamities were caused by the spread of the evil teaching of the *Collection of Passages on the Nembutsu?*

Answer: Prior to Buddhism being introduced in China sage rulers such as the Yellow Emperor governed their kingdoms by means of the five virtues. After the introduction of Buddhism we can see these five virtues are the same as the five precepts of Buddhism prohibiting killing, stealing, adultery, lying and drinking liquor. Ancient Chinese sages such as Lao-tzu and Confucius are the three sages whom the Buddha dispatched to China in order to propagate a Buddhism adapted to suit the land in the distant future. Therefore, the loss of kingdoms by such rulers as King Chieh of Hsia, King Chou Hsin of Yin, and King Yu of Chou through violating the five virtues, equals violating the five precepts.

Also, to be fortunate in being born a human being and becoming a king is due to the merit of having observed the five precepts and the 10 virtuous acts.[1] Although non-Buddhist scriptures* are superficial in teaching, not preaching the cause-and-effect relationship between merits in the past and rewards in the future, those who observed the five precepts and 10 virtuous acts became kings. Accordingly, when people transgress the five virtues, heavenly calamities and terrestrial disasters will occur in succession. Therefore, calamities and disasters in this life are also caused by all the people in Japan, high and low, who put faith in the *Collection of Passages on the Nembutsu.** Rejecting those who seek refuge in Buddhas other than the Buddha of Infinite Life and sutras other than the triple Pure Land sutras, those who believe in the *Collection of Passages on the Nembutsu* act rudely and refuse to express gratitude to them. Thus, the people in Japan all disregard courtesy, with both monks and lay followers not observing Buddhist precepts. They are like those who imitated Yüan-chi[2] destroying courtesy, and the followers of Wei Yüan-sung[3] bringing havoc to Buddhism in China.

Question: How do you know? What proof do you have to say that the five virtues prior to the introduction of Buddhism into China were the "five precepts" of Buddhism?

Answer: The *Sutra of the Golden Splendor** states, "All the teachings in the world encouraging to do good, stem from this sutra." The *Lotus Sutra,* chapter 19, The Merits of the Teacher of the Dharma, states, "When devout people expound scriptures of the secular world, talking about the government, or teaching the way to earn a livelihood, they all will be in accordance with the True Dharma." In the *Sutra of Meditation on Universal-Sage Bodhisattva,** "Ruling the country by the True Dharma without oppressing the people unjustly is the practice of the third repentance." And in the *Nirvana Sutra,** "All the non-Buddhist scriptures in the world are from the teachings of the Buddha, not from the teachings of non-Buddhists."

Sainan Kōki Yurai (ST 20)

The *Great Concentration and Insight,** of Grand Master T'ien-t'ai declares, "One who knows the true way of the world knows the Buddha Dharma." In the *Annotations on the Great Concentration and Insight,* Grand Master Miao-lê states, "Such worldly teachings as courtesy and music spread first, opening the way of the Buddha," and Priest Annen's *Comprehensive Interpretations** says this:

"The Buddha sent three wise men to China to teach the five precepts by means of the five virtues. In the past, when the prime minister of the Sung State asked Confucius whether or not the Three Emperors and Five Sovereigns in ancient China were sages, Confucius answered that they were not. The prime minister then asked whether Confucius himself was a sage, and he said he was not. The prime minister asked again whether or not there was anyone who was considered a sage. Confucius replied that he heard that there was a sage known as Śākyamuni in the land to the west."

The *Heterodox History of the Chou Dynasty* states:

"On the eighth day of the fourth month in the 24th year in the reign of King Chao of the Chou, rivers, springs, ponds and wells all suddenly overflowed while palaces, houses, mountains, rivers and the great earth all quaked. At night, rays of five colors went through the T'ai-wei Constellation,[4] shining in four directions. In the day, the rays turned blue-red. King Chao asked Historian Su-yu what caused this strange phenomenon. Su-yu replied that it was an omen of the birth of a great sage in the land to the west. Answering the king who asked what would be the effect upon the world, Su-yu declared that there would be no immediate effect, but his teaching would prevail over this land in 1,000 years. King Chao is said to have at once sent a man to Komen to have Su-yu's prediction inscribed on a stone and buried in the ground. It is in front of a heavenly shrine in the western outskirts.

"Also on the 15th day of the second month in the 52nd year during the reign of King Mu, a storm occurred suddenly destroying houses and toppling trees. Mountains, rivers and the great earth all trembled at once. In the afternoon the sky turned dark with black clouds. Twelve white rainbows hanging over the western sky passing from north to south, did not disappear for many nights. King Mu inquired of the Historian Hu-to about what these phenomena foretold. Hu-to replied that they predicted the death of a sage in the land to the west."

Now, as I contemplate these citations, the *Sutra of the Golden Splendor* assures us, "All the teachings in this world encouraging to do good, stem from this sutra." Before Buddhism was introduced into China, ancient rulers such as the Yellow Emperor first learned the five virtues from Hsüan-nü. The Buddha caused them to learn the teachings of the Eternal Buddha through learning Hsüan-nü's five virtues in order for them to govern the country. As their capacities for comprehension were not yet developed, they would not have understood the relationship between causes in the past and effects in the future, even if the five precepts of Buddhism had been preached. So they concentrated on governing the country and establishing themselves by strictly observing the moral codes of loyalty and filial piety in this world.

Citations from other sutras are the same. Also, the passage cited above from the *Heterodox History of the Chou Dynasty* shows that people knew of the birth of the Buddha in the land to the west more than 1,000 years before Buddhism was introduced to China. Lao-tzu was born during the Yin dynasty and was active during the reign of King Lieh of the Chou dynasty, and Confucius was his disciple while Yen-hui was a disciple of Confucius. It doesn't seem possible that they were unaware of the prediction made by Historians Su-yu and Hu-to during the reigns of the fourth and fifth rulers of the Chou dynasty, King Chao and King Mu, that Buddhism would spread over their country in 1,000 years.

Examining this further in Buddhist scriptures, I find in Grand Master T'ien-t'ai's *Great Concentration and Insight*, "I, the Buddha, sent the three sages: Yen-hui, Confucius and Lao-tzu, to China in order to enlighten the country." And in the *Annotations to the Great Concentration and Insight* by Grand Master Miao-lê, "The Buddha, in order to spread Buddhism in China, dispatched three bodhisattvas to China to teach the people the five virtues as an initial step to Buddhism." Considering these passages, we can assume that the five virtues in China before the introduction of Buddhism are identical to the "five precepts" of Buddhism.

Question (doubtfully): If so, why is it that some slanderers of the True Dharma, who believed in the *Collection of Passages on the Nembutsu*, did not suffer from this calamity?

Answer: Karmic powers of the people are not the same. Some people who commit the sin of slandering the True Dharma* in this life suffer retribution in this world. In the *Lotus Sutra*, chapter 28, The Encouragement of Universal-Sage Bodhisattva, it states, "Those who attack keepers of this sutra will suffer from white leprosy in their present life...and other serious diseases." And in the *Sutra of the Benevolent King*,* "Anyone destroying Buddhism will suffer from unfilial children, without peace among relatives, while no god will come to help him. Sickness and demons will haunt him day after day with calamities befalling him one after another without respite." The *Nirvana Sutra* preaches, "He who does not believe in this sutra...will be confronted with disorder and fighting at his deathbed, suffering from royal oppression and hatred of the people." These are examples of *jun-gengō*, suffering retribution in this life for actions in this life.

In the *Lotus Sutra*, chapter three, A Parable, it says, "Anyone who does not believe in this sutra and slanders it instead...will fall into the Hell of Incessant Suffering after death." And in the *Sutra of the Benevolent King*, "Those who destroy Buddhism...will after death fall into hell, the realm of hungry spirits, and that of beasts and birds." These are examples of *junji-shōgō*, suffering retribution in the next life for actions in this life. Examples of *jun-gogō*, suffering punishment in the life following the next for actions in this life are omitted.

Question (doubtfully): If so, why do believers of the Mahayana sutras, such as the Lotus-Shingon sutras, suffer from this calamity?

Answer: The *Sutra of the Golden Splendor* states, "Even the innocent are involved." And in the *Lotus Sutra*, chapter three, A Parable, "Unexpected disaster would be brought on him." The *Great Concentration and Insight* by Grand Master T'ien-t'ai states, "The karma of one not advanced in practicing Buddhism is slight. Therefore, even though his aspiration for Buddhahood is ripe, he cannot escape various misfortunes because of his grave karma in the past." Grand Master Miao-lê's *Annotations on the Words and Phrases of the Lotus Sutra* states, "If the karmic relation in the past and present is slight, one cannot escape even small suffering."

As I reflect upon these citations, those who practice the Lotus-Shingon teachings are not in an advanced stage, are without firm faith, and recite the sutras without knowing the meaning, solely for the purpose of gaining honors and profits. The residue of their sin for slandering the True Dharma in their past lives still exists. Outwardly they practice the Lotus-Shingon teachings, but at heart they believe in the *Collection of Passages on the Nembutsu*, solely chanting "*Namu Amida Butsu.*" They preach, probably without really believing, to the lay people, catering to the whim of the people, that the *Lotus Sutra* cannot save the people in the Latter Age of Degeneration. Thus, it is impossible for them to escape this calamity.

Question: Do you know any special method that would immediately stop this calamity?

Answer: You should rather get rid of books slandering the True Dharma and those who study such books. Otherwise, no matter how many gods and Buddhas you pray to, you would only spend your money in vain.

Question: How should we eradicate the slanderers of the True Dharma?

Answer: The method for dealing with the slanderers of the True Dharma is also preached in the sutras. The *Nirvana Sutra* declares, "The Buddha preached that you should give alms to all people except one...who commits the serious sin of slandering the True Dharma.... Everybody will praise and admire you if you give alms to all except this *icchantika*, one without Buddha-nature, who slanders the

True Dharma." Beside this passage, various ways to eradicate slanderers of the True Dharma, too many to explain here in detail, are preached.

Many people today, the clergy as well as the laity, put faith in the *icchantika*,* praising, admiring and giving alms to them. So when they happen to encounter those who do not study the teaching of slandering the True Dharma, far from praising such persons, they consider them slanderers and enemies of the True Dharma. Those, who do not know the truth of this, conversely think the keepers of the True Dharma to be slanderers of the True Dharma. They are exactly the same as those predicted in the *Lotus Sutra*, the 13th chapter, Encouragement for Keeping This Sutra,* "Monks in the Latter Age of Degeneration will be cunning, and their hearts flattering and crooked.... They will be delighted to point out our faults..., They will say to kings, ministers, Brahmans, and house-holders..., slandering and speaking ill of us who practice the True Dharma, saying that we are heretics who preach non-Buddhist doctrines."

Thus many people today, discarding preachers of the True Dharma whom the Buddha praised, laud, admire and give alms to the *icchantika*, whom He harshly admonished. As a result, greed grows profusely and the teachings of the slanderers of the True Dharma fill the world. How can calamities not occur? It is only natural that calamities befall this country.

Question: Is it a sin to stop giving alms to slanderers of the True Dharma and torment them?

Answer: The *Nirvana Sutra* tells us, "This supreme True Dharma is now entrusted to kings, ministers, officers, monks and nuns in various countries.... If anyone slanders the True Dharma, the King and his ministers, as well as the four kinds of Buddhists, monks, nuns, and lay men and women, should join hands to chastise him.... It does not constitute a sin at all." All sentient beings, even crickets, ants, mosquitoes and horseflies, necessarily possess Buddha-nature, but those who slander the True Dharma do not. Therefore, refusing to give alms to such people and tormenting them do not constitute a sin.

Question: You, a Buddhist monk, denounce Buddhist priests for committing a sin. Isn't it a violation of two Buddhist precepts: the precept against speaking ill of four kinds of Buddhists and the other against slandering the three treasures: the Buddha, the dharma, and the priesthood?

Answer: The Buddha admonishes us in the *Nirvana Sutra*, "Suppose there is a fine priest who, upon seeing a man slander and break the True Dharma, does not scold, chase out and correct him. Such a man is an enemy of Buddhism. If the priest chases out, scolds and corrects such a man, he is indeed a true disciple of the Buddha." Adhering to this admonition of the Buddha, I am predicting that slanderers of the True Dharma will all fall into the Hell of Incessant Suffering.

When this record spreads all over the land of Japan, rulers of Japan who read it should try to keep this in mind and root out slanderers of the True Dharma. Otherwise, they cannot escape the responsibility referred to in the *Sutra of the Great Assembly*, "Suppose a king, upon seeing that My Dharma is about to be destroyed, leaves it without trying to defend it... three ill omens will befall his land.... He will fall into a great hell upon death." And in the *Sutra of the Benevolent King*, "When the merit of good conduct by the king is all gone... seven calamities will inevitably occur."

If things occur as predicted in these passages, you should first of all ascertain the cause of the series of calamities. Or you had better look at and study hard the passage in the *Sutra of the Benevolent King*, "When a country is in disorder, demons first grow rampant. As demons grow rampant, all the people are disturbed." Today we are faced with wild demons and all the people are in trouble. Disorder in the country will inevitably follow according to the scripture. Such is my humble opinion regarding the cause of calamity and the way to get rid of it. It is up to the people to accept or reject it.

Written in the first 10 days of the second month in the second year of the Shōgen Period (1260).

Notes

1. The five precepts, *gokai*, are: (1) not to kill, (2) not to steal, (3) not to commit adultery, (4) not to lie, and (5) not to drink intoxicants. The 10 virtuous acts, or *jūzen:* 1 through 4 are the same as the first four of *gokai*, (5) not to speak harsh words, (6) not to say words causing enmity, (7) not to engage in idle talk, (8) not to be greedy, (9) not to be angry, and (10) not to have wrong views.
2. One of the Seven Sages of the Bamboo Grove. These were Taoistically inclined intellectuals of third-century China.
3. (Wei) Yüan-sung (-567-): a former Buddhist monk who turned against Buddhism in sixth-century China by inciting Emperor Wu of the Northern Chou to wage one of the severest anti-religious campaigns in the history of China.
4. *Tai-wei* or *Taibi* in Japanese: Constellation consisting of 10 stars near the Lion Constellation. It is considered the imperial palace or palaces of the Five Sovereigns.

Sainan Taiji-shō (ST 21)

Introduction

Sainan Taiji-shō was written in the second year of the Shōgen Period (1260), when Nichiren Shōnin was 38 years old. Fifteen pages of the original manuscript, an important cultural asset of Japan, have been enshrined at Hokekyōji Temple in the Nakayama district of Ichikawa City, Chiba Prefecture.

In this treatise, Nichiren examines the cause of various calamities such as the severe earthquakes, famines and epidemics that befell Japan centering at Kamakura in the 1250s, and proposes a way to put an end to them in light of all the scriptures of Buddhism. Concluding that such calamities are caused by the prevalence of false teachings such as Pure Land and Zen, and that the absence of the True Dharma causes the protective deities of Japan and Buddhism to grow powerless and abandon Japan, Nichiren insists that those evil teachings be immediately outlawed, especially the Pure Land teaching advocated by Hōnen.

Thus this treatise of Nichiren's expresses the same train of thought as his *Treatise on Protecting the Nation* and *The Cause of Misfortunes,* which is further developed in the *Risshō Ankoku-ron, Treatise on Spreading Peace Throughout the Country by Establishing the True Dharma.* Several of the scriptural citations in this writing used to explain the cause of calamities are the same as those found in *Risshō Ankoku-ron.*

Treatise on the Elimination of Calamities

This treatise examines the underlying cause of various calamities befalling our Land. These calamities include severe earthquakes, unseasonable high winds, widespread famine, epidemics, and large-scale wars. This treatise also addresses ways of eliminating the underlying cause.

It is stated in the *Sutra of the Golden Splendor** that the Four Heavenly Kings, four guardian kings of Buddhism, declared to the Buddha:

"Suppose there is a king in a country where this sutra has been transmitted but has never been spread at all because the king would not recognize the sutra, listen to it, make offerings to it, revere it, or praise it. Even if he meets the four kinds of Buddhists, monks, nuns, male followers and female followers, who uphold the sutra, he would not revere or make offerings to them. As a result we, the Four Heavenly Kings, our disciples and numerous gods would be unable to hear the teachings of this Wonderful Dharma, taste the nectar of the True Dharma, and bathe in the stream of the True Dharma. In the end we all would lose our authority and power, allowing only the spirits of the four evil realms, hell, realms of hungry spirits, beasts and birds, and fighting spirits, to grow rampant in the land at the cost of heavenly and human spirits. People would all fall into the river of birth and death, the realm of spiritual darkness and evil passion, losing the way to Nirvana.

"World Honored One! Seeing this, we the Four Heavenly Kings, our retainers and others like the *yakṣa* demons would all abandon this land, not wishing to defend it. It is not we alone who would abandon this king. Even if numerous protective gods existed to guard his country, we are sure that they all would abandon it. If we, the guardian deities and protective gods, all abandon this kingdom, various disasters would befall, and the king would be dethroned. All the people in the kingdom would lose compassion: arresting, killing, fighting, accusing, and flattering one another, causing even innocent people to suffer. Epidemics would spread widely. Comets would appear often. Two suns would appear simultaneously. The sun and moon would eclipse at random. Two rainbows, a black one and white one, would appear foretelling misfortune. Meteors would be seen. The earth would quake. Voices would be heard in wells. Unseasonable storms would occur. Famine would not end. Trees and plants would bear no fruit, And many foreign bandits would invade the land. Thus, the people would suffer in every way, finding no place to live in peace in this kingdom."

We read in the *Sutra of the Great Assembly*,* "Suppose there is a king who, upon seeing My dharma disappearing, gives up defending it. Even if he practiced charity, observed the precepts and cultivated wisdom in his numerous lives in the past, the amount of merit he accumulated would all disappear and the three misfortunes would befall his country.... Upon death he would be reborn in the worst hell."

The *Sutra of the Benevolent King** preaches, "Great King! When disorder takes over a country where the True Dharma is lost, the devils get out of control first. Because the devils are rampant, causing the people to suffer, the people grow wild." The sutra also states:

"Now, as I, the Buddha, observe lives in the past, present, and future clearly through My Buddha-eye,* all the present kings were enthroned due to the merit of having served 500 Buddhas during their lives in the past. Due to this merit, furthermore, all the sages and arhats will be born in the present kings' lands to help them greatly. When the merit which the present kings accumulated in the past is all gone, these sages will forsake them. When all the sages are gone, the seven calamities* will not fail to fall on them."

In the *Sutra of the Benevolent King*, the Buddha addresses King Prasenajit:

"Great King! In the 10 billion worlds where I now preach, 10 billion suns and moons exist. Each world has a Mt. Sumeru surrounded by four continents. On the southern continent of Jambudvīpa, 16 great, 500 medium sized, and 10,000 small states exist. The king in each of these states is fearful of the seven dreadful calamities. What are these dreadful calamities?

"Irregular revolution of the sun and the moon. The order of seasons reversed. The sun turning red or black, Two, three, four or five suns rising simultaneously, The sun losing its brightness because of eclipse. Or one, two, three, four or five rings appearing around the sun. This is the first calamity.

"Twenty-eight constellations* orbiting irregularly, and various stars such as the Metal Star (Venus), comets, the Ring Star, the Demon Star, the Fire Star (Mars), the Water Star (Mercury), the Wind Star, the Pot Star, the Southern Ladle Stars (Big Dipper), the Northern Ladle Stars (Little Dipper), the Earth Star (Saturn), all the King Stars, Three-Duke Stars and Hundred Official Stars leave their usual orbits appearing abnormal. This is the second calamity.

"Great fires sweeping the country burning all the people. Fires caused one after another by devils, dragons, thunderstorms, mountain wizards, human errors, trees rubbing against each other, or arsonists. This is the third calamity.

"Numerous floods drowning the people. Unseasonable rain in winter and snow in summer. Thunderstorms striking in winter, or ice, frost, and hail occurring in the warm month of June. Red, black, and blue rain falling. Mountains of dirt and rock as well as sand and pebbles, and stones in an avalanche. Rivers flowing upstream, carrying away mountains and rocks. These unusual phenomena constitute the fourth calamity.

"Severe winds blowing many people to their death, destroying at one stroke all the mountains, rivers and trees in the land. Untimely storms. Black, red and blue winds, wild winds, whirlwinds, winds as hot as fire or winds as cold as ice blowing. These monstrous winds make up the fifth calamity.

"Severe droughts drying up the heaven and earth with heat burning deep. Plants and grasses all perishing, so grains cannot be harvested. And heat scorching the earth killing off all the people. Such is the sixth calamity.

"Bandits approaching from four directions, invading the country, while rebels rise within the land. Bandits taking advantage of fires, floods or gale winds, with the devilish bandits devastating the people to cause an era of wars and disorder. These bandits coming from abroad and arising within the country make up the seventh calamity."

The *Lotus Sutra** declares in the 26th chapter, Dhāraṇīs, "I, the Heavenly King Vaiśravaṇa (Bishamon), will ensure that there will be no decline nor harm within the area of 100 *yojana*,[1] where this *Lotus Sutra* prevails."

The Nirvana Sutra* preaches, "You should know that the land in which this wondrous *Sutra on the Great Extinction (Nirvana Sutra)* is spread is a Pure Land as indestructible as a diamond. The people who reside here are also as indestructible as diamonds."

The *Sutra of the Benevolent King* states, "This sutra with a 1,000 lights always shines within 1,000 Chinese *li* assuring that the seven calamities will not befall in that area." The sutra also preaches, "Many evil priests who wish to win fame and material gain will preach false teachings before such men in power as the king, crown prince and princes, eventually destroying the teaching of Buddhism, leading the country to ruin. Unable to distinguish right from wrong, the king will put his faith in their false teachings and promulgate arbitrary laws and institutions contrary to the Buddha's commandments, ruining the teaching of Buddhism and destroying the country."

As I contemplate these scriptural passages, it is preached in the *Lotus Sutra*, "There will be no decline nor harm within the area of 100 *yojana*." In the *Sutra of the Benevolent King*, "The seven calamities will not befall the area within 1,000 Chinese *li*." And in the *Nirvana Sutra*, "You should know that the land is as indestructible as a diamond, and the people residing there as indestructible as diamonds."

A Statement of Doubt: Looking at the state of this country today, we are experiencing various disasters. From the eighth month in the eighth year of the Kenchō Period (1256) to the second month in the second year of the Shōgen Period (1260), disasters such as severe earthquakes, unseasonable high winds, and wide-spread famines and epidemics keep on occurring in succession without ending even today. It is as though almost all the people of this country have perished.

Many people have performed various devotional services without any effect. It is declared in the *Lotus Sutra*, which Śākyamuni Buddha asserted was the True Dharma after honestly discarding the expedient, with the Buddha of Many Treasures attesting to its truth and the Buddhas in manifestation from all the worlds in the universe verifying by extending their tongues to the Brahma Heaven, "there will be no decline nor harm within the area of 100 *yojana*." The *Nirvana Sutra*, the will of Śākyamuni Buddha preached last in the *sāla* forest* states, "The land is as indestructible as a diamond." The *Sutra of the Benevolent King* states, "The seven calamities will not befall an area within 1,000 Chinese *li*." All these scriptural statements seem false, do they not?

Answer: In my humble opinion, there are reasons why our prayers are not answered and we have disasters in this country, where various Mahayana sutras such as those mentioned above have been transmitted.

It is stated in the *Sutra of the Golden Splendor*, "In a country where this sutra has been transmitted but has never been spread because the king would not recognize the sutra and listen to it.... We, the Four Heavenly Kings ... all will abandon his kingdom and ... various disasters will befall it."

The *Sutra of the Great Assembly* preaches, "Suppose there is a king, who, seeing My dharma disappearing, gives up defending it.... Three misfortunes would befall his country." The *Sutra of the Benevolent King* states, "Being not in accordance with the commandments of the Buddha will cause destruction of the teachings of Buddhism and the country.... When sages all leave the country, the seven calamities will not fail to occur."

As we ponder these scriptural passages, although our country has various Mahayana sutras such as the *Lotus Sutra*, the four kinds of Buddhists, namely the clergy and laity, both male and female, have all abandoned these sutras, having no intention of listening and giving offerings to them. Because of this, the protective deities of Japan and sages have all left this country. In the absence of the protective deities and sages, demons and evil spirits grew rampant, causing various disasters to occur.

Question: What is the reason that the people in this country abandon and pay no attention to Mahayana sutras, having no intention of making offerings to them?

Answer: The *Sutra of the Benevolent King* states, "Many evil priests who wish to win fame and material gain will preach false teachings before such men in power as the king, crown prince, and princes, eventually destroying the teaching of Buddhism and leading the country to ruin. Unable to distinguish right from wrong, the king will put his faith in their teachings and promulgate arbitrary laws and institutions contrary to the Buddha's commandments."

The *Lotus Sutra* preaches in the 13th chapter, Encouragement for Keeping This Sutra, "Monks in the evil world will be cunning, flattering and crooked. Being proud in heart, they will boast of themselves as having attained enlightenment while they have not.... These men with evil hearts..., slandering and speaking ill of us who practice the True Dharma to kings, ministers, Brahmans, and householders, as well as other monks, say that we are heretics who preach non-Buddhist doctrines.... They are possessed by evil demons."

Reflecting on these passages, I feel sure that since this land is full of depraved monks preaching false teachings to cause the downfall of this country and destruction of the true teachings of Buddhism, kings as well as the four kinds of Buddhists, unable to distinguish between the false and the true, listen to such evil monks and put faith in their false teachings. Therefore, all the people abandon and ignore the various Mahayana sutras.

Question: You say that this land is full of depraved monks preaching false teachings to cause the downfall of this country and to destroy the true teachings of Buddhism. Do they stem from the disciples of the Buddha or preachers of non-Buddhism?

Answer: The *Sutra of the Benevolent King* states, "Destruction of the three treasures of Buddhism, the Buddha, dharma and priesthood, by those who should believe in and defend them is like parasites devouring the body of a lion. Destroyers of the teaching of Buddhism are not from among non-Buddhists." According to this passage, they are among the disciples of the Buddha who bring about the downfall of a country and corrupt Buddhism.

Question: Do those evil monks despoil the True Dharma by spreading teachings similar to it? Do they corrupt it by means of evil teachings?

Answer: Despoiling the expedient Mahayana* teachings by means of Hinayana* teachings, and the true Mahayana teachings by means of the expedient Mahayana teachings, they, both teachers and disciples, do not realize that they slander the True Dharma causing the downfall of a country. They thus violate the Buddha's commandments, causing national destruction and fall into the three evil realms of hell, the realm of hungry spirits and that of beasts and birds.

Question: Do you have any proof for this?

Answer: The *Lotus Sutra* in the 13th chapter, Encouragement for Keeping This Sutra, states, "Evil monks of the defiled world who do not know that the Buddha used expedient and provisional teachings will slander and scowl at those who practice the *Lotus Sutra*. We will often be chased out of monasteries."

It is also preached in the *Nirvana Sutra*, "After My extinction, there will be hundreds, thousands, and many more besides, who do not believe in the *Great Nirvana Sutra* and slander it…. The three kinds of Buddhists practicing the teachings for śrāvaka, pratyekabuddha, and bodhisattvas will likewise hate this supreme *Great Nirvana Sutra*."

Monk Valued-Opinion fell into the three evil realms, hell, the realm of hungry spirits, and that of beasts and birds, because of his sin of slandering Bodhisattva Happy-Root.[2] Thinking-of-Buddha and others suffered in the Hell of Incessant Suffering because of their sin of beating Never-Despising Bodhisattva.*[3] They all erred from not being able to distinguish between Mahayana and Hinayana and between provisional and true teachings in Buddhism. As even the ignorant know that the 10 evil acts[4] and the five rebellious sins* are grave crimes, they will hardly cause national destruction or the ruin of Buddhism. Consequently, it is stated in the *Sutra of the Benevolent King*, "Unable to distinguish right from wrong, the king will put his faith in evil priests' teachings." It is also stated in the *Nirvana Sutra*, "Those who commit the four major sins, killing, stealing, adultery and lying, and the five rebellious sins, with full knowledge of the seriousness of the sins they commit, have no abhorrence and repentance of their sins from the beginning, and no intention of confessing them."

These scriptural passages show that slanderers of the True Dharma, themselves as well as those who believe in them, do not know the meaning of slandering, so they commit this grave sin, destroying the country and ruining Buddhism.

Question: If so, is there anyone in this country who caters to the whims of the people destroying the true teaching by means of provisional teachings?

Answer: Certainly, there is.

Question: Do you have any evidence?

Answer: It is the *Collection of Passages on the Nembutsu** written by Hōnen Shōnin.* Now let me check its statements against the scriptural passages cited above to reveal its false teachings. If we can refute these, we will be able to pacify the country. The *Collection of Passages on the Nembutsu* asserts:

"Zen Master Tao-ch'o* in his *Collection of Passages Concerning Rebirth in the Pure Land* determines the Holy Way* and the Pure Land Gates while encouraging discarding the Holy Way and putting faith in the Pure Land.... First, regarding the Holy Way Gate there are two: Mahayana and Hinayana.* Within Mahayana, differences exist between exoteric and esoteric* teachings, or provisional and true* teachings. In his Collection, however, Tao-ch'o included only exoteric Mahayana and provisional Mahayana in the Holy Way, rejecting them as being roundabout practices needing immeasurably long periods of time to attain Buddhahood. From the context, however, I, Hōnen, believe that esoteric Mahayana and true Mahayana should also be included in the Holy Way teachings. Accordingly, the current eight schools of Buddhism — True Word (Shingon), Zen, T'ien-t'ai (Tendai), Flower Garland (Kegon), Three Discourse (Sanron), Dharma Aspect (Hossō), Ten-Stage Discourse (Jiron) and Consciousness Only (Shōron) — should all be included in the Holy Way, which should be discarded.... Priest T'an-luan* declares in his *Commentary on the Discourse on the Pure Land* that as we respectfully read the *Commentary on the Ten Stages* by the Bodhisattva Nāgārjuna, we find that there are two ways: 'difficult to practice' and 'easy to practice,' for bodhisattvas to attain enlightenment.... Of these two, the 'difficult to practice' way is the Holy Way Gate, and the 'easy to practice' way is the Pure Land Gate.... Those who study the Pure Land sect should first of all know this difference between the Holy Way and Pure Land Gates and 'difficult to practice' and 'easy to practice' ways. Even those who have studied the Holy Way teaching previously, if they wish to be reborn in the Pure Land, they should abandon the Holy Way Gate completely, taking refuge in the Pure Land Gate."

Hōnen also declares in his *Collection of Passages on the Nembutsu*, chapter two:

"Venerable Shan-tao* preaches in his Commentary on the *Sutra of Meditation on the Buddha of Infinite Life* that there are two kinds of practices: the correct and miscellaneous*, urging us to devote ourselves to the former and discard the latter. He states that the miscellaneous practices are five. The first miscellaneous practice is to uphold, read and recite sutras, either Mahayana or Hinayana or exoteric or esoteric, except for those preaching rebirth in the Pure Land such as the *Sutra of Meditation on the Buddha of Infinite Life*.... The third miscellaneous practice is to worship or revere Buddhas, bodhisattvas, or various gods, except for the Buddha of Infinite Life, Amida Buddha.... Judging from what Priest Shan-tao preaches, I, Hōnen, believe he meant to persuade us to discard the miscellaneous practices and concentrate solely on the correct practice of calling the name of the Buddha of Infinite Life. How can anyone discard the correct practice of solely calling the name of the Buddha of Infinite Life, which will enable 100 out of 100 persons to be reborn in the Pure Land? How can anyone attach himself to the miscellaneous practices, through which not even one out of 1,000 persons can attain Buddhahood? Those who practice Buddhism should ponder on this."

It is also stated in the 12th chapter of the *Collection of Passages on the Nembutsu*:

"The *Chen-yüan Era Catalogue of the Buddhist Canon* compiled during the Chen-yüan Period in T'ang China lists 637 Mahayana sutras, exoteric and esoteric, in 2,883 fascicles beginning with the 600-fascicled *Great Wisdom Sutra (Dai-hannya-kyō)* and ending with the *Sutra of the Eternal Dharma (Hō-jōjū-kyō)*. All these sutras must be included in 'reading and reciting Mahayana scriptures' as stated in the *Sutra of Meditation on the Buddha of Infinite Life*.... You should know this! Preaching expedient dharma according to the caliber of those who listened to Him, the Buddha temporarily opened the gate to two ways of practicing meritorious deeds, one with a concentrated mind and another with a scattered mind *(jōsan)*. However, in preaching the True Dharma in accordance with His true intent without considering the capacity of the listeners, the Buddha closed the gate to the two ways of practicing meritorious deeds. Opening the gate which, once opened, will never be closed forever, is solely by calling the name of the Buddha of Infinite Life."

In conclusion Hōnen also declares, "Given the choice between the two excellent teachings, the Holy Way and the Pure Land Gates, those who wish to leave the world of birth and death should choose to enter the Pure Land Gate, setting aside the Holy Way Gate for now. Between the two kinds of practices in Pure Land Buddhism, the correct and the miscellaneous, those who wish to enter the Pure Land Gate should take refuge in the correct, discarding various miscellaneous practices for the present."

Contemplating these citations from the *Collection of Passages on the Nembutsu*, I see people all over Japan today, both high and low, firmly believing in Hōnen Shōnin and revering this book. Consequently, ignorant people, clergy as well as laity, upon seeing such words as "abandon, close, set aside and cast away"* in this book, feel like "abandoning, closing, setting aside and casting away" all the sutras, Buddhas, bodhisattvas, gods and true deities, except for the triple Pure Land sutras and the Buddha of Infinite Life.* These ignorant people today in Japan not only do not wish to put faith in and make offerings to these Buddhas and sutras but also feel like deserting them.

Therefore, although great temples established by grand masters in the past to pray for the tranquility and safety of the country are ruined, nobody seems to regret this deplorable situation and try to rebuild them. As no one seems to feel regret enough to try to rebuild these ruined temples, the sound of reciting sutras and offering the taste of dharmas disappear. As protective deities can no longer savor the taste of dharmas, they lose their divine power and abandon this country. The sages called the Four Reliances, whom Buddhists can rely on for guidance, also leave this country and do not return.

This is exactly what is meant by sutras such as the *Sutra of the Golden Splendor* and the *Sutra of the Benevolent King* when they preach, "When sages all leave the country, the seven calamities will not fail to befall it," and "We, the Four Heavenly Kings... all will abandon this kingdom.... When we all abandon this kingdom, various disasters will befall it."

Is not Hōnen Shōnin, the author of the *Collection of Passages on the Nembutsu*, the very person referred to in the *Sutra of the Benevolent King* as "Many evil priests who wish to win fame and material gain" and in the *Lotus Sutra*, chapter 13, Encouragement for Keeping This Sutra, as "Monks in the evil world will be cunning, flattering and crooked"?

Question: If calamities and disasters occur in this land due to the spread of the *Collection of Passages on the Nembutsu*, would you say that there were no calamities and disasters in this land before it was written?

Answer: Of course there were calamities and disasters before that.

They occurred because the five virtues, benevolence, justice, courtesy, wisdom and fidelity, were violated and the teachings of the Buddha were contradicted. Examples are Emperor Wu of the Northern Chou and his anti-Buddhist advisor, Wei Yüan-sung.[5]

Question: If you say calamities and disasters today are also caused by the violation of the five virtues, how can you claim that they are necessarily caused by the prevalence of the *Collection of Passages on the Nembutsu*?

Answer: The *Sutra of the Benevolent King* preaches, "Great King! If in the future various petty kings, four kinds of Buddhists, clergy and laity, male and female... and evil monks,... arbitrarily promulgate laws and rules contradicting Buddhist precepts... or do not permit creation of Buddhist statues and stupas,... the seven disasters will not fail to befall such kingdoms."

It is also preached in the *Sutra of the Golden Splendor,* "When the King does not recognize this sutra, listen to it, make offerings to it, revere it, or praise it,... various disasters will befall his kingdom." And in the *Nirvana Sutra*, "The three kinds of Buddhists practicing the teachings for *śrāvaka, pratyekabuddha* and bodhisattvas will likewise hate this supreme *Great Nirvana Sutra.*" Are not these scriptural statements tallied exactly with Hōnen's calling the support, worship and praise of Buddhas and sutras, except for the Buddha of Infinite Life and the triple Pure Land sutras, the miscellaneous practices?

Question: Calamities and disasters also occurred in this country before Buddhism was introduced. How can we blame slanderers of the True Dharma for them?

Answer: Governing the country by means of the five virtues, before Buddhism was introduced, was the same as governing the country through the teaching of the Buddha who was in a distant land. So, violation of the five virtues, such as courtesy, was the same as violation of the five precepts established by the Buddha.

Question: Do you have proof for that?

Answer: The *Sutra of the Golden Splendor* preaches, "All the teachings in the world encouraging to do good stem from this sutra." In the *Lotus Sutra*, chapter 19, The Merits of the Teacher of the Dharma, "When pious people expound scriptures of the secular world, talk about the government, or teach the way to earn a livelihood, they all will be in accordance with the True Dharma." In the *Sutra of Meditation on Universal-Sage Bodhisattva*,* "Ruling the country by the True Dharma without oppressing the people unjustly is practice of the third repentance." And in the *Nirvana Sutra*, "All the non-Buddhist scriptures in the world are of the teachings of the Buddha, not the teachings of non-Buddhists."

It is declared in the *Great Concentration and Insight* by Grand Master T'ien-t'ai, "One who knows the true way of the world knows the Buddha dharma." In the *Annotations on the Great Concentration and Insight* by Grand Master Miao-lê, "Such worldly teachings as courtesy and music spread first, opening the way for the Buddha." In Priest Annen's *Comprehensive Interpretations:*

> "The Buddha sent three wise men to China to teach the five precepts by means of the five virtues. In the past, when the prime minister of Sung State asked Confucius whether or not the Three Emperors and Five Sovereigns in ancient China were sages, he answered that they were not. The prime minister then asked whether Confucius himself was a sage, and he said he was not. The prime minister asked again whether or not there was anyone who was considered a sage. Confucius replied that he heard that there was a sage known as Śākyamuni in the land to the west."

In considering these scriptural statements, it can be seen that the Three Emperors and Five Sovereigns of ancient China, before Buddhism was introduced, ruled their countries by means of the five virtues: benevolence, justice, courtesy, wisdom and fidelity. Such evil rulers as King Chieh of the Hsia, King Chou Hsin of the Yin and King Yu of the Chou dynasties violated the five virtues, such as courtesy, and ruined their lands. This is a question of whether or not they observed the commandments established by the Buddha from afar.

Question: If so, why do believers of Mahayana sutras such as the Lotus-Shingon encounter calamity?

Answer: It is stated in the *Sutra of the Golden Splendor*, "Even the innocent are involved." And in the *Lotus Sutra*, chapter three, A Parable, "Unexpected disaster would be brought on them." As I reflect upon these citations, those who practice the Lotus-Shingon teachings are not in an advanced stage, are without firm faith, and recite the sutras without understanding their meaning, solely for the purpose of gaining honor and profit. The residue of this sin for slandering the True Dharma in past lives still exists. Outwardly they practice the Lotus-Shingon teachings, but at heart they believe in the *Collection of Passages on the Nembutsu*, without knowing it is the fountainhead for calamity. Thus, it is impossible for them to escape disaster.

Question: If so, why is it that some slanderers of the True Dharma who believe in the *Collection of Passages on the Nembutsu* do not encounter calamity?

Answer: That is because the karmic powers of people are not the same. Regarding the receiving of retribution in this life for actions in this life *(jun-gengō)*, it is stated in the *Lotus Sutra*, chapter 28, The Encouragement of Universal-Sage Bodhisattva, "Those who slander the keepers of this sutra will suffer from white leprosy in their present life…and other serious diseases." And in the *Sutra of the Benevolent King*, "Anyone who tries to corrupt Buddhism will suffer from not having filial children or peace among relatives. The gods will not come to rescue him. Sickness and demons will haunt him day after day and calamities will befall him one after another without respite." The *Nirvana Sutra* states, "He who does not believe in this sutra…will confront disorder and fighting at his deathbed, suffering from royal oppression as well as hatred from the people."

Regarding the receiving of retribution in the next life for actions in this life *(junji-shōgō)*, it is stated in the *Lotus Sutra*, chapter three, A Parable, "Anyone not believing in this sutra and slandering it instead…will fall into the Hell of Incessant Suffering after death." And in the *Sutra of the Benevolent King*, "Those who corrupt Buddhism…will after death fall into hell, the realm of hungry spirits, and the realm of beasts and birds." Examples of receiving punishment in the life following the next for actions in this life *(jun-gogō)* are omitted.

Question: How can we stop such calamities?

Answer: You should get rid of slanderers of the True Dharma. Otherwise, no matter how many gods and Buddhas you pray to, you will not be able to avoid calamity.

Question: How can we uproot the slanderers of the True Dharma?

Answer: A method for dealing with the slanderers of the True Dharma is also preached in the sutras. The *Nirvana Sutra* declares, "The Buddha preached that you should give alms to all people except one...the one who commits the serious sin of slandering the True Dharma.... Everybody will praise and admire you if you give alms to all except this *icchantika*,* one without Buddha-nature, who slanders the True Dharma." According to this it seems that we should eradicate slanderers of the True Dharma by not giving alms to them. Beside this passage, many ways to uproot slanderers are preached, too many to explain here in detail.

Question: Isn't it a sin to stop giving alms to slanderers of the True Dharma and to torment them?

Answer: The *Nirvana Sutra* assures us, "This supreme True Dharma is now entrusted to kings, ministers, officers, monks and nuns in various countries.... Kings and ministers as well as four kinds of Buddhists, monks, nuns, and lay men and women, should join hands to chastise slanderers of the True Dharma.... It does not constitute a sin at all."

Question: You, a Buddhist monk, indict a sin committed by Buddhist priests. Isn't that a sin?

Answer: The Buddha admonishes us in the *Nirvana Sutra*, "Suppose a fine priest who, upon seeing a man slander and break the True Dharma, does not scold, chase out and correct him, such a priest is an enemy of Buddhism. If the priest chases out, scolds and corrects such a man, he is indeed a true disciple of the Buddha."

Upon seeing this passage in the sutra, I, Nichiren, in order not to be accused of being an enemy of Buddhism, clarify, without shirking from public criticism, the reason why Hōnen Shōnin and his disciples and followers will surely fall into the Hell of Incessant Suffering. A few of those who understand this reason, the clergy and laity, are converted.

If rulers of a country, though hearing this even once, do not stop giving alms to slanderers of the True Dharma as admonished by the Buddha in the *Nirvana Sutra* cited above, they cannot escape the prediction of the Buddha made in the *Sutra of the Great Assembly*: "Suppose a king upon seeing My dharma is about to be destroyed, ignored this without trying to defend it. Even if he gave alms, observed precepts and cultivated wisdom during his numerous lives in the past, all the merit will disappear and three misfortunes will befall his kingdom.... He will fall into a great hell upon death."

The *Sutra of the Benevolent King* states, "When the merit of virtuous conduct by the king is all gone...the seven calamities will inevitably occur." The *Sutra of the*

Great Assembly cited immediately above claims, "Even if he, the king, gave alms, observed precepts and cultivated wisdom during the numerous lives in the past, all the merit would disappear...."

Seeing these passages in the sutras, we should put aside everything else for now and first of all think hard of the cause of calamity. Otherwise, calamities will only increase. This is my humble opinion. It is up to individuals whether or not they accept my plan to eliminate the slanderers of the True Dharma.

Notes

1. The Sanskrit term *yojana* is said to be the distance covered by the royal army in a day. This is equivalent to 30 or 40 Chinese *li*.
2. *Shohō mugyō-kyō*.
3. *Lotus Sutra*, chapter 20, Never-Despising Bodhisattva.
4. The 10 evil acts: (1) killing, (2) stealing, (3) adultery, (4) lying, (5) harsh words, (6) words causing enmity, (7) idle talk, (8) greed, (9) anger, and (10) wrong views.
5. (Wei) Yüan-sung (-567-): a former Buddhist monk who turned against Buddhism in sixth-century China by inciting Emperor Wu of the Northern Chou to wage one of the severest anti-religious campaigns in the history of China.

Risshō Ankoku-ron (ST 24)

Introduction

Risshō Ankoku-ron was written on the 16th day of the seventh month in the first year of the Bunnō Period (1260), when Nichiren Shōnin was 38 years old. Thirty-six pages of the original manuscript, excluding the 24th page, are kept as a national treasure of Japan in the Nakayama Hokekyōji Temple, Chiba Prefecture. The "expanded edition" of this treatise, also in Nichiren's own handwriting, was probably completed in the last year of the Kenji or the first year of the Kōan Period (1278). The work consists of 24 pages and exists today in the Hongokuji Temple in Kyoto.

The reason for writing this treatise was a series of strange phenomena in the sky and natural calamities on earth that occurred in succession from the first year of the Shōka Period (1257) to the first year of the Bunnō Period (1260). For the purpose of rooting out those disasters, Nichiren searched the scriptures of Buddhism for both their cause and the means of eliminating them. His findings and conclusions, which were published earlier in *Treatise on Protecting the Nation*, *Treatise on Elimination of Calamities*, and others, were put together in the *Treatise on Spreading Peace Throughout the Country by Establishing the True Dharma*. This was then presented to former Shogunal Regent Lay Priest Hōjō Tokiyori, the *de facto* ruler of the Kamakura Shogunate, through Lay Priest Yadoya. That is to say, *Risshō Ankoku-ron* is a political proposal privately studied and submitted. This writing, consisting of 10 sections, proceeds with questions asked by a traveler, a believer of government ruled by a sage king, and answers by a master of a household who insists on government led by the dharma of Buddhism.

The first section explains the cause of disasters. Nichiren says that because people in Japan rejected the True Dharma and put faith in evil teachings, the protective deities of Japan and sages abandoned the land, causing devils and demons to grow rampant and calamities to occur in succession. In the second section, to prove his contention, Nichiren cites passages from the *Sutra of the Golden Splendor*, the *Sutra of the Great Assembly*, the *Sutra of the Benevolent King*, and the *Medicine Master Sutra*. In the third section, he declares that though

Buddhism flourishes in Japan, slanderers of the True Dharma exist among Buddhists themselves causing the destruction of Buddhism. In the fourth and fifth sections, Nichiren singles out Hōnen of the Pure Land sect, author of the *Collection of Passages on the Nembutsu,* as the slanderer of the True Dharma, concluding that Hōnen's teaching of the *nembutsu* is the source of the calamities that befall Japan. The sixth section justifies his appeal to the shogunate by stating that ridding the country of evil teachings is the duty of a Buddhist monk and that such an action has precedents. The seventh section proposes outlawing the slanderers of the True Dharma as a means of preventing natural disasters from occurring. The eighth section suggests ceasing to give alms to the slanderers as the best way of preventing calamities. In the ninth section Nichiren warns that domestic disturbance and invasion by foreign troops, two of the seven calamities, predicted by sutras, that have not taken place, will be sure to occur unless Japan as a nation establishes the True Dharma and stops giving alms to the slanderers. Thus he urges the shogunate to eradicate the slanderers of the True Dharma saying, "You should promptly discard your false faith, and take up the true and sole teaching of the *Lotus Sutra* at once...." This statement of Nichiren's in classic Chinese, consisting of 64 Chinese characters, explains the meaning of *Risshō Ankoku,* Spreading Peace Throughout the Country by Establishing the True Dharma, the title of the writing under discussion, and his basic religious concepts. Finally in the 10th and concluding section, the traveler, enlightened by the master's lectures, swears that he will not only stop being a slanderer of the True Dharma but that he will also admonish others to do likewise.

The main theme of this writing is that the Buddha land can be established on earth in this world through practicing the True Dharma. This idea of Spreading Peace Throughout the Country by Establishing the True Dharma constitutes the core of Nichiren Buddhism, which Nichiren upheld throughout his lifetime. Nichiren recopied this treatise several times during his life. The *Risshō Ankoku-ron* written sometime during the Kenji-Kōan Era (1275-1288) and supplemented with important passages that refute Shingon Buddhism and harshly criticizes Kūkai, Ennin and Enchin, Grand Masters Kōbō, Jikaku and Chishō, is known as the "expanded edition."

In this English translation, supplementary remarks found only in the "expanded edition" are placed between brackets.

Treatise on Spreading Peace Throughout the Country by Establishing the True Dharma
[by Buddhist Monk Nichiren][1]

I. The Cause of Disasters

A TRAVELER CAME TO LAMENT: In recent years, strange phenomena in the sky, natural calamities on earth,* famines, and epidemics have occurred and spread over all the land of Japan. Oxen and horses lie dead at crossroads and the streets are filled with skeletons. A majority of the population has perished and everyone has been touched by grief.

In the meantime, some try to avert disaster by chanting the name of the Buddha of Infinite Life, Lord of the Land of Bliss to the West,* putting sole faith in this practice as the "sharpest sword" to cut out sin and evil karma.[2] Others recite the *Medicine Master Sutra** of the Buddha in the Land of Emerald Light to the East,* relying on the vow of this Buddha to cure all disease. Some worship the *Lotus Sutra* as the message of the Buddha, believing in its statements from chapter 23, The Previous Life of Medicine-King Bodhisattva, that anyone can dispel sickness and will neither grow old nor die. Others put faith in a statement in the *Sutra of the Benevolent King* that the seven calamities[3] will disappear and seven fortunes[4] will rise when lectures are given on that sutra. So the Benevolent King Ceremony is held with 100 preachers lecturing on that sutra.

Some perform devotional services to ward off evil by sprinkling water over five vessels filled with offerings in accordance with the esoteric teachings of True Word (Shingon) Buddhism, while others practice the ritual of meditation to cleanse their minds thinking that they will see the emptiness of all phenomena, including natural calamities and evil fortune. Some write the names of the seven fierce gods on paper to paste on every gate hoping to escape epidemics. Others sketch the five mighty bodhisattvas, described in the *Sutra of the Benevolent King,* on paper to hang in every house hoping for protection. Still others worship various deities in heaven and on earth, trying to fend off epidemics by means of a Shinto ritual for purifying the four corners of the city. The emperor and his ministers, feeling pity for the misery of the common people, try to ward off national disaster by means of benevolent governing.

All these efforts, however, prove fruitless. Famines and epidemics only grow rampant. Only beggars and corpses are seen everywhere! Corpses are piled high as watchtowers, and lined up like a bridge. But realize! The sun and the moon shine bright day and night, and the five planets, Jupiter, Mars, Venus,

Mercury and Saturn, revolve regularly in the sky. On earth, the three treasures of Buddhism,* the Buddha, His teachings, and His disciples, continue to be respected. It is said that the Great Bodhisattva Hachiman vowed to protect the 100 rulers* of Japan. Why is this country in such decay though the number of Japanese emperors has not reached 100? Why is Buddhism in this country so powerless? How did this come about? What is the matter with this country?

THE MASTER ANSWERED: I have been worrying about this deeply in my mind without having anyone to talk to. Now that you have come to express your concern regarding this matter, let us discuss this.

Properly speaking, he who renounces family ties and enters the priesthood expects to attain enlightenment through the teachings of the Buddha. Observing carefully the state of affairs in our society today, however, the gods do not respond to our prayers and the Buddhas do not give any indication of their divine powers. I cannot help wondering whether a man as ignorant as I will ever be able to attain Buddhahood in the future. So I look up at the sky to calm my anger, and look down on the earth in great anxiety.

Knowing my limitations, I searched through some sutras and came to the conclusion that the cause of national calamities comes from all the people opposing the right dharma, and siding with false dharmas. Therefore, protective deities and sages have abandoned the country and will not return. This has allowed various evils and devils to invade, causing disasters and calamities. How can I not point this out! How can I not be afraid of this!

II. Predictions of Calamities in Sutras

THE TRAVELER INQUIRED: It is not I alone but all the people who are grieving over these calamities of recent years affecting the entire land of Japan. Now that I am able to see you and listen to your respected opinion, I would like to ask in what sutra is it stated that calamities and disasters occur in succession because the gods and sages deserted this country? What is your evidence for this?

THE MASTER RESPONDED: Many scriptures state this, and many attestations exist. Let me cite some of them. The Four Heavenly Kings,* four guardian kings of Buddhism, declare to the Buddha in the *Sutra of the Golden Splendor:**

> "Suppose there is a king in a country where this sutra exists but has never been spread at all because the king would rather not recognize the sutra, listen to it, make offerings to it, revere it or praise it. Even if he meets with the four kinds of Buddhists who uphold this sutra, monks, nuns,

male followers, and female followers, he would not respect them or make offerings to them. As a result we, the Four Heavenly Kings, our retainers and various gods will be unable to hear the teachings of this wonderful dharma, taste the nectar of the True Dharma, and bathe in the stream of the True Dharma. In the end we all will lose our authority and power, allowing only the spirits of the four evil realms, hell, realms of hungry spirits, beasts, and fighting spirits, to grow rampant in the land at the cost of heavenly and human spirits. People will all fall into the river of birth and death, namely the realms of spiritual darkness and evil passion, losing the way to Nirvana.

"World Honored One! Seeing this, we, the Four Heavenly Kings, our retainers and others like the *yakṣa* demons will give up this land, not wishing to defend it. It is not we alone who will abandon this king. Even if numerous protective gods exist to guard his country, we are sure that they all will abandon it. When we, the guardian deities and protective gods, all abandon this kingdom, various disasters will befall it, and the king will be dethroned. All the people in the kingdom will lose compassion, arresting, killing, fighting, accusing, and flattering one another, causing even innocent people to suffer.

"Epidemics will spread widely. Comets will appear often. Two suns will rise at the same time. The sun and the moon will eclipse at random. Two rainbows, a black one and a white one, will appear foretelling misfortune. Meteors will often be seen. The earth will quake. Voices will be heard in wells. Unseasonable storms will occur. Famine will not end. Trees and plants will bear no fruit. And many foreign bandits will invade the land. Thus the people will suffer in every way, finding no place to live in peace in this kingdom."

Next, it is stated in the *Sutra of the Great Assembly:**

"When Buddhism is about to disappear, the monks will grow whiskers and hair, their fingernails will lengthen and they will forget Buddhist manners and precepts.

"Then great voices will ring out in the sky, the earth will quake, and everything will revolve like a hydraulic turbine. City walls will collapse and houses will all crumble without exception. Tree roots, branches, leaves, flowers, and fruits, along with their flavors will disappear. With the exception of the Heaven of Pure Inhabitants (Jōgoten[5]), where reside sages who have reached the stage of not having to be reborn in the six realms of transmigration, everywhere else in the world of evil passion, the seven flavors, sweetness, hotness, sourness, bitterness, saltiness, astringency and lightness, and three energies, of the earth, dharma, and human beings, will be lost completely. Various discourses leading to emancipation will all disappear then.

"Trees and plants will not grow well, bearing fewer flowers and fruits, which will lack taste. Wells, springs, and ponds will dry up, while the earth will be salty and barren, and split into hills and ravines. All the mountains will be burning hot, and the heavenly dragons will send no rain. Grain-seedlings and plants will all die, and even weeds will not grow. Dust storms will darken the sky, eclipsing the sun and moon. Drought will be everywhere. Such ill omens will prevail.

"The 10 evil acts,[6] especially greed, anger, and false views will multiply. The people will be as unfilial to their parents as a timid deer is heedless of its herd when trying to run for its life. The people will decrease in number and their lives will be shorter. Their physical strength, authority, and pleasures will all diminish. Far from the pleasures of the realms of men and gods, they will without exception fall into the three evil realms of hells, hungry spirits, and beasts.

"When these evil kings and evil monks slander the True Dharma of the Buddha, hindering the way of humans and gods, even various protective gods, who feel pity for the people, will abandon this evil country."

It is stated in the *Sutra of the Benevolent King:**

"The first thing that happens when disorder takes over in a country where the True Dharma is lost, is that the devils will get out of control. Because the devils are rampant causing the people to suffer, the people will grow wild. Then foreign bandits will invade the country killing many people and causing quarrels among the king, his subjects, the crown prince, the royal princes, and the government officials. Strange phenomena will occur in heaven and on earth. Twenty-eight constellations* will change their positions, while the stars, the sun and the moon will revolve out of their regular orbits. Civil wars will break out everywhere."

The same *Sutra of the Benevolent King* also states:

"Now, as I, the Buddha, observe lives in the past, present and future* clearly through My Buddha-eye,* all the present kings were enthroned due to their having served 500 Buddhas during their lives in the past. Furthermore, due to this merit, all the sages and arhats will be born in their lands to help them greatly. When the merit which the present kings accumulated in the past is all gone, these sages will abandon them. When all the sages are gone, the seven calamities* will not fail to take place."

The *Medicine Master Sutra** asserts: "Calamities which befall warriors and kings will be of the following seven types: epidemics among the people, foreign invasion,* domestic disturbance,* irregularities in constellations, eclipses of the sun and moon, unseasonable storms and droughts."

In the *Sutra of the Benevolent King*, the Buddha addresses King Prasenajit:

"Great King! In the 10 billion worlds where I preach, 10 billion suns and moons exist. Each world has a Mt. Sumeru surrounded by four continents. On the southern continent of Jambudvīpa, 16 great, 500 medium sized, and 10,000 small states exist. The king in each of these states will be fearful of seven dreadful calamities. What are these seven calamities?

"First of all, irregular revolution of the sun and moon. The order of seasons reversed. The sun turning red or black. Two, three, four or five suns rising at the same time. The sun losing its brightness because of eclipse. Or one, two, three, four or five rings appearing around the sun. This is the first calamity.

"Next, 28 constellations orbiting irregularly, and various stars such as the Metal Star (Venus), the Ring Star, the Demon Star, the Fire Star (Mars), the Water Star (Mercury), the Wind Star, the Pot Star, the southern ladle stars (Big Dipper), the northern ladle stars (Little Dipper), the Earth Star (Saturn), king stars, three-duke stars, hundred-official stars and comets changing their courses. This is the second calamity.

"Great fires sweeping the country burning all the people. Or fires caused one after another by devils, dragons, thunderstorms, mountain wizards, human errors, trees rubbing against each other or arsonists. This is the third calamity.

"Great floods drowning the people. Unseasonable rain in winter and snow in summer. Thunderstorms striking in winter, or ice, frost, and hail occurring in the warm month of June. Red, black, and blue rain falling. Mountains of dirt and rock as well as sand, pebbles, and stones raining down. Rivers flowing upstream, carrying away mountains and rocks. These unnatural phenomena constitute the fourth calamity.

"Severe winds blowing many people to death, destroying in one stroke all the trees, mountains, and rivers in the land. Untimely storms. Black, red and blue winds, wild winds, whirl winds, winds hot as fire or winds cold as ice blowing. These unnatural winds constitute the fifth calamity.

"Severe droughts drying up the heaven and earth with heat burning deep into the earth. Plants and grasses all perishing, so grains will not be harvested. Heat scorching the earth killing off all the people. Such is the sixth calamity.

"Finally, bandits approaching from four directions, invading the country, while rebels rise within and outside of the ruling clan. Bandits taking advantage of fires, floods or gale winds, and devilish bandits devastating the people and causing an era of wars and disorder. These bandits coming from abroad and arising within the country make up the seventh calamity."

We also read in the *Sutra of the Great Assembly*:

"Suppose there is a king who practices charity, observes precepts, and cultivates wisdom in his numerous lives in the past, and suppose upon seeing My dharma disappearing, he gives up defending it. The immeasurable amount of merit he accumulated will all disappear and the three misfortunes will befall his country: famine, epidemics, wars and other disorders. As all the gods will leave the country and as people will not obey the king's orders and instructions, the country will always be invaded by neighboring countries. Violent fire will go out of control, fierce storms will run amuck often, swelling floods will drown the people, and royal relatives will band together in rebellion. Before long, the king will come down with a serious sickness and will be reborn in hell after his death.... Likewise his wife, crown prince, ministers, heads of cities, village heads, generals, county magistrates, and other officials will all meet the same fate."

The citations above, from the four sutras, the *Sutra of the Golden Splendor, Sutra of the Great Assembly, Sutra of the Benevolent King,* and *Medicine Master Sutra,* make it clear that not upholding the True Dharma is the source of calamities. Who in the world would doubt it?

Nevertheless, the blind and disturbed, not recognizing the true teaching, will indiscriminately put faith in false teachings. As a result, the people will abandon many Buddhas and sutras, having no intention of upholding them. So the gods who protect the country and the sages who teach the true teaching will abandon the country. This will allow evil demons and heretical doctrines to move in, causing calamities and difficulties.

III. Slandering the True Dharma.

ANGRY, THE TRAVELER FROWNED DEEPLY AND ASKED THE MASTER: Buddhism found its way to China when Emperor Ming, the second sovereign of the Later Han Dynasty, dreamed of a golden man and founded the White Horse (Pai-ma-ssu) Temple, inviting two monks from India. Buddhism became established in Japan when Prince Shōtoku* built the Shitennōji Temple after putting down the rebellion of Mononobe Moriya, the leader of the anti-Buddhist force. Since then everybody in Japan, from the Emperor down to the common people has worshipped Buddhist images and single-mindedly recited the sutras. Accordingly on Mt. Hiei, in the Southern Capital* of Nara, and in the Onjōji and Tōji Temples, all over Japan — in five central provinces and seven districts — sutras as numerous as stars in the sky were gathered, and temples as numerous as clouds were built. There are those as wise as Śāriputra, trying to attain Buddhahood by meditating on the moon over Mt. Sacred Eagle, while others as well disciplined as Halkena-yaśa,[7] try to observe precepts by following the way of Mahā-kāśyapa, who passed away on Mt. Cook's Legs (Kikkuṭapāda). In spite of all this, who in the world would you claim to have slighted the Buddha's lifetime teachings and destroyed the traces of the three treasures of Buddhism: the Buddha, His teachings, and the Buddhist priesthood? If you have proof for your allegations, I would like to hear about it in detail.

THE MASTER TRIED TO PERSUADE HIM: As you pointed out, Buddhist temples stand in rows and libraries of sutras are everywhere, while Buddhist priests are as numerous as bamboo stalks and reeds, or rice and hemp plants. Outwardly, they have been revered year after year and day after day. In reality, however, the priests are all flatterers and crooked in mind. They mislead the people, but both the king and his subjects are not wise enough to tell right from wrong.

It is stated in the *Sutra of the Benevolent King:* "Many evil priests who wish to win fame and material gain will preach false teachings to such men in power as the king, crown prince, and princes, which will eventually destroy Buddhism and lead the country to ruin. Unable to distinguish right from wrong, the king will put his faith in their teachings and promulgate laws arbitrary to the Buddha's commandments. This will ruin Buddhism and destroy the country."

[It is stated in the *Guardian Sutra:**

> "Great King, this evil monk will violate Buddhist precepts, commit sins, pollute residences of all high-ranking people, slander those monks who practice the True Dharma to the king, his ministers and office holders, speaking ill of them arbitrarily.... Blaming those who practice the True Dharma for everything wrong, not only in Buddhist temples but also throughout the country, this evil monk will fool the king, his ministers and officials until those who practice the True Dharma are driven out of the country so that this violator of precepts gains a free hand in the kingdom as an intimate friend of the king, his ministers and officials."

It also states, "There will be numerous disasters such as unseasonable winds and rains, droughts, continuous rains, successive crop failures, aggression by enemies, and epidemics."

The *Guardian Sutra* also declares:

> "The teachings of Śākyamuni Buddha will not be damaged at all by non-Buddhists such as all the heavenly devils, heretics, wicked men and supernatural beings with five supernatural powers. On the contrary, Buddhism will be destroyed internally by evil monks, who are Buddhist monks in name only. It is like Mt. Sumeru in the center of the world which will not be damaged at all even if it is being burned by fire for a long time fueled by all the trees and plants all over the world, but when the time for the end of the world arrives with the *kalpa*-fire erupting from within, it will burn to nothing, leaving not even ashes."

The *Sutra of the Golden Splendor** asserts: "When a violator of the law is revered and a law-abiding person is punished, constellations will revolve out of their regular orbits, it will rain and winds will blow out of season because evil is revered and the virtuous are punished." The sutra states also: "Everyone in the Heaven of the Thirty-three Gods is outraged, so that government will fall into disorder, flatteries and lies will be rampant, violent winds will blow constantly, and rainstorms will occur out of season." It is further stated in the sutra that various heavenly beings assert:

> "When this king violates the law and befriends evil persons, he will not be safe on the throne any longer and heavenly beings will be furious with him. As gods are furious with the king, his kingdom will be destroyed. His country will be ruined as Indra will have no intention of defending his land and all the other gods, too, will abandon it leaving it to perish. The king, himself, will be tormented by sufferings while his parents, wife and children, brothers and sisters all will have to suffer the sadness of separation from loved ones ... until they all die. Strange comets will pass through the sky, two suns will rise simultaneously, foreign bandits will invade the land, and the people in the kingdom will all suffer from the tragedy."

The *Sutra of the Great Assembly* preaches:

> "If any king and his clan members violate the law, harass, slander or abuse the Buddha's *śrāvaka* disciples, striking them with swords and sticks, rob them of their clothes or utensils, or persecute those who give alms to the disciples of the Buddha, we, gods and virtuous deities, will immediately cause his enemies to rise outside his kingdom. In addition we will cause his land to be plagued by civil wars, epidemics, famines, unseasonable winds and rains, fighting and lawsuits. Thus the king will be forced to lose his kingdom before long."

It is stated in the *Nirvana Sutra:*

> "When the True Dharma of Śākyamuni Buddha is about to expire,[8] many evil monks will not understand the profound teaching of the Buddha. They are like ignorant thieves who ignore the real treasure and get away with woods and grasses of no value. As they do not understand the profound teaching of the Buddha, they do not try to practice it. How sad it is! Fearful is the future world of corruption and degeneration after the passing away of the Buddha. These evil monks will steal this sutra, cutting it up into pieces to kill its original color, fragrance and flavor. In reading this sutra, unable to understand the essence of the Buddha's profound enlightenment, they will insert flowery phrases and meaningless sentences just to save appearances. They might put a beginning sentence at the end, and ending sentence at the beginning, a beginning or ending sentence in the middle, or a middle sentence at the beginning or at the end. You should know that these evil monks are not the Buddha's disciples but the Devil's companions."]

The *Nirvana Sutra* also warns of evil priests: "Bodhisattvas, you should not be afraid of wild elephants, but you should be of an 'evil friend.'* Even if you are killed by wild elephants, you will not be reborn in the three evil realms: hells, the realm of hungry spirits, and the realm of beasts and birds. But if your heart is lost to the evil priests, you will be reborn there without fail."

Next, the *Lotus Sutra,* chapter 13, Encouragement for Keeping This Sutra, discusses in detail the behavior of the evil priests in the Latter Age of Degeneration:

> "[Ignorant people will speak ill of us,
> Abuse us, and threaten us
> With swords or sticks.
> But we will endure all this.]
> Monks in the evil world
> Cunning, crooked, flattering, and arrogant,
> Boast of themselves as enlightened,
> While they are not.
> Some monks will stay in a monastery,
> Wearing robes, sitting quietly,
> Claiming to be preaching the true way.
> Despising the people,
> Attached to profit making,
> They will preach the dharma for the lay people
> And will be revered by the people
> As though they were arhats with Six Superhuman Powers....[9]

In order to slander us
Among the large crowd
They will speak ill of us
To the king, ministers, Brahmans,
Lay believers, and other monks
Saying that we are crooked in opinion
And preach heretical teachings....
In the evil world during the age of defilement
Many dreadful things
Such as demons entering their bodies
Cause them to abuse and shame us....
Evil monks of the defiled world,
Without knowledge of the Buddha
Using the expedient and provisional teachings,
Will slander us and frown at us.
Often we will be chased out of monasteries."

In the *Nirvana Sutra*, the Buddha also defines the behavior of the evil priests in the latter ages:

"In numerous centuries after My death, sages with four stages of Hinayana enlightenment[10] will all have died, too. After the Age of the True Dharma is over, in the Age of the Semblance Dharma, when the teaching of the Buddha remains only in form, those who claim to be monks will appear. Pretending to be observing Buddhist precepts, they will read and recite few sutras, while indulging in drinking and eating to nourish their bodies. Although they wear priestly robes, they will seek worldly gain just as a hunter stalks game with his eyes half-closed or a cat preys on a rat. They will always claim to have attained arhatship, pretending to be sages, but in their inner hearts they will be full of greed and jealousy. Just like a Brahman practicing a vow of silence, they will appear to be monks without being ones in reality. Their false views will spread far and wide and they will slander the True Dharma."

[The *Nirvana Sutra* also preaches: "Good men! Suppose a man of *icchantika** without root of goodness pretending to be an arhat stays in a remote corner of tranquility, slandering Mahayana sutras. Ordinary men who see him may think him to be an arhat or a great bodhisattva."

The six-fascicled *Nirvana Sutra** (*Hatsunaion-gyō*) states:

"There will be a man of *icchantika* who acts like an arhat but commits evil acts. And there will be an arhat who acts like a man of *icchantika* but has compassion. An arhat-like man of *icchantika* refers to the people who slander Mahayana Buddhism. An arhat who acts like a man of *icchantika* refers to a man who despises the Hinayana sages of *śrāvaka* and widely preaches Mahayana Buddhism, assuring the people that both he and they are bodhisattvas because everyone has Buddha-nature in himself. Nevertheless, those people will consider him a man of *icchantika*."

The sutra also preaches, "As people cannot see to the end, they do not know how evil a man of *icchantika* is. Nor have they seen Nirvana at the end of innumerable lives and deaths."]

Observing the world today through these scriptural passages, the state of the Buddhist world is exactly as they point out. How can we accomplish anything worthwhile without admonishing the evil monks who slander the True Dharma?

IV. Hōnen, Slanderer of the True Dharma

THE TRAVELER, STILL FURIOUS, PERSISTED: Wise kings lead the people under principles of heaven and earth, and sagacious rulers govern the country by discerning good from bad. Priests today are revered by all the people in the country. If they were evil priests as you claim, wise kings would not trust them. Were they not saintly masters, they would not be revered by men of wisdom and of intelligence. Since they are revered by wise kings and sagacious rulers, we know that eminent priests today are great monks. How dare you accuse them so falsely? Who would you say are evil priests? I would like to know exactly.

THE MASTER REPLIED: [I have many reasons, but in order to avoid complication I present just one example for now, so that you may infer all others.] During the reign of ex-Emperor Gotoba, a certain Buddhist monk called Hōnen* wrote the *Collection of Passages on the Nembutsu*, destroying the holy teaching of Śākyamuni Buddha in His lifetime and confusing all the people in the world. He asserts in this *Collection of Passages on the Nembutsu*:

> "Zen Master Tao-ch'o* preaches in his *Collection of Passages Concerning Rebirth in the Pure Land* that there are two ways in Buddhism: the Holy Way* and the Pure Land Way. We should discard the former and rightly follow the latter. As for the Holy Way, it can be divided into two: Mahayana and Hinayana Buddhism. Mahayana Buddhism itself consists of exoteric, esoteric, provisional and true teachings, while Tao-ch'o states that the Holy Way includes Hinayana Buddhism as well as exoteric and provisional teachings of Mahayana Buddhism. From the context, however, I, Hōnen, believe that both esoteric and true teachings of Mahayana should also

be included in the holy way. Accordingly, the current eight schools of Buddhism: True Word (Shingon), Zen, T'ien-t'ai (Tendai), Flower Garland (Kegon), Three Discourses (San-ron), Dharma Aspect (Hossō), Ten-Stage Discourse (Jiron), and Consciousness Only (Shōron) should all be included in the holy way, which should be discarded.

"Priest T'an-luan,* the founder of Chinese Pure Land Buddhism, declares in his *Commentary on the Discourse on the Pure Land:* 'Reading respectfully the *Commentary on the Ten Stages* by Bodhisattva Nāgārjuna, I see there are two ways through which a bodhisattva can attain enlightenment. They are the way difficult to practice and the way easy to practice.' What is referred to as the way difficult to practice by T'an-luan is the Holy Way, and the way easy to practice, the Pure Land Way. Those who study Pure Land Buddhism should first of all know this: the difference between the Holy and the Pure Land Ways. Even if one has studied the Holy Way, he should discard it completely, taking refuge in the Pure Land Way, if he wishes to be reborn in the Pure Land of the Buddha of Infinite Life."

Hōnen also declares in the second chapter of the *Collection of Passages on the Nembutsu*:

"Honorable Priest Shan-tao* preaches in his Commentary on the *Sutra of Meditation on the Buddha of Infinite Life* that there are two kinds of practices: correct and miscellaneous,* urging us to devote ourselves to the former and discard the latter in order for us to be reborn in the Pure Land. He states that the miscellaneous practices are five. The first of the five miscellaneous practices is to uphold, read and recite sutras, either Mahayana or Hinayana or exoteric and esoteric, except for the triple Pure Land sutras such as the *Sutra of Meditation on the Buddha of Infinite Life,* which preach rebirth in the Pure Land. The third miscellaneous practice is to worship or revere Buddhas, bodhisattvas, or gods except for the Buddha of Infinite Life, Amida Buddha. Judging from these words of Shan-tao, I, Hōnen, believe he meant to persuade us to discard all the miscellaneous practices and concentrate on the correct practice of calling the name of the Buddha of Infinite Life. How can anyone discard the true practice of solely calling the name of the Buddha of Infinite Life which will enable 100 out of 100 persons to be reborn in the Pure Land? How can anyone attach himself to the miscellaneous practices, through which not even one out of 1,000 persons is said to attain Buddhahood? He who wishes to practice Buddhism should think hard on this."

He also says in the 12th chapter of his *Collection of Passages on the Nembutsu*:

"The Chên-yüan Era Catalogue of the Buddhist Canon lists 637 Mahayana sutras, exoteric and esoteric, in 2,883 fascicles beginning with the 600-fascicled *Great Wisdom Sutra* and ending with the *Sutra of the Eternal Dharma*. Reading and reciting these sutras must be what the *Sutra of Meditation on the Buddha of Infinite Life* defines as "reading and reciting Mahayana scriptures," one of the meritorious deeds which can be practiced without concentration of mind through meditation. You should know this! Preaching expedient dharma according to the caliber of those who listened to Him, the Buddha temporarily opened the gate to two ways of practicing meritorious deeds, one with a concentrated mind and another with a scattered mind *(jōsan)*.* However, in preaching the True Dharma in accordance with His true intent without considering the caliber of listeners, the Buddha closed the gate to the two ways of practicing meritorious deeds. The only way to open the gate which, once opened, will never be closed, is by calling the name of the Buddha of Infinite Life."

The *Collection of Passages on the Nembutsu* also asserts in its eighth chapter:

"The *Sutra of Meditation on the Buddha of Infinite Life* preaches that those who practice Pure Land Buddhism should never fail to have the 'three minds' in reciting the name of the Buddha of Infinite Life: sincere mind, mind of deep faith and mind resolving to be reborn in the Pure Land. Shan-tao explains this in his *Commentary on the Sutra of Meditation on the Buddha of Infinite Life*: 'Those who understand and practice Buddhism differently from Pure Land Buddhists will insist that calling the name of the Buddha of Infinite Life will not guarantee rebirth in the Pure Land.... In order to protect one who practices Pure Land Buddhism against such heretic views, I will tell you a parable. There was a narrow white road, leading from the east bank to the west bank of a dreadful river of fire and water. The road was constantly burnt by flames and washed by waves. When a traveler began crossing the road, having taken a couple of steps, he was called back by a group of bandits on the east bank. This group of bandits calling back the traveler from using the narrow white road to cross the dreadful river is compared to those who understand and practice Buddhism differently, insisting on the evil opinion that rebirth in the Pure Land is impossible by means of calling the name of the Buddha of Infinite Life.' I, Hōnen, believe that all those who are referred to by Shan-tao here as having understood, practiced, and studied Buddhism differently and held opinions different from Pure Land Buddhists, are those who follow the Holy Way."

In conclusion Hōnen declares: "Given the choice between the two excellent ways, those who wish to leave the world of birth and death should choose the

Pure Land Way, setting aside the Holy Way for now. Between the two kinds of practices in Pure Land Buddhism, the correct and the miscellaneous, those who wish to follow the Pure Land Way should take refuge in the correct practice, discarding various miscellaneous practices for now."

Contemplating these citations from Hōnen's *Collection of Passages on the Nembutsu*, I can say that Hōnen based his conclusions on false interpretations put forth by T'an-luan, Tao-ch'o, and Shan-tao when he established the difference between the Holy and Pure Land Ways, that is ways difficult to practice* and easy to practice. He enclosed all the 637 Mahayana sutras in 2,883 fascicles, such as sutras of the Lotus, Hokke, and True Word (Shingon) schools, as well as all the Buddhas and bodhisattvas and various gods in the categories of the Holy Way, as ways difficult to practice, or the miscellaneous ways, saying that these should all be abandoned, closed, set aside, and cast away. With these four words, "abandon, close, set aside, and cast away," Hōnen misled many people. Besides, he slandered holy priests in India, China, and Japan, and the Buddha's disciples in the universe as "groups of bandits." Hōnen thus was against the vow of the Buddha of Infinite Life in the triple Pure Land sutras, basic canons of Pure Land Buddhism, which ensure all who call the name of this Buddha to be reborn in His Pure Land "except those who have committed the five rebellious sins* and slandered the True Dharma." Nor did he understand the warning in the second fascicle of the *Lotus Sutra*, the essence of all the sutras expounded in the lifetime of Śākyamuni Buddha throughout the five periods* of His preaching: "Suppose there is anyone who does not believe in this sutra and slanders it. Instead, he will fall into the Hell of Incessant Suffering upon his death."

Now we live in a Latter Age. People are not saints, astray in a dark alley leading to hell, and are forgetting all about the direct route to Buddhahood. How sad it is that no one awakens them! What a pity it is that only false faith grows rampant! As a result, everybody from the king down to the populace believes that there are no sutras except the triple Pure Land sutras and that there are no Buddhas except for the Buddha of Infinite Life and His two attendants.

In the past, such priests as Dengyō,* Gishin,* [Kōbō,*], Jikaku,* and Chishō* went far over the vast ocean to T'ang China. They visited various places in China and brought back to Japan sutras and Buddhist images, which were enshrined in temples and towers built atop high mountains and at the bottom of deep valleys. Śākyamuni and Medicine Master Buddha shone side by side keeping the people in awe in their present lives as well as the next. Bodhisattvas Sky-Repository and Earth-Repository enshrined on Mt. Hiei guided and benefited the people during and after their lives in this world. Therefore, rulers of Japan donated counties and villages to the temples so that the lights might be brighter on the altars, while stewards of landed estates donated farmlands for the upkeep of those temples.

Since the publication of the *Collection of Passages on the Nembutsu* by Hōnen, however, the people have forgotten all about Śākyamuni Buddha, Lord Preacher of our world, worshipping only the Buddha of Infinite Life in the Pure Land of Bliss to the West. They have discarded Medicine Master Buddha of the Land of Emerald Light to the East, who has been revered ever since the time of Grand Master Dengyō. Taking refuge solely in the triple Pure Land sutras in four fascicles, they have forgotten all other sutras preached by Śākyamuni Buddha during the five periods in His lifetime. Therefore no one makes offerings to any temples except those of the Buddha of Infinite Life, nor to Buddhist priests except those who recite the name of the Buddha of Infinite Life. As a result Buddhist temples, except for those of the Buddha of Infinite Life, are reduced to poverty, with moss growing on the roofs, living quarters left dilapidated, and weeds growing tall in the gardens. Nevertheless, nobody feels pity and attempts to rebuild them. Under the circumstances, saintly priests do not live there to watch them and guardian gods do not stay there to protect them. This is all due to Hōnen's *Collection of Passages on the Nembutsu*.

How sad it is that in the several decades since the publication of this *Collection of Passages* millions and tens of millions of people have been infatuated by this devilish work and have gone astray from true Buddhism! How can protective gods not be angry when the stray teaching is favored and the true one is forgotten? How can demons not take advantage when the one-sided Pure Land teaching is preferred and the perfect true teaching is discarded? Is not the best way to prevent calamities from overtaking the land to ban the one evil teaching, the source of all troubles, instead of having various devotional services?

V. Pure Land Buddhism as the Cause of Calamities

VERY ANGRY, THE TRAVELER FROWNED BACK: After our True Teacher, Śākyamuni Buddha, preached the triple Pure Land sutras, Priest T'an-luan of China discontinued preaching the four discourses[11] based on the principle of the void, and single-mindedly sought refuge in Pure Land Buddhism. Zen Master Tao-ch'o, also of China, put aside the five kinds of practices for bodhisattvas preached in the *Nirvana Sutra* and single-mindedly advocated the practice for rebirth in the Pure Land to the west. Venerable Priest Shan-tao of China discontinued the miscellaneous practices and practiced solely the recitation of the name of the Buddha of Infinite Life. [He discontinued practicing the *Lotus Sutra* as miscellaneous practices and solely chanted the *nembutsu* based on the *Sutra of Meditation on the Buddha of Infinite Life*.] Venerable Eshin,* a Tendai monk in Japan, collected essential passages from various sutras in his *Essential Collection Concerning Rebirth in the Pure Land*, advocating just the one practice of calling the name of the Buddha of Infinite Life *(nembutsu)*. [Precept Master Yōkan* abandoned both exoteric and esoteric teachings, entering the teaching of the *nembutsu*.] Thus the Buddha of Infinite Life has been revered by many great masters of Buddhism before us. Also imagine how many people there are who were able to be reborn in the Pure Land by calling the name of the Buddha of Infinite Life!

Above all, Saint Hōnen as a youth entered the Enryakuji Temple on Mt. Hiei, and mastered T'ien-t'ai commentaries on the *Lotus Sutra* in 60 fascicles[12] and the exquisite doctrines of the eight schools[13] of Buddhism by the time he was 17 years old. In addition, he read all the sutras and discourses as much as seven times. There were no commentaries or biographies which he did not study thoroughly. His wisdom was as bright as the sun and moon and he exceeded his predecessors in virtue.

Yet, Hōnen was unable to find the way to cut the chain of birth and death to enter Nirvana. Therefore, he read and contemplated all the Buddhist scriptures thoroughly, thinking hard and extensively about the times, and capacity of the people. Finally he gave up reading various sutras to concentrate on the practice of calling the name of the Buddha of Infinite Life. In addition he had a dream in which he was inspired by Venerable Priest Shan-tao to propagate the practice of the *nembutsu* widely among the people all over this country.

So, some people call him an avatar of Bodhisattva Mahāsthāmaprāpta, Gainer of Great Strength, while others looked up to him as Shan-tao's reincarnation. Thus, all the people in this country, high and low, or male and female, came to listen to him, bowing in front of him. Many years have gone by since then.

Despite all this, do you dare hold in contempt the teaching of Śākyamuni Buddha expounded in the triple Pure Land sutras, and slander the 48 vows of the Buddha of Infinite Life? This is terrible! How can you blame the august reign of the past emperor for calamities in recent years? How dare you speak ill of not only such earlier masters as T'an-luan, Tao-ch'o and Shan-tao but also Hōnen. What you are doing is the so-called "blowing someone's hair to expose his scar" or "cutting someone's skin to bleed him." When one looks for trouble, he will find it. I have never heard such abusive remarks as these. You should be afraid of this. You should refrain from this. You have committed a serious sin, for which you will never be able to escape punishment. It is awful for me just to sit before you. Taking my stick in hand, I would rather go home right away.

SMILING GENTLY, THE MASTER STOPPED THE TRAVELER AND SAID: They say that a knotgrass eater gets used to its sharp taste, and an insect living in a honey bucket does not smell its offensive odor. Affected by surroundings, people tend to lose their sense of judgement. So you take a good word for a bad one, call the slanderer of the True Dharma a holy man, and suspect the true teacher of being a false one. You are utterly confused and have committed a grave sin. Now listen carefully, I will explain in detail what caused your confusion.

Śākyamuni Buddha's lifetime preachings in five periods were done in sequence with proper use of provisional and true teachings.* He began with provisional doctrines which were easier to understand by less prepared people with lesser capacity. Gradually, the Buddha preached doctrines progressively closer to the truth and more difficult to comprehend, as the listeners became better prepared, until finally He revealed the ultimate truth in preaching the *Lotus Sutra*.

However, the founders of Pure Land Buddhism such as T'an-luan, Tao-ch'o and Shan-tao took refuge in provisional teachings, which had been preached in the first 40 years or so, discarding the *Lotus Sutra*, the true intent of the Buddha revealed during the last eight years by the Buddha. Certainly they did not know the ultimate truth of Buddhism. Hōnen especially, who belonged to the school of these masters, did not realize that their Pure Land Buddhism had its doctrinal base on provisional teachings. Why do I say this? It is because he misled all the people by preaching that they should "abandon, close, set aside, and cast away"* all the 637 Mahayana sutras in 2,883 fascicles as well as all Buddhas, bodhisattvas, and gods. This is solely Hōnen's arbitrary interpretation and has no scriptural basis whatsoever. His sin of having uttered false words and abusive language is very grave and without comparison. We cannot blame him too much.

[As I contemplate the doctrine of Hōnen in detail, it is more evil than the slanderous doctrines of such monks as Tz'ŭ-ên, who insisted that the three-vehicle teaching is true and the One Vehicle teaching is expedient. Or Kōbō who abused the *Lotus Sutra* as a joke. Or Fa-yün of the Kuang-chê-ssu Temple, who held that the *Nirvana Sutra* to be true and the *Lotus Sutra* evil. And Fa-tsang, who defined the *Flower Garland Sutra* to be fundamental and the *Lotus Sutra* unessential. It seems that Great Arrogant Brahman or Vimalamitra* of ancient India was reborn in Japan in the Latter Age of Degeneration. You should be careful of a poisonous snake and stay away from bandits. They are what the Buddha warned us as the cause of destruction of Buddhism and our country. Nevertheless,] people put complete faith in Hōnen's false words and revere his *Collection of Passages on the Nembutsu*. As a result they revere only the triple Pure Land sutras, discarding all others. And they worship only one Buddha of Infinite Life in the Land of Utmost Bliss, forgetting all others. Hōnen indeed is the archenemy of Buddhas and sutras, a deadly foe of sagacious priests as well as the populace. Yet this evil teaching has spread all over the country.

You are horrified when I attribute calamities in recent years to Hōnen's slandering of the True Dharma during the past years. I will dispel your fears by citing some precedents, showing that I am not without basis.

T'ien-t'ai's *Great Concentration and Insight,** fascicle two, cites from the *Historical Records,* stating: "Toward the end of the Chou dynasty in ancient China, there lived a man with disheveled hair wearing no clothes and observing no proprieties." Annotating this, Miao-lê cites Tso Ch'un-ming's *Commentary on the Spring and Autumn Annals* in his *Annotations on the Great Concentration and Insight,** fascicle two: "When King P'ing of Chou was defeated by northern barbarians and forced to move his capital eastward to Lo-i, he encountered a man with disheveled hair conducting a ceremony in a field near the I River. Then a wise man, Great Officer Hsin-yu, lamentingly predicted that the area near the I River would also be lost to Chou within 100 years, because the proper manners of Chou no longer existed there." We can tell from this that calamities are foretold by ill omens.

T'ien-t'ai's *Great Concentration and Insight,* fascicle two, cited above, continues:

"Yüan-chi of early Chin China in the third century CE, one of the Seven Sages of the Bamboo Forest, was a man of talent but indifferent to proprieties. His hair was disheveled and he wore clothes without a properly tied sash. The children of nobility gradually began to imitate his ill-manners, considering mutual abuse in vulgar words to be natural and observance of proprieties to be unrefined. This was an ill omen foretelling the downfall of the Ssu-ma clan, rulers of the Chin dynasty."

Grand Master Jikaku's *Account of Pilgrimage in China in Search of the Dharma* says in essence:

"In the first year of the Hui-ch'ang Era (841), Emperor Wu-tsung of the T'ang dynasty ordered Priest Ching-shuang of the Chang-ching-ssu Temple to propagate the doctrine of Pure Land Buddhism at various temples. Ching-shuang kept on going around to temples preaching for three days at each temple. Nevertheless, Uigur soldiers invaded the T'ang Empire across the border in the second year of the Hui-ch'ang Era. In the following year, the governor of the district north of the Yellow River suddenly rose in revolt against the emperor. Thereafter, the Tibetans once more refused to comply with the imperial order while the Uigurs invaded the empire again. Wars and disorder as devastating as during the transitional period from the Ch'in to Han dynasties ensued, and towns and villages were laid waste by fires caused by warfare. Moreover, Wu-tsung severely persecuted Buddhism, destroying many temples and towers. As a result, unable to put an end to the period of wars and disorder, the emperor died in agony in the sixth year of the Hui-ch'ang Era."

In view of these events in China, we can see that Pure Land Buddhism is the source of troubles in Japan today. Hōnen was actively propagating his faith in the Buddha of Infinite Life during the reign of ex-Emperor Gotoba, in the Kennin Era (1201-04). And as we all know, in the Jōkyū Incident in 1221, the ex-Emperor failed in his attempt to reassert his imperial authority to rule and died in exile on the Island of Oki. Pure Land Buddhism as the cause of calamities has been proved in the great T'ang Empire as well as in Japan. You should not have any doubt about it! In order to avert calamities and disasters in recent years, you must first of all discard the evil practice of calling out the Buddha of Infinite Life and take refuge in the good teaching of the *Lotus Sutra,* blocking Pure Land Buddhism at its source and cutting it off at the root.

VI. Appealing to the Authorities

HAVING CALMED DOWN SOMEWHAT, THE TRAVELER STATED: Though I am unable to understand you completely, I think I understand what you mean roughly. However, from Kyoto, the seat of the imperial court, to Kamakura, the capital of the shogunate, none of the eminent priests and able leaders of the Buddhist world has yet presented a written statement on this matter or made an appeal to the emperor or the shogun. It is not for you, a mere low-ranking priest, to venture to do so with your spiteful words. I can see your intention, but if you submit your appeal, you will be violating proprieties.

IN RESPONSE, THE MASTER DECLARED: Although I am a man of little capability, fortunately I have studied Mahayana Buddhism. It is said that a blue fly which rides on the tail of a fine horse can travel even 10,000 miles, and a green ivy vine which clings to a tall pine tree can climb up to 1,000 yards high. Likewise, born to be a disciple of the Buddha, I put my faith in the *Lotus Sutra,* the king of all the Buddhist sutras. Seeing the Buddha Dharma declining, how can I not feel sorrow?

The sorrow is even more so [in view of what the Buddha preached in the *Lotus Sutra,* in the 10th chapter, The Teacher of the Dharma, "Medicine-King Bodhisattva, listen carefully. Of the numerous sutras I have preached, this *Sutra of the Lotus Flower of the Wonderful Dharma* is the supreme," and "The sutras I have preached number immeasurable thousands, tens of thousands, and hundreds of millions. Of the sutras I have preached, am now preaching, and will preach, this *Lotus Sutra* is the most difficult to believe and to understand." In the 14th chapter, Peaceful Practices, "Mañjuśrī, this *Sutra of the Lotus Flower of the Wonderful Dharma* is treasured by all Buddhas and it is the supreme of all the sutras." In the 23rd chapter, The Previous Life of Medicine-King Bodhisattva, "As Mt. Sumeru is the highest of all mountains in the world, this *Lotus Sutra* is the supreme of all sutras. As the moon shines brighter than any other stars, this *Lotus Sutra* shines the brightest of all the sutras. As the sun eliminates all darkness, this *Lotus Sutra* eliminates all kinds of darkness. As the Great King of the Brahma Heaven is the king of all the people, those who uphold this *Lotus Sutra* are first of all the people."]

The Buddha also warns us in the *Nirvana Sutra:* "Suppose there is a monk, to all appearances 'good', who encounters a destroyer of the dharma but does not take any measures in accusing him, chasing him out or punishing him. You must know that such a man is not a 'good' monk at all but an enemy of Buddhism. On the other hand if he accuses the destroyer of the dharma, chases him out, or punishes him strictly, such a man is My disciple, one who truly hears Me."

[Numerous bodhisattvas, 80 trillions in number, vow in the 13th chapter of the *Lotus Sutra,* Encouragement for Keeping This Sutra, "We will not spare even our lives. We treasure only the unsurpassed way."

The *Nirvana Sutra* preaches: "Suppose an eloquent speaker was sent to a foreign country as a royal emissary. Even at the cost of his life, he must convey the words of his king without concealing anything. Likewise, without sparing even his own life, a wise man must widely spread among the ignorant people the true teaching of the Buddha, the existence of Buddha-nature in all."]

Although I am not a man worthy of being called a good monk, I do not want to be accused of being a foe of Buddhism. Therefore, I must explain some principles showing just a portion of the Buddha's teaching.

In addition, during the Gennin Era (1224-25) the temples of Enryakuji on Mt. Hiei and Kōfukuji in Nara repeatedly appealed to the imperial court to suppress Pure Land Buddhism. By orders of the emperor and the shogun the printing blocks of Hōnen's *Collection of Passages on the Nembutsu* were confiscated and sent to the Great Hall of the Enryakuji Temple, where they were burnt as an act of gratitude to the Buddha for His favors received during the past, present, and future lives. Hōnen's grave was ordered to be destroyed by bearers of the portable shrine of the Gion Shrine, and his disciples such as Ryūkan, Shōkō, Jōkaku, and Sasshō were banished to remote provinces. They have never been pardoned. How can you claim that nobody has appealed to the authorities to reject Pure Land Buddhism?

VII. The Means to Prevent Calamities

THE TRAVELER SPOKE IN A MILD MANNER: It is hard for me to blame Hōnen for slighting sutras and slandering priests. However, it is without question that Hōnen "abandoned, closed, set aside, and cast aside" all 637 Mahayana sutras, in 2,883 fascicles, together with all Buddhas, bodhisattvas, and gods. This is clearly stated in his writing. For this fault, which is like a slight flaw in jade, you are calling him a slanderer of the True Dharma. I do not know whether or not you are suffering from delusion, whether or not your action is wise, and whether or not you are right. Nevertheless, you strongly insist that it is Hōnen's *Collection of Passages on the Nembutsu* that is causing the recent calamities and disasters.

After all, world peace and tranquility of a nation is what both the sovereign and subjects alike desire, and all the people of a nation wish for. Now, the prosperity of a nation depends on the dharma, which is revered by the people. When the nation is destroyed and its people perish, who will revere the Buddha and who will put faith in the dharma? Therefore, we should first pray for the peace and tranquility of a nation before trying to spread Buddhism. If you know the means to prevent calamities and disasters, I would like to hear about it.

THE MASTER REPLIED: I am ignorant and do not know exactly how to address these issues. I just would like to express my humble opinion based upon Buddhist sutras. Generally speaking, there are too many references to the means of countering calamities and disasters in both Buddhist and non-Buddhist scriptures. They are too numerous to be mentioned here thoroughly. However, as I have often contemplated the matter in view of Buddhism, I have come to the conclusion that putting a ban on the slanderers of the True Dharma, and highly esteeming the upholders of the True Dharma will lead to the tranquility of the nation and world peace.

Thus, it is stated in the *Nirvana Sutra:*

"The Buddha said to Cunda, a disciple of His: 'Giving alms is an act of merit. Everybody will praise you if you give alms to anyone except just one.' Cunda asked Him who is the one to whom alms should not be given. The Buddha told him that he who violates precepts as preached in the sutra does not deserve to receive alms. Unable to understand what the Buddha meant, Cunda beseeched Him to explain in detail. So the Buddha explained to Cunda: 'He who violates precepts is an *icchantika*.* If you give alms to anyone except *icchantika*, everyone will praise you and you will gain great rewards.'

"Cunda then asked the Buddha for the meaning of *icchantika*, and the Buddha again explained: 'Cunda! Suppose there is a Buddhist — a monk or a nun, a layman or a laywoman — who slanders the True Dharma in abusive language without ever repenting this grave sin. Such people, I should say, have taken the way of *icchantika*. Suppose there are people who have committed the four major sins: killing, stealing, adultery, and lying, and the five rebellious sins: killing one's own father, mother, or an arhat, injuring the Buddha, and destroying the harmony of a Buddhist order.

Suppose these people realized the seriousness of their offenses but never had or showed a sense of guilt or repentance from the beginning. Suppose they have no intention of protecting the True Dharma to establish it forever, instead they slander and despise it in false words. Such people, I should say, have taken the way of *icchantika*. Giving alms to anyone except just one category of people, *icchantika*, will be praised by everyone.'"

Relating an episode in the previous life of the Buddha, the *Nirvana Sutra*, also asserts: "As I contemplate the past, I was once the king of a great kingdom in the human world. My name then was King Sen'yo* and I loved and revered Mahayana sutras. Gentle in mind, I harbored no evil thought, no jealousy of anyone, and no stinginess. Good man! I then esteemed Mahayana Buddhism highly, and upon hearing a Brahman slandering it, I instantly slaughtered him. Good man! Because of this karma of my killing the Brahman, I have never fallen to hell ever since then." The sutra also states that when the Buddha was a king practicing the bodhisattva way once in His previous life, He killed many Brahmans. The same sutra explains killing:

"There are three categories of killing: the lower, the intermediate, and the upper. The lower category means killing all beasts beginning with an ant, except those into which bodhisattvas transformed themselves in order to save others. For committing a killing of the lower category one will fall into hell, the realm of hungry spirits, or that of beasts and birds, where he will undergo all the sufferings of the lower category. Why is this? Because each beast possesses Buddha-nature, though it may be little, those who kill such a beast will receive full punishment for this offense.

"The intermediate category means murdering people, including ordinary people, as well as those sagacious people, who have reached the stage of not being reborn in the world of transmigration.[14] Those who commit this sin will fall into hell, the realm of hungry spirits or that of beasts and birds to bear all the sufferings of the intermediate category.

"The upper category of killing means to kill one's parents, arhats, *pratyekabuddha*, or bodhisattvas who have reached the stage of no regression. He who commits this sin will fall into the Hell of Incessant Suffering. Good man! Killing a man of *icchantika*, however, is not included in these three categories. Good man! Those Brahmans who slander the True Dharma are all without exception men of icchantika; Murdering them does not constitute a sin."

The Buddha addressed King Prasenajit in the *Sutra of the Benevolent King*: "Therefore, I will transmit this sutra to kings, not to monks or nuns, who are not as powerful as kings."

The *Nirvana Sutra* restates this: "Now I will transmit this supreme True Dharma to kings, ministers, prime ministers, and the four categories of Buddhists: monks, nuns, laymen, and laywomen. Ministers and the four categories of Buddhists should chastise those who slander the True Dharma."

The Buddha preached to Kāśyapa Bodhisattva in the same sutra: "Kāśyapa! Because of the karma from upholding the True Dharma in My previous lives, I was able to attain Buddhahood with My body as indestructible as a diamond. Good man! Those who wish to uphold the True Dharma should arm themselves with swords, bows and arrows, and halberds, instead of keeping propriety, and observing the five precepts against killing, stealing, adultery, lying, and drinking alcohol."

It also states: "Those who keep the five precepts do not necessarily practice Mahayana Buddhism. Even those who do not observe the five precepts can be called the men of Mahayana if they protect the True Dharma. Protectors of the True Dharma should arm themselves with swords and sticks. Even if they carry swords and sticks, they should be called the keepers of the precepts."

The Buddha then related to Kāśyapa in the same sutra the merit of His having defended the True Dharma in His previous lives:

"Good man! Once in the past a Buddha named the Buddha of Joy lived in the City of Kuśinagara. The True Dharma of this Buddha lasted for countless hundreds of millions of years after His death. During the last 40 years of this period, a monk called Virtue Consciousness* appeared, and he strictly observed the precepts. As it was toward the end of the Age of the True Dharma, there were many monks who violated the precepts. Upon hearing Monk Virtue Consciousness preach the True Dharma, these evil monks hated and persecuted him with swords and sticks.

"The king, named Virtuous,* heard about this. In order to protect the dharma he hurried to this preacher and battled to the utmost of his power against those evil monks who did not keep the precepts. The preacher, Virtue Consciousness, was rescued unharmed but the king was wounded by swords and halberds so not any part of his body, even the size of a poppy seed, was left unharmed. Virtue Consciousness praised the king saying, "Excellent! Excellent! Now you, King Virtuous, are truly the protector of the True Dharma. You will be able to become a preacher of immeasurable strength."

"Hearing this, the king felt great joy in his heart and passed away. He was reborn in the land of Immovable Buddha* to be the first disciple of this Buddha. Those of the king's generals, soldiers, people, and clansmen who followed him in the battlefields or felt happy at seeing the king fight for the True Dharma all aspired for Buddhahood without ever falling back.

When they died, they all were reborn in the land of Immovable Buddha. When Monk Virtue Consciousness died, he, too, was reborn in the land of Immovable Buddha, becoming the second disciple of this Buddha among all those who heard Him preach.

"When the True Dharma is about to disappear, this is the way one should uphold and defend it. Listen, Kāśyapa! King Virtuous then was I, Śākyamuni Buddha, today. And Preacher Virtue Consciousness was Kāśyapa Buddha.[15] Kāśyapa! Those who defend the True Dharma will gain such an immeasurable reward as this. Due to this karma of Mine in the past, I was able to attain various physical characteristics and attain Buddhahood with the indestructible Dharma Body."

The Buddha continued to instruct Kāśyapa Bodhisattva.

"Therefore, those laymen who wish to defend the True Dharma should arm themselves with swords and sticks in order to defend it just as King Virtuous did. Good man! In the decadent world after My death, countries will be in chaos, plundering one another, and the people will be at the brink of starvation. Faced with starvation, many will aspire to enter the priesthood. Such people should be called 'shaven-heads', monks in form only. These 'shaven-heads', will chase out, harm, or even kill those who defend the True Dharma. Therefore, I now allow monks who keep precepts to ally with lay people who arm themselves with swords and sticks for the purpose of defending the True Dharma. Although these people may hold swords and sticks, it is for the purpose of defending the True Dharma. Therefore, I call them keepers of the precepts. Although they may hold weapons for the defense of the True Dharma, they may not kill people at random."

The third chapter of the *Lotus Sutra,* A Parable, points out the graveness of the sin of slandering the True Dharma: "He who does not put faith in this sutra and slanders it will destroy the seed of Buddhahood of all the people in the world. [Also, he who slights, hates, envies, and bears a grudge against those who read, recite, copy and uphold this sutra]...will fall into the Hell of Incessant Suffering upon death."

The meaning of the above citations is quite clear. Yet, how they need my words of explanation! According to the *Lotus Sutra,* slandering the Mahayana sutras is countless times more sinful than committing the five rebellious sins, such as killing one's own parents. Therefore, such sinners will fall into the Hell of Incessant Suffering, from which they will never be able to escape.

According to the *Nirvana Sutra,* even if offerings to offenders of the five rebellious sins are permitted, it is not permitted to give offerings to slanderers of the True Dharma. One who kills an ant will without fail fall into the three evil realms, hell, the realm of hungry spirits, and that of beasts and birds. But one who eliminates a slanderer of the True Dharma will reach the stage of non-regression, and eventually will attain Buddhahood. Monk Virtue Consciousness, who preached the True Dharma in the past despite persecution by slanderers of the True Dharma, became Kāśyapa Buddha, and King Virtuous, who killed slanderers to defend the True Dharma, was reborn in this world as Śākyamuni Buddha.

The *Lotus* and *Nirvana Sutras* are the essence of Śākyamuni Buddha's lifetime teaching preached in five periods[, the gist of 80,000 Buddhist teachings]. His warnings in them should weigh very heavily. Who should not obey them?

Nevertheless, slanderers of the True Dharma are ignoring the upholders of the True Dharma. Moreover, they have been blinded and made fools of by Hōnen's *Collection of Passages on the Nembutsu*. Thus some of them remembered him by carving wooden images of him, or drawing portraits of him, while others, believing in his false teaching, carved wood blocks to print this writing and spread it throughout the land, beyond cities to the countryside. People revere only the teaching of Hōnen and give alms only to his disciples. As a result some cut off fingers of Śākyamuni's images to be replaced by the finger sign of the Buddha of Infinite Life. Others renovated temples dedicated to Medicine Master Buddha of the Land of Emerald Light in the East in order to enshrine the Buddha of Infinite Light, the Lord Buddha of the Land of Bliss in the West. Or they discontinued the practice of copying the *Lotus Sutra*, which had continued more than 400 years on Mt. Hiei, substituting it with copying the triple Pure Land sutras. Still others suspended the lecture-meeting on the memorial day of Grand Master T'ien-t'ai, to hold a lecture-meeting in memory of Shan-tao. There are countless numbers of these people. Are they not slanderers of the Buddha, the Dharma, and the Buddhist priesthood? [Are they not the cause of national destruction?] These evil practices all stem from Hōnen's *Collection of Passages on the Nembutsu*.

It is really sad that the people do not follow the true commandments of the Buddha. It is indeed a pity that they are misled by the false doctrine of Hōnen. If you wish to bring about the tranquility of the empire as soon as possible, you must first of all put a ban on the slanderers of the True Dharma throughout the nation.

VIII. Outlawing the Slanderers

THE TRAVELER THEN ASKED THE MASTER: In order to eliminate the slanderers of the True Dharma in compliance with commandments of the Buddha, is it necessary to put them to death as preached in the *Nirvana Sutra*? If so, killing will beget killing. What should we do about sinful karma then?

The Buddha declares in the *Sutra of the Great Assembly*: "Gods and men should give offerings to those with shaven heads wearing monks' robes, regardless of whether or not they keep the precepts. Giving offerings to them means giving offerings to Me because they are My sons. If someone strikes them, it is My sons whom he strikes. If someone insults them, it is Me whom he insults."

[It is preached in the *Sutra of the Benevolent King*: "Great King, in the latter age when the Buddha Dharma is about to expire..., those kings of petty kingdoms who commit the sin of illegally arresting a Buddhist monk ... will all lose the throne in return."

It is also preached in the *Sutra of the Great Assembly*:

"The Buddha said to the King of the Brahma Heaven, 'I shall briefly explain this for you. Suppose a person injured and caused the bleeding of numerous Buddhas, how grave do you think his sin is?' The King of the Brahma Heaven replied, 'For injuring and causing bleeding to just one Buddha, the offender suffers immeasurably in the Hell of Incessant Suffering. How much more one has to suffer if he injures and causes the bleeding of numerous Buddhas! No one, except the Buddha Himself, can describe the suffering.' The Buddha then told the King of the Brahma Heaven, 'Great King of the Brahma Heaven, suppose someone torments, abuses, humiliates, strikes or arrests a Buddhist monk, who shaves his head and wears Buddhist robes for Me, though he may not have received precepts or violated them even if he received them. Such a man will be punished more severely than those who caused injury and bleeding of the Buddha.'"

It is also preached in the same sutra: "Kings and those who pass judgment on cases..., you should not... strike, abuse, humiliate and inflict punishment in any way upon those who follow My teaching and have become Buddhist monks, even if they committed such sins as killing, stealing, adultery, lying and other evil acts. If you fail to comply with this rule..., you will inevitably fall into the Hell of Incessant Suffering."

The *Sutra of the Great Assembly* further continues: "In the world in the future, people with an evil mind will become Buddhists, carry out a few meritorious deeds, give some alms, observe precepts and practice meditation. Due to the merit of these virtuous deeds they will be kings. Being ignorant, shameless, self-conceited, and without compassion, they do not even think of how dreadful their lives in the future will be. These evil kings will torment, strike, abuse and humiliate all the disciples of the Buddha.... Due to these evil deeds, they will all fall into the Hell of Incessant Sufferings."]

According to this scriptural statement we have to give offerings to monks regardless of whether or not they are good ones or whether or not they keep the precepts. How dare you beat and insult the children of the Buddha to make their Father sad?

Those Brahmans with bamboo sticks who killed Venerable Maudgalyāyana* sank to the bottom of the Hell of Incessant Suffering for endless time. Devadatta,* who murdered a nun named Utpalavarṇā, also suffered for ages in the choking flames of the Hell of Incessant Suffering. These are clear testimonies to retribution for killing monks and nuns, which we in the later generation should take most seriously. Killing slanderers of the True Dharma, as is preached in the *Nirvana Sutra*, seems to be a warning against slandering the True Dharma. Nevertheless, does it not violate the commandment preached in the *Sutra of the Great Assembly*? I can hardly believe that such is the proper course to take. How can I justify it?

THE MASTER STATED IN RESPONSE: You, my guest, have seen clear statements in the *Nirvana Sutra* outlawing slanderers of the True Dharma. Yet you ask me such a question. Is it because you don't understand them, or is it because you don't know the reason for them? What the *Nirvana Sutra* means is not that we should outlaw disciples of the Buddha at all but that we should solely chastise slanderers of the True Dharma.

[The scriptural statements you cited above concern monks with right views who may or may not observe precepts, and who have not received them, while what I am urging to eliminate are those with evil views who may or may not keep precepts or who have not received them.]

Speaking of the previous lives of Śākyamuni Buddha, the *Nirvana Sutra* states that the Buddha, appearing as King Sen'yo and King Virtuous, killed slanderers of the True Dharma. However, the present Śākyamuni Buddha preaches not to give offerings to such slanderers. [Nevertheless, this is a special method applicable only to certain occasions. King Śīlāditya of ancient India was a sage who protected Buddhism. Punishing only the ringleader, the king spared the lives of all other members who rebelled against him, banishing them from his kingdom. Emperor Hsüan-tsung of T'ang China was a wise ruler who protected Buddhism. He executed 12 Taoist masters, eliminating enemies of the Buddha and restoring Buddhism.

These examples in India and China are of non-Buddhists and Taoist masters trying to destroy Buddhism. Their sins were comparatively light. On the contrary today in Japan, a disciple of the Buddha is about to destroy Buddhism. His sin is extremely grave. He must be strictly punished without delay.] Therefore, if all the countries in the world and the four kinds of Buddhists, monks, nuns, laymen and laywomen, all stop giving offerings to the evil priests who slander the True

Rissho Ankoku-ron (ST 24)   125

Dharma, putting all their faith instead in the defenders of the True Dharma, how can any more calamities arise or disasters confront us?

IX. Establishing the True Dharma

KNEELING ON THE FLOOR AND ADJUSTING HIS ROBE, THE TRAVELER RESPECTFULLY SAID TO THE MASTER: There are various schools of Buddhism, each with a doctrine hard to comprehend. I have many questions and cannot tell which is right or which is wrong. Nevertheless, Saint Hōnen's *Collection of Passages on the Nembutsu* does exist, asserting that all the Buddhas and sutras [including Śākyamuni Buddha, Lord Preacher of the *Lotus Sutra*,] bodhisattvas and gods [such as Goddess Amaterasu and Bodhisattva Shō-Hachiman, Protectors of Japan,] should be "abandoned, closed, set aside and cast away." This is clearly stated in it. As a result sages and protective gods have abandoned our country, causing famine and epidemics to spread all over it. Now, you have clearly shown me what is right and what is wrong by quoting many passages from a wide range of sutras. Thanks to you, I am now free from my earlier prejudices, and can see and hear things clearly.

After all, peace and tranquility of the nation is what the one person above, as well as all the people below, desire and pray for. Let us immediately stop giving offerings to men of *icchantika*, [root out the slanderers of the True Dharma,] and instead support the many good monks and nuns [and look up to them] for ages to come. If we thus quell the pirates in the ocean of Buddhism and kill the bandits on the mountain of dharma, our land will be as peaceful and tranquil as it was under the sagacious rule of Fu-hsi, Shen-nung, Yao, and Shun of ancient China. After that we should compare the profoundness of doctrines held by the different schools of Buddhism, [both exoteric and esoteric, to find out whether the Shingon or Lotus teaching is superior] in order to decide whom to honor as the leader of the Buddhist world [and in order for us to strive to spread the One Vehicle *Lotus* teaching].

DELIGHTED, THE MASTER SAID: They say that a dove will be a hawk, and a sparrow will transform itself into a clam. How wonderful it is that you have changed your mind so quickly! It is like going into a house of orchids and picking up its scent or like a mugwort plant growing straight among flax plants. If you put faith in my words in dealing with the calamities and disasters confronting us today, there is no question that the winds will calm down, the waves will subside, and years with bountiful harvests will return before long.

However, human minds change with time, and matters change in nature according to circumstances. They are like the moon's reflection in the water moving with the waves, or soldiers in the battleground afraid of swords. You may believe in me now, but you will probably forget me completely. If you wish to bring about peace in our country and pray for happiness in this life, as well as in the future, then waste no time. Think hard and take the necessary measures to thoroughly deal with slanderers of the True Dharma.

Why do I say this? It is because five of the seven calamities predicted in the *Medicine Master Sutra* have already taken place, leaving just two still to occur: foreign invasion* and domestic disturbance.* Moreover, two of the three calamities predicted in the *Sutra of the Great Assembly* have already happened, leaving just one yet to come: war and disorder. And each of the various calamities and disasters which the *Sutra of the Golden Splendor* predicts have indeed fallen upon us except one: invasion of our land by foreign bandits. At this moment, six of the seven calamities foretold in the *Sutra of the Benevolent King* are seriously confronting us, leaving just one yet to come: invasion of our land by foreign armies from four directions. Moreover, the same sutra warns: "When disorder takes over in a country where the True Dharma is lost, the devils will seize control first. When the devils are rampant, the people suffer, and grow wild!"

Comparing our present situation carefully with this passage, there is no doubt that the devils are rampant and many people are dying. Some of the predicted calamities have already taken place. How can we doubt the possibility of the remaining predictions all being realized? What will you do if the remaining predictions, domestic disturbance and foreign invasion, take place at once as punishment for upholding the evil dharma?

The king governs the empire holding his country together, and the people make a living by cultivating their farmlands. However, if the country [our country] is invaded by foreign armies and the people's lands are plundered by domestic disorder, how can there be anything but terror and confusion? Where can the people escape when they lose their country and homes? If you wish to have peace for yourself, you should first of all pray for the peace of the country.

People in this world are afraid of the next life to such an extent that they seek refuge in false teachings or revere slanderers of the True Dharma. I hate to see them confuse right and wrong, trying to seek refuge in Buddhism in the wrong way. If they are to put faith in Buddhism, why should they revere the words of false teachings? Should they refuse to change their minds and cling to false teachings, they will soon leave this world and fall into the Hell of Incessant Suffering without fail. I am sure of this because the Buddha preaches in the *Sutra of the Great Assembly*:

"Suppose there was a king who practiced charity, observed precepts, and cultivated wisdom in his numerous lives in the past. If he sees My dharma disappearing and does not defend it, the immeasurable amount of merit he accumulated will all vanish.... Before long, the king will come down with a serious sickness and will be reborn in hell after his death.... Likewise the queen, the crown prince, ministers, heads of cities, village heads, generals, county magistrates, and other officials will all meet the same fate."

The *Sutra of the Benevolent King* also states the same in effect:

"Destroyers of Buddhism will not have filial children, peace among relatives, or divine help from gods. They will be visited daily by diseases and devils, accompanied by calamities and disasters throughout their lives, wherever they may be. Upon death, they will fall into hell, the realm of hungry spirits, or that of beasts and birds. If they happen to be born human beings, their lot will be miserable like slaves or soldiers. One must pay for retribution as definitely as sound is followed by echo, and form is accompanied by shadow. Just as letters written at night with the help of a light continue to exist even if the light is extinguished, evil karma caused by offenses committed in this triple world of the unenlightened will never disappear."

[It is preached in the *Wisdom Sutra:*

"Slanderers of the True Dharma will suffer in a large hell due to their cumulative evil karma of destroying the True Dharma. They will be shifted around from one large hell to another. When the world is destroyed by *kalpa*-fire, they will be reborn in a large hell in another world, moving around from one large hell to another.... They will go around large hells in the worlds throughout the universe.... When their serious crime is reduced and they are allowed to be reborn in the human world, they will be born in the family of the blind, as outcasts, or as base people who clean toilets and bury dead bodies. Or, they will be born without eyes, mouth, ears, or hands functioning properly."

The *Sutra of the Great Assembly* preaches:

"Great King, suppose there are four classes of people in the future world: warriors, Brahmans, commoners and slaves.... If an ignorant man among them, having no faith in Buddhism, snatches alms given to others, he will receive 20 kinds of bad retribution within this life. What are they? First of all, virtuous gods and good deities will all leave him. In the fourth place, evil people who bear a grudge against him and hate him will crowd around him. In the sixth place, he will become crazy and always wander around the town. In the 11th, he will be separated from his beloved ones. In the 15th, his fortune will all be dispersed. In the 16th, he will always contract serious sickness. And finally in the 20th, he will always be in a very filthy place... and fall into the Hell of Incessant Suffering upon death."

The same sutra states also:

"Born in a desert without eyes and four limbs, he will suffer from hundreds and thousands of kinds of unbearable sufferings such as hot air blowing hard as if he were cut up by a sword and forced to writhe on the ground in agony. Upon death, he will be born in an ocean to be eaten up by men. He then will have a huge body as long as 100 *yojana*.[16] The water where he lives will be as hot as melting copper, and he will be the prey of savage birds and beasts for many hundreds and thousands of years.... Even when he is able to reduce his sin gradually so he may be reborn a human being, he will be in a country without the Buddha or a country filled with defilement and corruption. He will be born blind, without six organs properly functioning, and he will be so ugly that people will turn their faces away."

The *Six Pāramitā Sutra* preaches in effect:

"He will fall into hell to undergo various sufferings. His entire body will be burnt by 13 flames of fire. A set of two flames will go through his body from the toes to the head. Another set will begin burning his body from the head down to the toes. Two flames will enter his body from the back and go out from his chest, while another two go through his body in the opposite direction. Two more flames will burn his body from the right side to the left side, while another two from left to right. Lastly a flame will burn his body from the neck down to the toes. As the bodies of those in hell are as soft as butter, nothing will remain after being burnt by 13 flames of fire, just as those flames in hell will reduce pieces of woolen fabric with flower designs to ashes]."

The *Lotus Sutra,* fascicle two, the third chapter, A Parable, states:

"He who does not put faith in this sutra and slanders it, [will commit the sin of exterminating the seed of Buddhahood in all the people in the whole world. Or suppose those who frown at and harbor doubt about the teaching of this sutra...despise, hold in contempt, hate, envy, and bear a deep grudge against those who read, recite, copy, and uphold this sutra. What would such people get in return? You should listen carefully.] Such people will fall into the Hell of Incessant Suffering upon death, [where their suffering will last endlessly, for a *kalpa* after another... until they fall into the world of beasts becoming a huge serpent as long as 500 *yojana* in length.]"

The same sutra, fascicle seven, the 20th chapter, Never-Despising Bodhisattva, also asserts: "[Some of the four categories of Buddhists, monks, nuns, laymen and laywomen, had impure minds.

They got angry, spoke ill of him, saying, 'Where did this ignorant monk come from?' They struck him with a stick, a piece of wood, a piece of tile or a stone.] They were tormented in the Hell of Incessant Suffering for as long as 1,000 *kalpa* for the sin of persecuting one who practices the *Lotus Sutra*."

The *Nirvana Sutra*, too, declares: "If one avoids good teachers who preach the True Dharma and instead takes refuge in false dharmas, one will sink into the Hell of Incessant Sufferings, undergoing all the sufferings with his huge body of 84,000 square *yojana*."

Examining many sutras, we thus see they all regard slandering the True Dharma the most serious crime. How sad it is that people [in Japan] all should wander out of the gate of the True Dharma into the prison of evil dharma! Such ignorance is causing everyone [in Japan, high and low,] to be pulled by the rope of evil teachings and caught forever by the net of slandering the True Dharma! In this life such wanderers are lost in the mist of delusions. In the next life they will sink to the bottom of flaming hells. How sad it is! How terrible it is!

You should promptly discard your false faith, and take up the true and sole teaching of the *Lotus Sutra* at once. Then this triple world* of the unenlightened will all become Buddha lands. Will Buddha lands ever decay? All the worlds in the universe will become Pure Lands. Will Pure Lands ever be destroyed? When our country does not decay and the world is not destroyed, our bodies will be safe and our hearts tranquil. Believe these words and revere them!

X. Confession and Conversion

FINALLY CONVINCED, THE TRAVELER SAID: In considering the possibility of tranquility in this life and the attainment of Buddhahood in future lives, who will not be cautious? Who will not be afraid? Listening to the words of the Buddha carefully as preached in those sutras, I now realize how serious a crime it was to have slandered the Buddha and destroyed the True Dharma. It was not due to my arbitrary opinion that I took refuge only in the Buddha of Infinite Life, throwing away all others, revering only the triple Pure Land sutras, setting aside all others. I only followed the leaders of Pure Land Buddhism. Probably other Pure Land Buddhists everywhere must have done the same. It is clearly stated in the sutras and is logically obvious that such people's nerves will be worn out in this life and they will all fall into the Hell of Incessant Suffering in the next life. There is no doubt about it.

I hope to continue receiving your compassionate instructions so that I may completely eliminate my ignorance, devise the best means to chastise slanderers of the True Dharma at once, and bring about peace in the world soon. Let us first secure tranquility in this life, and then try to attain Buddhahood in future lives. I not only believe in this but also will try to lead others in correcting their misconceptions.

Notes

1. Words, phrases or sentences found only in the "expanded edition" are bracketed.
2. As preached in the *Hymns on the Pan-chou San-mei (Pan-chou-tsan)* by Shan-tao, a patriarch of Pure Land Buddhism in China.
3. Irregular revolution of the sun and moon, irregular revolution of constellations, fire, floods, gales, droughts, and bandits according to the *Ninnō-kyō*.
4. Meaning the disappearance of the seven calamities.
5. Said to be the three top layers of heaven in the *shiki-kai*, world of form.
6. Killing, stealing, adultery, lying, harsh words, slandering, idle talk, greed, anger, and false views.
7. 23rd patriarch of Buddhism in India.
8. The period after the death of the Buddha is sometimes divided into three ages. In the Age of the True Dharma, the first 10-century period, the Buddha's teaching is practiced and enlightenment can be attained. In the Age of the Semblance Dharma, the second 10-century period, the teaching is practiced but enlightenment is not possible. In the last period of 10,000 years, the Latter Age of Degeneration, the teaching exists but it is no longer practiced.
9. Six transcendental faculties of a Buddha, bodhisattva, or arhat: (1) ability to go anywhere, (2) heavenly eye, (3) heavenly ear, (4) ability to read other people's minds, (5) ability to know former lives, and (6) ability to destroy all evil passions.
10. The four stages of sainthood in Theravada Buddhism are: (1) *sudaon*, one entering the stream of enlightenment; (2) *shidagon*, one who has destroyed gross evil passions and will be reborn in the human and heavenly realms once more before entering Nirvana; (3) *anagon*, one who has destroyed more of his evil passions, and will not be reborn in the realm of desire, the world of transmigration; and (4) *arakan*, arhat, who has destroyed all evil passions.
11. *Discourse on the Middle (Chū-ron), Twelve Gate Discourse (Jūnimonron),* and *Great Wisdom Discourse (Daichido-ron)* by Nāgārjuna (Ryūju); and *One Hundred Verse Discourse (Hyaku-ron)* by Āryadeva (Daiba).
12. T'ien-t'ai's *Profound Meaning of the Lotus Sutra, Words and Phrases of the Lotus Sutra,* and *Great Concentration and Insight,* each in 10 fascicles, and Miao-lê's commentaries on them, also in 10 fascicles each.
13. Six schools of Nara plus Tendai and Shingon schools.
14. See note 10.

15. The sixth of the Seven Buddhas in the past, the seventh being Śākyamuni Buddha.
16. Unit of length, said to be the distance covered by a royal chariot in a day.

Ankoku-ron Soejō (ST 48)

Introduction

Nichiren Shōnin wrote the *Ankoku-ron Soejō* in the fifth year of the Bun'ei Period (1268), when he was 46 years old. Because the last half of this covering letter is missing, we do not know to whom it was addressed, although it is believed to have been to Hōjō Tokimune, Shogunal Regent of the Kamakura Shogunate. The original manuscript was kept in the Kuonji Temple on Mt. Minobu until 1875, when it was lost in a fire.

On the 18th day of the first month in the fifth year of the Bun'ei Period, a Mongol emissary arrived in Japan with Khubilai Khan's state letter. For the purpose of reminding the Kamakura military regime of the *Risshō Ankoku-ron, Treatise on Spreading Peace Throughout the Country by Establishing the True Dharma*, submitted nine years earlier to Hōjō Tokiyori, Nichiren made a copy of the work and sent it to Tokimune together with this letter. He declared in it that what he had predicted nine years before had become true and urged the shogunate to adopt the policy he had suggested.

Covering Letter to the Risshō Ankoku-ron

Although I have not had the honor of meeting you, I believe it is not improper for me to respectfully send a letter to you regarding a matter of importance to our country. Concerning the severe earthquake at about nine o'clock in the evening on the 23rd day of the eighth month in the first year of the Shōka Period (1257), I had contemplated its cause in the light of various scriptural statements, reaching the conclusion that because people in Japan, high and low, all sought refuge in such evil teachings as those of the Pure Land* and Zen* schools, various deities and virtuous gods who protect this country harbored resentment, causing the disaster to occur. I, therefore, composed a fascicle of written opinion* in which I warned that the disaster was an evil omen for the destruction of Japan by foreign invasion unless these Buddhist schools spreading evil teachings were extinguished. I named the treatise the *Risshō Ankoku-ron* and presented it to the late Lay Priest Hōjō Tokiyori through Lay Priest Yadoya Mitsunori* on the 16th day of the seventh month in the second year of the Shōgen Period (1260). (hereafter missing)

Ankoku-ron Gokanyurai (ST 49)

Introduction

Addressed to a certain monk named Hōkan-bō, this letter is dated the fifth day of the fourth month in the fifth year of the Bun'ei Period (1268). The original manuscript, consisting of five pages, has been preserved at the Hokekyōji Temple in the Nakayama section of Ichikawa City near Tokyo as an important cultural asset of Japan.

The state letter from Khubilai Khan's Great Mongol Empire proved that what was predicted by Nichiren Shōnin nine years before in his *Risshō Ankoku-ron, Treatise on Spreading Peace Throughout the Country by Establishing the True Dharma*, was becoming a reality. Taking this opportunity, Nichiren renewed his campaign of national admonition. In writing this letter to Hōkan-bō, Nichiren attempted to cause him, and the military regime at Kamakura through him, to realize the grave crisis facing the country and to understand what was said in the treatise he had submitted to the Shogunate nine years before.

This letter first explained the reason for writing the treatise and how it was conveyed to the Shogunate. After summarizing the treatise, Nichiren asserted that the huge comet appearing in the first year of the Bun'ei Period (1264) and the arrival of the Mongol state letter proved that his prediction had come true. In conclusion, Nichiren warned that having high priests of various Buddhist schools perform prayer services to repel national enemies would only bring about the destruction of Japan because Nichiren alone knew how to deal with them.

The Reason for Submitting the Risshō Ankoku-ron

At about nine o'clock in the evening of the 23rd day in the eighth month in the first year of the Shōka Era (1257), Japan's most severe earthquake took place. It was followed by a typhoon on the first day of the eighth month in the second year of the Shōka Era (1258), a serious famine in the third year of the same era (1259), and widespread epidemics in the first year of the Shōgen Era (1259), which remained rampant throughout the four seasons in the following year, causing more than half the people to die. Meanwhile, rulers of Japan, greatly alarmed, had Buddhist and non-Buddhist priests perform devotional services. None, however, availed to avert these national calamities. They only intensified the severity of famines and epidemics.

Encountering this terrible state of the nation, I, Nichiren, studied all the scriptures of Buddhism,* in which I found scriptural proofs* answering why various prayer services were of no avail, only intensifying disasters. Finally, I could not refrain from composing a written opinion,* entitling it the *Risshō Ankoku-ron, Treatise on Spreading Peace Throughout the Nation by Establishing the True Dharma*. I submitted this to the late Lay Priest Lord Saimyō-ji, Hōjō Tokiyori, at eight o' clock in the morning on the 16th day of the seventh month in the first year of the Bunnō Era (1260) through his chamberlain, Lay Priest Yadoya.* It was nothing but a way for me to repay what I owe my country.

THE GIST OF THE REPORT IS: "The line of Japanese sovereigns, beginning with the seven generations of heavenly deities and five generations of terrestrial deities, is supposed to be followed by 100 generations of human emperors (*hyakuō*).* During the reign of the 30th human emperor, Emperor Kimmei, Buddhism was introduced for the first time from the country of Paekche on the Korean Peninsula to Japan. It has been over 260 years since then to the reign of Emperor Kammu, a reign of more than 50 sovereigns. During this period all the scriptures of Buddhism, as well as the six schools of Buddhism in Nara, Kusha, Jōjitsu, Ritsu, Sanron, Hossō and Kegon schools, were introduced to Japan. Tendai and Shingon schools, however, were not.

"During the reign of Emperor Kammu, there lived a poor monk, Saichō, a disciple of Venerable Gyōhyō of the Yamashinadera (Kōfukuji) Temple in Nara. He was later called Grand Master Dengyō.* Saichō studied thoroughly the doctrines of the six schools of Nara, which had been transmitted to Japan earlier, and also Zen Buddhism, without finding any of them satisfactory. Later he read the T'ien-t'ai school's writings transmitted to Japan by Venerable Chien-chên* (Ganjin) of T'ang China 40 years or so earlier during the reign of Emperor Shōmu, and was awakened to the profound meaning of Buddhism.

"Thereupon Saichō founded the Enryakuji Temple on Mt. Hiei in the fourth year of the Enryaku Period (785) in order to pray for peace and tranquility of the country. Taking refuge in the temple, Emperor Kammu named it the 'Temple of the Imperial Guardian Star.' He gave up faith in the six schools of Nara, putting sole faith in the 'perfect' Tendai school.

"In the 13th year of the same Enryaku Period (794), the imperial capital was moved from Nagaoka to the newly founded city of Heian: Kyoto. On the 19th day of the first month in the 21st year of the same period (802), the Emperor ordered 14 scholars of the six schools of Nara, such as Gonsō and Chōyō, from seven great temples in the southern capital, Nara, to meet with Saichō in the Takaodera Temple for debate. The brilliant scholars of the six schools could not answer even one question, keeping their mouths shut tightly.

"The doctrine of five teachings* of the Flower Garland (Kegon) sect,* the three-period teaching* of the Dharma Characteristics (Hossō) sect* and the doctrines of two storehouses* and three periods of the Three Discourse (Sanron) sect* were all refuted by Saichō. Not only were their doctrines destroyed but it also became clear that they were all slanderers of the True Dharma. On the 29th of the same month, 10 days later, an imperial edict was issued censuring the 14 scholars of the six schools of Nara, who respectfully submitted a letter of apology to the emperor.

"Successive emperors since then have devoted themselves to the Enryakuji Temple on Mt. Hiei in a way more filial than filial children serve their parents or more respectfully than the people respect their king. On behalf of the temple some emperors issued imperial decrees, while others went so far as to bend the law.

"Emperor Seiwa especially owed his enthronement to the religious power of Venerable Eryō of the Enryakuji Temple. Fujiwara Yoshifusa, the imperial grandfather on the maternal side, sent a letter of gratitude to the temple, promising imperial support. Minamoto Yoritomo, the founder of the Kamakura Shogunate, was a descendant of Emperor Seiwa. Nevertheless, the policies of the Kamakura military government do not comply with the wishes of the Enryakuji Temple, whether right or wrong. Are they not inviting heavenly wrath?

"Moreover, during the reign of ex-Emperor Gotoba, in the Kennin Period, two overly proud priests named Hōnen* and Dainichi,* possessed by evil spirits, fooled all the people in Japan, high and low. As a result, the entire Japanese people became followers of either Pure Land or Zen Buddhism. Imperial patronage of the Enryakuji Temple decreased unexpectedly while scholars of Lotus (Hokke) and True Word (Shingon) Buddhism were abandoned.

"As a result, the protective deities of Mt. Hiei, the Sun Goddess Amaterasu, Shō-Hachiman Shrine, and the Seven Sannō (Hie) Shrines, as well as the various great gods and protectors of the entire land of Japan, were all unable to taste the flavor of the *Lotus Sutra*, lost power and left the land. Taking advantage of the situation, evil spirits took possession of Japan, causing various calamities and disasters, foreshadowing the foreign invasion of this land."

This is what I predicted in my *Risshō Ankoku-ron*.

Afterwards, on the fifth day of the seventh month in the first year of the Bun'ei Era (1264), a comet appeared in the eastern sky shining over almost the entire land of Japan. It was the worst omen we have ever had since the beginning of the world. None of the scholars, Buddhist and non-Buddhist alike, knew what caused it. I felt all the more saddened as I knew it was an omen foretelling the foreign invasion of Japan.

As I feared, in the intercalary first month this year, nine years after I had submitted my *Risshō Ankoku-ron*, a letter of state came from the Great Mongol Empire. Looking at the letter, I see that it turned out to be exactly what I had predicted in the *Risshō Ankoku-ron* just as two halves of a tally matched each other.

Śākyamuni Buddha predicted: "100 years or so after My death, Great King Aśoka will appear to spread My dharma."[1] During the reign of King Chao, the fourth ruler of the Chou dynasty in ancient China, Historian Su-yu predicted that Buddhism would spread in China in 1,000 years. Prince Shōtoku* predicted: "The city of Heian (Kyoto) will be founded in the Province of Yamashiro 200 years or so after my death." And Grand Master T'ien-t'ai said: "200 years or so after my death, I will be reborn in a country to the east to spread my True Dharma."[2] These predictions all proved to be true.

I, Nichiren, encountering a severe earthquake, a typhoon, and famine in the Shōka Era* (1257-59), and wide-spread epidemics in the first year of the Shōgen Era (1259), predicted that these were omens foretelling the invasion of this country, Japan, by foreign troops. I may sound as though I am singing my own praises, but I dare say this because, should this land of Japan be destroyed, there is no doubt that Buddhism also will be destroyed.

High priests these days, however, are in one mind with slanderers of the True Dharma, or they do not even know the exquisite doctrine of their own schools. I suppose these high priests will probably receive an imperial decree or shogunal order to pray for repulsing foreign invaders, but I am afraid that it will only intensify the anger of the gods and Buddhas, resulting in the destruction of the land of Japan.

I, Nichiren, also know how to repulse the impending foreign invaders. Except for those at Mt. Hiei, I am the only one who knows this in Japan. It is because two sages will not appear at the same time, just as there never will be two suns or two moons. If this is a lie, I will receive the punishment of the 10 female rākṣasa demons, guardians of the *Lotus Sutra*, which I, Nichiren, uphold. It is solely for the sake of the country, the dharma, and the people, not for myself, that I say this to you. I say this to you also because I was able to see you earlier. If you do not accept my words, you will regret it.

Sincerely yours,
5th day of the 4th month
in the 5th year of the Bun'ei Era (1268)
Nichiren (seal)
To Reverend Hōkan-bō*

Notes

1. Aśoka was the third king of the Maurya dynasty in Magadha in Central India (268-232 BCE) who was responsible for building the Aśoka Pillars with inscriptions of Buddhist messages throughout the kingdom and ruled according to Buddhist ideals. It is stated in the *Miscellaneous Āgama Sutra* (*Zō-agon Gyō*), fascicle 23, that two small boys in the town of Rājagṛha offered a mud pie to the Buddha, who predicted that 100 years after His death these two boys would be reborn to be great kings to unify the country and restore Buddhism.
2. No such statement is found in existing writings of T'ien-t'ai, but it was widely believed that Dengyō of Japan was the reincarnation of T'ien-t'ai.

Yadoya Nyūdō Sai-gojō (ST 51)

Introduction

Nichiren Shōnin wrote the *Yadoya Nyūdō Sai-gojō* sometime around the ninth month of the fifth year of the Bun'ei Era (1268), when he was 46 years old. The letter was probably addressed to Lay Priest Yadoya though we do not know for certain, as the last portion of this letter has not been found. The original manuscript of 11 lines on one page is kept in the Hongokuji Temple in Kyoto.

Having failed to receive a response to a previous correspondence, Nichiren demanded an answer in this writing. The letter helps to clarify the trend of Nichiren's activities during this period following the advent of the Mongol state letter in 1268.

Still unable to receive an answer, Nichiren wrote letters to 11 leading figures in the political and Buddhist worlds in Japan, warning them against national destruction and making demands for public debate. These letters are known as the "Eleven Letters of Nichiren Shōnin."

Second Letter to Lay Priest Yadoya

Sometime last month, the eighth month, I had my letter delivered to you. Since then until this month I have not yet received your answer, negative or affirmative, and I cannot help being in low spirits. You may have been so busy that you have forgotten my letter, or you may have considered it unimportant, not worthy of writing even one line in response.

A proverb says that a lion does not slight a small hare, nor does it fear a huge elephant. You should not slight a poor monk. In the event of foreign troops attacking this land of Japan, you will have to bear sole responsibility for failing to inform the authorities.

One studies Buddhism in order to repay what one owes to one's country even at the cost of one's life. It is not at all for one's own sake. Grand Master T'ien-t'ai declares in his *Words and Phrases of the Lotus Sutra:* "Looking at heavy rainfall, one can tell the size of the dragon which causes it. Looking at the abundance of lotus flowers, one can tell the depth of the pond." Likewise, we should realize the seriousness of the coming event by looking at unusual omens. National disaster seems imminent, so I have written to you repeatedly. No one listens to me. Yet I keep warning. (hereafter missing)

Ankoku-ron Okugaki (ST 69)

Introduction

The *Ankoku-ron Okugaki* was written at the end of the *Risshō Ankoku-ron* which was copied anew by Nichiren Shōnin himself on the eighth day of the 12th month in the sixth year of the Bun'ei Era (1269). The original manuscript is kept in the Nakayama Hokekyoji Temple as a national treasure of Japan.

The state letter of the Mongol Empire was delivered to Japan in the first intercalary month of the fifth year in the Bun'ei Era (1268) and again in the ninth month of the following year. It seemed that what had been prophetically warned by Nichiren in his *Risshō Ankoku-ron* was about to come true. Nichiren Shōnin made a new copy of the nine year old writing, adding supplementary remarks in the form of a postscript. This writing makes it clear that Nichiren was motivated by the great earthquake that occurred in the first year of the Shōka Era (1257) to write the *Risshō Ankoku-ron* which was submitted to Hōjō Tokiyori through Lay Priest Yadoya. As the nine-year old prediction had come true, Nichiren was convinced that there would be no doubt about the need for widespread conversion to the Lotus teaching, and he confidentially stated, "This writing of mine has been attested to be true."

Postscript to the Risshō Ankoku-ron

I finished writing this *Risshō Ankoku-ron* in the first year of the Bunnō Era (1260). I began writing it during the Shōka Era (1257-59).

I began writing the *Risshō Ankoku-ron* upon experiencing a severe earthquake at around nine o'clock in the evening on the 23rd day of the eighth month in the first year of the Shōka Era (1257). Three years later, on the 16th day of the seventh month in the first year of the Bunnō Era (1260), I submitted this to the late Lay Priest Lord Hōjō Tokiyori through his chamberlain, Lay Priest Yadoya.*

Afterward, on seeing a great comet on the fifth day of the seventh month in the first year of the Bun'ei Era (1264), I felt convinced that I knew the cause of this calamity. It had been nine years since I finished writing the *Risshō Ankoku-ron* in the first year of the Bunnō Era (1260) when a letter of state from the Great Mongol Empire in the west arrived on the 18th day of the first intercalary month in the fifth year of the Bun'ei Era (1268), making clear its threat to invade Japan. A written challenge came again in the sixth year of the Bun'ei Era.

The prediction in my written opinion,* the *Risshō Ankoku-ron* has proven to be true. Contemplating the future on the basis of this, I should say that my prediction in it will also not fail to be true in the future. Though this writing of mine has been attested to be true, it is not due to my own power. But rather it is a divine response to the true words of the *Lotus Sutra*.

This copy of the *Risshō Ankoku-ron* was written on the eighth day of the 12th month in the sixth year of the Bun'ei Era (1269).

Ko Saimyōji Nyūdō Kenzan Gosho (ST 71)

Introduction

This writing contains only a fragment of the original letter of Nichiren Shōnin believed to have been written in the sixth year of the Bun'ei Era (1269). Consisting of five lines on one page, this document is kept in the Myōjōji Temple at Takidani, Ishikawa Prefecture.

Although the beginning as well as the ending portions are missing, this letter indicates that Nichiren Shōnin met Hōjō Tokiyori, advising him of the falsehood of Pure Land and Zen Buddhism before submitting the *Risshō Ankoku-ron*. It is an important document in the biographical study of Nichiren, showing that he had an interview with Tokiyori to admonish him.

Meeting the Late Lay Priest Saimyōji Letter

(hitherto missing) Meeting with the late Lay Priest Lord Hōjō Tokiyori, I told him that it is nothing but an evil act of a heavenly devil for him to stop seeking refuge in the existing Tendai and Shingon temples and to begin having faith in the new Zen temples. I also submitted the *Risshō Ankoku-ron* to him, pointing out that the practice of the *nembutsu* is an evil teaching which leads people into the Hell of Incessant Suffering. The Zen and Pure Land temples in Japan all... (hereafter missing)

Kingo-dono Gohenji (ST 73)

Introduction

The *Kingo-dono Gohenji* is a letter addressed to Ōta Jōmyō, (or Shijō Kingo, by an alternate opinion) written on the 28th day of the 11th month in the seventh year of the Bun'ei Era (1270) according to the *Shōwa Teihon* (ST). Judging from its content, however, it was most likely written in the sixth year (1269). Four pages of the original manuscript, except supplementary remarks in the beginning and the ending portions of the letter, are preserved as an important cultural asset of Japan in the Nakayama Hokekyōji Temple in Ichikawa City, Chiba Prefecture, near Tokyo.

This letter was written to express gratitude for the donation Lord Ōta sent to support the annual lecture service in memory of Grand Master T'ien-t'ai. After reporting that the service gathering was most successful, Nichiren Shōnin refers to the unrest caused by the arrival of the Mongol state letter, reports about his writing letters to 11 leading figures in the political and Buddhist worlds, in which he demanded a debate open to the public, and expresses his unwavering conviction as one who practices the *Lotus Sutra*, who fully expects banishment or even the death sentence. Regarding the national crisis of impending Mongol attack, foretold by the arrival of letters from the Mongol state in 1268 and 1269, Nichiren expresses his conviction that slanderers of the True Dharma should be dealt with even if the consequence is loss of life.

A Reply to Lord Ōta Jōmyō

Beginning on New Year's Day, I intend to read the *Great Concentration and Insight** of Grand Master T'ien-t'ai, fascicle five, praying for "tranquility in this life and rebirth to a better world in the next life." Kindly send it to me at your convenience, even if it is dilapidated. I can have it repaired here. Forgive me for bothering you, as I need many books.

With gratitude I received the five strings of coins that you sent for the Grand Master's Memorial Lecture.* It has been three or four years since we started this series of lectures in memory of Grand Master T'ien-t'ai, and it was most successful this year.

I believe that the spread of the teaching of the *Lotus Sutra* depends on the truth of the prediction of domestic disturbance and foreign invasion that I made in a written opinion,* the *Risshō Ankoku-ron, Treatise on Spreading Peace Throughout the Country by Establishing the True Dharma*. Last year, when the Mongol state letter arrived foretelling the coming of foreign invasion, I wrote letters to various people, leaders in the political and religious worlds in Japan, demanding a public debate. But I received no answer, negative or affirmative. As another Mongol state letter came again this year, I wrote letters again to various places around the 11th month with some of them responding. It seems that the feeling of the people in general has calmed down so as to make them think that I, Nichiren, might be right. Or, it may be that those letters of mine caught the eye of the ruler, the Shogunal Regent.

At any rate, as I ventured to speak up on such a grave matter, which seemed unreasonable to most of the people, I fully expected to be punished by death or banishment. I feel it indeed strange, however, that nothing has happened to me until today. Does it prove that what I insisted on was quite reasonable?

As the scriptural prediction of foreign invasion has proven to be true, the remaining prediction of domestic disturbance* will not fail to be true. I hear that the Enryakuji Temple on Mt. Hiei has been shaken up a hundred, thousand, ten thousand, and a hundred million times more than in the past. This is not a trivial matter. There must be a reason.

As China and Korea were converted to Zen and Pure Land Buddhism, protective deities gave up the countries, leaving them to be conquered by the Mongols. In Japan, too, as these evil dharmas of Zen and Pure Land spread and the Tendai-Lotus sect was neglected, Mt. Hiei is trembling hard. As both Buddhist ministers and their followers in Japan have become slanderers of the True Dharma, I am afraid, chances are eight or nine out of 10 that this country will be conquered by the Mongols as China and Korea were.

Fortunately, I have already been born to the human world without being misled by an evil teacher. For the sake of the *Lotus Sutra*, I was sentenced to banishment to Izu, but regrettably I have not been executed yet. Hoping that such a thing will happen so that I will be executed for the sake of the *Lotus Sutra*, I have exerted myself to write strongly worded letters to various people.

I am almost 50 years old, and do not know how many more years I will be able to live. I pray that I may sacrifice my body, which otherwise will be thrown away in a wild field, for the sake of the One Vehicle teaching of the *Lotus Sutra*. I pray that I may follow the examples of Young Ascetic in the Snow Mountains,* who was willing to sacrifice his own life in search of the dharma, and Medicine-King

Bodhisattva,* who burned his own arm in order to offer light to the *Lotus Sutra*. And I pray that I may live up to Kings Sen'yo* and Virtuous,* defenders of the True Dharma, leaving my name in future lives so that the future Buddha will mention my name when He preaches the *Lotus* and *Nirvana Sutras*.

Namu Myōhō Renge-kyō!

28th day of the 11th month
Nichiren (seal)
Response

Ankoku-ron Sōjō (ST 108)

Introduction

Nichiren Shōnin's letter from Sado was written on the 26th day of the fifth month in the ninth year of the Bun'ei Era (1272). One page of the original manuscript without the name of addressee has been kept at the Nakayama Hokekyōji Temple in Ichikawa City, Chiba Prefecture.

This letter requests that a copy of the *Risshō Ankoku-ron* be made and sent to him at Sado. It shows that Nichiren did not have time to take it with him. Although this letter is known as the *Ankoku-ron Sōjō*, literally *Covering Letter to the Risshō Ankoku-ron*, it does not represent the content of this letter.

A Letter Requesting the "Risshō Ankoku-ron"

The original of the *Risshō Ankoku-ron* has been kept by Lord Toki.* Please make a copy and send it to me. As for the copyist, in case Lord Toki is unavailable, anyone else will do.

26th day of the 5th month
Nichiren (written seal)

Musō Gosho (ST 111)

Introduction

Nichiren Shōnin recorded the *Musō Gosho* on or around the 24th day of the 10th month in the ninth year of the Bun'ei Era (1272). The original manuscript consisting of two lines exists in the Myōhokkeji Temple in the Tamazawa section of Mishima City, Shizuoka Prefecture.

This short remark was jotted down in the form of explanatory notes on the reverse side of sheets of paper used by Nikkō Shōnin, one of the five elder disciples of Nichiren, to copy the *Risshō Ankoku-ron*. It says that according to the dream Nichiren had on the 24th day of the 10th month in the ninth year of the Bun'ei Era, troops would be dispatched from Sagami Province on the ninth day of the first month in the following year to repulse the Mongols. It reflects the state of crisis caused by the impending invasion of Japan by Mongol troops, which Nichiren had predicted in the *Risshō Ankoku-ron*. It also indicates that Nichiren had inspiration characteristic of a prophet.

Record of a Dream

During the night on the 24th day of the 10th month in the ninth year of the Bun'ei Era (1272), I had a dream to the effect that various numbers of troops will be dispatched from Sagami Province on the ninth day of the first month next year for the purpose of getting rid of the Mongols.

Kassen Zai-Genzen Gosho (ST 155)

Introduction

The *Kassen Zai-Genzen Gosho* is believed to have been written around the 11th month of the 11th year of the Bun-ei Era (1274). A three-line fragment of the original manuscript is kept at the Hongakuji Temple in Mishima City, Shizuoka Prefecture.

This document concerns the first Mongol Invasion of Japan that took place in the 10th month of the 11th year. It briefly but vividly shows the deep impact of the war upon the people. Some consider it a draft for the writing *Soya Nyūdō-gari Gosho*, Letter to Lay Priest Soya and Ōta Jōmyō.

A War Right Under Your Nose

(hitherto missing) Of the five 500-year periods which the *Sutra of the Great Assembly* predicts to take place after the death of Śākyamuni Buddha, four periods proved exactly as foretold by the Buddha. The fifth 500-year period, the period of steadfast engagement in disputes, falls today, in the Latter Age of Degeneration. Accordingly, as we look at the world today, the country of Japan and the Mongol Empire are fighting a war right under your nose. Judging from this, the *Lotus Sutra*... (hereafter missing)

Ken Risshō-i Shō (ST 156)

Introduction

Written on the 15th day of the 12th month in the 11th year of the Bun'ei Era (1274), shortly after the first Mongol Invasion of Japan, the *Ken Risshō-i Shō* addresses all disciples and followers of Nichiren Shōnin. The original manuscript has not been found, but a copy made by his disciple Nisshun (-1303-) has been kept in the Kōchōji Temple in Numazu City, Shizuoka Prefecture.

Nichiren points out in this writing that what he predicted in the *Risshō Ankoku-ron*, domestic disturbance and foreign invasion, were proven true when an internal revolt broke out in the second month of the ninth year (1272) and the Mongols invaded Japan in the 10th month of the 11th year (1274). Nevertheless, the Japanese people have not been awakened at all. He thus warns the country that there is no doubt that the people in Japan all will fall into the Hell of Incessant Suffering for their sin of slandering the True Dharma, as foretold in the *Risshō Ankoku-ron*. He also admonishes his own disciples and followers saying that they will also fall into the Hell of Incessant Suffering unless they give up their lives for the sake of the *Lotus Sutra*.

A Tract Revealing the Gist of the Risshō Ankoku-ron

The *Risshō Ankoku-ron*, which I wrote with deliberation upon experiencing the great earthquake on the 23rd day of the eighth month in the first year of the Shōka Era (1257), states:

> "Five of the seven calamities* predicted in the *Medicine Master Sutra** have already taken place, leaving just two still to occur: foreign invasion* and domestic disturbance.* Two of the three calamities* predicted in the *Sutra of the Great Assembly** have already happened, leaving just one yet to come: war and disorder. Each calamity or disaster predicted in the *Sutra of the Golden Splendor** has indeed fallen upon us except one: invasion of our land by foreign bandits. Six of the seven calamities foretold in the *Sutra of*

the Benevolent King* are menacing us at this moment, leaving just one yet to come: invasion of our land by foreign armies from the four directions. Moreover, the same sutra warns: 'When disorder is about to prevail in a country, devils will get out of control first. When devils are rampant, causing the people to suffer, the people will grow wild.'

"Examining the present conditions carefully in comparison with this passage, there is no doubt that devils are rampant and many people are dying. Some of the calamities predicted have already taken place. How can we doubt the possibility of the remaining predictions taking place? What will you do if the remaining predictions, domestic disturbance and foreign invasion, should occur at once as punishment for your upholding evil dharmas?

"The king governs the empire for the good of his country and the people make a living by cultivating their farmlands. However, if the country is invaded by foreign armies and the people's lands are plundered by domestic disorder, how can there be anything but terror and confusion? Where can the people escape if they lose their country and homes?"

These are the predictions in the *Risshō Ankoku-ron*. Now I, Nichiren, would like to add my views to them. The Buddha once predicted that Kutoku, a Jain, would die in seven days and be reborn a hungry spirit. Refuting the Buddha, Kutoku declared that he would not die in seven days and that he would be an arhat, who would not be reborn in the realm of hungry spirits. Nevertheless, Kutoku died in seven days, showing the very appearance of the hungry spirit just as predicted by the Buddha.

When the wife of a rich man in the city of Campā, in central India, became pregnant, six non-Buddhist masters insisted that she would give birth to a baby girl. However, just as the Buddha predicted, a baby boy was born.

Upon finishing the preaching of the *Lotus Sutra*, the Buddha predicted in the *Sutra of Meditation on Universal-Sage Bodhisattva* that He would enter Nirvana within three months. Although non-Buddhist masters all called it a lie, the Buddha entered Nirvana on the 15th day of the second month.

It is stated in the *Lotus Sutra*, fascicle two, chapter three, A Parable, "Śāriputra! After a countless, inconceivable number of *kalpa* from now... you will become a Buddha called Flower Light Buddha." The sutra also asserts in the third fascicle, chapter eight, The Assurance of Future Buddhahood, "This Mahā-kāśyapa, a disciple of Mine, will see 300 trillions of Buddhas in future lives.... After that in the final stage of his physical existence, he will become a Buddha called Light Buddha." It is declared in the fourth fascicle, chapter 10, The Teacher of the Dharma, "If anyone rejoices even for a moment at hearing a verse or a phrase of the *Sutra of the Lotus Flower of the Wonderful Dharma* after My death, I also assure him of his future attainment of Perfect Enlightenment."

These passages in the *Lotus Sutra* are predictions of the Buddha about future lives. Nevertheless, who would believe in them if His three predictions cited above, such as the death of Kutoku, a Jain, had not proved to be true? It would be difficult to believe in them even if the Buddha of Many Treasures* attested them to be true, and Buddhas in manifestation* swore to their truth with their long tongues touching the Brahma Heaven. The same can be said about me today. Even if I, Nichiren, were able to preach as fluently as Pūrṇa,* or show the divine powers of Maudgalyāyana,* who would believe in me if my predictions had not proven to be true?

When a letter of state came from the Mongol Empire in the fifth year of the Bun'ei Era (1268), a wise man, if there had been one in Japan, should have wondered whether or not my prediction was proving to be true. I uttered harsh words to Hei no Saemonnojō who arrested me on the 12th day of the ninth month in the eighth year of the Bun'ei Era (1271). Those harsh words have proved to be true on the 11th day of the second month in the following year, when a domestic disturbance erupted. Anyone with a human mind should have believed me. People should have believed me even more so, as Mongol troops have invaded Japan this year, plundering the two provinces of Iki and Tsushima. Even pieces of wood and stone or birds and beasts would be startled by the exact agreement between what I predicted and what actually happened. Yet, nobody listens to me. This is no trivial matter. Possessed by evil spirits, all the people in this country are drunk and insane. It is sad, pitiful, fearful, and hateful.

Predicting their future lives, I also declared in the *Risshō Ankoku-ron*, "Should the people refuse to change their minds, clinging to false teachings, they will soon leave this world and fall into the Hell of Incessant Suffering without fail." Judging from my predictions in this present life having proven to be true, I am sure that this prediction of mine about their future lives will also become true. It is as certain as shooting an arrow at the great earth that all the people in Japan, high and low, will fall into the Hell of Incessant Suffering.

Aside from these people, some of my disciples might not be spared from this calamity of falling into the Hell of Incessant Suffering upon death. Those who disdained and hurt Never-Despising Bodhisattva, Fukyō, fell into the Hell of Incessant Suffering upon death for as long as 1,000 *kalpa*. It was due to their great sin of slandering that bodhisattva that they were paid such a hard fate, although they later believed in, respected, followed, and obeyed the bodhisattva while in this life.

Now, the same could be said of disciples of Nichiren. If they believe in, respect, follow, and obey me in name only without heart, they will no doubt suffer in the

Hell of Incessant Suffering for the period of one, two, 10, or 100, if not 1,000, *kalpa*. If you wish to be saved from this, you should each practice just as Medicine-King Bodhisattva* did, who set his arm afire to offer it as a light to the Buddha. Or as Aspiration Dharma Bodhisattva (Gyōbō Bonji)* who skinned himself to write the dharma on his own skin. Just as Young Ascetic in the Snow Mountains* and King Suzudan did, you should sacrifice your own life or serve your masters from the bottom of your heart in search of the dharma. Otherwise, you should beseech the Buddha for help, bowing to Him with your four limbs and face touching the ground, dripping with sweat. Or you should pile up rare treasures in front of the Buddha as an offering to Him. If that is not possible, you must become servants to the upholders of the dharma. Or you should practice some other ways suitable to the time according to the principle of the four ways of preaching Buddhism.* Among my disciples those whose faith is shallow will show at the moment of death, the sign of falling into the Hell of Incessant Suffering. Do not blame me for it then!

Written by Nichiren
15th day of the 12th month
in the 11th year of the Bun'ei Era (1274)

Shinkoku-ō Gosho (ST 168)

Introduction

Nichiren Shōnin wrote the *Shinkoku-ō Gosho*, in the second month of the 12th year in the Bun'ei Era (1275). 44 pages of the original manuscript are treasured in the Myōkenji Temple of Kyoto as an important cultural asset of Japan, even though the last portion of the work as well as part of the 22nd page are missing.

The *Shinkoku-ō Gosho* begins with a description of the land of Japan and her sovereigns, followed by the introduction of various schools of Buddhism into Japan, culminating in the establishment of Buddhism based on the teaching of the *Lotus Sutra* by Grand Master Dengyō on Mt. Hiei. Nichiren states that this Lotus tradition of Buddhism on Mt. Hiei, however, was converted to Shingon esotericism by Grand Masters Jikaku and Chishō.

Nichiren also points out that the defeat of the imperial forces and banishment of three ex-emperors by Shogunal Regent Hōjō Yoshitoki in the Jōkyū Incident of 1221 stemmed from the prayers performed by the priests of Shingon esotericism. Stating that his motivation to enter the priesthood was due to his childhood question of whether Buddhism had anything to do with the rise and fall of a country, Nichiren writes that he has found the answer to the question: the confusion and demise of a country is caused by the prevalence of slandering the True Dharma. He then describes how he has been persecuted simply because he has aggressively propagated the Lotus teaching in order to rectify the mistakes of other schools and for spreading the True Dharma of the *Lotus Sutra*. Calling himself one who practices the *Lotus Sutra*, who has overcome many persecutions, Nichiren urges various gods and virtuous deities to protect him. This is one of Nichiren's most important writings as he discloses his own motive for entering the priesthood and reveals his own philosophy of history, nationhood, and Shinto gods.

Sovereigns of Our Divine Land

Japan: Land and Sovereigns

As I contemplate, Japan is also known variously as Mizuhonokuni, that is the Land of Luxuriant Rice Plants, Yamato, Akitsushima or Fusō. It consists of 66 provinces and two islands of Iki and Tsushima, totaling 68 provinces, extending 3,000 *ri* east to west, though the measurement from north to south is not positively known.

The land of Japan is divided into five provinces in the Central District and seven circuits. The five central provinces are Yamashiro, Yamato, Kawachi, Izumi and Settsu. The seven circuits are: Tōkai-dō covering 15 provinces, Tōsan-dō eight provinces, Hokuriku-dō seven provinces, San'in-dō eight provinces, San'yō-dō eight provinces, Nankai-dō six provinces, and Saikai-dō, which is also called Chinzei or Dazaifu, 11 provinces. This is the land of Japan.

Next considering the rulers of Japan, 12 gods, seven heavenly and five terrestrial, reigned over Japan during the pre-historic legendary period. The first of the seven heavenly rulers was Kunitokotachi no Mikoto...the seventh being Izanagi no Mikoto and his wife, Izanami no Mikoto. The first of the five terrestrial sovereigns was Amaterasu Omikami, who is the Sun Goddess enshrined at the Grand Shrine of Ise. She is the daughter of Izanagi and Izanami.... The fifth terrestrial sovereign, Hikonagi Satake Ugaya Fukiaezu no Mikoto, was a son of Hikohohodami no Mikoto, the fourth sovereign. His mother was the daughter of the dragon king. These five reigns of terrestrial gods, together with the seven reigns of heavenly gods constitute the twelve reigns of divine rulers.

Human sovereigns, I suppose, will number about 100, beginning with Emperor Jimmu, son of Hikonagi Satake Ugaya Fukiaezu no Mikoto.... The 14th was the Emperor Chūai, father of Great Bodhisattva Hachiman, and the 15th was Empress Jingū, Mother of Great Bodhisattva Hachiman. The 16th was Emperor Ōjin, who is a son of Emperor Chūai and Empress Jingū and is now worshipped as Great Bodhisattva Hachiman*.... Heretofore, until the 29th reign of Emperor Senka, Buddhism had not been transmitted to Japan, although it existed in India and China.

Introduction of Buddhism

The 30th sovereign was Emperor Kimmei, eldest son of the 27th Emperor Keitai. He reigned for 32 years. On the 13th day of the 10th month during the 13th year of his reign (552), King Sông-myông of Paekche presented to the Japanese

Emperor a gilt-copper statue of Śākyamuni Buddha, which all the people of Japan today, from the emperor down, regard as the Buddha of Infinite Life.*

The Paekche king's letter of presentation stated: "I, a subject of Your Highness, have heard that Buddhism is the best of all teachings and supreme of all ways in the world. In order for Your Highness to practice it, I respectfully present you this Buddhist statue, scriptures and monks through my emissary. I pray that Your Highness may have faith in Buddhism and practice it."

For 30 years or so during the three reigns of Emperors Kimmei, Bidatsu and Yōmei, however, no one had faith in Buddhism. Strange phenomena in the sky and natural calamities on earth,* similar to those today, did occur during these years, though with less severity.

Introduction of the Six Sects in Nara

During the 33rd reign of Emperor Shushun, Buddhism began spreading in Japan, gaining momentum during the reign of the 34th Emperor Suiko, whose Imperial Regent, Prince Shōtoku, did much for the rise of Buddhism. The Prince was responsible for the promulgation of the 17 Article Constitution based on Buddhist doctrines. It was during Emperor Suiko's reign that schools of Buddhism called Sanron,* or Three Treatises, and Jōjitsu,* or Completion of Truth, were transmitted to Japan for the first time. This Sanron sect was the first of the Buddhist sects, Mahayana* or Hinayana, appearing in India, China or Japan. Therefore, it is called the mother or father of Buddhist sects.

Thereafter, the Zen sect* was transmitted to Japan in the reign of Emperor Kōgyoku, the 36th sovereign. The Hossō, or Dharma Characteristics sect,* was introduced during the reign of Emperor Temmu, the 40th sovereign. The *Great Sun Buddha Sutra,** was introduced during the reign of Emperor Genshō, the 44th sovereign. And the Kegon, or Flower Garland sect,* was introduced during the reign of the 45th Emperor Shōmu. Both the Ritsu, or Precepts, and Tendai-Hokke, or Lotus sects were introduced to Japan by Venerable Priest Chien-chên, that is Ganjin, in the reign of the 46th Emperor Kōken, but Chien-chên propagated only the Ritsu sect* without spreading the Tendai-Lotus sect.

Spread of the Tendai-Lotus Sect

During the reign of the 50th sovereign, Emperor Kammu, a sage priest named Saichō, Grand Master Dengyō, founded the Lotus sect which was superior to other Buddhist schools. Saichō defeated in debate the six sects of Nara: Kusha,* Jōjitsu, Ritsu, Hossō, Sanron and Kegon.

Learning about the school of Buddhism called Dainichi, Great Sun Buddha or Shingon sect in China, Grand Master Dengyō, went to China during the reign of the same emperor in the 23rd year of the Enryaku Period (804) to study and transmit the four schools of Buddhism. In China he studied the Lotus, Shingon* (True Word), Zen and Mahayana Ritsu sects. Upon returning to Japan, however, Grand Master Dengyō spread only the Lotus and Mahayana Ritsu sects without spreading the Zen sect. As for the Shingon sect, Dengyō did not recognize its independence, merely permitting monks of the seven great temples of Nara to perform the esoteric "sprinkling water on the head" ceremony.* Not knowing the true intent of the Grand Master, however, people in those days conjectured that he studied the profound teaching of the Tendai-Lotus school, but not the doctrine of Shingon esotericism.

Introduction of the Shingon Sect

During the same reign of Emperor Kammu, a monk named Kūkai went to China to study Shingon Buddhism. Not returning to Japan during Kammu's reign, Kūkai, however, returned in the first year of the Daidō Period (806) during the reign of the 51st sovereign, Emperor Heizei. On the 19th day of the first month in the 14th year of the Kōnin Period (823) during the reign of the 52nd Emperor Saga, Kūkai was granted the Tōji Temple in Kyoto as the headquarters of Shingon esotericism, which was named Kyōō Gokoku-ji Temple. It was a year after the death of Grand Master Dengyō.*

In the fifth year of the Jōwa Period (838) during the reign of Emperor Nimmei, the 54th sovereign, Venerable Priest Ennin, also known as Grand Master Jikaku,* went to China for further study of the Tendai-Lotus and Shingon teachings, returning to Japan in the 14th year of Jōwa (847). During the Ninju and Saikō Periods (851-857), in the reign of Emperor Montoku, the 55th sovereign, Ennin wrote commentaries on the *Diamond Peak Sutra* and the *Sutra of the Act of Perfection*, totaling 14 fascicles, calling them, together with the *Annotations on the Great Sun Buddha Sutra*, or *Dainichi-kyō Gishaku*, the "triple works of the Shingon sect." Ennin built the Sōjiin Temple on Mt. Hiei and began spreading Shingon Buddhism. Thus the Shingon sect was permitted to spread on Mt. Hiei, and it became customary that the chief ministers of the Tendai sect, thereafter, concurrently studied both Lotus and Shingon doctrines. Nevertheless, as the Lotus sect was compared to the moon while the Shingon sect to the sun, people as a whole assumed that the Shingon teaching was superior. At any rate, the head priests of Mt. Hiei studied both Tendai and Shingon Buddhism and so did all other priests on the mountain.

During the same reign of Emperor Montoku, Venerable Enchin, also known as Grand Master Chishō,* went to T'ang China. Studying both the Lotus and Shingon schools of Buddhism, he returned to Japan in the second year of the Ten'an Period (858). In Japan, Venerable Enchin had mastered Lotus and Shingon Buddhism under the guidance of of Gishin,* who was the first Chief Priest of Mt. Hiei, Enchō,* the second Chief Priest, Grand Master Bettō or Kōjō*, and Ennin, the third Chief Priest. Venerable Enchin also mastered the Shingon doctrine of the Tōji Temple. He then ventured to China, to study both the Lotus and Shingon teachings further. Grand Master Chishō founded the Tendai-esoterism of today's Miidera Temple.

These are the so-called four grand masters of Shingon Buddhism in Japan. Generally speaking, eight streams* exist within Japanese esotericism, of which five belonging to the Tōji Temple were founded by Grand Master Kōbō* and three belonging to the Tendai sect were originated by Grand Master Jikaku.*

The Juei and Jōkyū Incidents

The 81st sovereign, Emperor Antoku, was the eldest son of Emperor Takakura, and his mother, Kenrei Mon'in, was a daughter of Lay Priest Prime Minister Taira no Kiyomori. Emperor Antoku, defeated by the army of Minamoto Yoritomo, was drowned in the Sea of Yashima on the 24th day of the third month in the first year of the Genryaku Period (1184).[1]

The 82nd sovereign, Emperor Gotoba, was later called "ex-Emperor in Buddhist Robes on Oki Island." He was the third son of Emperor Takakura and was enthroned in the first year of the Bunji Period (1185). The 83rd sovereign was Emperor Tsuchimikado, known as "ex-Emperor of Awa Province." He was the first son of Emperor Gotoba and was placed on the throne in the second year of the Kennin Period (1202). The 84th sovereign was Emperor Juntoku, known also as "ex-Emperor on the island of Sado." He was the second son of Emperor Gotoba who ascended the throne on the 26th day of the second month in the third year of the Jōkyū Period (1221) but was exiled to Sado Island in the seventh month of the same year. Thus, the 82nd, 83rd, and 84th emperors were a father and his two sons. Defeated by Hōjō Yoshitoki, vassal of Minamoto Yoritomo of Kamakura, these three sovereigns were banished respectively to Oki, Awa, and Sado Provinces, an event of disgrace that has never been paralleled in history.

Buddha Dharma, State, and Society

Here I, Nichiren, have a great doubt. The Buddha is a teacher, master, and parent of various kings of the triple world* such as the King of the Brahma Heaven, King of Devils in the Sixth Heaven,* Indra,* the sun, the moon, Four Heavenly Kings, the Wheel-turning Noble King* and others. These kings of the triple world have received lands divided by Śākyamuni Buddha so they can be the rulers of various provinces or special territories. Therefore, the King of the Brahma Heaven, Indra and other kings revere the wooden statues and portraits of Śākyamuni Buddha. If they go against the teaching of the Buddha even

Shinkoku-ō Gosho (ST 168) 159

slightly, the imposing palace of the King of the Brahma Heaven and the Joyful Sight Palace of Indra will instantly crumble, and the crown of the Wheel-turning Noble King will fall off.

Also, gods are past rulers of countries who are revered as though they were alive. Therefore, gods are parents, masters and teachers of kings and their subjects. When they act only slightly contrary to the expectations of gods, their countries will not be at peace even for a day. When they worship gods, three calamities* and seven calamities* will disappear, people will be healthy and live long lives. In their next lives people, gods, as well as the three vehicles,* the three kinds of Buddhist practictioners: *śrāvaka, pratyekabuddha* and bodhisattvas, all will be rewarded with Buddhahood.

Our country of Japan is superior to 80,000 countries in the world including India and China. The reason I say this is because Buddhism in India has spread only in 70 or so states according to such documents as the *Record of the Western Regions* by Hsüan-chuang. Other states in India are all non-Buddhist.* Buddhist temples in China are 108,040 in number whereas there are as many as 171,037 temples in Japan. Japan compared to India or China in size is like Oshima Island of Izu against the whole of Japan, but there is all the difference in the world between the number of Buddhist temples in Japan and China or India. Moreover, in India and China some states believe in Hinayana while others in Mahayana Buddhism, though these are nothing but provisional. In Japan, on the other hand, doctrines of the eight or 10 schools of Buddhism are mastered in each temple and Mahayana sutras are recited in each home. Buddhists in India and China are one out of 1,000 people whereas in Japan everybody is a Buddhist and nobody believes in a non-Buddhist religion.

Furthermore, we have various gods enshrined in about 3,000 shrines in Japan, beginning with Goddess Amaterasu* in the first place, Great Bodhisattva Hachiman in the second place and Sannō Gongen in the third place, guarding our country day and night and watching the nation morning and evening. Besides, it is said that Goddess Amaterasu's spirit abides in the mirror enshrined in the sanctuary called Kashikodokoro within the imperial palace, and Great Bodhisattva Hachiman forsakes his palace to stay in the head of the emperor to protect him all the time.

Regarding the protection of Buddhas and gods, the circumstances should be especially favorable to our country. Why is it then that such Japanese sovereigns as Emperor Antoku, ex-Emperors Gotoba, Tsuchimikado and Juntoku were attacked by their own subordinates for generations to be killed, banished, become demons in exile, or sent to hell?

It is customary for any of the Buddhist temples in Japan, totaling 171,037, beginning with Mt. Hiei, the seven great temples in Nara, Tōji and Onjōji

Temples, to pray for peace in the country and security of the emperor even when they hold minor services. Furthermore, Great Bodhisattva Hachiman has sworn to protect the emperor especially. Entering the imperial body of the 48th sovereign of Japan, Emperor Kōken, the spirit of Hachiman declared: "Ever since its founding, no subject has ever ascended the Japanese throne. Emperors must be of imperial blood." In the first year of the Jōgan Era (859), Hachiman also announced through the mouth of Priest Gyōkyō of the Daianji Temple: "I made a vow to protect 100 rulers of Japan."* The 100 emperors of Japan beginning with Emperor Jimmu, therefore, should be safe and sound no matter what might happen. Nobody will try to usurp the throne.

It is said in Buddhism that bodhisattvas of the highest stage who have attained Enlightenment equal to the Buddha's and will take the Buddha's place in the next life will never die on the way, and that a holy man will not die of an accident. How did it happen that those four emperors of Japan were not only deprived of the throne and country, but also drowned at sea or exiled to islands? I wonder why Goddess Amaterasu, protector of Japan, did not enter the bodies of the four emperors to replace them? What happened to the vow of Great Bodhisattva Hachiman to protect the 100 rulers of Japan?

Doubt About Shingon Prayers

Furthermore, during the reign of Emperor Antoku, Lay Priest Minister-President Taira Kiyomori and his clan members requested Chief Priest Myōun of the Enryakuji Temple on Mt. Hiei to be the state master and submitted the following written pledge to the temple: "In ancient times, the Fujiwara clan established the Kōfukuji Temple as their clan temple and worshipped at the Kasuga Shrine as their clan shrine. Likewise hereafter we, the Taira clan, will worship at Enryakuji as our clan temple and at Hie Shrine as our clan shrine." Thus 3,000 monks on Mt. Hiei beginning with Chief Priest Myōun performed the grand prayer service using five altars,* while the families of ministers of state and others each recited the *Sonshō Darani Sutra* and said prayers to the fierce spirit of Fudō, and made donations to various temples. Thus they prayed in vain for the subjugation of Minamoto Yoritomo using all the great secret dharmas available, but in the end Emperor Antoku was drowned in the western sea.

Again, at the time of the Jōkyū Incident,* the Imperial House summoned such high priests as Archbishop Jien of the Tendai sect, Prince Reverend Dōjō of the Ninnaji Temple, and the head priest of the Onjōji Temple to have them perform prayer services with all kinds of great secret dharmas known in Japan for the purpose of forcing the Kamakura forces to surrender. On the 19th day of the fourth month in the third year of the Jōkyū Era (1221), a prayer service was held at the Imperial Palace using the 15 altars* with the Archbishop Jien conducting the Ichiji Konrin Dharma Service. On the second day of the fifth month, the head priest of the Ninnaji Temple presided over the Nyohō Aizen Myōō Dharma Service in the Shishinden, the Main Hall of the Imperial Palace. On the eighth day of the sixth month he further conducted the *Guardian Sutra* Dharma Service. Thus altogether 41 high priests, one by one, performed prayer services using the 15 altars. This was only the second time when these great prayer services were performed in Japan.

In Kamakura, on the other hand, since Lord Hōjō Yoshitoki, the leader of the military regime, was unaware of the Imperial Court having prayer services conducted, he did not specially order one. Even if he had, he could not have mustered the high priests with great secret dharmas comparable to those mobilized by the Imperial Court.

Speaking of the power of Buddhism and the prestige of the king, the emperor is the ruler of Japan protected by various kings and gods in the triple world. In contrast, the shogun is a subject of this country, protected merely by minor gods. Minamoto Yoritomo is a vassal of the emperor for generations and Yoshitoki is his rear vassal.

For the king to chastise his subject should be as easy and simple as for a hawk to hunt a pheasant, a cat to prey on a rat, a snake to swallow a frog, or a lion to kill a rabbit. Why, then, did the Imperial Court thoughtlessly pray to the gods in heaven and the deities on earth and request assistance from Buddhas and bodhisattvas? A lion king does not need to exhaust himself in hunting a rabbit. Is it necessary for a hawk to pray when catching a pheasant? For a king to destroy his subject without praying should be as simple as extinguishing a small fire with a large quantity of water or a strong wind blowing away a small cloud.

Besides, just like wood added to fire or a heavy rain over a great river, the great power of the king is reinforced by prayer services with the great secret dharma of Shingon Buddhism, causing the King of the Brahma Heaven and Indra to extract the life and spirit from Yoritomo and Yoshitoki. Therefore, it should have been as easy for the Imperial House to defeat the Kamakura forces as killing a man drunk with old sake or a snake snatching the spirit from a frog.

As the spirits and names of Yoritomo and Yoshitoki, written on paper, were stepped on by Buddhas, bodhisattvas and gods while prayers were said for their repulse, they seemed to be defeated in no time. However, it was the imperial forces that were destroyed, not in a month or a year, but merely in one or two days. Why was this so? For the sake of their future lives, those who will be the rulers of a Buddhist country should contemplate the reason and pray.

True and False Dharmas and Rise and Fall of a Country

Pondering these two great events in the history of Japan, I, Nichiren, since my childhood have seriously studied both exoteric and esoteric* Buddhism, as well as all the sutras of various Buddhist schools. I have done this by either learning from others or reading the sutras and contemplating them. Finally, I discovered the reason for these events.

To see our own faces, we must look at them reflected upon a spotless mirror. Likewise, to see the rise and fall of a country, there is no way better than to see that country reflected upon the mirror of the Buddha Dharma. As we respectfully read such Mahayana sutras as the *Sutra of the Benevolent King,* *Sutra of the Golden Splendor,* *Guardian Sutra,* *Nirvana Sutra,* and *Lotus Sutra,* it is preached that the rise and fall of a country and the life span of people in it depend on the Dharma they believe; whether they believe in the True Dharma or a false dharma. It is like water that keeps a boat afloat but also destroys it, or staple grains which nourish human bodies but often damage them. Small winds and waves would not damage large ships, but small ships can easily be destroyed by gale winds and huge waves. Unjust government, like small winds and waves, would not cause the downfall of a great country and a great man. However, there is no doubt that a false dharma in Buddhism, like gale winds and huge waves destroying small boats, will destroy a country.

Śākyamuni Buddha predicts in the *Guardian Sutra:*

> "In the Latter Age of Degeneration after My passing, even if evil dharmas and evil persons try to destroy the country and Buddha Dharma, they will not succeed. For instance even if we try to burn Mt. Sumeru*with grass and wood of a whole world as fuel, the mountain will not be burnt. However, when the *kalpa*-fire starts at the end of this world, a fire as small as a bean started at the foot of Mt. Sumeru will burn it down to ashes. Likewise, My True Dharma will be destroyed not by evil people, non-Buddhists and devils, but by those precept masters who always wear Buddhist robes like Buddhas, or arhats with six superhuman powers* who strictly observe the practice of begging alms with alms bowls in their hands, and by those high priests who are revered by people, just as strong winds sway grass and trees. Then such gods as the King of the Brahma Heaven, Indra, the sun and moon, and the Four Heavenly Kings will become so angry that they will admonish the country by creating strange phenomena in the sky and disasters on earth. When their admonition is unheeded, they will further cause the seven calamities in the country, making parents, brothers, the lord, subjects, and all the people to fight one another and to bring about the ruin of their country.

This is just as an owl eats up his own mother and a beast called *hakei* kills his own father. In the end they will cause a foreign force to attack the country."

The Spotless Mirror of the Lotus Sutra and the Current State of Japan

As I look at the existing state of Japan reflected upon the clear mirrors of all the holy teachings of the Buddha's lifetime,* those Japanese appearing in the mirror are without doubt enemies of the country and the Buddha. Among the spotless mirrors of the holy teachings preached in His lifetime, the *Lotus Sutra* is the special divine mirror. A copper mirror can show the figure of a man but not his mind. The divine mirror of the *Lotus Sutra* shows not only a man's figure but also his mind. Not only the current mind of a man but also his karma in the previous life and his reward and retribution in the future can clearly be spotlighted.

The *Lotus Sutra,* fascicle seven, the 21st chapter, The Supernatural Powers of the Tathāgata, preaches: "Suppose that after the Buddha passed away, someone who knows the causes and conditions and proper sequence of the sutras expounded by the Buddha will preach them truthfully according to the true meaning. As the light of the sun and moon can eliminate all darkness, so this person will wipe out the darkness of living beings as he walks about in the world."

This scriptural passage means that he who expounds even a word or a phrase of the *Lotus Sutra* should know well the comparative profundity of the holy teachings preached during His lifetime and the sequence of preaching them. For instance, speaking of the calendar consisting of more than 360 days a year, a mistake by one day will cause mistakes for 10,000 days. In a 31-syllable Japanese poem, a mistake in a syllable or a phrase makes the whole 31 syllables unpoetic. Likewise, in reading or reciting a sutra. If one is confused about the sequence and comparative profundity of the holy teachings of the Buddha, beginning with the *Flower Garland Sutra* preached first at the Hall of Enlightenment,* to the *Nirvana Sutra* expounded last in the *śāla* forest,* one will inevitably fall into the Hell of Incessant Suffering without committing the five rebellious sins. Those who believe in this one, despite his confusion, will also fall into the Hell of Incessant Suffering.

Therefore, when a wise man appears in the world to declare correctly the comparative profundity of the holy teachings preached during the Buddha's lifetime, aristocratic families or those priests who have transmitted false doctrines from the founders of their respective sects and are revered as the teachers of the state will make a false charge against the wise man to the rulers of the country or incite a popular protest against him. Otherwise, the weakness of their sects would be revealed, causing them to be despised by the people. Then, it is preached, the protective deities of Buddhism will be so enraged that they will destroy this country just as gale winds tear up the leaves of banana plants or high waves overturn small boats.

Criticism of Various Sutras and Sects

Enumerating all the Buddhist sutras beginning with the *Flower Garland Sutra* preached first by the Buddha at His Hall of Enlightenment, and ending with the *Nirvana Sutra,* or those sutras preached during the period of 40 years or so, the *Sutra of Infinite Meaning** declares that "The truth has not been revealed in them." In the *Nirvana Sutra* preached last by the Buddha, it is stated also, just as the *Sutra of Infinite Meaning* declares, that of the 50 years of the Buddha's preaching beginning with the attainment of Buddhahood at the age of 30, sutras expounded during the first 42 years are of false opinions, confirming the *Lotus Sutra* preached during the last eight years to be the lord of sutras.

In the *Lotus Sutra* preached between these two: the *Sutra of Infinite Meaning* and the *Nirvana Sutra,* the Buddha stated that this *Lotus Sutra* was far superior to any of those which have already been preached during the 42-year period, the *Sutra of Infinite Meaning* which is being preached, and the *Nirvana Sutra* which will be preached hereafter.* Then the Buddha of Many Treasures of the Treasure Purity World and Buddhas coming from all the worlds throughout the universe attested this to be true. After that they all returned to their respective worlds.

The twenty-four successors to the Buddha's teaching who spread it in India after the passing of the Buddha, however, propagated only Hinayana and provisional Mahayana sutras, not the true teaching of the *Lotus Sutra.* They were like Bodhisattvas Gyōki* and Chien-chên* of Japan who knew about the True Dharma of the *Lotus Sutra* without disseminating it.

The three Southern and seven Northern masters in China did not know the comparative superiority of the various Buddha Dharmas and were confused about the comparative profundity of sutras outwardly. Such masters as Chi-tsang, that is Grand Master Chia-hsiang* of the Three Treatises school, Ch'êng-kuan* of the Flower Garland school, and Tz'ŭ-ên* of the Dharma Characteristics school did not realize the comparative profundity-superiority among the various Buddha Dharmas both inwardly and outwardly. However, their faith in Buddhism was so firm that they followed T'ien-t'ai disregarding their own positions and reputations. So I do not know whether or not these masters were able to gain emancipation from the illusion of birth and death because of their merit of repentance. They might have gone to hell because their sin of slandering the True Dharma was too serious to be acquitted, just as King Ajātaśatru* and Vimalamitra* fell into hell despite their repentance.

Slandering the True Dharma
by the Three High Priests of the Shingon Sect

Shingon priests all say that the three *Tripiṭaka* Masters Śubhākarasiṃha,* Vajrabodhi* and Pu-k'ung* were the fifth or sixth transmitters of the dharma from the Great Sun Buddha* and that they are the originators of the teaching which claims that one can become a Buddha with one's present body.* To me, however, they are the founders of stealing the dharma and the authors of theft.

They brought from India such scriptures as the *Great Sun Buddha Sutra*, the *Diamond Peak Sutra** and the *Sutra on the Act of Perfection*,* which are not only inferior to the *Flower Garland Sutra*, *Wisdom Sutra*, *Nirvana Sutra* and others but also are ranked seven steps below the *Lotus Sutra*. This is clearly stated in sutras.

Seeing the 30 fascicles of Grand Master T'ien-t'ai's* three major works such as the *Great Concentration and Insight** on arriving to China, Śubhākarasiṃha was speechless with admiration and said to himself: "The *Great Sun Buddha Sutra* does not amount to the *Lotus Sutra*, so it is impossible to spread its teaching in China. If I say that the *Great Sun Buddha Sutra* is superior, it is obvious that I am a liar. What should I do?"

After contemplation Śubhākarasiṃha finally contrived a great lie. He insisted that the 31 chapters of the *Great Sun Buddha Sutra* corresponded to the 28 chapters of the *Lotus Sutra* and the three chapters of the *Sutra of Infinite Meaning*, and that the mental practice of the three mystic practices, mental, verbal and bodily, of the *Great Sun Buddha Sutra* was identical to that of the *Lotus Sutra*, which abbreviated the bodily and verbal mystic practices of *mudrā* and mantras.* As the *Lotus Sutra* was the abbreviated version of the *Great Sun Buddha Sutra*, Śubhākarasiṃha maintained that the *Great Sun Buddha Sutra* did not belong to either category of sutras preached before, at the same time as, and after the *Lotus Sutra* was preached. Thus Śubhākarasiṃha craftily sided with the *Lotus Sutra* in order to avoid the criticism from the standpoint of the *Lotus Sutra* claiming itself to be supreme of all sutras preached before, at the same time as and after the *Lotus Sutra* was. Claiming that the *Great Sun Buddha Sutra* was superior because it preached *mudrā*, that is finger signs, and mantras, which the *Lotus Sutra* did not, Śubhākarasiṃha in the end demoted the *Lotus Sutra* and established the Shingon or True Word sect.

This big lie of Śubhākarasiṃha is like the three imperial consorts of ancient China who destroyed the last three kings of Yin, Hsia and Chou. The Buddha predicted in fascicle nine of the *Nirvana Sutra*, the epilogue of the *Lotus Sutra:* "After My death evil priests will destroy My True Dharma just as a woman causes the destruction of a country." The Buddha must have referred to the lie of Śubhākarasiṃha.

Accordingly, *Tripiṭaka* Master Śubhākarasiṃha upon death was accused by King Yama and was tied with seven chains of iron. Later he was barely resuscitated, but as his biographer says, at the last moment of his life, his entire skin blackened and he looked emaciated. As stated in scriptures, his corpse showed the appearance of the Hell of Incessant Suffering.* It is clearly stated in the holy teachings preached in the Buddha's lifetime that blackening of the corpse upon death foretells falling into the Hell of Incessant Suffering. The countenance of Śubhākarasiṃha upon death was exactly what is stated in sutras, so we can conjecture the fate of two of his successors, *Tripiṭaka* Masters Vajrabodhi and Pu-k'ung, after death. They seem to have repented in their closing years, but as they did not repent from the bottom of their hearts, they would not be able to avoid going to hell. Shingon ministers today do not know anything about this. When they know the big lie of Śubhākarasiṃha, they will automatically understand why Emperor Hsüan-tsung of T'ang China, who had faith in the *tripiṭaka* master, lost his throne.

The Decline of the Tendai-Lotus Sect

In Japan, such priests as Kōbō, Jikaku and Chishō, not to speak of other Shingon priests, transmitted the evil doctrine of Shingon Buddhism propagated by Śubhākarasiṃha and others without knowing them to be slanderers of the True Dharma. For a while, Shingon Buddhists in Japan quarreled with those of the Tendai-Lotus sect, which gradually declined until Shingon Buddhism dominated Mt. Hiei completely when Myōun became the 55th Chief Priest (*zasu*) of the Enryakuji Temple during the reign of the 81st sovereign, Emperor Antoku.

Moreover, the 61st Chief Priest Kenshin Gonsōjō not only moved to the Shingon sect while being the head of the Enryakuji Temple but also abandoned both Lotus and Shingon Buddhism to become a disciple of Hōnen,* the leading slanderer of the True Dharma. Also, Jien Sōjō, who prayed for the defeat of the Hōjōs in the Jōkyū Incident, became the 62nd, 65th, 69th and 71st Chief Priests of the Enryakuji Temple and was the teacher of ex-Emperor Gotoba.

These high priests of Mt. Hiei transmitted the esoteric teaching of such Shingon masters as Śubhākarasiṃha, Vajrabodi, Pu-k'ung, Jikaku and Chishō as it had been. Like the same water in different containers, they were Tendai priests in name but the same old Shingon priests in reality. Besides, they disgraced the reputation of the Chief Priest of Enryakuji Temple while managing the fief of the temple for many years. They headed the 3,000 priests on Mt. Hiei and were revered as National Teachers. However, they regarded the *Great Sun Buddha Sutra*, which was seven steps below the *Lotus Sutra*, as their basic canon, believing that it was eight steps above the *Lotus Sutra*. This is like calling heaven earth, taking the subjects for the king, or mistaking a pebble for a gem. Not only that, they are like people who insist that a gem is a pebble.

These high priests of Mt. Hiei are not only loathsome enemies of Lord Śākyamuni Buddha, the Buddha of Many Treasures* and Buddhas in 10 directions* in the worlds throughout the universe, but are also those who gouge out eyes of all living beings, block the gate to the three virtuous realms of gods, humans and *asura*, and open the gate to the three evil realms of hell, hungry spirits and beasts. How can various deities, protectors of the *Lotus Sutra* such as the King of the Brahma Heaven, Indra, the sun and moon, and the Four Heavenly Kings, not punish them? How can these deities protect the followers of such priests? How can the oaths of Goddess Amaterasu, enshrined in the Naijidokoro in the imperial palace, and Great Bodhisattva Hachiman, for protecting the Imperial House for 100 generations be fulfilled?

One Who Practices the Lotus Sutra and His Persecution

Ever since I realized the cause of the Gempei War in the Juei Period, 1185, and the Jōkyū Incident in 1221, I was so moved by compassion that I could not ignore it. At first, I mentioned it to some of my disciples. My realization gradually spread until it reached the shogunate. Rulers of the country should give priority to reason and reject injustice. I don't know what happened to the shogunate, but they believed false charges against me and rejected me, Nichiren, who advocated righteousness.

The three Southern and seven Northern masters in China slandered Grand Master T'ien-t'ai, but as the two sovereigns of the Ch'ên and Sui dynasties revered him, people did not hate him bitterly. In Japan, Grand Master Dengyō was spoken ill of by priests of the seven great temples in Nara. However, as Dengyō was deeply trusted by the three emperors Kammu, Heizei and Saga, even his loathsome enemies could not do much to him.

Now, I, Nichiren, am not only hated by priests of 171,037 temples in Japan but also am not in good grace with the national rulers, so all the Japanese people despise me more than one who has killed their parents, or their old foe. Consequently, I was banished twice, to Izu and Sado, and was almost beheaded once at Tatsunokuchi.

My persecution was more severe than the one endured by Monk Fuji in the remote past during the Latter Age of Degeneration after the death of Great Splendor Buddha. This monk strove to uphold the Buddha's True Dharma and was persecuted by four evil monks and their numerous followers. It was more unbearable than the hardship Monk Kikon encountered when he was insulted by Monk Shōi and his numerous disciples during the Latter Age of

Degeneration after the passing of Lion Voice King Buddha. The persecutions of Monk Virtue Consciousness* by slanderers of the True Dharma as preached in the *Nirvana Sutra,* and the difficulty of Never-Despising Bodhisattva* being beaten with sticks and wood, and having pieces of tiles and stones thrown at him as mentioned in the *Lotus Sutra,* probably do not equal what I had to endure. By any chance, if I am one who practices the *Lotus Sutra,** people in Japan will fall into the Hell of Incessant Suffering in the next life for the sin of persecuting me. Leaving this aside for now, rulers of Japan, like Hui-tsung and Ch'in-tsung, the last two emperors of the Northern Sung in China, will lose the country in this life. Or they will be like two examples from ancient India who were destroyed by foreign invaders: King Udayana, who did not trust Monk Piṇḍlabharadvāja, and King Kirīta, who persecuted Buddhist monks. As for other people, there is no doubt that for the sin of slandering the True Dharma, they will suffer from serious sickness such as white leprosy and black leprosy. If there is no such factual proof, then I do not practice the *Lotus Sutra,* and I with this present body will contract those grave illnesses and will fall into the Hell of Incessant Suffering upon death just as Devadatta* and Kokālika* did.

It is said that an *asura* who tried to shoot the sun and moon shot his own eye and a dog who barked at the king of lions exploded his own belly. King Virūdhaka, who murdered the Buddha's disciples, was burnt to death while at a drinking party aboard a ship on a river. Devadatta, who injured the Buddha, felt the flaming fire of the Hell of Incessant Suffering while alive. In Japan, Mononobe Moriya, who burnt the gilt bronze statue of Śākyamuni Buddha was shot to death by the arrows of the Four Heavenly Kings. Lay Priest Taira no Kiyomori, who burnt down the Tōdaiji and Kōfukuji Temples at Nara, suffered from a high fever as though being burned alive. To be sure they are all serious sins, but compared to the persecution of Nichiren they are rather insignificant. Even insignificant sins such as the above received actual punishment. What can we say of such a grave sin as persecuting Nichiren. It is only natural that various gods punish those who persecute me.

Delight and Sorrow of Persecution

My delight is to have been born during the fifth 500-year period* to spread the *Lotus Sutra* in the Latter Age of Degeneration as predicted in the sutra, and wait for the time for its wide dissemination. My sadness is to have been born in this period of quarrels and fighting to witness this country being in the realm of *asura*.

Lay Priest Taira no Kiyomori and Minamoto Yoritomo, heads of the Taira and Minamoto clans respectively, were as unfriendly to each other as dogs and monkeys. Nevertheless, when Kiyomori was in power he mistreated poor

Yoritomo and incurred the latter's enmity as an old foe of many generations. As a result, the whole Kiyomori clan was destroyed. Moreover, innocent infant Emperor Antoku was sadly drowned in the western sea.

Now, I, as the messenger of Lord Śākyamuni Buddha, the Buddha of Many Treasures, and Buddhas in manifestation in all the worlds in the universe, spread only the teaching of the *Lotus Sutra* without committing any worldly crime. Nevertheless, the Kamakura Shogunate not only allowed all the people in Japan to hate me but also exiled me twice, disgracing me by taking me along the streets of Kamakura in broad daylight as though I were a national traitor. Besides, they tore down my hermitage enshrining Śākaymuni Buddha as the Most Venerable One, my *honzon,* and all the Buddhist scriptures.* They made people not only trample the statue of the Buddha and scrolls of sutras but also threw them in the mud and excrement. Furthermore, they took out the *Lotus Sutra* from my bosom and hit me on the head with it mercilessly. My persecution as severe as this was neither due to any long standing enmity nor any crime I have committed. It was solely due to my disseminating the *Lotus Sutra* that I have been persecuted so severely.

Admonition of Gods

Thereupon I, Nichiren, loudly declare facing heaven:

"As we look at the first Introductory chapter of the *Lotus Sutra,* we see that the King of the Brahma Heaven, Indra, the sun and moon, the Four Heavenly Kings, the Dragon King, *asura,* various gods of the realms of desire and of form *(nikai hachiban)** and heavenly beings from numerous worlds are gathered in the assembly. When they heard that the *Lotus Sutra* was supreme of all the sutras preached in the past, those being preached at present and those which would be preached in the future,* they felt enthusiastic about protecting this sutra just as Young Ascetic in the Snow Mountains* sacrificed his own body for the dharma and Medicine-King Bodhisattva* burnt his elbow to offer light to the Buddha. Then Lord Śākyamuni Buddha admonished* them in front of the Buddha of Many Treasures and various Buddhas from the worlds throughout the universe: "You should now swear to protect the *Lotus Sutra.*" Encouraged by the Buddha's advice like sailing in the wind, listeners in the three meetings at two places* all swore in unison: 'We will protect those who practice the *Lotus Sutra* according to the words of the Buddha,' did they not? What happened to this vow?

"Having heard this oath in their presence, the Buddha of Many Treasures and numerous Buddhas from the worlds throughout the universe felt assured and returned to their respective worlds. It has been many years since Śākyamuni Buddha passed away. Therefore, it could be that although one who practices the *Lotus Sutra* exists today in the Latter Age of Degeneration in a remote land of Japan, such gods as the King of the Brahma Heaven, Indra, the sun and moon have forgotten their oath before the Buddha and do not protect him. To me, one who practices the *Lotus Sutra* in the Latter Age of Degeneration, it is merely a temporary grief. In my numerous lives since the remote past, I have often been a pheasant in front of a hawk, a frog before a snake, a rat before a cat, a monkey before a dog. As this world is as transient as a dream, I can reconcile myself to have been fooled by Buddhas, bodhisattvas and gods.

"The saddest thing to me, however, is for such heavenly beings as the King of the Brahma Heaven, Indra, the sun and moon and the Four Heavenly Kings to use up the good fortune of heaven and fall into the Hell of Incessant Suffering for their sin of not having protected one who practices the *Lotus Sutra*, who chants *Namu Myōhō Renge-kyō* and encounters persecution. As flowers are blown away by a storm, as it rains from the sky to the ground, and as it is stated in the sutra: 'He will go to the Hell of Incessant Suffering upon death,' they will all go to hell. It is indeed a pity.

"Even if they, supported by numerous Buddhas in all the worlds throughout the universe in the past, present and future, insist that they have no knowledge of such an oath made before the Buddha, I, Nichiren, will be their strong enemy. Unless the Buddha is unjust, I am sure that I will send the King of the Brahma Heaven, Indra, the sun and moon and the Four Heavenly Kings to the Hell of Incessant Suffering. If they are afraid of my eye and mouth, they had better carry out the oath before the Buddha immediately. The mouth of Nichiren…" (hereafter missing)

P.S. With gratitude I also received one box of barley, two *kammon* of coins, one bale each of *wakame* and *kachime* seaweeds, one bag each of dehydrated rice and roasted rice. I am so grateful that I feel like describing each in detail, but as I wrote about a number of important doctrines, I should lay down my brush now. I have written teachings of vital importance, so be careful not to reveal them to people in other sects.

Note

1. Historically, Emperor Antoku is believed to have been drowned in the Sea of Dannoura in the fourth year of the Juei Period (1185).

Senji-shō (ST 181)

Introduction

Nichiren Shōnin wrote *Senji-shō* in the sixth month of the first year in the Kenji Period (1275), when he was 53 years old. The original manuscript of this essay, designated an important cultural asset of Japan, is known to have consisted of 110 pages, of which 107 exist today at the Myōhokkeji Temple at Tamazawa in Mishima City, Shizuoka Prefecture. Of the missing parts, altogether two pages are kept separately at four temples including the Ryūhonji Temple of Kyoto.

The foreign invasion of Japan predicted by Nichiren in his *Risshō Ankoku-ron* proved true in the 10th month of the 11th year of the Bun'ei Period (1274) when Mongol troops invaded western Japan. At that critical moment, Nichiren could not sit and watch Japan fall, and began writing this essay. In it Nichiren declared that the only way to save Japan from annihilation was through the *Lotus Sutra* and that Nichiren himself was none other than the one who practices the *Lotus Sutra* entrusted by Śākyamuni Buddha to spread its teaching and save all the people in the Latter Age of Degeneration.

At the beginning of this writing, Nichiren discusses the "right time." Maintaining that the spread of the *Lotus Sutra* depends on the "time," Nichiren describes the history of Buddhism after the death of the Buddha during the three Ages of the True Dharma, the Semblance Dharma and the Latter Age of Degeneration, in the three lands of India, China and Japan, to prove that the "right time" for the spread of the *Lotus Sutra* is none other than the Latter Age of Degeneration.

As the Buddha's messenger entrusted to propagate the teaching of the *Lotus Sutra*, Nichiren harshly criticizes those who stand in his way and the evil teachings that confuse people and slander the True Dharma. Censuring the three sects of Pure Land, Zen and Shingon, especially the last mentioned, Nichiren derogatorily calls such masters as Kûkai, Ennin, Enchin, Annen, Genshin and Hōnen parasitic worms in one's bosom. With unwavering conviction that the great dharma of the *Lotus Sutra* is the only way to save Japan from national destruction and that he himself was the messenger of the Buddha, Nichiren dedicated his life to the dissemination of the Lotus teaching. He, therefore, expects all his disciples and followers to do the same: to practice the *Lotus Sutra* even at the cost of their lives

Selecting the Right Time:
A Tract by Nichiren, the Buddha's Disciple*

Buddhism and Time

To study Buddhism, first of all we must know the right time.*

In the past, Great Universal Wisdom Buddha* appeared in the world, but he did not preach at all for as long as 10 small *kalpa*. It is said in the *Lotus Sutra*, chapter seven, The Parable of a Magic City, "He sat in meditation for 10 small *kalpa*," and "Though begged to preach, the Buddha sat in silence because He knew the time was not yet ripe." Our Lord Śākyamuni Buddha did not expound the *Lotus Sutra* for more than 40 years.* As said in the sutra, chapter two, Expedients, it was because "the time was not ripe." Lao-tzu is said to have spent as long as 80 years in his mother's womb before he was born. Bodhisattva Maitreya,* future Lord Buddha of this *Sahā* World, is expected to stay in the inner chamber of the Tuṣita Heaven, *Tōsotsu-ten*, for as long as 5,670,000,000 years, waiting for the time to attain perfect enlightenment. As nightingales wait for summer to sing and roosters wait for dawn to crow, even beasts know the time. How much more should we choose the right time in practicing Buddhism?

When the Buddha preached the *Flower Garland Sutra* at the Hall of Enlightenment,* various Buddhas appeared from the worlds in 10 directions, and all great bodhisattvas gathered together. Moreover, the Great King of the Brahma Heaven, Indra, and the Four Heavenly Kings danced for joy. Eight kinds of gods and semi-gods such as dragon gods held their hands together in reverence. The wiser among ordinary men bent their ears to Him. And various bodhisattvas such as Moon of Emancipation, *Vimuki-candra*, who have attained enlightenment during their present lives, begged Him to preach. However, Śākyamuni did not even reveal the names of His two most important teachings: "Obtaining Buddhahood by men of the Two Vehicles, *śrāvaka* and *pratyekabuddha*" (*nijō-sabutsu*)* and "Śākyamuni's attaining Enlightenment in the eternal past" (*kuon-jitsujō*).* Nor did He expound the fundamental doctrines of the "becoming a Buddha with one's present body" (*sokushin-jōbutsu*)* and "3,000 existences contained in one thought" (*ichinen-sanzen*).* It was not that He did not speak of those doctrines because no one had the capacity* to understand them. It was solely because, as stated in the *Lotus Sutra,* chapter two, Expedients, "The time was not ripe."

When the *Lotus Sutra* was preached on Mt. Sacred Eagle, King Ajātaśatru,* the most unfilial man in the world, attended the assembly. Even Devadatta,* who had abused the True Dharma throughout his life, was guaranteed to be *Tennō,* Heavenly King Buddha, in the future. Furthermore, even though females were considered incapable of becoming a King of the Brahma Heaven, an Indra, a King of Devils, a Wheel-turning Noble King, or a Buddha, nevertheless a dragon girl* became a Buddha without changing her dragon-body. Attainment of Buddhahood by men of the Two Vehicles, and those with fixed nature* who had been considered doubtlessly incapable of becoming Buddhas, was as wondrous as a toasted seed germinating, flowering and bearing fruit. When Śākyamuni Buddha's "attaining Enlightenment in the eternal past" was revealed, the audience was so astonished as to wonder how a 100-year old man could be the son of a 25 year old man. The "3,000 existences contained in one thought" doctrine explained that unenlightened beings in the Nine Realms and enlightened ones in the Realm of the Buddha are one and inseparable, opening the way for the unenlightened to attain Buddhahood. Therefore, each letter of this sutra represents a wish-fulfilling gem* that pours out 10,000 treasures. Each phrase of it is the seed of Buddhahood. The preaching of these most profound teachings was not done because of the capacity of the audience, their intelligence to understand or faith to uphold them. It was because the time was ripe. The *Lotus Sutra,* chapter two, Expedients, therefore says: "Now is the time to expound the Mahayana teaching definitely."

Teaching, Capacity of People and Right Time

Question: Suppose this great dharma is preached to those whose intelligence and faith are not ready, ignorant people are bound to slander it, and as a result they would fall into evil realms. Isn't this the fault of he who preaches it?

Answer: Suppose a road was built, and someone got lost on the way. Can we blame the person who built the road for that? Or, suppose a patient refused to take the medicine a great doctor prescribed for him and died. Is this the fault of the doctor?

Question: It is said in the *Lotus Sutra,* fascicle two, chapter three, A Parable, "Do not preach this sutra to ignorant people." In the fourth fascicle, chapter 10, The Teacher of the Dharma, it declares: "Do not give it to others carelessly." The fifth fascicle, chapter 14, Peaceful Practices, further states: "This *Lotus Sutra* is the treasured teaching of Buddhas. This is supreme of all sutras. Keep it and refrain from expounding it for a long period of time." Don't these statements in the *Lotus Sutra* enjoin us not to preach unless the audience has sufficient intelligence and faith?

Throwing back the question: In the 20th chapter of the *Lotus Sutra*, Never-Despising Bodhisattva,* it is said that once there was a bodhisattva named Never-Despising, who bowed to anyone saying, "I respect you deeply." Some of the people with impure minds became angry, spoke ill of him and abused him saying, "What an ignorant monk he is!" They struck him with a stick or a piece of wood or a tile or a stone. Again, it is said in the 13th chapter, Encouragement for Keeping This Sutra,* "Ignorant people will speak ill of us, and threaten us with swords or sticks." These statements in the *Lotus Sutra* make clear that men such as Bodhisattva Never-Despising preached the True Dharma despite being spoken ill of, abused, and beaten. Would you say that they made a mistake in preaching?

Question: Those two sets of statements in the *Lotus Sutra* are as incompatible as water and fire. How am I supposed to accept this?

Answer: Grand Master T'ien-t'ai* says in his *Words and Phrases of the Lotus Sutra*, "It all depends on the situation." His disciple Grand Master Chang-an* states in the *Annotations on the Nirvana Sutra*, "Selection must be made carefully, without being one-sided." What they meant is that (1) preaching should be suspended sometimes when people are abusive; (2) but other times it would be better to preach even if people are abusive; (3) sometimes preaching should be suspended when most people are abusive although there are a few faithful people; (4) but sometimes preaching must be done even if all people are abusive.

When Śākyamuni Buddha first attained Perfect Enlightenment under the *bodhi* tree and began preaching the *Flower Garland Sutra,* such great bodhisattvas as Dharma Wisdom, Forest of Merit, Diamond Banner, Diamond Piṭaka, Mañjuśrī, Samantabhadra, Maitreya, and Moon of Emancipation gathered together. The crowd included also an incalculable number of such ordinary beings with great intelligence as the King of the Brahma Heaven, Indra, and the Four Heavenly Kings.

When He preached the Āgama sutras at Deer Park, a huge crowd appeared. This included His first five disciples: Kauṇḍinya, Kāśyapa* and 250 of his disciples, Śāriputra and 250 of his disciples. 80,000 gods also appeared. In both cases, however, the Buddha did not preach His true intention, the *Lotus Sutra*.

Next, while preaching the Hōdō sutras, at the earnest request of His father, King Śuddhodana, Śākyamuni Buddha visited the King in his royal palace and preached the *Meditation on the Buddha Sutra*. For His mother, the Buddha went up to the Trāyastriṃśa Heaven, where He preached the *Māyā Sutra* for 90 days.

What treasured teaching should He have concealed from His beloved parents? Nevertheless, He did not preach the *Lotus Sutra* for them. After all it was not because of the lack of understanding of the audience that He did not preach the sutra. It was because the time was not ripe.

Five 500-year Periods After the Death of the Buddha

Question: If so, when should the Hinayana or provisional sutras be preached, and when should the *Lotus Sutra* be preached?

Answer: We don't know. Even bodhisattvas, from the lowest 10 rankings to the highest, second only to the Buddhas, would not know clearly the capacity of people as well as the time. How can we, ordinary men* know?

Question: Can't we know at all?

Answer: Yes, we can. Contemplate the time and capacity of people through the Buddha-eye,* and observe the land illuminated by rays of the Buddha's wisdom as brilliant as the sun.

Question: What do you mean by that?

Answer: In the *Sutra of the Great Assembly*,* Śākyamuni Buddha speaks to Bodhisattva Moon Piṭaka, predicting the future ages after His death. According to this, during 500 years after the death of the Buddha there will be many who attain Buddhahood. The second 500 years will be the period of solid meditation in which many will study Buddhism and practice meditation. This will be the state of Buddhism during the first 1,000 years after the death of the Buddha.

The third 500 years will be the era in which people read sutras extensively to increase their knowledge. The fourth 500-year period will be the time when many people build temples and towers, trying to find happiness and virtue. This will be the state of Buddhism during the 2,000 years after the death of Śākyamuni. The fifth 500-year period will be a time of increasing disputes and quarrels within Buddhism itself, resulting in destruction of the pure dharma.

Many scholars have various interpretations of this prediction from the *Sutra of the Great Assembly* concerning the state of Buddhism during the five 500-year periods, together comprising 2,500 years after the death of the Buddha. Meditation Master Tao-ch'o* of T'ang China said: "Although both Mahayana and Hinayana Buddhism will flourish for 2,000 years following the death of Śākyamuni, namely during the Ages of the True Dharma and the Semblance Dharma, they will all perish during the Latter Age of Degeneration.* Then only those who believe in the Pure Land teaching and recite the name of the Buddha of Infinite Life will be able to go to the Pure Land of this Buddha, Amida, by cutting the chain of birth and death."

Hōnen* of Japan maintains that current Japanese Buddhism, which includes such Mahayana sutras such as *Lotus, Flower Garland,* and *Great Sun Buddha,* various Hinayana sutras, as well as such Buddhist schools as Tendai, Shingon, and Ritsu, is the pure dharma predicted in the *Sutra of the Great Assembly* to flourish during the 2,000-year Ages of the True and Semblance Dharmas. According to the prediction, however, they are to disappear during the Latter Age of Degeneration. Hōnen insists that even if someone practices those teachings in the Latter Age, no one will be able to escape the chain of birth and death. These teachings are what Bodhisattva Nāgārjuna's *Commentary on the Ten Stages* and Monk T'an-luan's* *Commentary on the Discourse on the Pure Land* call the "difficult way." According to Tao-ch'o, in his *Collection of Passages Concerning Rebirth in the Pure Land* "no one has ever attained Buddhahood" and according to Shan-tao,* in his *Praise of Rebirth in the Pure Land* "not even one out of 1,000 has attained Buddhahood" through this "difficult way." They insist that after the disappearance of those pure dharmas, the triple Pure Land sutras* and calling the name of the Buddha of Infinite Life will appear as the only great pure dharma to save the people of the time. They maintain those who practice calling the name of this Buddha in the Latter Age of Degeneration, no matter how evil and ignorant they may be, will all be able to be reborn in this Buddha's Pure Land without exception, 10 out of 10 and 100 out of 100. According to them, this is the only way to be reborn in the Pure Land of Bliss.

Thus Hōnen spread faith in the Buddha of Infinite Life saying: "Those who wish to be reborn in the Pure Land of Utmost Bliss should stop believing in all the Buddhist temples in Japan beginning with such temples as Enryakuji on Mt. Hiei, Tōji, Onjōji, and the seven great temples in Nara. Take back all the landed estates donated to them and donate them to the temples of the Buddha of Infinite Life. There is no doubt that such people will be reborn in this Buddha's Pure Land." As a result, people in Japan all have been his followers for 50 years. It also has been a long time since I, Nichiren, refuted this heresy.

The Spread of Buddhism in the Fifth 500-year Period

The fifth 500-year period, the period of destruction of the pure dharma referred to in the *Sutra of the Great Assembly,* is without doubt happening today. After the destruction of the pure dharma, however, the great pure dharma of *"Namu Myōhō Renge-kyō,"* the gist of the *Lotus Sutra,* should spread widely among all the people and subjects of 80,000 kings of 80,000 lands in the world, just as today in Japan people all recite the name of the Buddha of Infinite Life. This has been decided by the Buddha, so we must make it a reality.

Question: Do you have any proof for this?

Answer: It is said in the *Lotus Sutra,* fascicle seven, chapter 23, "It will spread throughout the world in the fifth 500-year period after the death of the Buddha, lest it should be lost." This means that the *Lotus Sutra* will spread in the period after the destruction of the pure dharma predicted in the *Sutra of the Great Assembly.* The *Lotus Sutra* also makes such references as: "those who uphold it in the evil world during the Latter Age of Degeneration" in fascicle six, chapter 17; "at the time when the dharma is about to disappear in the future latter age" in fascicle five, chapter 14; "even during the time of the Buddha much hatred and jealousy is raised against this sutra. How much more after His death!" in fascicle four, chapter 10; and "much hate exists toward this sutra in the world, making it difficult to uphold it" in fascicle five, chapter 14. Speaking of the fifth 500-year period after the death of the Buddha, namely, the period of increasing disagreements and quarrels, the *Lotus Sutra* in its seventh fascicle, chapter 23, declares: "Devils, devils' subjects, dragons, *yakṣa* demons, and *kumbhāṇḍa* devils will be trying to take advantage." It is stated in the *Sutra of the Great Assembly:* "Disputes and quarrels will arise within Buddhism itself." And in the *Lotus Sutra,* fascicle five, chapter 13: "Monks in the evil world will be cunning, flattering, and arrogant," "some monks will live in monasteries and appear to be practicing the true ways," and "devils will enter the bodies of those monks and cause them to abuse those who uphold the True Dharma."

These citations meant to say that a large number of great monks will be haunted by a devil's spirit all over the country in the fifth 500-year period. Suppose a wise man appears then. Those high priests haunted by a devil's spirit would induce the king and his ministers and populace into speaking ill of him, abusing him, beating him with sticks or pieces of wood, throwing stones or tiles at him, and banishing or even executing him. Then Śākyamuni Buddha, the Buddha of Many Treasures and Buddhas in all the worlds in 10 directions would order the great bodhisattvas appearing from underground,* who in turn would order the King of the Brahma Heaven, Indra, the sun, the moon, and the Four Heavenly Kings to inflict strange phenomena in the sky and natural calamities on earth.* If those kings do not heed the divine punishments, their neighboring countries would be ordered to chastise those evil kings and monks, resulting in the most terrible war the world has ever had.

Then all the people in the world living under the sun and moon, desirous of the welfare of their countries or of themselves, would pray in vain to all Buddhas and bodhisattvas. Finally, believing in the poor monk whom they have hated, an incalculable number of high priests, 80,000 great kings, and all the people would bow low with their heads touching the ground and holding their hands together in reverence, reciting *"Namu Myōhō Renge-kyō, Homage to the Lotus Sutra!"* It would be just as when the Buddha revealed the eighth of His 10 supernatural powers* in the 21st chapter of the *Lotus Sutra,* The Supernatural Powers of the Tathāgata,that all the people without exception in all the worlds throughout the universe faced this *Sahā* World, resoundingly reciting in unison *"Homage to Śākyamuni Buddha! Homage to Śākyamuni Buddha! Homage to the Lotus Sutra! Homage to the Lotus Sutra!"*

The Spread of the Lotus Sutra Predicted by Teachers in China and Japan

Question: I see you have solid proofs in scriptures. Have T'ien-t'ai, Miao-lê* and Dengyō* also predicted the same?

Answer: Your question is out of order. You may ask for scriptural proofs to back up statements in later commentaries, but you may not look for proofs in later commentaries when statements in sutras are clear. Are you going to side with commentaries against sutras in case you find them contradictory?

Inquirer Insists: You are absolutely right, but as an ordinary man I feel that the sutras were preached thousands of years ago, while commentaries are closer to us because they are works of later people. As such if what is said in commentaries are made clear, I may be able to deepen my faith in sutras.

Answer: Since your question is so sincere, I shall cite from some commentaries. Grand Master T'ien-t'ai states in his *Words and Phrases of the Lotus Sutra,* "The wonderful way of the *Lotus Sutra* will spread benefit far into the fifth 500-year period!" Grand Master Miao-lê explains it in his *Annotations on the Words and Phrases of the Lotus Sutra:* "Not necessarily will there be no divine favor of the *Lotus Sutra* at the beginning of the Latter Age." Grand Master Dengyō declares in his *Treatise on the Protection of the Nation:* "The Age of the True Dharma and that of the Semblance Dharma are about to end, and the Latter Age of Degeneration is around the corner. This is the time for the One Vehicle teaching of the Lotus to spread. How can we say this? We know it because it is stated in chapter 14 of the *Lotus Sutra,* Peaceful Practices, that it should be spread at the time when the dharma is about to disappear in the latter world." He also says in his *Outstanding Principles of the Lotus Sutra:*

> "The time now is toward the end of the Age of the Semblance Dharma and the beginning of the Latter Age of Degeneration. The place is east of T'ang China and west of Katsu[1] when people live in the world of defilement and corruption, full of disputes and quarrels. The *Lotus Sutra,* chapter 10, states that much hatred and jealousy existed even during the lifetime of Śākyamuni Buddha, not to speak of after His death. This is a meaningful statement indeed!"

According to Buddhist scriptures, the world goes through four *kalpa*,* periods of construction, continuance, destruction, and emptiness, each of which consists of 20 small *kalpa*. In the period of continuance, the average human lifespan increases by a year per century from 10 years until it reaches the maximum human longevity of 84,000 years. Thereafter the human life grows shorter by a year per century until it reaches the minimum average human life span of 10 years. Now, Śākyamuni Buddha was born to this world during the ninth small *kalpa*, within the *kalpa* of continuance, when the human life span was decreasing to 100 years. The 50 years of Śākyamuni's appearance in this world, the 2,000-year period of Ages of the True Dharma and the Semblance Dharma, and the 10,000 years of the Latter Age of Degeneration are all included in this period, during which human longevity decreases from 100 years to the minimum of 10 years. It includes two periods in which the *Lotus Sutra* flourishes: the last eight years of Śākyamuni Buddha and the first 500 years of the Latter Age of Degeneration after His extinction. Grand Masters T'ien-t'ai, Miao-lê and Dengyō missed the preaching of the *Lotus Sutra* by the Buddha, nor were they able to be born in the Latter Age after His death. Regretting their misfortune for being born in between the two occasions, those grand masters made the statements cited above, wishing to have been born in the Latter Age.

This is like Hermit Asita's lament. Seeing the birth of Prince Siddhārtha, the Indian hermit deplored: "Being over 90 years old, I will not be able to live long enough to see the Prince attain Buddhahood in this world. Since I will be reborn in the realm of non-form,[2] I will not be able to attend Śākyamuni's preachings for 50 years in this world. Nor will I be able to be reborn after His death in the Age of the True Dharma, the Semblance Dharma, or the Latter Age of Degeneration." Those who have aspiration for enlightenment should be glad to see and hear these comments. Those who care for future lives should rather be born as common people today in the Latter Age than great kings during the 2,000-year period after the death of Śākyamuni Buddha, the Age of the True Dharma and that of the Semblance Dharma. How could they not believe in this? They should rather be suffering from leprosy in the Latter Age reciting *"Namu Myōhō Renge-kyō*, Homage to the *Lotus Sutra*" than to be the revered chief abbot of the Enryakuji Temple, grand temple of the Tendai school of Buddhism, during the Age of the Semblance Dharma. Emperor Wu of Liang in ancient China prayed: "I would rather be Devadatta, who sank to the worst Hell of Incessant Suffering but who eventually was able to attain Buddhahood through the *Lotus Sutra*, than be Hermit Udraka-rāmaputra, who was able to be born in heaven but never succeeded in attaining Buddhahood."

Buddhism in India in the Age of the True Dharma

Question: Besides Grand Masters T'ien-t'ai, Miao-lê and Dengyō, did such great Indian commentators as Nāgārjuna and Vasubandhu express similar opinions?

Answer: Nāgārjuna and Vasubandhu felt the same way, but they did not express it.

Question: Why not?

Answer: There are many reasons. First of all, people would not understand them. In the second place, the time was not ripe for them to speak up. In the third place, being disciples of Buddhas in manifestation *(shakke),** they were not entrusted to spread the *Lotus Sutra* in the Latter Age of Degeneration.

Question: I would like to hear more about this.

Answer: The Age of the True Dharma began on the 16th day of the second month, a day after the death of Śākyamuni Buddha. Entrusted by the Buddha, Venerable Kāśyapa spread His teaching for 20 years. In turn he was succeeded by Venerable Ānanda, Śāṇakasvāsa, Upagupta, and Dhrtoka, for 20 years each. During these 100 years they spread only the Hinayana teachings without even mentioning names of the Mahayana sutras, not to speak of spreading the *Lotus Sutra*. They were succeeded by several men such as Mikkaka, Buddha-nandiya, Buddhamitra, Pārśva, and Puṇyayaśas, who mostly spread Hinayana Buddhism during the first 500 years of the Age of the True Dharma. Although it was not that they did not preach the Mahayana teachings at all, they did not make much effort in spreading them. This is the first 500-year period referred to in the *Sutra of the Great Assembly* as the period of solid liberation.

During the latter half of the Age of the True Dharma, namely between 600 and 1,000 years after the death of the Buddha, a dozen or so men continued the succession of the dharma: Bodhisattva Aśvaghoṣa, Venerable Kapimāla, Bodhisattva Nāgārjuna, Bodhisattva Kāṇa-deva, Venerable Rāhulabhadra, Saṅghanandi, Saṅghayhośas, Kumāralāta, Jayana, Vasubandhu, Manura, Haklena-yaśa, and Siṃha. These dozen or so reverends at first studied non-Buddhist teachings before studying the Hinayana sutras, which they later refuted completely when they studied the Mahayana sutras.

Although they refuted the Hinayana sutras with the Mahayana sutras, they did not clarify the relative importance of the *Lotus Sutra* and other Mahayana sutras. They seem to have talked about it a little, but they did not clarify such fundamental doctrines as the "20 profound doctrines preached in the theoretical and essential sections of the *Lotus Sutra*," "obtaining Buddhahood by Two Vehicles,"* "attaining Enlightenment by Śākyamuni in the eternal past,"* "superiority of the Lotus among all the Buddhist scriptures preached, being preached, and going to be preached,"* "100 realms and 1,000 aspects of existence,"* and "3,000 existences contained in one thought."* They only touched upon them as vaguely as pointing a finger at the moon. They wrote a little about them but did not even touch upon such important doctrines of the Lotus as the "beginning and ending of the Buddha's guidance,"* "eternal relationship between the Buddha and His disciples," and "attainment of Buddhahood by all people." This was the state of Buddhism during the latter half, 500 years, of the Age of the True Dharma, referred to in the *Sutra of the Great Assembly* as the period of solid meditation.

After 1,000 years of the Age of the True Dharma, Buddhism was still prevalent all over India. However, Buddhism reached a state of confusion with Mahayana Buddhism being refuted by Hinayana Buddhism, or the true teaching being concealed by provisional ones. As a result less and less people attained Buddhahood, while an incalculable number of people ended up in evil realms by slandering Buddhism.

Buddhism in China During the Age of the Semblance Dharma

After 1,000 years of the Age of the True Dharma, in the 15th year during the Age of the Semblance Dharma, Buddhism spreading eastward reached China. During the first century of the first half, 500 years, of the Age of the Semblance Dharma, Chinese Taoism and Indian Buddhism fought for supremacy, neither side having the upper hand. Even if the issue had been decided, Chinese faith in Buddhism was not firmly established yet. Therefore, it was feared that if Buddhism was divided into Mahayana and Hinayana, provisional and true,* or exoteric and esoteric,* people might suspect Buddhism for its lack of uniformity and desert it for non-Buddhist scriptures.* This was the reason why Mo-t'eng (Mātaṅga) and Chu Fa-lan, first transmitters of Buddhism to China, did not differentiate Mahayana from Hinayana Buddhism. Nor did they talk about true and provisional teachings although they knew of them.

Afterwards, during the five dynasties of Wei, Chin, Sung, Ch'i, and Liang, Chinese Buddhism was in disarray with disputes continuing between Mahayana and Hinayana, provisional and true, and exoteric and esoteric Buddhism. Since no one knew which was superior, everybody, from the emperor down to his subjects, grew increasingly suspicious. Chinese Buddhism was split into 10 schools: three Southern and seven Northern.* The San-shih, Ssŭ-shih, and Wu-shih schools in the South and Wu-shih, Pan-wan, Ssŭ-tsung, Wu-tsung, Lu-tsung, Erhtsung-ta-ch'eng and I-tun schools in the North fought among themselves like fire and water, stubbornly insisting on their own contentions. However, they were in a general agreement that among all the holy teachings of the Buddha's lifetime* the *Flower Garland Sutra* ranked first, the *Nirvana Sutra* second, and thirdly the *Lotus Sutra*. They insisted that compared to such sutras as the *Āgama*, *Wisdom*, *Vimalakīrti*, and *Shiyaku*, the *Lotus Sutra* was the true and righteous sutra, thoroughly revealing the truth.* However, compared to the *Nirvana Sutra*, they claimed, the *Lotus* was a false sutra preached by a temporary Buddha without revealing all the truth.

During the Ch'ên and Sui dynasties, roughly between 450 years and 500 years or so after the introduction of Buddhism to Later Han China, there lived a monk called Chih-i. Later called Grand Master T'ien-t'ai, he refuted the false teachings of three Southern and seven Northern schools, and he advocated a theology stating that the *Lotus Sutra* ranks first among all the holy sutras, the *Nirvana Sutra* second, and the *Flower Garland Sutra* third. This was the first 500-year period of the Age of the Semblance Dharma, which is referred to in the *Sutra of the Great Assembly* as the period of wide reading and discussions.

In the latter 500-year period of the Age of the Semblance Dharma, Venerable Hsüan-chuang visited India during the reign of Emperor T'ai-tsung in the early T'ang dynasty. He spent 19 years[3] visiting various temples in 130 lands, meeting many scholars, and mastering the heart of 80,000 holy teachings of the Buddha, grouped in the twelve kinds of scriptures. Among them, he specially studied the two schools of Fa-hsiang (Hossō)* and San-lun (Sanron).* Of the two, Fa-hsiang, that is Mahayana Buddhism, originated by Maitreya and Asaṅga in the past, was transmitted to Hsüan-chuang by Master Sīlabhadra. Hsüan-chuang brought it back to China and presented it to Emperor T'ai-tsung.

This Fa-hsiang school maintains:

> "Buddhism must be preached according to the intellectual capacity of people and firmness of their faith. For those who are suited to the One Vehicle* teaching, it is preached that Three Vehicle* teachings for *śrāvaka*, *pratyekabuddha* and bodhisattvas are expedient, and that only the One Vehicle teaching is the true teaching. This is the teaching of the *Lotus Sutra*. However, for others who are suited to the Three Vehicle teachings, it is preached that the Three Vehicle teachings are true teachings whereas the One Vehicle teaching is merely expedient. This is the teaching of the *Revealing the Profound and Secret Sutra** and the *Srīmālā Sutra*. Grand Master T'ien-t'ai did not understand this."

T'ang T'ai-tsung was a wise emperor. Not only did his fame spread over all the lands under heaven, the entire world knew that he was superior even to such ancient sage rulers as the Three Emperors and Five Rulers. He was a wise ruler who not only controlled the entire land of China, but also swayed more than 1,800 lands from Kao-ch'ang in the west to Koguryô in the east. He was respected inside and outside the empire. Hsüan-chuang was revered most by this great Emperor of T'ang. Therefore, not even one T'ien-t'ai scholar criticized Hsüan-chuang. As a result, the true teachings of the Lotus Sutra have already been forgotten by the entire people of China.

During the reign of Emperor Kao-tsung, who was T'ai-tsung's crown prince, and Empress Wu, who was Kao-tsung's stepmother, a monk named Fa-tsang appeared. Having seen the T'ien-t'ai school eroded by the Fa-hsiang school, he chose the *Flower Garland Sutra,* which had been rejected by Grand Master T'ien-t'ai as not having revealed the whole truth. Fa-tsang advocated that among all the sutras preached by the Buddha in His lifetime the *Flower Garland Sutra* ranks first, the *Lotus* second, and the *Nirvana* third.

In the fourth and eighth years of the K'ai-yüan Era (716, 720) during the reign of Emperor Hsüan-tsung, four generations after T'ai-tsung, Tripiṭaka Masters Śubhākarasiṃha* (Shan-wu-wei), Vajrabodhi* (Chin-kang-chi), and Amoghavajra (Pu-k'ung)* came from India. They brought with them the *Great Sun Buddha Sutra,** the *Diamond Peak Sutra,** and the *Sutra on the Act of Perfection** and established the Chen-yen (Shingon) school in China. According to the theology of this school, there are two kinds of teaching in Buddhism. One is the exoteric teachings such as the *Flower Garland Sutra* and the *Lotus Sutra* preached by Śākyamuni Buddha. The other is the esoteric teaching of the *Great Sun Buddha Sutra* preached by the Great Sun Buddha. Although the *Lotus* is prime among exoteric sutras, Shingon theology declares that it does not fully reveal the truth. The *Lotus Sutra* is somewhat similar to the Great Sun Buddha's esoteric teaching in their ultimate doctrines, but it lacks finger signs and mantric words of Shingon mysticism. Since the *Lotus* does not preach all three mystic practices, bodily, verbal, and mental, they say it does not wholly reveal the truth.

Thus the three schools of Chinese Buddhism, Fa-hsiang (Dharma Characteristics), Hua-yen (Flower Garland), and Chen-yen (True Word), were all attacking the T'ien-t'ai Lotus school. However, since there was no man as wise as Grand Master T'ien-t'ai within the Lotus school at that time, while feeling their attack was unreasonable, nobody stood in public to declare so. As a result, everyone, from the king and his ministers to all his subjects, was confused about Buddhism, blocking the way for attaining Buddhahood. This was the state of Buddhism during the first 200 years in the latter half, 500 years, of the Age of the Semblance Dharma.

Buddhism in Japan During the Age of the Semblance Dharma

After 400 years or so from the beginning of the Age of the Semblance Dharma, monks, nuns, and all the scriptures of Buddhism together with the wooden statue of Lord Śākyamuni, were sent from Paekche in Korea to Japan. This was towards the end of the Liang and the beginning of the Ch'ên dynasties in China, and during the reign of Emperor Kimmei in Japan, the 30th ruler of Japan counting from Emperor Jimmu. Then, Prince Shōtoku, the first son of Emperor Yōmei, and grandson of Emperor Kimmei, not only spread Buddhism but also designated the *Lotus Sutra,* the *Vimalakīrti Sutra,* and the *Śrīmālā Sutra* to be the fundamental dharmas for pacification of the country.

Afterwards, during the reign of Emperor Kōtoku, the 37th sovereign of Japan, Bishop Kanroku transmitted the two schools of Sanron and Jōjitsu from Paekche, and Monk Dōshō introduced the Hossō and Kusha schools from China. During the reign of Emperor Genshō, the 44th emperor of Japan, *Tripiṭaka* Master Śubhākarasiṃha (Shan-wu-wei) transmitted the *Great Sun Buddha Sutra* from India, but he returned to China without spreading it in Japan. In the reign of the 45th ruler, Emperor Shōmu, Monk Shinjō introduced the Kegon (Flower Garland) school from Silla, and transmitted it to Bishop Ryōben and Emperor Shōmu, causing them to build the Great Buddha of the Tōdaiji Temple. During the same reign, Venerable Chien-chên* (Ganjin) of T'ang China transmitted the Tendai (T'ien-t'ai) and Ritsu* (Lü) schools of Buddhism. Of the two, Chien-chên spread Ritsu Buddhism in Japan and established the Hinayana precept platform at the Tōdai-ji Temple. However, he never even mentioned the Lotus school before his death.

After that, during the reign of Emperor Kammu, the 50th emperor, 800 years after the beginning of the Age of the Semblance Dharma, a monk called Saichō appeared, who was later known as Grand Master Dengyō. At first, he studied the six schools of Buddhism, Sanron, Hossō, Kegon, Kusha, Jōjitsu, and Ritsu, as well as Zen Buddhism, from such masters as Bishop Gyōhyō. Meanwhile, he himself established the Kokushōji Temple, later renamed the Enryakuji Temple, on Mt. Hiei, There he checked basic sutras and commentaries of the six schools against the interpretations by scholars of those schools. He found many discrepancies between interpretations of scholars and the sutras and commentaries on which they were based. Moreover, they produced so many false opinions that he felt that all those who believed in them would fall into the three evil realms: hell, the realm of hungry spirits, and that of beasts.

Additionally, Saichō found that those scholars of the six schools each boastfully claimed mastery of the true teaching of the *Lotus Sutra* without actually mastering it. He tormented himself thinking: "If I point this out, there will be disputes. If I keep silent, I will be going against the Buddha's warning." Fearful of the Buddha's warning, he finally appealed to Emperor Kammu, who was astonished and ordered the scholars of the six schools to meet Saichō in debate. At the beginning their banner of self-pride waved as high as a mountain and their evil thoughts were more vicious than poisonous snakes. However, they finally had to surrender to Saichō in front of the Emperor, and the six schools and seven temples all became his disciples. It was just like the time those scholars from Northern and Southern China became the disciples of Grand Master T'ien-t'ai after being defeated in debate by him in front of the Emperor of Ch'ên.

While Grand Master T'ien-t'ai's comparison of the Lotus to other sutras was limited to the areas of meditation *(jō)* and wisdom *(e)*, without covering the area of observing precepts *(kai)*, Grand Master Dengyō refuted the specific granting of Hinayana precepts and performed the ceremony for the specific granting of Mahayana precepts* according to the *Brahma-net Sutra* for eight monks of the six schools in Nara. In addition, Grand Master Dengyō established the "perfect and sudden" Lotus precept platform on Mt. Hiei for the granting-the-precepts ceremony. Therefore, the "perfect and sudden" specific granting-the-precepts ceremony on Mt. Hiei was not only the first of its kind in Japan, but also the first ever held in India, China, and the world for over 1,800 years since Śākyamuni performed it on Mt. Sacred Eagle.

In this sense, Grand Master Dengyō's accomplishments were greater than those of Nāgārjuna, Vasubandhu, T'ien-t'ai, and Miao-lê. Not a single monk of Japanese Buddhism today — including those of the Tōji Temple, the Onjōji Temple, the seven great temples at Nara, the eight schools of Buddhism, and those of the Pure Land, Zen, and Ritsu schools — was opposed to these "perfect and sudden" precepts of Grand Master Dengyō. Though Buddhist monks in the entire land of China seemed to be disciples of T'ien-t'ai as far as perfect meditation and wisdom are concerned, since there was no platform for the "perfect and sudden" precept established in China, some Chinese monks may not have been disciples of T'ien-t'ai in this regard. In Japan, on the other hand, Buddhist monks who were not disciples of Grand Master Dengyō were either non-Buddhists or villains.

As for the comparative superiority between T'ien-t'ai (Tendai) and Chen-yen (Shingon) Buddhism in China and Japan, Grand Master Dengyō knew this personally, but such public debates in the presence of the emperor as in the case between the six schools of Nara and the Tendai school were not held. Perhaps because of that, all of Japan after the time of Grand Master Dengyō, beginning with the Tōji Temple, seven great temples of Nara, Onjōji Temple, and everybody from the emperor down to the people, believed that the Shingon school was superior to the Tendai school. Therefore, it was only during the time of Grand Master Dengyō that the Tendai-Lotus school was regarded to be the prime school of Buddhism. This was towards the end of the Age of the Semblance Dharma, referred to in the *Sutra of the Great Assembly* as the period of solid temple construction. It was not yet the fifth 500-year period, the Latter Age, in which disputes and quarrels would be rampant within the Buddhist world, and the true teaching of the Buddha would disappear.

Japanese Buddhism in the Latter Age of Degeneration

We have been in the Latter Age for over 200 years now, and this is the time when the *Sutra of the Great Assembly* predicted disputes and quarrels within Buddhism would be rampant and the true teaching of the Buddha would disappear. If this prediction by the Buddha is true, this would be the time for a world filled with fighting. I heard that the entire land of China, 360 states and 260 provinces, have been conquered by the Mongols. I heard also that the capital of the Sung dynasty had already been destroyed, while its two emperors, Hui-tsung and Ch'in-tsung, who had been taken captives by northern barbarians, died in the land of the Tartars. Chased out of Ch'ang-an, Emperor Kao-tsung, grandson of Emperor Hui-tsung, has been living in a temporary capital, Lin-an, Hangchow today, for several years now without seeing Ch'ang-an again. Over 600 lands of Koryô, as well as Silla and Paekche in Korea were all attacked by the great Mongol emperor just as today in Japan, the islands of Iki, Tsushima, and Kyushu are under fire. The Buddha's prediction foretelling the time of disputes and quarrels is proving to be as certain as the ebb and flow of the ocean!

Looking at things from this angle, is there any doubt about the spread of the *Lotus Sutra*, the true teaching of the Buddha, all over Japan and the world following the period of the disappearance of the True Dharma predicted in the *Sutra of the Great Assembly*? The *Sutra of the Great Assembly* was preached by the Buddha, but it is a quasi-Mahayana sutra. It does not show the true way to cut the chain of birth and death and attain Buddhahood. Therefore, we cannot claim it to be the true sutra for those who have not heard the *Lotus Sutra*. Nevertheless, does not the sutra seem exactly like the *Lotus Sutra* in describing the transmigration of beings born in the four modes of birth[4] in the six base realms[5] throughout the lives in the past, present, and future?*

Moreover, it was in reference to the *Lotus Sutra* that Śākyamuni Buddha declared in the second chapter, Expedients, "He would reveal His true intention," and that the Buddha of Many Treasures attested it to be all true, and all the Buddhas throughout the universe declared it to be true by reaching the Brahma Heaven with their long, wide tongues.[6] His never-lying tongue touching the highest heaven in the realm of form,[7] Śākyamuni Buddha again declared to the King of the Brahma Heaven, Indra, the sun god, the moon god, the Four Heavenly Kings, and dragon gods: "In the fifth 500-year period, when all the teachings of the Buddha are about to disappear, Superior-Practice Bodhisattva* will be entrusted with the five ideograms of *myō*, *hō*, *ren*, *ge*, and *kyō*, *Sutra of the*

Lotus Flower of the Wonderful Dharma, as the cure for those slanderers and non-believers of Buddhism who suffer from white leprosy." How could these words of the Buddha be false? Even if the earth turned upside down, high mountains crumbled, summer did not follow spring, the sun set in the east, and the moon fell on the earth, there would be no mistake about this.

Persecution of Those Who Practice the Lotus Sutra

If there is no mistake about the words of the Buddha, the Buddha of Many Treasures and all the Buddhas throughout the universe, how can the king of Japan, his vassals and all the people feel at peace abusing, speaking ill of, banishing and striking me, Nichiren, and inflicting much suffering on my disciples and followers? After all I, as a messenger of the Buddha, am only trying to spread *"Namu Myōhō Renge-kyō"* in this period of disputes and quarrels. With my saying this, ignorant people might think that I, Nichiren, am cursing the entire land of Japan. Actually, however, those who spread the *Lotus Sutra* in Japan are parents of all the Japanese people. Grand Master Chang-an's *Annotations on the Nirvana Sutra* teaches us that pointing out a man's mistake to help him get rid of it was doing him a favor. Then, I, Nichiren, am the parent of the reigning emperor of Japan. For followers of the Buddha of Infinite Life, Zen Buddhists, and Shingon monks, I am the teacher and master. Nevertheless, everyone in Japan does me harm, from the emperor down to the populace. How do you expect the sun and moon to shine over their heads, or the earth god to sustain their feet?

When Devadatta struck Śākyamuni Buddha, the earth trembled and threw out flames. When the anti-Buddhist King Mihilakula beheaded Venerable Siṃha, his right hand fell off still holding the sword. Within half a year after Emperor Hui-tsung of the Sung dynasty banished *Tripiṭaka* Master Fa-tao to the South of the River with the mark of a branding iron on his face, the emperor became a captive of barbarians. The imminent attack on Japan by Mongols could be the same divine punishment! Even if all the soldiers in all of India are mobilized and even if the Surrounding Iron Mountains are fortified, you cannot defend Japan. All the people in Japan are bound to suffer from the calamity of war. Then you will know whether or not I, Nichiren, truly practice the *Lotus Sutra.*

Lord Śākyamuni declared that those who speak ill of and abuse a propagator of the *Lotus Sutra* in the latter-day period of the evil world would be many hundreds of thousands of billions times more sinful than those who harm the Buddha for as long as a *kalpa.*[8] Nevertheless, the sovereign of Japan and his people persistently harbor enmity against such a propagator more than against their parents' enemies and their enemies from previous lives, and revile him more than they do traitors and murderers. Yet the earth does not split open to swallow them or thunder does not shatter them into bits. I wonder why?

Is it because I, Nichiren, am not one who truly practices the *Lotus Sutra*? If so, it is regrettable indeed. How sad it is for me to be persistently accused by everyone, leaving no time for rest in this life and falling into evil realms in the next life! Also, if I, Nichiren, am not one who truly practices the *Lotus Sutra*, who then is the upholder of the One Vehicle teaching, the *Lotus Sutra*? Is Hōnen, who advised people to discard the *Lotus Sutra* in his *Collection of Passages on the Nembutsu*, Shan-tao, who said in the *Praise of Rebirth in the Pure Land* that not even one out of 1,000 people can attain Buddhahood through the *Lotus Sutra*, or Tao-ch'o who declared in the *Collection of Passages Concerning Rebirth in the Pure Land* that no one attains Buddhahood by means of the *Lotus Sutra*. Do any of them practice the *Lotus Sutra*? Or, is Grand Master Kōbō, who stated in his *Treatise on the Ten Stages of Mind* that practicing the *Lotus Sutra* was merely a joke, is he one who practices the *Lotus Sutra*?

It is preached in the *Lotus Sutra* that we must uphold it and propagate it in the 17th and 11th chapters respectively. What does propagating this sutra mean? As it is said in the 14th chapter that the *Lotus Sutra* is supreme of all sutras, only those who insist that the *Lotus Sutra* is superior to such sutras as the *Great Sun Buddha*, *Flower Garland*, *Nirvana*, and *Wisdom*, truly practice the *Lotus Sutra*. If this is so, those who practice the *Lotus Sutra*, except for Grand Master Dengyō and I, Nichiren, have not existed for more than 700 years since Buddhism was introduced to Japan. I have been wondering why those who abuse and speak ill of me, one who truly practices the *Lotus Sutra*, are left unpunished. I now know, however, why their "heads have not been split into seven pieces" or their "mouths have not been sealed" as predicted in the 26th and 14th chapters of the sutra. Such punishments are relatively light and concern only a few people.

In the whole world, Nichiren is primary among those who practice the *Lotus Sutra*. Those who abuse me, hate me, and others who side with such people, should suffer from the most severe calamities in the world. The great earthquake of the Shōka Era* that shook all of Japan and the great comet of the Bun'ei Era* that ran across the sky were such punishments. Think on this carefully! Many have harmed those who practice Buddhism after the death of Śākyamuni Buddha, but calamities as severe as the ones we have now never occurred before. This means that never before has there been a person admonishing all the people to recite *"Namu Myōhō Renge-kyō."* Is there anyone in the whole world who can see eye to eye, and stand shoulder to shoulder with me, to evaluate the merits of spreading the *Lotus Sutra*?

The Lotus Sutra During the Ages of
the True Dharma and the Semblance Dharma

Question: In the Age of the True Dharma, the intelligence of the people and their faith were inferior to those who lived during the time of the Buddha, but they were superlative compared to those in the Semblance and Latter Ages. And yet why was not the *Lotus Sutra* spread at the beginning of the Age of the True Dharma? After all, was it not in the 1,000-year period of the Age of the True Dharma that such great Buddhist leaders as Aśvaghoṣa, Nāgārjuna, Deva, and Asaṅga appeared, and Bodhisattva Vasubandhu, author of 1,000 tracts, wrote the *Commentary on the Lotus Sutra,* declaring the sutra to be first among all sutras? According to *Tripiṭaka* Master Paramārtha, furthermore, more than 50 people propagated the *Lotus* in India, and Vasubandhu was only one of them. Does this not mean that the *Lotus Sutra* was widely spread during the Age of the True Dharma?

At about the middle of the Age of the Semblance Dharma, Grand Master T'ien-t'ai, appearing in China, wrote the 30 fascicled triple work of the *Profound Meaning of the Lotus Sutra,* the *Words and Phrases of the Lotus Sutra,* and the *Great Concentration and Insight,* revealing the heart of the *Lotus Sutra.* Toward the end of the Age of the Semblance Dharma, Grand Master Dengyō appeared in Japan, and spread the perfect meditation and perfect wisdom of the *Lotus Sutra* transmitted from Grand Master T'ien-t'ai. Not only did he achieve that, he also established the great "perfect and sudden" precept platform on Mt. Hiei, making Japan entirely the land of the perfect precepts, where everyone from the emperor down to the populace looked up to the Enryakuji Temple as their leader. Does it not mean that the *Lotus Sutra* was widely spread in the Age of the Semblance Dharma?

Answer: Although scholars in the world often say that the Buddha preached according to the intelligence and faith of the audience, actually it is not so according to the Buddha. If great dharmas are to be preached for those with superior intelligence and faith, why is it that the *Lotus Sutra* was not preached upon attainment of Buddhahood by Śākyamuni? Mahayana sutras should have been spread during the first half, 500 years, of the Age of the True Dharma. If great dharmas are to be preached for close relations, the Buddha should have preached the *Lotus Sutra* instead of such quasi-Mahayana sutras as the *Meditation on the Buddha Sutra* and the *Māyā Sutra* to his father, King Śuddhodana, and mother, Queen Māyā. If secret teachings are not to be revealed to those evil people without close relation to and slanderers of the True Dharma, Monk Virtue Consciousness* should not have preached the *Nirvana Sutra* to those numerous violators of the precepts of the Buddha. Or, why did Bodhisattva

Never-Despising* preach the *Lotus Sutra* to slanderers of the True Dharma? Therefore, I think it a great mistake to say that dharmas are preached taking the intelligence and faith of the audience into consideration.

Question: If it is so, did not such great commentators of Buddhism as Nāgārjuna and Vasubandhu, who appeared in the Age of the True Dharma, preach the truth of the *Lotus Sutra*?

Answer: No, they did not.

Question: What kind of Buddhism did they preach?

Answer: They preached quasi-Mahayana exoteric and esoteric sutras such as the *Flower Garland Sutra*, Hōdō sutras, the *Wisdom Sutra*, and the *Great Sun Buddha Sutra*, but not the teaching of the *Lotus Sutra*.

Question: How do you know?

Answer: It is not easy to know the truth, because not all the religious tracts produced by Bodhisattva Nāgārjuna, amounting to as many as 300,000 verses, were transmitted to China and Japan. However, we can conjecture what he said in his commentaries left in India from those brought to China such as the *Commentary on the Ten Stages*, the *Middle Doctrine*, and the *Great Wisdom Discourse*.*

Question: Among those tracts by Nāgārjuna left behind in India, are there not any superior to those brought over to China?

Answer: I dare not conjecture about Bodhisattva Nāgārjuna, because the Buddha predicts in the Sutra of Transmission of the Buddhist Teaching that after His death a man called Bodhisattva Nāgārjuna will appear in Southern India, expressing his basic ideas in the *Middle Doctrine*. And in India as many as 70 branch schools descended from Bodhisattva Nāgārjuna exist with 70 great commentators, all of whom regard the *Middle Doctrine* as the basic canon. The gist of the *Middle Doctrine*, 27 chapters in four fascicles, is the four-phrase verse saying, "Everything is begotten by causes and conditions, which is consistent with the Triple Truth[9] of emptiness, temporariness, and the middle path." This four-phrase verse stands for the Four Doctrinal Teachings* and Triple Truth of the Kegon, Hōdō and Hannya doctrines, but it does not go as far as to reveal the perfect and interfused Triple Truth preached in the *Lotus Sutra*.

Question: Has there ever been anybody else who also asserted this?

Answer: T'ien-t'ai says in his *Profound Meaning of the Lotus Sutra*, "The *Lotus Sutra* is so profound that the *Middle Doctrine* cannot be compared to it." He also states in the *Great Concentration and Insight*, "Vasubandhu and Nāgārjuna deep in their hearts knew exactly the teaching of the *Lotus Sutra*, but outwardly they preached as they saw to fit the time." Explaining what is meant by T'ien-t'ai in the *Profound Meaning of the Lotus Sutra*, Miao-lê declares in his *Commentary on the Profound Meaning of the Lotus Sutra*, "No one can be compared to the *Lotus Sutra* in rectifying the fallacies of the various sutras and revealing the truths." Then in the *Additional Annotations to the Three Major Works of T'ien-t'ai*, Ts'ung-i interprets T'ien-t'ai's words in the *Great Concentration and Insight*, "Both Nāgārjuna and Vasubandhu are not comparable to T'ien-t'ai in perceiving the true intent of the Buddha."

The Treatise on the Aspiration for Buddhahood and Pu-k'ung's Fallacies

Question: Toward the end of the T'ang dynasty, *Tripiṭaka* Master Pu-k'ung (Amoghavajra) brought from India to China a fascicle of a tract entitled the *Treatise on the Aspiration for Buddhahood*. It is said to have been a work of Bodhisattva Nāgārjuna. According to Grand Master Kōbō it is the core of the 1,000 tracts written by Nāgārjuna. What do you say about this?

Answer: This tract, consisting of merely seven written pages, includes many words which cannot have been taught by Nāgārjuna. Catalogues of Buddhist scriptures cannot determine whether Nāgārjuna or Pu-k'ung wrote it. Besides, this is not a summary of all the sutras preached by the Buddha during His lifetime, and it often lacks accuracy. First of all, its main point is not true. It insists that one cannot attain Buddhahood with his present body except through Shingon Buddhism. It denies the possibility of becoming a Buddha with one's present body* as preached in the *Lotus Sutra*, which has both scriptural proof* and factual proof,* while insisting that becoming a Buddha with one's present body is possible in Shingon sutras, though they have neither scriptural nor factual proof. The character "except for" meaning "exclusively with Shingon Buddhism" is the prime mistake. I believe it is an arbitrary work of *Tripiṭaka* Master Pu-k'ung, claimed to have been written by Nāgārjuna for the purpose of greater credibility.

Moreover, *Tripiṭaka* Master Pu-k'ung's works have many mistakes. Calling the Buddha who was revealed in the 16th chapter of the *Lotus Sutra*, The Duration of the Life of the Tathāgata, the Buddha of Infinite Life, as he does in his *Esoteric Rites Based on the Lotus Sutra*, was apparently a blunder. It is not worthy of discussion that he mixed up the arrangement of the chapters in the *Lotus Sutra* by placing the 26th chapter, Dhāraṇīs, next to the 21st chapter, The Supernatural Powers of the Tathāgata, and moving the 22nd chapter, Transmission, to the end. On the other hand, through plagiarizing the Mahayana precepts of T'ien-t'ai, he received an imperial decree from Sung Tai-tsung to establish the Mahayana precept platform at his five temples on Mt. Wu-t'ai. He also insisted on adopting the T'ien-t'ai doctrine to establish the doctrine of Chen-yen (Shingon) Buddhism. Thus he blundered much.

Sutras and treatises translated by anyone but Pu-k'ung must be depended on sometimes, but this man's translation cannot be trusted. There were, altogether, 187 men, old* and new, who transmitted and translated Buddhist scriptures from India to China. All, except one, *Tripiṭaka* Master Kumārajīva,* committed errors. *Tripiṭaka* Master Puk'ung especially erred much. Besides, he apparently had false ideas.

Question: How do you know that all, except *Tripiṭaka* Master Kumārajīva, erred in translating Buddhist scriptures? Are you not only trying to destroy the seven schools of Buddhism such as Zen, Pure Land, and Shingon but also discrediting all translators who transmitted Buddhism to China and Japan?

Answer: This is something I consider quite confidential. You may ask me for details later. However, let me explain briefly now. *Tripiṭaka* Master Kumārajīva used to say from his own pulpit:

> "All the scriptures of Buddhism in Chinese do not represent the true meaning of the original Sanskrit. Hoping to reveal this, I have made a great vow: 'I have made my body impure by getting married, but as far as my tongue is concerned, I will keep it pure and refrain from speaking falsely on Buddhism.' To prove it, cremate my body after my death. If my tongue burns together with my body, you should consider my translations of scripture as false and discard them all."

Therefore, everybody, from the emperor down to the populace, wished to live long enough to see the death of *Tripiṭaka* Master Kumārajīva. Later, when he died and was cremated, his impure corpse all became ashes, but his tongue alone remained unburnt on the blue lotus that appeared in the fire. Radiating rays of five colors, it shone so brightly, that the night looked as bright as the day, and even the sun in the day paled in comparison. As a result, estimation of the sutras translated by all other masters began to decline while those translated by Kumārajīva, especially the *Lotus Sutra*, began to spread quickly in China.

Question: You may be right about translators before the time of Kumārajīva. But how about those after him such as Śubhākarasiṃha and Pu-k'ung?

Answer: Even after him, it remained the same. If a translator's tongue does not remain unburnt after the cremation of his corpse, you should know that his translations are false. This is the reason why Grand Master Dengyō attacked the Hossō (Dharma Characteristics) school, then spreading in Japan saying, "*Tripiṭaka* Master Kumārajīva's tongue remained unburnt while those of Hsüan-chuang and Tz'ŭ-ên, who had translated Hossō canons, were burnt." Accepting this to be reasonable, Emperor Kammu converted to the T'ien-t'ai Lotus school.

It is predicted in the *Nirvana Sutra,* in such fascicles as the third and ninth, that in the process of transmission from India to foreign lands, Buddhism would beget many misinterpretations, and as a result few people would be able to attain Buddhahood. Therefore, Grand Master Miao-lê says, "Whether or not there are mistakes in Buddhist scriptures, it all depends on translators. It has nothing to do with the Buddha Himself." He means that no matter how hard people today try to attain Buddhahood according to sutras, they would be unable to do so if the sutras are false, and that they can't blame the Buddha for it. In studying Buddhism, besides knowing the differences between Mahayana, Hinayana, provisional, real, exoteric, and esoteric teachings, one must first of all know whether or not scriptures are correctly translated.

Grand Master T'ien-t'ai in the Age of the Semblance Dharma

Question: I do not fully agree with your view that those commentators in the 1,000 year Age of the True Dharma propagated only provisional Mahayana teachings while knowing the true teaching of the *Lotus Sutra* was superior to all other sutras, exoteric as well esoteric. However, I think I am beginning to understand you.

In the middle of the 1,000 year Age of the Semblance Dharma, Grand Master T'ien-t'ai appeared and write the 10 fascicled *Profound Meaning of the Lotus Sutra,* exhaustively explaining the five characters of *miao, fa, lien, hua,* and *ching* in 1,000 written pages. He also wrote the 10 fascicled *Words and Phrases of the Lotus Sutra* in 1,000 written pages, interpreting each word and phrase of the *Lotus Sutra,* beginning with the opening phrase "thus I heard" to the closing words "they bowed to Him and retired," using four guidelines of causes and effects *(innen),* correlated doctrines *(yakkyō),* theoretical and essential teachings of the *Lotus Sutra (honjaku),* and spiritual contemplation *(kanjin).*

In writing these two works in 20 fascicles, Grand Master T'ien-t'ai likened the relationship between the *Lotus Sutra* and all other Buddhist scriptures to that between the ocean and rivers. He stated that as all rivers flow into the ocean, the teachings of the Buddha in all the dharma worlds in the universe without exception lead to the *Lotus Sutra.* The Grand Master, moreover, adopted interpretations by great Indian commentators all without exception into the *Lotus Sutra.* As for the interpretations by the 10 masters in Northern and Southern China, he refuted or adopted what he should, establishing the doctrines of the five periods and eight teachings to classify all the scriptures of Buddhism under the *Lotus Sutra.*[10]

The Grand Master further wrote the 10 fascicled *Great Concentration and Insight*, recapitulating in one moment of thought the whole teaching of the lifetime of the Buddha, and classifying all creatures in the Ten Realms, from the Buddha land on top to hell at the bottom, into 3,000 categories. His writing style is superior to those of commentators faraway in India in the past 1,000 years, to say nothing of those masters nearby in China during the past 500 years.

Therefore, Grand Master Chia-hsiang (Chi-tsang)* of the Sanlun school, together with more than 100 leaders and elders of Northern and Southern China, invited Grand Master T'ien-t'ai to lecture saying:

> "It is said that a sage appears in 1,000 years and a wise man in 500 years. It has come true today in the persons of the wise sage Nan-yüeh and the great philosopher T'ien-t'ai. In the past lives they upheld the *Lotus Sutra* physically, verbally, and mentally, and in this life have they been the master and his disciple, transmitting the sutra. Not only have they spread this teaching, as sweet as nectar, in the land of China but also their fame has reached as far as India. Having the natural ability to master the profound teaching of the Buddha, they are incomparably superior in lecturing on Buddhist scriptures to anyone since the time of Wei and Chin. This is the reason why I, together with some 100 monks who practice meditation, would like to invite Grand Master T'ien-t'ai to lecture on the *Lotus Sutra*."

Precept Master Tao-hsüan of Mt. Chung-nan praised Grand Master T'ien-t'ai in these words:

> "His understanding of the *Lotus Sutra* is as penetrating as the sun at high noon shining on the bottom of deep valleys. He preaches Mahayana sutras like strong winds blowing in the great sky. Even if 10 million scholars of letters tried to learn his eloquence, no one would be able to master it. His lectures are like a finger pointing to the moon. Without sticking to the text, he freely expounds the dharma, always pointing to the truth of the *Lotus Sutra*."

Monk Fa-tsang* of the Hua-yen (Flower Garland) school admired Grand Master T'ien-t'ai praising: "Men like Nan-yüeh and T'ien-t'ai are extraordinary. Their minds naturally penetrate the truth and they conduct themselves as bodhisattvas. They listened to Śākyamuni Buddha preach on Mt. Sacred Eagle in the past and still remember what they heard then."

There is a story in the *Biographies of Buddhist Patriarchs of Sung* that *Tripiṭaka* Master Pu-k'ung (Amoghavajra) and his disciple, Priest Han-kuang of the Chen-yen school, deserted their school to surrender to Grand Master T'ien-t'ai. It says that when Priest Han-kuang accompanied his master to India, a priest said to him, "I heard that T'ien-t'ai in China teaches superbly, differentiating true Buddhism from the false and judging the comparative superiority of the Buddhist sutras. Is it not possible for you to translate and transmit this to India?" This is what Grand Master Miao-lê heard from Han-kuang. Hearing this, Grand Master Miao-lê wondered and recorded in his *Annotations on the Words and Phrases of the Lotus Sutra,* "Does this not mean that Buddhism has been lost in India and that the people in India are trying to find it in lands in the four directions? Yet very few people in China knew about T'ien-t'ai just as very few people in the state of Lu knew about Confucius." If there had been in India such great commentaries as T'ien-t'ai's 30 fascicled *Profound Meaning of the Lotus Sutra,* the *Words and Phrases of the Lotus Sutra* and the *Great Concentration and Insight,* how could it be that Indian priests wished to see the works of T'ien-t'ai? Does this not mean the revelation of the true meaning of the *Lotus Sutra* was spreading all over the world in the Age of the Semblance Dharma?

Answer: Grand Master T'ien-t'ai for the first time in China spread the perfect meditation and wisdom of the *Lotus Sutra,* supreme of all sutras preached by the Buddha during His lifetime. No commentators had ever propagated this sutra before during the 1,400 years after the death of the Buddha, that is, the 1,000-year Age of the True Dharma and the first 400 years of the Age of the Semblance Dharma. Moreover, Grand Master T'ien-t'ai's fame has reached as far as India. It appears that the *Lotus Sutra* was widely propagated, but the Grand Master did not establish the "perfect and sudden" precept platform. It will not do for Hinayana precepts to be side by side with the perfect meditation and wisdom of Mahayana Buddhism. It is just like an eclipse of the sun or the moon. Moreover, the time of Grand Master T'ien-t'ai was in what the *Sutra of the Great Assembly* called the period of "wide reading and much hearing," that is, the third 500-year period after the death of the Buddha. It was not yet the fifth 500-year period, when the *Lotus Sutra* was predicted to spread widely.

Grand Master Dengyō in the Age of the Semblance Dharma

Question: Grand Master Dengyō is Japanese. Living during the reign of Emperor Kammu, he refuted the false teachings of the six schools of Nara, which had spread during more than 200 years since the reign of Emperor Kimmei, and propagated the perfect wisdom and meditation established by Grand Master T'ien-t'ai. He also refuted the three Hinayana precept platforms established in Japan by Master Chien-chên, and established on Mt. Hiei the perfect and sudden precept platform for specific granting of the Mahayana precepts.* This happened 1,800 years after the death of the Buddha. It was a wondrous event not only for India, China, and Japan, but also throughout the entire world. Dengyō's inner understanding of Buddhism may or may not have been equal to Nāgārjuna and T'ien-t'ai. Nevertheless, he seems superior to Nāgārjuna and Vasubandhu, or Nan-yüeh and T'ien-t'ai, in that he was able to bring about a unity to the Buddhist world by means of the perfect precepts.

Generally speaking, only these two, T'ien-t'ai and Dengyō, practiced the *Lotus Sutra* in the 1,800 years after the death of the Buddha. Grand Master Dengyō, therefore, cites in his *Outstanding Principles of the Lotus Sutra* the words of the *Lotus Sutra*, chapter 11, Beholding the Stupa of Treasures, which states that lifting up Mt. Sumeru and throwing it to numerous Buddha lands is not as difficult as spreading the *Lotus Sutra* in the Latter Age of Degeneration after the death of the Buddha. Interpreting this, he then declares: "Śākyamuni Buddha said that it is easy to uphold the sutras that are shallow in meaning, but it is difficult to uphold those sutras profound in meaning. Therefore, it is natural for men of valor to believe in the *Lotus Sutra*, which is profound in meaning, just as Grand Master T'ien-t'ai following the wishes of Śākyamuni spread the Lotus school in China in the past. Today we on Mt. Hiei, following the teaching of T'ien-t'ai, are propagating the Lotus school in Japan."

Here is the meaning of this interpretation. Suppose there was a short man, five feet tall, living between the ninth small *kalpa* within the *Kalpa* of Continuance[11] when the human life span was 100 years and decreasing, and within the last 50 years of Śākyamuni Buddha's life and 1,800 years after His death. Even if such a man could throw a gold mountain, 168,000 *yojana*[12] or 6,620,000 *ri* in height, over the Surrounding Iron Mountains as though it were a one or two inch piece of tile thrown a few hundred yards at a speed faster than a sparrow, it would be more difficult for this man to expound the *Lotus Sutra* in the Latter Age of Degeneration as the Buddha did during His lifetime. Only Grand Masters T'ien-t'ai and Dengyō spread it in a way similar to that of the Buddha.

Commentators in India had not gone to preach the true meaning of the *Lotus Sutra*. In China, Buddhist masters before T'ien-t'ai had gone either too far or too short. Those after him, such as Tz'ŭ-ên, Fa-tsang, and Śubhākarasiṃha, blundered calling the "east" the "west" or the "heaven" the "earth." Those words in the *Outstanding Principles of the Lotus Sutra* are not those of self-conceit on the part of Grand Master Dengyō!

On the 19th day of the first month in the 21st year of the Enryaku Era (802), Emperor Kammu traveled to the Takaozan Temple, where he ordered a dozen or so high priests of the six schools and seven great temples in Nara such as Zengi, Shōyū, Hōki, Chōnin, Kengyoku, Ampuku, Gonsō, Shūen, Jikō, Gen'yō, Saikō, Dōshō, Kōshō, and Kambin to challenge Priest Saichō, that is Grand Master Dengyō, in debate. Marveling at Grand Master Dengyō's first word, without even listening to his second and third words, they all surrendered to him at once, bowing their heads and holding their hands together. Such Sanron doctrines as the two storehouses,* three periods, and three preachings by Śākyamuni Buddha, the Hossō doctrines of the three-period teaching,* and five mutually distinctive natures* of sentient beings, and the Kegon doctrines of the four teachings, five teachings,* basic and unessential teachings, and six forms and 10 mysteries of all phenomena,[13] all these doctrines were refuted from their foundations as if the ridge-beam of a large house was broken. The banner of pride of these schools' 10 high priests was pulled down!

Greatly surprised, the emperor on the 29th day of the same month sent his emissaries, Wake no Hiroyo and Ōtomo no Kunimichi, to the seven great temples and six schools in Nara demanding their answers again. Each of them presented a letter of submission stating:

> "Having read in our hearts the exquisite commentaries on the *Lotus Sutra* by Grand Master T'ien-t'ai, we believe that they summarize Śākyamuni's teaching preached in His lifetime, clearly explaining its meanings. Revealing the One Vehicle way of the *Lotus Sutra*, what he preaches in them is a profound and wonderful truth incomparable to the doctrine of any other school. Students of the seven great temples and six schools of Nara had never heard or seen such commentaries before. The long feud between the Sanron and Hossō schools dissolved as quickly as ice melting away, making everything clear just like the rays of the sun, moon, and stars shining through after clouds and fog have dissipated.
>
> "Many sutras and commentaries have been preached during the 200 years since the dissemination of Buddhism by Prince Shōtoku, and discussions about the comparative superiority of the doctrines have been endless. Yet this most superb Tendai sect has not spread. Is it because people do not have the intelligence and faith in Buddhism to be able to listen to the perfect teaching?
>
> "We respectfully believe that Emperor Kammu, who had been entrusted by the Buddha far in the distant past to spread the *Lotus Sutra*, saw the time was ripe for it. So the emperor initiated the establishment of the One Vehicle teaching of the *Lotus Sutra*, enabling students of the six schools at Nara to see the ultimate teaching of the Buddha for the first time. We should say that from now on, all the people in this world would be able to reach the shore of enlightenment quickly aboard the vessel of the *Lotus Sutra*. Today we, Zengi and others, are fortunate to be in this auspicious era and hear the enlightening words in these commentaries to the *Lotus Sutra*. Our karma from the past lives has given us this fortune. Without it, how could we be born in this auspicious era?"

Chia-hsiang (Chi-tsang) and others in China over 100 in number, determined Grand Master T'ien-t'ai to be a sage. Today in Japan, 200 monks in those seven great temples of Nara also call Grand Master Dengyō a sage. In the 2,000 years after the death of the Buddha, only two sages were seen in China and Japan. Moreover, Grand Master Dengyō established, on Mt. Hiei, the great "perfect and sudden" precept platform which even Grand Master T'ien-t'ai had not propagated. Does this not mean that the *Lotus Sutra* was propagated toward the end of the Age of the Semblance Dharma?

Answer: As I said above, Aśvaghoṣa, Nāgārjuna, Deva, Vasubandhu, and others propagated the great dharma which such masters as Kāśyapa and Ānanda had not. I also mentioned before that what had not been propagated by such masters as Nāgārjuna and Vasubandhu was spread by Grand Master T'ien-t'ai. It is also clear that Grand Master Dengyō established the great "perfect and sudden" precept platform, which Grand Master T'ien-t'ai had not.

What I am not sure of, however, is the greatest and most profound secret dharma clearly seen in the face of the *Lotus Sutra*. I wonder very much whether or not this profound True Dharma, which the Buddha had preached exhaustively for those in the Latter Age but had not been spread by such masters as Kāśyapa, Ānanda, Aśvaghoṣa, Nāgārjuna, Asaṅga, Vasuabandhu, T'ien-t'ai, and Dengyō during the 2,000-year Ages of the True Dharma and the Semblance Dharma, would spread all over the world now at the beginning of the Latter Age, during the fifth 500-year period after the death of the Buddha, as the Buddha predicted.

The Most Profound and Secret Dharma and Fallacies of Nembutsu, Zen, and Shingon Buddhism

Question: What is the secret dharma? First, we would like to know its name, and then its meaning, please. If there is really such a secret dharma, is it Śākyamuni Buddha appearing in this world again, or Superior-Practice Bodhisattva emerging out of the earth once again? Please be kind enough to explain it right away.

Reborn six times to this world, *Tripiṭaka* Master Hsüan-chuang finally reached India, where he spent 19 years studying and concluded that the One Vehicle teaching of the *Lotus Sutra* was merely provisional while Hinayana *Āgama* sutras were the true teaching of the Buddha. *Tripiṭaka* Master Amoghavajra (Pu-k'ung) returning to India from China wrote that the Buddha revealed in the 16th chapter of the *Lotus Sutra* was "the Buddha of Infinite Life." Their blunders were as obvious as calling the east the west or taking the sun for the moon. What is the use of toiling with soul and body in such a blundering study? Born in the Latter Age of Degeneration, we are fortunate to be able to surpass, without taking a step, those who have been seeking the dharma for an incalculably long period of time, and to become a Buddha with the noble countenance of the Buddha without sacrificing our heads to feed hungry tigers.

Answer: It is easy to talk about this secret dharma as it is clearly stated in the sutra. However, it is necessary to point out three serious sins before revealing this dharma. A great ocean is vast but will not retain a corpse. The earth is deep but will not sustain the unfilial. In Buddhism, even those who commit the five rebellious sins and those who are unfilial children will be saved, but those of incorrigible disbelief, who slander the True Dharma *(icchantika)*, and those who pretend to be holy men by ostentatiously keeping precepts, will never be saved. In fact, these slanderers are men of the Pure Land, Zen, and Shingon schools, which are the three calamities.

First of all, the Pure Land school has been spread all over Japan and all Buddhists, clergy and laymen, chant *"Namu Amidabutsu"* as though they are merely singing a song. Next, self-conceited Zen monks with three robes and one alms-bowl* fill the land behaving like leaders of the whole world. In the third place, the Shingon school is worse off still. Shingon monks are in command of such influential temples as the Enryakuji Temple on Mt. Hiei, the Tōji Temple, seven great temples at Nara, and the Onjōji Temple. They insist that although the divine mirror, part of the imperial regalia enshrined in the Imperial Sanctuary, was burnt to ashes, they can depend on the finger sign of the Great Sun Buddha as the mirror of the Buddha. They insist also that although the divine sword, another part of the imperial regalia, was sunk in the western sea, Japan can be protected against enemies by the strength of the five great protective deities of Shingon Buddhism. Their stubborn belief does not seem to be shaken even if a *kalpa* rock, 10 cubic miles in size, should be worn away by the touch of an angel's garment once in three years.[14] They do not seem to have any doubt about their faith even if the earth should turn upside down.

This Shingon school of Buddhism had not been introduced to China yet when Grand Master T'ien-t'ai refuted the three Southern and seven Northern masters of Chinese Buddhism. It was also not present in Japan when Grand Master Dengyō chastised the six schools of Nara. Having escaped its two strongest enemies, Shingon Buddhism is about to destroy the True Dharma of the *Lotus Sutra*. Moreover, Grand Master Jikaku, disciple of Grand Master Dengyō, having sided with the Shingon school, destroyed the Tendai school on Mt. Hiei and converted it to the Shingon. Who would dare to stand up against him? Under the circumstances, no one tried to question the false teachings of Grand Master Kōbō. Venerable Annen* criticized Kōbō a little, but his criticism was limited to Kōbō's assertion that the *Lotus Sutra* was inferior to the *Flower Garland Sutra*, verifying, in effect, that the *Lotus Sutra* was inferior to the *Great Sun Buddha Sutra*. He was merely a so-called "go-between."

Refutation of the Pure Land School

Question: What is wrong with these three schools of Buddhism?

Answer: The Pure Land school was founded by Priest T'an-luan during the reign of the Ch'i dynasty in China. Originally he studied the San-lun school, but upon reading Bodhisattva Nāgārjuna's *Commentary on the Ten Stages,* he insisted that in Buddhism there are ways easy-to-practice and difficult-to-practice. During the T'ang dynasty, Zen Master Tao-ch'o, who had originally been preaching the *Nirvana Sutra,* converted to the Pure Land school upon reading the writings of Priest T'an-luan which revealed his conversion to the Pure Land. He maintained that there were two ways of attaining Buddhahood: the Holy Way, by putting into practice the holy teachings of the Buddha, and the Pure Land Way, by being born in the Pure Land of the Buddha of Infinite Life. In addition, a disciple of Tao-ch'o, Shan-tao by name, differentiated the correct practice from the miscellaneous practices in Buddhism, calling the recitation of the *nembutsu* the correct practice leading to birth in the Pure Land.

A priest named Hōnen appeared in Japan during the reign of ex-Emperor Gotoba, 200 years after the beginning of the Latter Age. He propagated the recitation of the name of the Buddha of Infinite Life, *nembutsu,* to everybody, monks and nuns, as well as lay followers of Buddhism by saying:

> "The teachings of the Buddha must be preached according to the time as well as the intelligence and faith of the congregation. Such sutras as the *Lotus Sutra* and the *Great Sun Buddha Sutra,* and eight or nine schools of Buddhism such as the Tendai and Shingon, that is to say, all the Buddhist sutras and practices of Mahayana, Hinayana, exoteric, esoteric, provisional, and the true teachings preached by the Buddha during His lifetime, are for those with superior intelligence and firm faith during the 2,000-year Ages of the True Dharma and the Semblance Dharma. They are of no use in the Latter Age of Degeneration, no matter how rigidly they are put into practice.
>
> "Moreover, if one tries to put them into practice while reciting the name of the Buddha of Infinite Life, the recitation of the *nembutsu* would not help him to be reborn in the Pure land of the Buddha of Infinite Life. This is not my own arbitrary statement. Bodhisattva Nāgārjuna and Priest T'an-luan said that all sutras and practices other than the recitation of the *nembutsu* were ways too difficult to practice. Tao-ch'o reviled them saying that no one had ever attained Buddhahood by means of them, and Shan-tao declared that not even one out of 1,000 would attain Buddhahood through their ways.

"Being masters of different Buddhist schools, they might have some doubts about being reborn in the Pure Land by recitation of the *nembutsu*. Venerable Eshin, probably the wisest among the scholars of the Tendai and Shingon schools, has written in the preface to his *Essential Collection Concerning Rebirth in the Pure Land* that teachings of exoteric and esoteric Buddhism are not the way for ignorant men like himself to attain emancipation from sufferings of birth and death. You should also look at such writings as the *Ten Reasons for Rebirth in the Pure Land* by Yōkan of the Sanron school.

"Therefore, you should throw away such teachings as the *Tendai, Lotus,* and *Shingon,* concentrating solely on reciting the *nembutsu*. Then all of you, 10 out of 10 and 100 out of 100, will be able to be reborn in the Pure Land of the Buddha of Infinite Life."

Although such temples as the Enryakuji on Mt. Hiei, the Tōji, the Onjōji and the seven great temples in Nara at first seemed to argue against Hōnen, Abbot Kenshin of the Enryakuji Temple was converted to be a disciple of Hōnen as words in the preface to the *Essential Collection Concerning Rebirth in the Pure Land* seemed reasonable to him. Even those who did not become disciples of Hōnen recited the name of the Buddha of Infinite Life as though humming a song, in a way different from reciting the names of the other Buddhas, greatly favoring this. As a result it seemed that everybody in Japan was a disciple of Priest Hōnen.

As all the people in Japan without exception have become disciples of Priest Hōnen during these past 50 years, everybody in Japan without exception has become a slanderer of the True Dharma. For example, if 1,000 children get together in killing one parent, all of them are guilty of committing the five rebellious sins. If one of them falls into the Hell of Incessant Suffering, why not all of the rest?

Resentful of having been banished, Hōnen became an evil spirit haunting the ruler of Japan and the monks on Mt. Hiei and in the Onjōji Temple, who had been responsible for punishing him and his disciples, causing them to rebel and do evil. In the end, they were all destroyed by the Kamakura Shogunate. The remaining few monks on Mt. Hiei and in the Tōji Temple have been slighted by lay men and women just as monkeys are laughed at by people or prisoners are disdained even by children.

Refutation of the Zen School

Taking advantage of the decline of Mt. Hiei, Tōji and other temples, Zen monks deceive the people by pretending to be sages upholding precepts. As they appear so noble in countenance, nobody feels any suspicion, no matter how madly they preach their false doctrines.

The Zen school insists on "transmission of the dharma outside of the sutras," that is to say, Śākyamuni Buddha's enlightenment was not revealed in Buddhist scriptures but was transmitted directly to Venerable Kāśyapa when He talked to the Venerable in whispers. Therefore, the Zen school insists that trying to study Buddhist scriptures without knowing the Zen school is just like a dog barking at thunder or a monkey trying to grasp the reflection of the moon.

Because this false teaching is suited to those in Japan who have been abandoned by their parents because of their disobedience, disowned by masters because of their discourtesy, young monks who are lazy in studying, or those who have the maddening character of prostitutes, people such as this are all converted to the Zen school. Pretending to behave properly according to Buddhist precepts, they all have been grasshoppers feeding on all the farmers of Japan. So, the heaven stares its eyes out and terrestrial deities tremble, causing strange phenomena in the sky and natural calamities on earth.

Refutation of the Shingon School

The Shingon school is a false teaching bringing calamities incomparably greater than those of the two schools mentioned above. Briefly speaking, it originates from *Tripiṭaka* Masters Śubhākarasiṃha, Vajrabodhi and Amoghavajra (Pu-k'ung) who brought the *Great Sun Buddha Sutra*, the *Diamond Peak Sutra*, and the *Sutra on the Act of Perfection* from India to China during the reign of Emperor Hsüan-tsung of the great T'ang dynasty. What these sutras preach is clear. The ultimate doctrine preached in them is the One Vehicle teaching leading to bodhisattvahood, sublating or negating the two kinds of teachings applicable to men of the Two Vehicles: *śrāvaka* and *pratyekabuddha*.

To differentiate them from other sutras, they preach only finger signs and mantras. Their doctrines are not comparable to the One Vehicle teaching leading to Buddhahood, sublating the three kinds of teaching applicable to the men of the Two Vehicles and bodhisattvas, preached in the *Flower Garland Sutra* and the *Wisdom Sutra*. Still less do they equal what the Tendai doctrine[15] refers to as "distinct" *(bekkyō)* and "perfect" *(engyō)* teachings among the sutras preached before the *Lotus*. They are merely Hinayana *(zōkyō)* and introductory Mahayana *(tsūgyō)* teachings. Nevertheless, *Tripiṭaka* Master Śubhākarasiṃha seems to have opinionated: "These sutras would be derided by the Flower Garland (Kegon) and the Fa-hsiang (Hossō) schools and made a laughing stock by the T'ien-t'ai school if they are known as they are. It's a pity, however, not to propagate them in China after having brought them from India as important documents."

Senji-shō (ST 181) 203

Then there was a fool called Zen Master I-hsing* among the T'ien-t'ai monks in China. Śubhākarasiṃha talked him into discussing the doctrines of Chinese Buddhism prevalent at the time. Completely fooled, I-hsing described not only the gist of the Sun-lun, Fa-hsiang, and Flower Garland doctrines but also the T'ien-t'ai doctrine as well. Upon listening to him talk, Śubhākarasiṃha determined that the T'ien-t'ai school was so great, greater than what he had heard in India, that he would not be able to add anything to it. Therefore he fooled I-hsing by saying that I-hsing was a wise man of China and the T'ien-t'ai school was great and that what the Shingon (Chen-yen) school could offer, and the T'ien-t'ai school could not, were only finger signs and mantras. As I-hsing agreed with him, Śubhākarasiṃha further said to him: "Just as Grand Master T'ien-t'ai wrote commentaries on the *Lotus Sutra*, I want commentaries to the *Great Sun Buddha Sutra* to be written as a means of spreading Shingon Buddhism. Would you care to write them?" I-hsing answered:

> "I would be glad to do so, but I wonder in what way I should write them. The T'ien-t'ai school is an irritating school. It has an advantage that no other school can defeat it in debate, no matter how hard it tries. In the *Sutra of Infinite Meaning*, an introductory teaching to the *Lotus Sutra*, it is definitely stated that the truth was not revealed in any sutras preached during 40 years or so before the *Lotus Sutra*. Further it is stated in the 10th chapter of the *Lotus Sutra*, The Teacher of the Dharma, and 21st chapter, The Supernatural Powers of the Tathāgata, that sutras preached after the Lotus will not show the true way leading to Buddhahood. The *Lotus Sutra* also makes clear in the 10th chapter that it is the supreme sutra compared to those being preached, and that none of those sutras preached at the same time as the *Lotus* equals it. Now, in which group should we include the *Great Sun Buddha Sutra*, among those sutras preached in the past, those being preached at present, or those to be preached in the future?"

With a crafty design, Venerable Śubhākarasiṃha then told I-hsiang:

> "The *Great Sun Buddha Sutra* has a chapter entitled Stages of Mind. Just as the *Sutra of Infinite Meaning* repelled all the sutras preached during 40 years or so preceding the *Lotus Sutra*, it can also do the same. The chapters of the *Great Sun Buddha Sutra* following the Introducing the Mandala chapter are separated into two sutras of the Lotus and Great Sun Buddha in China, but they were originally one sutra in India. Śākyamuni Buddha preached only the pure doctrine of the *Great Sun Buddha Sutra*, exclusive of its teaching on finger signs and mantras, to Śāriputra and Bodhisattva Maitreya, calling it the *Lotus Sutra*. Tripiṭaka Master Kumārajīva transmitted it to China, which Grand Master T'ien-t'ai read. The Great Sun Buddha called the *Lotus Sutra*

the *Great Sun Buddha Sutra* when he preached it to Vajrasattva. It is called the *Great Sun Buddha Sutra*, which I personally saw in India.

"Therefore, what you should stress when you write is that the *Great Sun Buddha Sutra* and the *Lotus Sutra* are of one taste like a mixture of water and milk. Then we can claim that the *Great Sun Buddha Sutra* is superior to all the sutras preached, those being preached, and those to be preached just as the *Lotus Sutra* is claimed to be.

"In addition, if we decorate the 3,000 Existences Contained in One Thought doctrine, which is a pure doctrine, with finger signs and mantras, it will be a secret dharma equipped with the three mystic practices, physical, verbal, and mental. Considering these three mystic practices, the Tendai (T'ien-t'ai) school has mental mystic practice alone, lacking finger signs and mantras. The Shingon school is like a brave general wearing armor and a helmet and armed with a bow and arrow. Equipped with only the mental mystic practice, the Tendai school is like a brave general who is naked."

So, Master I-hsing wrote his commentary on the *Great Sun Buddha Sutra* as instructed above. It seems there was no one in the 360 states in China who knew this. Although there were some who enthusiastically discussed the comparative superiority of the *Lotus Sutra* and the *Great Sun Buddha Sutra* at the beginning, they were converted to Shingon Buddhism day by day until such discussion ceased to exist. Śubhākarasiṃha was highly esteemed while the followers of the T'ien-t'ai school were not, and no man alive then had T'ien-t'ai's wisdom. As years passed, the deception of the Shingon school became deeply rooted until it was completely hidden.

Grand Master Dengyō's View on Shingon Buddhism

When Grand Master Dengyō* of Japan went to T'ang China to introduce T'ien-t'ai (Tendai) Buddhism to Japan, he transmitted Chen-yen (Shingon) Buddhism as well. He transmitted Tendai Buddhism to the emperor of Japan, and had the high priests of the six schools of Nara study Shingon Buddhism. As the comparative superiority of the six schools of Nara and Tendai had been decided upon prior to his going to China, he should have settled the issue on the comparative superiority of Tendai and Shingon after his return. However, as arguments for and against the establishment of the "perfect and sudden" Mahayana precept platform seemed to last forever, he did not say anything about Shingon Buddhism before the emperor. Nor did he make clear-cut statements to his disciples about it, perhaps because he felt it unwise to make many enemies who might block the establishment of the precept platform, or perhaps because he intended to leave the chastising of Shingon Buddhism for those who practice the *Lotus Sutra* in the Latter Age of Degeneration. However, he wrote a secret essay entitled the "Effects of T'ien-t'ai on Buddhist schools" in a fascicle describing how the seven schools of Buddhism, six schools of Nara and Shingon school, surrendered to the Tendai school. In the preface, he wrote a few words about the deception of the Shingon school.

Refuting Grand Master Kōbō's False Teaching

Grand Master Kōbō* went to China during the same Enryaku Era as Grand Master Dengyō and studied Shingon Buddhism under Hui-kuo of the Ch'ing-lung-ssu Temple. In his writings after returning from China, judging the comparative superiority among all the sutras Śākyamuni Buddha preached during His lifetime, Grand Master Kōbō insisted "Shingon sutras are the first, the *Flower Garland,* the second, and the *Lotus,* the third." Although this Grand Master has been extremely highly esteemed, I dare say that his understanding of Buddhism is surprisingly shallow.

Thinking about this matter briefly, I suppose Grand Master Kōbō went to China to bring back only the ritualism of Shingon Buddhism, namely, the finger signs and mantras, without deeply contemplating the doctrine. Upon returning to Japan he observed the world carefully and saw that the Tendai school had grown so strong that it might be difficult to spread Shingon Buddhism in Japan. Therefore, by adopting the Flower Garland doctrine, which he had studied before going to China, he insisted that Shingon Buddhism was superior to the *Lotus Sutra*. However, perhaps because he thought that people would not believe him if he said it just as the Flower Garland school maintained, he added a little color by saying it was the true teaching of the *Great Sun Buddha Sutra,* Bodhisattva Nāgārjuna's *Treatise on the Aspiration for Buddhahood,* and Śubhākarasiṃha. It was an extraordinary lie, but the followers of the Tendai school did not strongly protest against it.

Question: Grand Master Kōbō says in his *Treatise on the Ten Stages of Mind, Jewel Key to the Store of Mysteries,* and *Comparison of Exoteric and Esoteric Buddhism* that all exoteric teachings claim to be the path leading to Buddhahood, but they are merely useless arguments compared to Shingon esotericism preached later. He says that compared to the Great Sun Buddha, Śākyamuni Buddha is still in the realm of spiritual darkness, unenlightened, and that the *Lotus Sutra* is of the fourth, butter, taste according to the five-flavor* classification. He also says that Chinese scholars of Buddhism competed with one another in stealing the ultimate taste of clarified butter *(daigo)* from Shingon Buddhism in order to bolster their own. What do you think of these comments of Kōbō?

Answer: Surprised at these comments, I looked through all the Buddhist scriptures as well as the triple sutras of the *Great Sun Buddha*. Nowhere is it said, not even one word or phrase, that the *Lotus Sutra* is merely a useless argument in contrast to the *Flower Garland Sutra* and the *Great Sun Buddha Sutra*, a robber compared to the *Sutra of the Six Pāramitā*, and in the realm of spiritual darkness compared to the *Guardian Sutra*. This does not have any factual basis whatsoever. Nevertheless, since these comments have been accepted by many wise men of Japan for the past three or four hundred years, people came to think there were reasons for them. For now, I will point out their very simple lies to make it clear that others are not worth discussing.

It was during the time of the Ch'ên-Sui dynasties in China that the *Lotus Sutra* was likened to the taste of clarified butter *(daigo)*, while the *Sutra of the Six Pāramitā* was introduced to China by *Tripiṭaka* Master Prajñā (Hannya Sanzō) in the middle of the T'ang dynasty. If the *daigo* taste of the sutra had been transmitted to Ch'ên-Sui China, it might have been possible that Grand Master T'ien-t'ai plagiarized the *daigo* taste of Shingon Buddhism. How could he steal it, when it was introduced to China after his death?

There is a similar example readily available. Monk Tokuitsu of Japan once accused Grand Master T'ien-t'ai of destroying the three-period teaching expounded in the *Revealing the Profound and Secret Sutra*, saying it was like a three-inch tongue murdering a five-foot body. Then Grand Master Dengyō pointed out his mistake saying: "The *Revealing the Profound and Secret Sutra* was introduced to China by Hsüan-chuang at the beginning of the T'ang dynasty. Grand Master T'ien-t'ai is a man of the preceding Ch'ên-Sui period. It was several years after the death of Grand Master T'ien-t'ai that the sutra was introduced. How could anyone destroy a sutra transmitted after his death?" Monk Tokuitsu not only was at a loss for an answer, but died with his tongue split in eight pieces.

Now, Kōbō's slandering of Grand Master T'ien-t'ai is incomparably worse than Tokuitsu's. He said that Fa-tsang of the Hua-yen school, Chia-hsiang of the San-lun school, Hsüan-chuang of the Fa-hsiang school, Grand Master T'ien-t'ai, masters of Northern and Southern China, and scholars and commentators since the Later Han period were all thieves. This is the worst slander that has ever been uttered. Moreover, describing the *Lotus Sutra* to be the taste of *daigo* is not an arbitrary statement of Grand Master T'ien-t'ai. In the *Nirvana Sutra*, the Buddha called the *Lotus Sutra* the taste of *daigo*. Bodhisattva Vasubandhu has written in his *Commentary on the Lotus Sutra* that the *Lotus Sutra* and the *Nirvana Sutra* are of *daigo*. And Bodhisattva Nāgārjuna named the *Lotus Sutra* a golden remedy in his *Great Wisdom Discourse*.

Therefore, if those who call the *Lotus Sutra* the taste of *daigo* are thieves, then are not Śākyamuni Buddha, the Buddha of Many Treasures, all the Buddhas in all the worlds in the universe, Nāgārjuna, and Vasubandhu also thieves? Disciples of Kōbō and Shingon monks of the Tōji Temple in Japan, even if you cannot see whether your own eyes are black or white, you must see your own sins of slandering the True Dharma when using the words of the Buddha, commentators and masters as a mirror.

Besides, if there is a clear statement in the *Great Sun Buddha Sutra* or the *Diamond Peak Sutra* to the effect that the *Lotus Sutra* is a useless argument as Kōbō wrote it to be, you had better show it to me. Even if there could be such statements in those sutras, you had better think hard because they could be mistranslations. It is said that Confucius thought about something nine times before uttering a word. The Duke of Chou is said to have interrupted washing his head and having a meal as often as three times in order to meet his guests and listen to them. Even among those who study shallow temporal matters in non-Buddhist scriptures, wise men are as careful as this. How could Kōbō make such a shameful statement that the *Lotus Sutra* was a useless argument?

Shōgakubō Kakuban, a distant student of Kōbō who had such a wrong view, calling himself the founder of the Denbōin Temple, states in his *Liturgy for the Ceremony Dedicated to the Buddha's Relics*: "Supreme is the Great Sun Buddha, the lord of esoteric Buddhism. The threefold body[16] of Śākyamuni Buddha, who is like a donkey or an ox compared to the Great Sun Buddha, cannot even pull a wagon for the Great Sun Buddha. Most secret and profound is the teaching of the Two Mandalas, in front of which the four teachings of exoteric Buddhism cannot even be its sandal-carriers."

What is referred to as the four teachings of exoteric Buddhism here are the four schools of Hossō, Sanron, Kegon, and Lotus. The threefold body of donkey and ox refer to four Buddhas as the lords of the *Lotus, Flower Garland, Great Wisdom,* and the *Revealing the Profound and Secret Sutras*. Thus, it is stated that compared to the Shingon monks, monks of those four schools and their Buddhas are inferior even to cattlemen and sandal-carriers of Shōkakubō and Kōbō.

Refuting the Fallacies of the Three Schools

Brahman, the Boaster of India was born wise, studied both exoteric and esoteric Buddhism, and mastered thoroughly all books, Buddhist as well as non-Buddhist. Therefore, both the king and his subjects bowed down to him, and all the people looked up to him as their teacher. Self-conceited, he said to himself, "Those respected most by the people are the four sages of Maheśvara, Vāsudeva, Nārāyaṇa and the Buddha. Let them be the four legs of my pulpit." Thus he made their statues the four legs of his pulpit on which he preached. This is just the same as present day Shingon priests, performing ceremonies while sprinkling water on the head *(kanjō)* and sitting on a mandala with Śākyamuni Buddha and all other Buddhas drawn on it. It is also the same as Zen priests who boast that theirs is the school of Buddhism which steps on the head of the Buddha.

Then, Commentator Bhadraruci appeared, a young priest, insisting on chastising Brahman, the Boaster. However, the king, his subjects and all the people would not listen to him. Instead they incited the disciples and followers of the Boaster to speak ill of Bhadraruci and beat him up on a countless number of trumped-up charges. Nevertheless, Bhadraruci continued his accusations at the risk of his life. Annoyed, the king tried to silence him in debate.But it was Brahman, the Boaster who was silenced. Looking up to heaven and throwing himself on the ground, the king lamented: "I was able to see this with my own eyes and get rid of my false view, but my father was completely fooled by this man. He must have fallen into the Hell of Incessant Suffering." Holding Bhadraruci's legs, the king shed tears of regret. Upon Bhadraruci's suggestion, Brahman, the Boaster was put on a donkey's back and taken all over India to expose his shame. As a result his evil heart grew rampant, and he fell alive into the Hell of Incessant Suffering. Are followers of the Shingon and Zen schools today different from this Brahman, the Boaster?

Zen Master San Chiai (Hsin-hsing) of Sui China, the founder of San-chiai Buddhism, maintained:

> "The *Lotus Sutra* of Lord Śākyamuni Buddha is the teaching for the first step, the Age of the True Dharma, and the second step, the Age of the Semblance Dharma. What is needed in the third step, the Latter Age of Degeneration, is the *Fukyō, General Sutra,* which I wrote. Therefore, those who practice the *Lotus Sutra* in this world today will fall into the Hell of Incessant Suffering in 10 directions. It is because the *Lotus Sutra* does not fit the intelligence and faith of people in the Latter Age of Degeneration."

He strictly observed worship and repentance six times a day and meditation four times as though he were a living Buddha. He was respected by many people and had more than 10,000 disciples.

Challenged by a mere girl who had faith in the *Lotus Sutra,* however, San-chiai lost his voice on the spot. Later he transformed himself into a large snake, which swallowed a number of disciples, followers, girls, and virgin women.

The fallacy of Shan-tao and Hōnen of the Pure Land school today, who say that not even one out of 1,000 will attain Buddhahood by putting their faith in the *Lotus Sutra* in the Latter Age of Degeneration, is not different at all from what San-chiai said. The fallacies of these three schools — Pure Land, Zen and Shingon — have been around for so long that it would not be easy to rectify them. Nevertheless, there may be some who would now believe me as I have pointed out these fallacies for so long. The worst fallacy, however, is hundreds of thousands of billions times harder to believe than these.

Refuting Grand Master Jikaku

Everybody in Japan, from the emperor down to the populace, believes that Grand Master Jikaku, the third disciple of Grand Master Dengyō, is superior to his own master. Having mastered the doctrines of both the Shingon and Lotus schools, Jikaku said that Shingon was superior to the *Lotus Sutra*, which 3,000 monks on Mt. Hiei and all the scholars of the entire country of Japan accepted without reservation.

Disciples of Kōbō felt that their master might have gone too far in insisting that the *Lotus Sutra* was inferior to the *Flower Garland Sutra*. They were convinced, however, that the teaching of the Shingon school was superior to that of the *Lotus Sutra* according to the interpretation of Grand Master Jikaku. The monks on Mt. Hiei among all the Buddhists in Japan should have spearheaded a movement opposing such a heretic idea that the teaching of Shingon was superior to that of the *Lotus Sutra*. Contrary to such a movement, Grand Master Jikaku silenced 3,000 monks on Mt. Hiei, allowing the Shingon school to spread at will. Thus, the best friend of the Shingon temple of Tōji was none other than Grand Master Jikaku.

Jikaku's role in relation to Shingon Buddhism was just like those played by Venerables Annen* and Eshin in spreading the Zen and Pure Land schools in Japan. Even if these doctrines might spread to some other lands, they did not seem to have any chance in Japan even in a million years so long as the Enryakuji Temple on Mt. Hiei opposed them. Nevertheless, when Venerable Annen, the high ranking Elder of Mt. Hiei, wrote the *Debate on the Teaching and Time* comparing the superiority of the nine schools of Buddhism, he insisted on placing the Shingon school first, the Zen school second, the Tendai-Lotus school third, and the Flower Garland school fourth. It was due to this great mistake of his that the Zen school spread all over Japan, forcing the country to the verge of destruction. Also, it was due to the preface to the *Essential Collection Concerning Rebirth in the Pure Land* of the Tendai monk Eshin, that the Pure Land school of Hōnen spread all over Japan forcing the country to face destruction. As the Buddha pointed out, parasites living in the body of a lion feed on the body of the lion. How true it is!

Theological Differences Between Dengyō and Jikaku

Grand Master Dengyō studied Tendai and Shingon doctrines by himself for 15 years in Japan. Wise by nature, he was able to master them without anyone guiding him. Nevertheless, he went to China for further study of the Tendai and Shingon schools in order to dispel the doubts of the people. Although there were various opinions among Chinese scholars, the Grand Master was convinced that the teaching of the Lotus was superior to that of the Shingon. Upon returning from China, therefore, he propagated Tendai Buddhism only. He avoided using the name of the "Shingon school" when he petitioned the Imperial Court and was granted a fellowship, which allowed him to choose annually two students to study and practice meditation *(shikan)* and mantras *(shingon)* of the Tendai school for twelve years. Moreover, receiving the imperial edict defining the *Lotus Sutra,* the *Sutra of the Golden Splendor,* and the *Sutra of the Benevolent King* as the three sutras for the tranquility of the nation, the Grand Master enshrined them at Shikan-in, the Main Hall of Enryakuji, to be revered forever as though they were the Three Imperial Treasures, the divine jewel, treasured sword, and sacred mirror enshrined in the Imperial Sanctuary, the most precious of all treasures in Japan. During the time of Venerable Gishin, the first abbot of the Enryakuji Temple on Mt. Hiei, and Grand Master Enchō,* the second abbot, these rules were unchanged.

The third abbot, Grand Master Jikaku, had gone to China for 10 years to study the comparative superiority of exoteric and esoteric teachings from the eight great masters, as well as such T'ien-t'ai masters as Kuang-hsiu and Wei-chüan. He thought privately that the Shingon school was superior to the Tendai school and that his master Dengyō had not studied the Shingon doctrine very thoroughly but only briefly during his short stay in China. So upon returning to Japan, he built a great lecture hall called Sōji-in to the west of the Shikan-in at the Eastern Tower section of Enryakuji Temple, enshrining in it the Great Sun Buddha of the Diamond Realm Mandala as the Most Venerable One. In front of this Great Sun Buddha, Grand Master Jikaku wrote the commentaries to the *Diamond Peak Sutra* and *Sutra on the Act of Perfection,* seven fascicles each, altogether 14 fascicles, based upon Venerable Śubhākarasiṃha's commentary on the *Great Sun Buddha Sutra.* These commentaries can be summarized as follows:

> "There are two kinds of Buddhism, exoteric and esoteric. The former is for those who are called Three Vehicles, that is to say, bodhisattvas, *pratyekabuddha,* and *śrāvaka.* It does not preach the perfect fusion of absolute truth and relative truth. The latter is the One Vehicle teaching, the single path to enlightenment, preaching the perfect fusion of absolute truth and relative truth. This esoteric Buddhism can further be divided into two categories. Such sutras as the *Flower Garland, Great Wisdom, Vimalakīrti, Lotus,* and *Nirvana* belong to one group, which is esoteric only in doctrine. These sutras preach the perfect fusion of the absolute truth and the relative

truth but not the ritual aspects of the mantra words and finger signs (mudrā). The second group consists of such sutras as the *Great Sun Buddha Sutra, Diamond Peak Sutra,* and *Sutra on the Act of Perfection.* These sutras preach not only the perfect fusion of the absolute truth and relative truth but also ritualism of mantra words and finger signs."

The main idea in Jikaku's commentaries is that comparison of the *Lotus Sutra* and the three canons of Shingon Buddhism shows that both preach the same 3,000 Existences Contained in One Thought doctrine. However, since the former lacks the ritual aspect of finger signs and words of spells, which the latter preaches, the *Lotus Sutra* is esoteric only in doctrine while the three Shingon canons are esoteric in both doctrine and ritualism. Therefore, the latter is incomparably superior to the former. Grand Master Jikaku believed that what he wrote in his commentaries was not his personal opinion but the heart of Śubhākarasiṃha's commentary to the *Great Sun Buddha Sutra.* Nevertheless, it seems that he was not yet so sure about the comparative superiority of the Lotus and Shingon schools, or perhaps he was still trying to dispel the doubts about it raised by others. So it is said in a biography of Grand Master Jikaku:

"After writing the commentaries to the two sutras, the Grand Master thought about whether or not they represented the Buddha's intention, determining not to publish them unless they did. Placing them in front of the Buddha's statue, he prayed from the depths of his heart for seven days and seven nights. At dawn of the fifth day, he dreamed he shot an arrow to the sun at noon, hit it and the sun trembled. He realized from this dream that his commentaries represented the true intent of the Buddha and decided that they should be transmitted to posterity."

Grand Master Jikaku completely mastered both the exoteric teaching of Dengyō and esoteric Buddhism of Kōbō in Japan. Moreover, he stayed in China as long as 10 years to study Shingon Buddhism, the most secret of all esoteric teachings, from the eight great masters and *Tripiṭaka* Master Pao-yüeh of South India among others. After completing the commentaries on the two Shingon sutras, he prayed to the Most Venerable One asking whether or not they were acceptable. Then he had a dream which ended with an arrow of wisdom hitting the sun representing the ultimate truth. Overjoyed with the dream, Jikaku requested and received imperial permission from Emperor Nimmyō to publish his commentaries. Thus, he, in effect, converted from the head of the Tendai school to that of the Shingon school, propagating the three Shingon sutras for the tranquility of the nation. Since then for more than 400 years they have been studied by scholars as numerous as rice and hemp plants and worshipped by the people in crowds like bamboo forests and reed bushes. As a result all the temples which had been built by Emperor Kammu and Grand Master Dengyō all over Japan, without exception, have become Shingon temples. Both court nobles and warriors have invited Shingon monks to be their masters and appointed them to the priest-officers in charge of Buddhist temples. All eight schools of Buddhism in Japan have come to use the finger signs and mantras of the Great Sun Buddha in the eye-opening ceremony for Buddhist wooden statues and portraits.

Evil Teachings of Grand Master Jikaku

Question: What should those who believe that the *Lotus Sutra* is superior to Shingon Buddhism do with this interpretation of Grand Master Jikaku? Should they accept it, or reject it?

Answer: Concerning the judgment of the comparative superiority of the Buddhist sutras in the future, the Buddha preached in the *Nirvana Sutra*, "Rely upon reason, not upon men." Bodhisattva Nāgārjuna stated in his *Commentary on the Ten Stages*, "It is right to depend on the sutra. It is not right not to depend on the sutra." T'ien-t'ai said in the *Profound Meaning of the Lotus Sutra*, "Accept what is in accordance with the sutra. Do not believe in what is not said in the sutra in letter or in spirit." Grand Master Dengyō in his *Outstanding Principles of the Lotus Sutra* said, "Rely upon what the Buddha preached. Never believe in what is transmitted orally."

According to these sutras, commentaries, and interpretations, we should not depend upon such things as dreams. What we need is a sutra directly comparing the superiority of the *Lotus Sutra* and the *Great Sun Buddha Sutra*. Śākyamuni Buddha declared in the *Lotus Sutra* that of all sutras the Lotus is the prime sutra and that it is the king of sutras. No such statement can be found in the *Great Sun Buddha Sutra*.

However, it is strange to say that it is impossible to perform the eye-opening ceremony for Buddhist wooden statues and portraits without finger signs and mantras of Shingon Buddhism. Had not there been the ceremony for opening the eyes of wooden statues and portraits prior to the emergence of Shingon Buddhism? Although there had been such miracles as Buddhist wooden statues and portraits walking, preaching, or speaking in India, China, and Japan prior to the time of Shingon Buddhism, there have been no such miracles ever since the eye-opening ceremonies began to be conducted with finger signs, and mantras of Shingon Buddhism. This is what I have been telling you always. However, regarding the contention of Grand Master Jikaku that Shingon teaching is superior to that of the *Lotus Sutra*, it is not necessary for me to cite distinctive proof. We have only to believe in what he said in his commentaries. Grand Master Jikaku's own words prove his fallacy.

Question: How should we understand him?

Answer: Grand Master Jikaku's having such a dream was due to his preconception that Shingon Buddhism was superior to the *Lotus Sutra*. If his dreams were auspicious, Shingon Buddhism might be superior as the Grand Master judged. However, is a dream of shooting the sun auspicious? I wish to see any proof, if there is any, in Buddhist scriptures, over 5,000 or 7,000 scrolls or in 3,000-odd scrolls of non-Buddhist scriptures,* showing that the dream of shooting the sun is a good omen.

If I may, I will show some proof contradicting this. When King Ajātaśatru dreamed of the moon falling from the sky, his minister, Jīvaka, predicted the death of the Buddha. Subhadra dreamed of the sun falling from the sky and foretold the death of the Buddha. In the battle against Indra, the *asura* demon at first shot the sun and moon. King Chieh of Hsia and King Chou of Yin, wicked rulers of ancient China, destroyed themselves and lost their kingdoms by shooting the sun. Queen Māyā gave birth to Prince Siddhārtha after dreaming she was pregnant with the sun. So the Buddha's infant name was Sun-seed. This country is called Japan, meaning the origin of the sun, because Goddess Amaterasu, the founder of Japan, is the Goddess of the Sun. Therefore, the dream of Jikaku meant that his commentaries to the two Shingon sutras are the arrow that shot through Goddess Amaterasu, Grand Master Dengyō, Śākyamuni Buddha, and the *Lotus Sutra*.

I, Nichiren, am an ignorant fool who does not know anything about sutras and commentaries. Nevertheless, I know for sure that those who insist because of such a dream like this that Shingon Buddhism is superior to the *Lotus Sutra* would destroy their country and lose their houses in this life, and fall into the Hell of Incessant Suffering after death.

Factual Proof of Shingon as the Cause of National Destruction

Let me present the real proof that Shingon Buddhism leads to the destruction of the nation. Since all the Shingon monks in Japan pray for the defeat of the Mongols in the present war between Japan and the Mongols, if Japan should win the war, we may believe in the superiority of Shingon Buddhism. However, we have as precedence the Jōkyū Incident, in which the Shogunal Regent, Hōjō Yoshitoki, for whose chastisement many Shingon monks prayed, won the war. As a result it was as though they prayed for the banishment of ex-Emperor Gotoba to Oki Province and his son, Emperor Juntoku, to Sado Island. In the end, as howling foxes are killed by dogs, all the 3,000 monks on Mt. Hiei were attacked and forced by the shogunal army to surrender. It was exactly as predicted in the *Lotus Sutra*, chapter 25, that when someone curses others, the cursing will come back to himself. Nevertheless, the Kamakura Shogunate is again asking Shingon monks to pray. Does it have them pray for the destruction of Japan? One who knows this well is the wisest in the world. We certainly must remember this.

Now is the age of warriors at Kamakura. So "Shingon" monks of the Tōji Temple, Mt. Hiei, the Onjōji Temple, and seven temples of Nara as well as those slanderers of the True Dharma, who read the *Lotus Sutra* without knowing what it stands for, have gone to Kamakura in the Kantō District to kneel down, bow their heads, and cater to the whims of the warriors in order to win leadership of the temples. They pray for the tranquility of the nation with the false teaching which caused the downfall of the imperial house at the time of the Jōkyū Incident. The shogun, his retainer-warriors and others all believe that peace in the land will be ensured by their prayers. Meanwhile, since those in the shogunal service are monks who are against the *Lotus Sutra* and are fountainheads of calamities, this land will certainly be destroyed.

First of Those Who Practice the Lotus Sutra in the Latter Age of Degeneration

Because it is lamentable to see the possibility of our land and ourselves destroyed, I have determined to point this out even at the cost of my life. If the ruler of the land wishes to maintain peace, he should have already begun to wonder and investigate what I have said. On the contrary, believing only in the words of slanderers, he is persecuting me, Nichiren. The King of the Brahma Heaven, Indra, the sun, the moon, the Four Heavenly Kings, and the terrestrial gods, whose duty it is to protect the *Lotus Sutra*, in the past regarded slanderers of the True Dharma as outrageous. However, when nobody pointed out such slanderers, these deities sometimes ignored them just as parents overlook the mischief of their sole child, although at other times they punished him with as little as a warning. Today, however, the ruler not only appoints slanderers of the True Dharma to official positions but also persecutes the man who happened to admonish* him, not just for one or two days, one or two months, and one or two years, but for many years. Nichiren has been persecuted more severely than Never-Despising Bodhisattva, who was beaten with sticks and pieces of wood, and Monk Virtue Consciousness, who was about to be murdered, upholding the True Dharma in the past. Therefore the King of the Brahma Heaven, Indra, the sun, the moon, the Four Heavenly Kings, the stars, and the terrestrial gods all are angry with the ruler and often warn him by sending strange phenomena in the sky and natural calamities on earth. Since he does not perceive their warnings and only intensifies the persecution of the man who admonishes, they order the sagacious ruler of a neighboring land to chastise the ruler of Japan and send demons into his land to deceive the people and cause internal disruption.

Great events, regardless if they are good or bad, are foreshadowed by great omens. We saw the largest comet we have ever seen in 2,230 years or so since the death of the Buddha and experienced the severest earthquake we have ever had in history. They foretell the destruction of Japan, at the same time they are omens of the appearance of the one who truly practices the *Lotus Sutra* in Japan. There have been many sages endowed with wisdom and talent in China and Japan, but none has ever believed in the *Lotus Sutra* as firmly as I, Nichiren. Nor has anyone had as many strong enemies in the land as I do. From these facts, you should recognize Nichiren to be first among those who practice the *Lotus Sutra* in the world.

It has been more than 700 years since Buddhism was introduced to Japan, bringing with it 5,000 or 7,000 scrolls of Buddhist scriptures and the development of eight or 10 Buddhist schools. Men of wisdom have been as numerous as rice and hemp plants and Buddhism has spread as briskly as bamboo forests or reed plants. Since no Buddhas have been as popular as the Buddha of Infinite Life, calling the name of this Buddha has spread most widely.

As for those who spread the practice of calling the name of the Buddha of Infinite Life, Eshin (Genshin) who wrote the *Essential Collection Concerning the Rebirth in the Pure Land*, converted one third of the Japanese people to Pure Land Buddhism. When Yōkan wrote the *Ten Reasons for Rebirth in the Pure Land* and the *Order of Service for Rebirth in the Pure Land*, two-thirds of the people in Japan were converted to Pure Land Buddhism. Finally Hōnen wrote the *Collection of Passages on the Nembutsu and the Original Vow*, completing the conversion of all the people in Japan. So not all those who recite the *nembutsu*, calling the name of the Buddha of Infinite Life, today are disciples of one master.

The *nembutsu* is the title of the three canons of Pure Land Buddhism. Namely, the *Sutra of the Buddha of Infinite Life*, the *Sutra of Meditation on the Buddha of Infinite Life*, and the *Pure Land Sutra*, which are provisional Mahayana sutras. Is not the spread of the title of provisional Mahayana sutras preliminary to the spread of the title of the true Mahayana *Lotus Sutra*? Thoughtful people should contemplate this. The true sutra will spread after provisional sutras. The title of the true sutra will spread after that of provisional sutras.

I have never seen or heard of any man of knowledge who recited *"Namu Myōhō Renge-kyō"* himself and advised others to do so during the 700-year period between the reigns of Emperor Kimmei, when Buddhism was introduced to Japan, and the latest emperor. It is only natural that when the sun rises, stars disappear. When a wise king rises to power, an ignorant king is destroyed. So when the True Dharma spreads, provisional ones decline. When a man of knowledge recites *"Namu Myōhō Renge-kyō,"* ignorant people follow him, just as a body is followed by its shadow and a sound is followed by its echo. Consider what is said above. I, Nichiren, undoubtedly am first among those who practice the *Lotus Sutra* in Japan. No one in China, India, or anywhere in the whole world is comparable to me.

The Cause of Calamities and the Reappearance of Superior-Practice Bodhisattva

Question: How did the great earthquake of the Shōka Era* and the great comet of the Bun'ei Era happen?

Answer: T'ien-t'ai* has said, "Men of knowledge know the causes of phenomena, and snakes only know the way of snakes."

Question: What does that mean?

Answer: It means that when Superior-Practice Bodhisattva* emerged from the earth as described in the 15th chapter of the *Lotus Sutra,* even such bodhisattvas as Maitreya, Mañjuśrī, Avalokiteśvara, and Medicine-King, who had reached only one step below Buddhahood by conquering the 41 steps of darkness of mind, did not know that he had been called upon to spread *"Namu Myōhō Renge-kyō,"* the essence of the 16th chapter of the *Lotus Sutra,* The Duration of the Life of the Tathāgata, in the Latter Age of Degeneration. It was because they had not yet conquered the fundamental darkness of mind* and therefore were still considered ignorant.

Question: Is there anyone in Japan, China, or in India who knows the cause of these calamities?

Answer: Even the great bodhisattvas, who have extinguished delusions arising from false views and thoughts and conquered the 41 steps of darkness of mind, reaching the state just one step below Buddhahood, do not know it. How can anyone who has not extinguished delusions at all know it?

Question: How can we deal with these calamities without the man of knowledge who knows the cause of them? For instance, if a man tries to cure an illness without knowing what causes it, his patient is bound to die. So it is without doubt that when prayers are said by persons who do not know the cause of calamities, the country will be ruined. How sad it is!

Answer: Snakes can foretell a heavy rain a week in advance and crows know what will happen all year round, either good or bad. This is because snakes are retainers of great dragons and crows learn from their long traditions. Being an ordinary man, I, Nichiren, do not know the cause of calamities. With the help of the Buddha, however, I can try to explain the cause.

During the reign of King P'ing in Chou China, when a naked man with disheveled hair appeared, a man called Hsin-yu predicted the downfall of the Chou dynasty within a century. When a violent earthquake crumbled mountains and destroyed rivers during the reign of King Yu of the same Chou dynasty, a man named Pai-yang predicted that the great king would encounter a great difficulty within a dozen years. The calamities today such as the great earthquake of the Shōka Era and the great comet of the Bun'ei Era are sent by heaven, angry at the ruler of Japan, because he hates Nichiren and patronizes monks of the Zen, Pure Land, and Shingon schools, teachings leading to national destruction!

Question: How can I believe in this?

Answer: It is said in the *Sutra of the Golden Splendor** that when evil men were regarded highly and good men were persecuted, constellations, rains and winds all went out of control. If this passage of the sutra is correct, undoubtedly there are evil men in this country, whom its ruler and his subjects believe in. It is also without doubt that there are men of knowledge in this country, whom the ruler of Japan hates and begrudges.

The same sutra also states that when all the gods of the Thirty-three Heavens are angry, a strange comet will fall, two suns will rise at the same time, and the people will suffer from foreign invasion. Japan has already experienced strange phenomena in the sky and calamities on earth as well as foreign invasion. Undoubtedly the gods of the Thirty-three Heavens have all been angry.

It is said in the *Sutra of the Benevolent King* that many evil monks seek fame and profit by preaching false dharmas to the king, crown prince, and princes. These false dharmas destroy Buddhism and ruin the country while the king, unable to distinguish the True Dharma from the false ones, listens to them and believes in them. The sutra also declares that the sun and moon will not rise with regularity. Seasons will reverse their order. A red or black sun will rise, Two, three, four or five suns will rise at the same time. An eclipse of the sun will occur, making it completely dark. Or one, two, three, four or five halos, will appear around the sun.

The heart of these passages is that if a country is full of evil monks who deceive their king, his crown prince, and princes by preaching to them false dharmas for the ruin of Buddhism as well as of the country, the king and others will be deceived by those evil monks and mistake their false dharmas for true Buddhism and True Dharma that would bring about the tranquility of the country. When they accept the words of these evil monks and put them into practice, the revolution of the sun and moon will change, and such calamities as strong winds, heavy rains, and big fires will occur. Next will come internal revolt, severe fighting among relatives, in which those who should be on the king's side will all be killed. After that this country will be invaded by foreign soldiers, with people either committing suicide, being captured, or surrendering. This is how evil monks destroy Buddhism and demolish the country.

It is said in the *Guardian Sutra:*

> "All the teachings of Śākyamuni Buddha are indestructible from the outside, even by all the heavenly kings, non-Buddhists, evil men, and hermits with mastery of five superhuman powers. However, they will be completely destroyed without a trace internally by evil monks who are monks in name and appearance only. This is just like Mt. Sumeru, which will not be hurt at all even if it is burned for a long time with all the grasses and trees in the whole world as fuel. However, when the time comes for destruction of the world and the conflagration at the end of the *kalpa* of destruction[17] begins within the world, it will be burned up in no time without leaving even ashes."

It is also said in the *Lotus Flower Mask Sutra:* "The Buddha declared to Ānanda that when lions die, no creatures in the sky, the earth, water, or on land would eat their corpses. Only those worms begotten by the lions themselves would eat the corpses. So it is with Buddhism. Buddhism would not be destroyed from the outside. Evil monks within His own Buddhist order would destroy the True Dharma, which He had attained through hard work for an incalculably long period of time, three great *asaṃkhya kalpa.*"

As for the meaning of these sutras, Kāśyapa Buddha, the sixth of the seven Buddhas in the past, preached to King Kṛki about the Latter Age of Degeneration after the death of Śākyamuni Buddha. Considering what kind of men could destroy the teaching of Śākyamuni Buddha, it is stated, even such a wicked man as King Mihirakula, who burned down all the Buddhist temples in all of India and murdered monks and nuns of 16 great kingdoms in India, or Emperor Wu-tsung of T'ang China, who destroyed over 4,600 temples and towers in nine states and drove 260,500 monks and nuns from their monasteries, could not destroy the Buddhism of Śākyamuni Buddha. It would be destroyed by those Buddhist monks who wear the three robes, carry a bowl for begging around their necks, know 80,000 Buddhist teachings by heart, and recite the twelve kinds of Buddhist scriptures. It is just as Mt. Sumeru, a mountain made of gold, will not be damaged at all even if it is burned with all the grasses and trees of the entire world piled high up to the heaven for not only a year or two but for millions of billions of years. However, when a conflagration starts at the end of the *kalpa* of destruction, a fire as small as a pea will begin at the base of Mt. Sumeru, and it soon will burn to ashes not only Mt. Sumeru but also the entire world.

If what is predicted in these sutras is right, does it not mean that monks of the ten or eight schools of Japanese Buddhism will burn down Mt. Sumeru of Buddhism? The angry spirit of Hinayana monks of the Kusha, Jōjitsu, and Ritsu schools being envious of Mahayana Buddhism is the fire that will burn down Buddhism. Such monks as Śubhākarasiṃha of Shingon Buddhism, San-chiai of the Zen school, and Shan-tao of the Pure Land school are like grasshoppers who germinate from the lion, Buddhism, to eat up its corpse. Grand Master Dengyō called the eminent masters of the six schools of Nara "six worms." I, Nichiren, name the founders of the Shingon, Zen, and Pure Land schools "three worms." Such Tendai monks as Jikaku, Annen, and Eshin are "three worms" germinating in the body of a lion, the *Lotus Sutra* and Grand Master Dengyō.

As rulers of Japan persecute me, Nichiren, who prosecute the fountainhead of slanderers of the True Dharma, heavenly gods feel pity for me and terrestrial deities are angry at these rulers, causing various calamities. You must remember, therefore, that since the most important dharma in the world is being preached, you are witnessing the best omens.

It is pitiful that all the people in Japan are about to fall into the Hell of Incessant Suffering. It is my great pleasure, however, that I, though unworthy, am able to have just planted the seed of Buddhahood in the bottom of my heart.

You shall see that such a time will soon come when the Great Mongol Empire will attack Japan with several tens of thousands of warships. All the people in Japan, from the emperor down to his subjects, casting aside all the Buddhist temples and Shinto shrines, shall recite in unison *"Namu Myōhō Renge-kyō, Namu Myōhō Renge-kyō."* Holding their hands together in *gasshō*, they will cry: "Please help us, Priest Nichiren, please help us." They are like King Mihirakula of India, who attacked a neighboring ruler, King Bālāditya, only to be captured and had to apologize to King Bālāditya with hands together in *gasshō*. They are like Taira no Munemori of Japan, the head of the Taira Clan, who was defeated and captured by the Minamoto Clan and had to show respect to Kajiwara Kagetoki, a Minamoto vassal. They represent the principle that the conceited will have to submit to their enemies.

Those self-conceited monks, who had slighted and abused Bodhisattva Never-Despising, at first beat him with sticks and pieces of wood, but later they regretted what they had done, holding their hands together in *gasshō*. Devadatta, who had tortured Śākyamuni Buddha until He bled, chanted *"Namu"* at the moment of his death. If he had said *"Namu* Buddha," he would have not fallen into hell. However, because of his bad karma, he said merely *"Namu"* without saying "Buddha." High priests of Japan, today, too, seem to say merely *"Namu,"* although what they would like to say is *"Namu* Nichiren Shōnin." What a pity!

Three Outstanding Predictions

It is said in a non-Buddhist writing that those who can predict things before they actually take place can be called sages. In Buddhism, those who see life in the past, present, and future are called sages. I made three outstanding predictions. First, on the 16th day of the seventh month in the first year of Bunnō (1260), upon presenting my *Risshō Ankoku-ron, Treatise on Spreading Peace Throughout the Country by Establishing the True Dharma*, to the former Shogunal Regent, Hōjō Tokiyori, I told Lay Priest Yadoya, a member of the entourage of Tokiyori: "Please tell the former Regent to ban the Zen and Pure Land schools. Otherwise fighting will break out within the Hōjō Clan and Japan will be attacked by foreign powers."

In the second place, around 4:00 p.m. on the 12th day of the ninth month in the eighth year of Bun'ei (1271) I declared to Hei no Saemonnojō when he came to arrest me at Matsubagayatsu:

> "I, Nichiren, am the chief support of Japan. When you kill me, you will cut the pillar of Japan. Before long, there will be a civil war, in which the Japanese people fight among themselves, and foreign invasion, in which many people in Japan will not only be killed but also captured by foreign invaders. Unless all the temples of the Pure Land and Zen schools such as Kenchōji, Jufukuji, Gokurakuji, Great Buddha, and Chōrakuji are burned down and their priests all beheaded at Yuigahama Beach, Japan is bound to be destroyed."

In the third place, last year, on the eighth day of the fourth month in the 11th year of Bun'ei (1274), I declared to Hei no Samonnojō:

> "Since I was born in the land under the Hōjō's control, my body appears to follow your order. However, I cannot obey you in my heart. There is no doubt that Pure Land Buddhism leads to falling into hell and Zen is the work of a heavenly devil. Especially, the Shingon school of Buddhism is the cause of calamities in Japan. Therefore, Shingon priests should not be entrusted to perform prayers for the expulsion of the Mongols. If they are entrusted with this great task, they will only speed up the destruction of Japan."

Then Hei no Samonnojō asked me when, in my opinion, the Mongols would attack Japan. I told him: "No sutras specifically state when, but as the heavens seem quite angry, it will not be long before they do. Most likely it will be before the year ends."

It was not I, Nichiren, who made these three important predictions. I believe it was solely the spirit of Śākyamuni Buddha, entering my body, who made them.

I am overwhelmed with joy. This is the important 3,000 Existences Contained in One Thought doctrine of the *Lotus Sutra*. According to it, the mind of any person is equipped with the seed of Buddhahood, which could grow to blossom in his mind when he upholds the right faith. As a result, his mind could function like that of the Buddha. This is what happened to me, Nichiren, when I made these three predictions. Due to my faith in the *Lotus Sutra*, I was able to see things before they actually took place. What is the meaning of "appearances of all phenomena as they are" as stated in the *Lotus Sutra*? Since "appearance" is mentioned first among the 10 factors of existence,[18] it is the most important among them and the Buddha has come into this world in order to expound it. The appearance of a thing represents its reality. So we can grasp its reality when we see through its appearance clearly, and in turn we can predict what would happen in the future. This is what Grand Master Miao-lê meant when he said that wise men know the cause of phenomena, and snakes only know about snakes.

Rivers come together to form an ocean. Particles of dust accumulate to become Mt. Sumeru. When I, Nichiren, began having faith in the *Lotus Sutra*, it was like a drop of water or a particle of dust in Japan. However, when the sutra is chanted and transmitted to two, three, ten, a million, and a billion people, it will grow to be a Mt. Sumeru of perfect enlightenment or the great ocean of Nirvana. There is no way other than this to reach Buddhahood.

Second Outstanding Prediction

Question: Regarding your second prediction, when you were punished by the shogunate on the 12th day of the ninth month in the eighth year of Bun'ei (1271), how had you known that if you, Nichiren, were persecuted, there would be internal disturbance and foreign invasion?

Answer: It is said in the *Sutra of the Great Assembly*, 50th fascicle:

> "Again, if there are kings who commit evil to hinder the Buddha's disciples, speak ill of them, beat them with sticks or kill them with swords, rob them of robes or iron bowls for begging and many other things, or stand in the way of those who want to give offerings to them, we will make sure that soon there will be foreign invasion as well as civil wars in their lands. We will cause epidemics, famines, unseasonable storms, quarrels, fighting, and abuse among them with those kings losing their lands before long."

There are similar statements in various sutras. I have chosen this, however, because it fits me, Nichiren, and is specifically valuable to me in this Latter Age of Degeneration. "We" in this passage refers to the King of the Brahma Heaven, Indra, the King of Devils in the Sixth Heaven, and all the heavenly beings and dragons in the triple world* such as the sun and moon and the Four Heavenly Kings. Leaders of these went to see the Buddha, and made an oath before Him saying:

> "During the Ages of the True and Semblance Dharmas and the Latter Age of Degeneration after the extinction of the Buddha, monks of evil teachings will appeal to the king, slandering those who practice the True Dharma. Because they are close and friendly to the king and are revered by the king, he will uncritically persecute without reason those wise men, who will practice the True Dharma. Then for some unknown reason a great civil war will suddenly break out, which will be followed by foreign invasion. In the end the king will lose his life and his kingdom will be destroyed."

I am in a great quandary. When my prediction comes true, it will prove that I am a sage, but Japan will be destroyed. I, Nichiren, have not committed any crime in this life. I am only sorry that what I said for the sake of my country and in order for me to repay the debt of gratitude to my native land was not appreciated. In addition, I was arrested and badly beaten with the fifth fascicle of the *Lotus Sutra*, which I had kept in my bosom. Finally I was taken through the streets of Kamakura like a criminal. So I said loudly to the heavenly beings:

> "The sun and moon gods are still in heaven as they had been at the time of the Lotus Assembly on Mt. Sacred Eagle. Yet now they don't come to rescue me, Nichiren, when I am severely persecuted. Does it mean first of all, that I am not one who truly practices the *Lotus Sutra*? If so, I will not hesitate to correct my false view right away. If I, Nichiren, am one who truly practices the *Lotus Sutra*, please show proof immediately all over Japan. Otherwise, the sun and moon today are great liars who fool Śākyamuni Buddha, the Buddha of Many Treasures and Buddhas in all the worlds in the universe. Their lies are a hundred, a thousand, ten thousand, and ten million times larger than those committed by Devadatta and his disciple Kokālika."

In prompt response they immediately caused civil disturbance, throwing Japan into confusion. Although I am an ordinary man not worth mentioning, in regard to upholding the *Lotus Sutra*, I am the greatest man in Japan today.

The Wisest in the World

Question: Self-conceit, which is a form of evil passion, can be divided into seven, eight, or nine categories. The great self-conceit of yours is a hundred, a thousand, ten thousand, and ten million times larger than the self-conceit preached in Buddhism. Commentator Guṇaprabha did not show respect to Bodhisattva Maitreya. Brahman, the Boaster, sat on a chair with statues of the four sages, including the Buddha, as its four legs. Mahādeva claimed to be an arhat while being merely an ordinary man. And Commentator Vimalamitra called himself the greatest in India. They all fell into the Hell of Incessant Suffering. They were criminals committed to hell. Why do you claim to be the wisest in the world? How can it be that you will not fall into a great hell? How dreadful it is!

Answer: Do you know anything about seven, eight or nine kinds of self-conceit? When Śākyamuni Buddha claimed to be the first in the triple world, all the non-Buddhists predicted that He would soon be punished by heaven or that the earth would split open and crumble. He was not punished, however. Instead He was protected by heaven both on the right and left, and the earth was as solid as a diamond and did not split open. In the seven temples of Nara, 300 monks wondered whether or not Priest Saichō, Grand Master Dengyō, was a self-conceited Mahādeva or Daiten, and Teppuku or Daisha of India reincarnated in Japan. However, Grand Master Dengyō established the Enryakuji Temple on Mt. Hiei, and he became the eye of all the people. In the end, the seven temples in Nara surrendered to the Grand Master and became his disciples, while people in various provinces in Japan became members of his congregation. Therefore, it is not self-conceit, though it sounds like it, to call something excellent when it is actually excellent. It is an act of great merit. The Grand Master says in his *Outstanding Principles of the Lotus Sutra,* "The Tendai-Lotus school is superior to other schools of Buddhism because its basic canon, the *Lotus Sutra,* is superior to those of other schools. This is not self-conceit slandering others."

It is said in the *Lotus Sutra,* fascicle seven, chapter 23, "Mt. Sumeru is the greatest of mountains. Likewise, this *Lotus Sutra* is supreme of all sutras." This means that the the *Lotus Sutra* transmitted to Japan is like Mt. Sumeru while all other sutras, that is 5,000 or 7,000 fascicles of pre-*Lotus* Sutras such as the *Flower Garland, Great Wisdom,* and *Great Sun Buddha Sutras,* the *Sutra of Infinite Meaning,* which was preached at the same time as the *Lotus Sutra,* and post-*Lotus* Sutras such as the *Nirvana Sutra,* as well as all the Buddhist sutras in India, the dragon's palace, the heavens of the Four Heavenly Kings, Trāyastiṃsa Heaven, the sun and moon, and all the worlds in the universe, all these are like the earth mountains, black mountains, Small Surrounding Iron Mountains and Great Surrounding Iron Mountains, which encircle Mt. Sumeru.

It is also said in the same chapter, "Those who put faith in the *Lotus Sutra* and uphold it are likewise the greatest of all people!" This means that those who upheld the *Flower Garland Sutra* are Bodhisattvas Samantabhadra, Moon of Emancipation, Nāgārjuna, and Aśvaghoṣa, and Grand Master Fa-tsang, State Master Ch'ing-liang, Empress Wu, Masters Shinjō and Ryōben, and Emperor Shōmu. The *Revealing the Profound and Secret Sutra* and the *Wisdom Sutra* have been upheld by Bodhisattva Shōgishō, Venerable Subhūti, Grand Master Chia-hsiang, Venerable Hsüan-chuang, Emperors T'ai-tsung and Kao-tsung of T'ang China, Priests Kanroku and Dōshō and Emperor Kōtoku of Japan. The *Great Sun Buddha Sutra* of the Shingon school has been upheld by Vajrasattva, Bodhisattvas Nāgārjuna and Nāgabodhi, King Sātyavahona, *Tripiṭaka* Masters Śubhākarasiṃha, Vajrabodhi and Amoghavajra, Emperors Hsüan-tsung and Tai-tsung of T'ang, Hui-kuo, and Grand Masters Kōbō and Jikaku. The *Nirvana Sutra* has been upheld by Bodhisattva Kashōdōji, 52 groups of those who listened to the preaching of the *Nirvana Sutra, Tripiṭaka* Master Dharmarakṣa, Fa-yün of the Kuang-chê Temple and the 10 masters of Northern and Southern China. However, ordinary people in the Latter Age of Degeneration, who single-mindedly believe that the *Lotus Sutra* is supreme of all the sutras which have been preached, are being preached, and will be preached and that it is the only way leading to Buddhahood, are a hundred, a thousand, ten thousand, and ten million times superior to those Bodhisattvas and great masters. This is true even if they may not be able to keep one precept, may be regarded by others as *icchantika*, who have no faith in Buddhism, and may not have any ability to understand things at all. So says the passage.

Some of those great bodhisattvas and masters spread those sutras among the people so that they would be converted later to the *Lotus Sutra*. Others attached themselves to those sutras without moving into the *Lotus Sutra*, while still others not only remained in those sutras but also attached themselves so much to them that they insisted that the *Lotus Sutra* was inferior to those sutras.

Therefore, those who practice the *Lotus Sutra* today should remember what is preached in The Previous Life of Medicine-King Bodhisattva chapter: "Just as the ocean is the largest of all bodies of water, upholders of the *Lotus Sutra* are above all other people." They should also remember: "Just as the moon is brighter than any star, upholders of the *Lotus Sutra* are the first among the people." Wise men today in Japan are like numerous stars while Nichiren is like the full moon.

Question: Did anyone say this before?

Answer: Grand Master Dengyō has said in his *Outstanding Principles of the Lotus Sutra:* "You should know this. As basic canons of other schools are not the supreme sutras, those who uphold those sutras are not enlightened above all the people. The basic canon of the Tendai-Lotus school is the supreme sutra, so those who uphold it are enlightened above all the people. These are the words of the Buddha. How can this be self-conceit?" When a mite riding on the tail of a dragon-horse, which can run 1,000 *ri* a day boasts that it, the mite, can run 1,000 *ri* a day, or when a follower of the Wheel-turning Noble King claims to run around the world in a second, who would blame or suspect him? We should remember by heart: "How can this be self-conceit?" If so, since those who uphold the *Lotus Sutra* exactly as it is are above the King of the Brahma Heaven and Indra, they should be able to have Mt. Sumeru carried by *asura* demons and a great ocean swallowed up by dragons.

According to Grand Master Dengyō, "Those who praise the *Lotus Sutra* accumulate merits as high as Mt. Sumeru, and those who slander it fall into the Hell of Incessant Suffering." It is said in the *Lotus Sutra*, chapter three: "If someone despises, hates, envies or bears a grudge against the person who reads, recites, or upholds the *Lotus Sutra*...such a person will fall into the Hell of Incessant Suffering upon his death." If the golden words of the Lord Śākyamuni Buddha are true, if the testimony of the Buddha of Many Treasures is correct, and if the testimony by the Buddhas from all the worlds in the universe with their long and wide tongues is certain, how can there be any doubt that all the people in Japan will fall into the Hell of Incessant Suffering?

It is said in the *Lotus Sutra*, fascicle eight, chapter 28: "If someone will uphold, read, and recite this sutra in the future, his wishes will be fulfilled, and he will receive a happy reward in his present life." It is said also: "If someone reveres and praises the *Lotus Sutra*, he will receive a real reward in his present life." Regarding these two passages, there are eight characters meaning "he will receive a happy reward in his present life" and another eight characters meaning "he will receive a real reward in this life." If these 16 characters are not realized and I, Nichiren, do not receive a great reward in this life, the golden worlds of the Buddha would be as worthless as the empty words of Devadatta, and the testimony of the Buddha of Many Treasures would be no different from the lies of Kokālika, the disciple of Devadatta. All the people who slander the *Lotus Sutra* would not fall into the Hell of Incessant Suffering, and there would be no Buddhas throughout life in the past, present and future. Therefore, I urge you, my disciples, to practice Buddhism as preached in the *Lotus Sutra* without sparing your life and prove the truth of Buddhism once for all. *Namu Myōhō Renge-kyō! Namu Myōhō Renge-kyō!*"

Exhortation Not to Spare One's Own Life for the Sake of the Supreme Way

Question: Now, in this *Lotus Sutra*, 13th chapter, it is said: "I will not spare my life. I will treasure only the supreme way." It is also said in the *Nirvana Sutra*:

> "Just as a royal emissary, skillful in talking and dealing, is sent to a foreign land and carries out the royal order even at the cost of his own life by stating the king's words without concealing them, likewise, wise men should expound the Mahayana teaching secretly held by the Buddha. Namely, that

each person possesses Buddha-nature. This should be expounded among ordinary people even at the cost of life."

I would like to hear you explain why it is necessary for them to sacrifice their lives.

Answer: At first I wondered whether or not the dangerous trips to China by Dengyō, Kōbō, Jikaku, and Chishō under imperial order were what is referred to as "I will not spare my life." I also wondered whether *Tripiṭaka* Master Hsüan-chuang almost losing his life six times trying to reach India from China, Young Ascetic in the Snow Mountains* sacrificing his own life in order to hear half a verse, and Medicine-King Bodhisattva burning his own elbow to offer a light to Sun Moon Pure Bright Virtue Buddha for as long as 72,000 years referred to "I will not spare my life." According to sutras, however, this is not so.

Before the phrase "I will not spare my life" is mentioned in the *Lotus Sutra*, it is preached that the three kinds of enemies* of the *Lotus Sutra* will abuse and accuse those who believe in it and attack them with sticks and swords until they die. The phrase "even at the cost of life" in the *Nirvana Sutra,* is followed by: "An *icchantika,* who does not have faith in the True Dharma, disguised as an arhat, lives in a quiet mountain, slandering Mahayana sutras. Having seen such a man, ordinary people would say that he is a true arhat and a great bodhisattva!"

Speaking of the third of the three kinds of enemies of the *Lotus Sutra,* the sutra says: "There are some who will live in a quiet mountain monastery, wearing patched clothing. They will be respected by the people as though they were arhats with six superhuman powers." It is also said in the six-fascicled *Nirvana Sutra (Hatsunaion-gyō)*: "There are some *icchantika* who resemble arhats and do evil deeds." These passages mean that the worst enemies of the True Dharma are not to be found among wicked kings and his wicked subjects, among heretics and the King of Devils, or among monks without precepts. The worst slanderers of the True Dharma are to be found among those high-ranking monks who uphold precepts and are regarded to be wise men. Therefore, Grand Master Miao-lê writes: "Among the three kinds of enemies, the third one is the worst. As we go through the first kind, second kind, and the third kind, the latter ones are more cunning in pretending to be sages. Therefore, it is harder to reveal their wickedness."

It is said in the *Lotus Sutra,* fascicle five, chapter 14: "This *Lotus Sutra* is the secret treasure of all Buddhas. It is supreme of all sutras." Please note that "it is supreme of all sutras." According to this sutra, therefore, he who insists that the *Lotus Sutra* is supreme of all sutras is one who truly practices the *Lotus Sutra,* isn't he? Nevertheless, many who are revered in the land insist that there are sutras superior to the Lotus. Standing against these monks, who are revered by the king and his subjects, the one who practices the *Lotus Sutra* is poor and powerless, with all the people in the land despising him. Under such circumstances, if he points out their sin of slandering the True Dharma as stubbornly as Never-Despising Bodhisattva or as decisively as Commentator Bhadraruci defeated Brahman, the Boaster, his life will be in jeopardy. This seems of prime importance. This fits me, Nichiren.

In my present status, it is not easy to state that such monks as Grand Masters Kōbō and Jikaku or *Tripiṭaka* Masters Śubhākarasiṃha, Vajrabodhi, and Amoghavajra are enemies of the *Lotus Sutra,* and that if the sutra is true, there is no doubt that they will all fall into the Hell of Incessant Suffering. For example, as preached in the *Lotus Sutra,* chapter 11, it is easy to walk through a great fire, grab Mt. Sumeru and throw it away, or walk on an ocean carrying a huge rock. It is most difficult, however, to establish the teaching of the *Lotus Sutra* in Japan. Without constant support extended by Lord Śākyamuni Buddha in the Pure Land of Mt. Sacred Eagle, the Buddha of Many Treasures in the Treasure Purity World, Buddhas in manifestation, *funjin* Buddhas, in all the worlds in the universe, numerous bodhisattvas emerged from the earth, the King of the Brahma Heaven, Indra, the sun and moon, and the Four Heavenly Kings, how can we have tranquility even for an hour or a day?

Notes

1. Probably refers to the Mo-ho tribes in Manchuria.
2. The highest layer of the world of transmigration, *sangai*. It consists of a part of heaven. Its inhabitants have no physical form. See "Triple world" *(sangai)* in the glossary.
3. Actually 16 years, 629-645.
4. Birth from the womb, *taishō,* birth from an egg, *ranshō,* birth from moisture, *shisshō,* and metamorphosis, *keshō.*
5. Six lower states of existence: hell, realms of hungry spirits, beasts, *asura* demons, men and heavenly beings, and gods. These are the lower six of the so-called Ten Realms, or *jikkai,* of T'ien-t'ai.
6. Having a long tongue is one of the Buddha's 32 physical excellences, considered a sign of truly spoken words.
7. One of the three realms of the world of the unenlightened, the *sangai* or triple world. The realm of form is a part of heaven, and its inhabitants have no desires.
8. Aeons: an inconceivably long period of time, explained as the period needed to empty a city full of poppy seeds by taking away one seed every three years, or to wear away a 10-mile-cubic stone by the touch of an angel's garment once in three years.

9. The T'ien-t'ai term to explain reality in three aspects: (1) "truth of voidness," i.e., all existence is non-substantial in essence; (2) "truth of temporariness," i.e., all existence is temporarily manifested, produced by causes and conditions; and (3) "truth of the middle," i.e., the absolute reality of all existence cannot be explained in either negative or affirmative terms.
10. The T'ien-t'ai doctrine classifies Buddhist doctrines into four in ascending order: *zōkyō*, the Hinayana teaching, *tsūgyō*, common teaching, *bekkyō*, Mahayana teaching, and *engyō*, perfect teaching.
11. See "Four kalpa" *(shikō)* in the glossary.
12. Distance covered by the royal army in a day, said to be 40 or 30 Chinese *li*.
13. *Rokusō-jūgen*: Kegon doctrine analyzing the phenomenal world from the standpoint of difference and identity.
14. See note 8.
15. The four teachings of the doctrine, *kehō no shikyō*: T'ien-t'ai's classification of Śākyamuni Buddha's teachings according to their content. They are in ascending order: (1) *tripiṭaka* teaching, *zōkyō*, i.e., Hinayana teaching; (2) common teaching, i.e., introductory Mahayana teaching; (3) Mahayana teaching; and (4) perfect teaching.
16. A Buddha is supposed to have the threefold body of Dharma Body, the ultimate truth to which He was enlightened, Reward Body, the body of a Buddha rewarded by religious practices, and Accommodative Body, the body of a Buddha who appears for the benefit of the unenlightened in this world.
17. It is believed a great fire will break out at the end of the world. See note 11.
18. The 10 factors of existence according to the Tendai doctrine: appearance, nature, subsistence, function, action, cause, indirect cause, effect, reward, and the ultimate equality of all of them.

Gōnin-jō Gohenji (ST 200)

Introduction

Dated on the 26th day of the 12th month in the first year of the Kenji Era (1275), when Nichiren Shōnin was 53 years old, this letter was addressed to Priest Gōnin. Consisting of eight pages, the original manuscript of the letter is preserved at the Myōkenji Temple in Kyoto as an important cultural asset of Japan.

Gōnin, a Shingon priest residing in Fuji, Suruga Province, present-day Shizuoka Prefecture, sent a letter to Nichiren two months earlier, accusing Nichiren of aggressive propagation activities and demanding a debate. In response, Nichiren wrote this letter, stating that a private debate in the countryside would be fruitless and bound to cause a useless fight. Nichiren proposed that they instead appeal to the imperial court in Kyoto and the military government in Kamakura to hold a public discussion. He further harshly refuted the fallacies of Shingon and Tendai esoteric teachings established by Kōbō and Jikaku for the loss of the True Dharma in Japan, and how these fallacies transformed Japan into a land of slanderers at the brink of national destruction.

Response to Gōnin's Letter

Dear Priest Gōnin.* Your letter chastising me dated on the 25th day of the 10th month reached me on the 26th day of the 12th month in the same year. Regarding the debate you propose, I too have been appealing for a public debate during these years. Therefore, I am quickly writing this reply to answer your questions and those of the people in the world.

I am afraid, however, knowing right from wrong in the remote countryside will be useless, like wearing a brocade kimono and strolling in the darkness or a master carpenter searching for tall pine trees in a deep valley. Moreover, private debates tend to cause useless fights. Therefore, if you wish to carry out the desire of having a debate against me, let us appeal to the imperial court and the Kamakura Shogunate for permission before discussing the veracity of dharmas in public. It will please the emperor above and dispel the doubt of the populace. Besides, Śākyamuni Buddha has entrusted the dissemination of His Buddha Dharma to the kings and their ministers. Therefore, the right and wrong of the world as well as those of Buddha Dharmas must be decided in a public place.

Especially, as we consider the condition of Japan today, we are faced with two calamities of domestic disturbance* and foreign invasion.* As I contemplate the cause of these great calamities in the light of the great collection of sutras,* I am sure there are serious problems in the state as well as with Buddha Dharmas in Japan.

Startled by the great earthquake in the first year of the Shōka Era (1257) and the huge comet in the first year of the Bun'ei Era (1264), I examined all the Buddhist scriptures.* They preach that two calamities that had never happened in Japan would occur: domestic disturbance and foreign invasion. These serious calamities were induced by the fallacies of Hinayana and provisional Mahayana teachings of Shingon, Zen, Pure Land and Ritsu Buddhism, destroying the True Dharma of the *Lotus Sutra* in Japan.

I had already known that foreign troops would attack Japan sooner or later. Therefore, making a vow in front of Buddhas and gods to save my country from destruction even at the cost of my life, I admonished the shogunate during the day and talked to my disciples at night ignoring the threat of execution by sword and spear, or punishment by the military government. Nevertheless, as priests of the Shingon, Zen, Pure Land and Ritsu schools repeatedly made false charges with various fabrications, my admonitions were not accepted. Not only that, I was attacked with sticks and swords everywhere, twice banished to Izu and Sado in disgrace by the shogunate, and was about to be beheaded at Tatsunokuchi.

Setting aside the veracity of Buddha Dharmas in India and China for now, let me contemplate what brought our land of Japan to the brink of extinction. Confused with the comparative superiority between the *Lotus* and the *Great Sun Buddha Sutras*, Grand Masters Kōbō,* the founder of the Shingon school in Japan, and Jikaku,* the third Chief Priest of the Enryakuji Temple on Mt. Hiei, concealed the right teaching of Grand Master Dengyō,* who was the greatest sage in Japan. Ever since then temples on Mt. Hiei sided with the fallacy of Jikaku, and the Jingoji Temple of Takao and the seven great temples in Nara all followed the false teaching of Kōbō. For over 400 long years both the emperors and their ministers have revered those evil masters while the populace has believed their false teachings. Meanwhile the country of Japan has progressively declined with the result that the imperial rule is at the brink of extinction.

King Puṣyamitra of India burned down as many as 84,000 Buddhist temples and towers and beheaded countless number of Buddhist priests, while Emperor Wu-tsung of T'ang China destroyed more than 4,600 Buddhist temples and drove priests and nuns from their monasteries in nine states. Though wrongdoers of magnitude, they nevertheless cannot compare to those slanderers of the True Dharma in Japan. Thus, gods in heaven glare at the country and deities on earth tremble with rage, causing strange phenomena in the sky and natural calamities on earth.

The emperor does not know what causes them because they are not ordinary worldly disasters, while his ministers do not contemplate the cause of the disasters because they are not Confucian scholars. Moreover, they trust Shingon priests to ward off the disasters and give offerings to Ritsu priests in the hope of avoiding these national calamities. This is a great mistake. It is like adding fuel to a fire to extinguish it or pouring water to defrost ice: it will only increase the amount of ice. The more fervently they believe in the wrong teachings, the greater the difficulty of Japan will be. The country of Japan is now about to be destroyed.

As I had contemplated the reason for the advent of this national crisis, I have tried to preach it at the cost of my life in order to save my country in crisis and repay what I owe her. However, it is customary for ignorant people to respect people in the remote past and slight those near by, or believe the opinions of the majority and abandon the words of one person. As a result, my words of truth have been in vain for years. Fortunately you, Priest Gōnin, have sent me a letter reprimanding me, Nichiren. If you really wish to debate, is this not an opportune time for us to get imperial permission for holding a public debate to decide who is superior and right in doctrine?

Furthermore, your letter shows your prejudice stemming from a mistaken preoccupation. If you do nothing throughout your life to rectify your mistake, you and your congregation together will have to endure the unbearable pain of the Hell of Incessant Suffering. Based on self-conceit in this life, you will create the karma of wandering in the world of delusion forever. Therefore as soon as possible, you ought to register an appeal for the imperial permit to hold a public debate in order to change your evil ways. My letter cannot fully express my thoughts. My words do not completely convey what is in my heart. Let me therefore fully express myself in the format of a public debate.

Respectfully yours,
Nichiren (signature)
On the 26th day of the 12th month
To Priest Gōnin

Kangyō Hachiman-shō (ST 395)

Introduction

The *Kangyō Hachiman-shō* was written in the 12th month in the third year of Kōan (1280). Of the original manuscript's 47 pages, 32 are treasured in the Fuji Taisekiji Temple in Shizuoka Prefecture as an important cultural asset of Japan.

Nichiren Shōnin was motivated to write this treatise when the Tsurugaoka Hachiman Shrine in Kamakura burnt down in the 11th month of the third year of Kōan. He claims that the fire may have been caused by the sun god, the moon god, and the Four Heavenly Kings in order to reprimand Bodhisattva Hachiman for allowing the Hōjōs to persecute Nichiren, one who practices the *Lotus Sutra* and who is trying to save Japan. As an alternative, Nichiren also suggests that Bodhisattva Hachiman, who is the manifestation of Lord Śākyamuni Buddha, abandoned the land of slanderers, burned his palace, and ascended to heaven. Saying that even if Bodhisattva Hachiman went to heaven, whenever he finds an honest man practicing the *Lotus Sutra*, he will dwell in the head of whoever practices the *Lotus Sutra*, Nichiren admonished the Bodhisattva urging him to protect the one who practices the *Lotus Sutra*. In the end, Nichiren expressed his belief that a sage will appear in the Latter Age of Degeneration in Japan to reveal the Buddha dharma, which will spread back to India, the birthplace of Buddhism. This treatise reveals Nichiren's unique views on Shinto gods and the sovereignty of Japan. The *Kangyō Hachiman-shō* is also an important document in the sense that Nichiren expresses his awareness of being the one who, like the Buddha, bears the suffering of all people.

Admonition of Bodhisattva Hachiman

Strength of Heavenly Beings

A colt, one or two-years old, does not look sick even if its joints grow long, legs become round and thin, and upper legs are long. When it becomes seven or eight years old and is heavier, all kinds of trouble become apparent as the blood vessels become larger and the upper part of the body grows bigger while the lower part remains small. The horse is no longer useful to people, as it is weak in strength and short in longevity. It is like a small boat loaded with huge rocks or a tiny tree with huge fruits.

The same is true with heavenly beings. At the beginning of the *Kalpa* of Construction,[1] when the world was being created, gods were born with excellent rewards from virtuous acts in previous lives, and men were not evil. Therefore, heavenly beings were shiny in body, pure in spirit, bright as the sun and moon, and as brave as the lion and elephant. When the *Kalpa* of Construction was over and the world entered the *Kalpa* of Continuance,[2] heavenly beings from the previous period grew old and declined like the waning moon, and newly born gods were mostly equipped with inferior rewards of actions in their previous lives. As a result, the three calamities* and seven calamities occurred all over the world and people everywhere began experiencing suffering and joy.

Then the Buddha appeared in this world and prepared the panacea of life, that is Buddhism, for the gods and people. Like oil added to a lamp or a cane supporting an elderly person, heavenly beings regained the authority and power they possessed in the *Kalpa* of Construction.

Buddhism and Divine Help

The sutras preached by the Buddha can be divided into five flavors.* The people born during the lifetime of the Buddha had some rewards for virtuous acts in their previous lives, though not as much as those born in the *Kalpa* of Construction. Hence their authority and power increased upon tasting any of the five flavors of sutras. After the passing of the Buddha, however, as time continued through 2000 years of the Ages of the True Dharma and the Semblance Dharma into the Latter Age of Degeneration, heavenly beings, gods, *asura* demons, and great dragons of the former period grew older, tired in body and weak in mind. The newly born heavenly beings, men, and *asura* demons in the Latter Age of Degeneration are either born with little reward from the virtuous acts in their previous lives, or are evil gods and wicked men, who cannot do any good even if they taste the four flavors of Hinayana or provisional Mahayana sutras: milk, cream, curdled milk, and butter. It is like providing an elderly person with coarse food and a person of high standing with rice cooked with barley.

Not knowing anything about this, however, scholars today follow the way of the world and recite for pleasure scriptures such as the Hinayana sutras, Hōdō sutras, and the *Wisdom, Flower Garland,* and *Great Sun Buddha Sutras* in front of all the gods in Japan. Based on these sutras, they also appoint priests of such

Buddhist schools as Kusha, Jōjitsu, Ritsu, Hossō, Sanron, Kegon, Jōdo, and Zen, to be priests who protect the land. It is as useless as feeding coarse food to elderly persons and hard rice to children.

Moreover, Hinayana sutras and schools and Mahayana sutras and schools today are no longer the same as those in the past. The words of the Buddha in Hinayana and Mahayana sutras were mixed with the private words of translators when Buddhism was transmitted from India to China. The same is true with Buddhist schools, both Hinayana and Mahayana. Commentators* in India and teachers* in China made such mistakes as calling Hinayana, Mahayana or vice versa, writing Mahayana doctrines into Hinayana sutras or vice versa, placing earlier sutras behind later ones or later ones in front of earlier ones, attaching earlier sutras to the later sutras, and designating exoteric sutras as esoteric ones or vice versa. It is like adding water to milk or mixing poison with medicine. Such impure sutras are useless.

The Buddha predicts in the *Nirvana Sutra*, "Thereupon bandits, evil priests, diluted the flavor of *daigo*, ghee. As they added too much water, it tasted like neither milk, cream or ghee." Hinayana Āgama sutras are of milk flavor. Such Hōdō sutras as the *Sutra of the Great Assembly*,* the *Pure Land Sutra*,* the *Revealing the Profound and Secret Sutra*,* the *Entering Laṅkā Sutra* and the *Great Sun Buddha Sutra** are of cream flavor. The *Wisdom Sutra*,* of curdled milk. The *Flower Garland Sutra*,* of butter. And the *Lotus* and *Nirvana Sutras*,* of ghee. Although Hinayana sutras are like the milk flavor, how can it not have any medicinal value at all according to the words of the Buddha? How much more valuable are those Mahayana sutras with flavors of cream and curdled milk, not to speak of the *Lotus Sutra* with the best flavor of ghee!

However, translators who transmitted Buddhist scriptures from India to China number 187. Excepting *Tripiṭaka* Master Kumārajīva,* those 186 translators preceding and following him diluted pure milk with water and prescribed poison for medicine. All those Buddhist priests and scholars who do not know this cannot get rid of the delusion of birth and death even if they read and recite all the scriptures of Buddhism and learn the twelve kinds of scriptures* by heart. Even if their prayer seems somewhat effective, it cannot be as powerful as moving heaven and earth. With a helping hand extended by the King of Devils and his subordinates, their prayer may appear temporarily responsive. In the end, however, both they and their followers will not be at peace. It is like medicine mixed with poison by an evil physician, which his disciple steals or unknowingly uses on his patients. How can it be safe?

Scholars of seven Buddhist schools such as Shingon as well as the Pure Land and Zen sects today in Japan do not realize that Kōbō, Jikaku, Chishō and others diluted the *daigo*, ghee flavor of the *Lotus Sutra* as supreme of all sutras by mixing it with arbitrary opinions of the *Lotus Sutra* that are second or third rate. How can they escape the sin of "destroying the flavor of ghee by diluting it" stated in the *Nirvana Sutra* cited earlier?

To begin with, the *Great Sun Buddha Sutra* is inferior to the *Lotus Sutra* by seven steps. Nevertheless such priests as Kōbō, on the contrary, decided that the *Great Sun Buddha Sutra* is supreme of all sutras and spread it in Japan. It is like diluting milk, the *Lotus Sutra*, with water, the *Great Sun Buddha Sutra*, in a ratio of one to seven. Such a mixture is neither water nor milk, neither the *Great Sun Buddha Sutra* nor the *Lotus Sutra*. It is so ambiguous that it resembles the *Lotus Sutra*, and at the same time it is like the *Great Sun Buddha Sutra*. Śākyamuni Buddha criticized this in the *Nirvana Sutra*:

> "After My passing...at the time when the True Dharma is about to collapse, many evil priests will appear.... They will act like a milkmaid desirous of making quick money by selling four parts milk diluted with one part water.... This milk is watery.... This sutra then will spread widely in this world. Thereupon those evil priests will abbreviate this sutra and divide it into many parts, destroying the color, scent and excellent flavor of the True Dharma. Even if these evil priests read and recite the sutra as it is so mutilated, they will not convey the essence of the Buddha's profound enlightenment.... They will extract a front part placing it in the rear and vice versa, or placing the front and rear parts in the middle and the middle part in front or in the rear. You should know that such evil priests are the devil's companions."

Punishment of the Gods Who Protect
Slanderers of the True Dharma

Now, when I contemplate the situation of Japan, I note that it has been a long time since her inception. Accordingly the future of Japan's original protective deities must have been exhausted, their life span having grown shorter, and their authority and power having declined. Their authority and power will increase only when they taste the flavor of the True Dharma. The True Dharma, however, has been lost, allowing evil dharmas to prosper and protective deities to grow old. How can they repulse national disasters and protect parishioners?*

Moreover, while Japan has been the country of slanderers of the True Dharma, those protective deities of the community not only fail to chastise the Japanese people for committing the grave sin of slandering the True Dharma but they also protect them as parishioners. We must conclude that they broke their vow sworn before the Buddha to protect those who practice the True Dharma. Just as parents do not abandon their child who committed a crime, however, protective deities such as the Great Bodhisattva Hachiman protected their parishioners. Therefore, is it not the case that they were punished and their palaces burnt down by the King of the Brahma Heaven, Indra, and others for not punishing the ruler of Japan and his subjects who hated and slandered the one who practices* the *Lotus Sutra,* but protected them instead? This is a matter of great importance. It must be kept a secret.

It is stated in a sutra that Śākyamuni Buddha called such heavenly beings as the King of the Brahma Heaven, Indra, the sun, the moon, the Four Heavenly Kings, and dragons of this *Sahā* World as well as other worlds together and had them make written pledges in front of Himself, the Buddha of Many Treasures, and various Buddhas from other worlds throughout the universe, stating:

> "In the Ages of the True, Semblance, and Latter Dharmas* after the passing of Śākyamuni Buddha, evil spirits such as the King of Devils in the Sixth Heaven* and other devils will enter the bodies of the king and his subjects, causing trouble to disciples of the Buddha regardless of whether or not they observe precepts or break them. If those heavenly beings who made written pledges to Buddhas see or hear about the Buddha's troubled disciples but do nothing to punish the king and his subjects, the King of the Brahma Heaven and Indra will inevitably send a messenger to the Four Heavenly Kings* ordering punishment for them. In case the community deities do not punish the king and his subjects who trouble the Buddha's disciples, such deities will be dealt with by the King of the Brahma Heaven, Indra and the Four Heavenly Kings. The same will be true with the King of the Brahma Heaven and Indra. The King of the Brahma Heaven, Indra and the Four Heavenly Kings in other worlds will never fail to punish their counterparts in this world, who do not carry out their promised duty. If they don't, they will be unable to see Buddhas in their past, present and future lives, lose the ranks of the King of the Brahma Heaven and Indra forever, and fall into the Hell of Incessant Suffering."

Bodhisattva Hachiman as the Protector of the True Dharma

As I contemplate this, those who become the king and deities of Japan are bodhisattvas in the rank of *sangen,* three wisdoms, according to Hinayana Buddhism and bodhisattvas in the rank of the initial 10 ranks, *jūshin,* of the 52 ranks in Mahayana. In the six-stage practice of the *Lotus Sutra,* they are at the second stage called *myōji-soku,* notional understanding, the stage at which one hears the name of the *Lotus Sutra* and thereby has faith in it. Or they are at the third stage called *kangyō-soku,* perception and practice, perceiving and practicing the "five stages" after the death of the Buddha: rejoicing on hearing the Sutra, reading and reciting the Sutra, expounding it to others, practicing the six *pāramitā*, and perfecting the six *pāramitā*. Therefore, no matter how much merit community deities accumulate, if they are not moved to believe in the *Lotus Sutra* upon hearing its name and practice the spiritual contemplation of the "3,000 existences contained in one thought"* doctrine, they will become former bodhisattvas who will sink to the Hell of Incessant Suffering forever. Thus, it is stated in the *Concise Chronicle of Japan*:

> "When Grand Master Dengyō* lectured on the *Lotus Sutra* for Great Bodhisattva Hachiman in the Jingūji Temple of Usa, the Great Bodhisattva Hachiman* declared in a divine message when he had finished listening to the Grand Master: 'I have been unable to hear the voices of Buddhist sutras. Fortunately today I was able to see the venerable Buddhist priest and listen to him speak about the true teaching of the Buddha. Moreover, he has accumulated much merit for me, for which I am deeply grateful. How can I express my gratitude to him? I will donate my treasured robe to him.' Thereupon, the Shinto priest who received the divine message opened the door of Hachiman's palace, respectfully held up a purple robe and a purple sash, and made a request of the Grand Master saying, 'With your great compassion, please accept these donations.' Surprised at the miraculous event, subordinate Shinto priests all uttered that they had never seen or heard anything as wonderful as this. This robe donated by the Great Bodhisattva Hachiman exists today in the Sannōin Temple on Mt. Hiei."

Contemplating this, I now believe that the Great Bodhisattva Hachiman was Emperor Ōjin, the 16th sovereign of Japan. Buddhism had not yet been introduced to Japan then, so Buddhist robes and sashes could not have existed in Japan. In the 32nd year of Emperor Kimmei, the 30th sovereign of Japan, Hachiman manifested himself as a god. Since then to the fifth year of Kōnin (814), when Grand Master Dengyō lectured on the *Lotus Sutra* for Hachiman, minor Shinto priests of *negi* and *hafuri* continued to protect the palace of the Great Bodhisattva Hachiman. In which emperor's reign were the robe and sash donated? Whenever it was, those Shinto priests said that they had never seen or heard about the treasures. How then, did the Great Bodhisattva obtain the robe and sash? This is indeed inexplicable.

Also from the reign of Emperor Kimmei to the fifth year of Kōnin, there were 22 emperors, and it has been more than 260 years since Buddhism was introduced to Japan. During this period, six or seven Buddhist schools such as Sanron, Jōjitsu, Hossō, Kusha, Kegon, Ritsu, and Zen were transmitted to Japan and numerous people had read and recited sutras in front of the Great Bodhisattva Hachiman.

There must have been those who lectured on the *Lotus Sutra*. There is a Buddhist temple called Jingūji which gives lectures on all the Buddhist scriptures such as the *Lotus Sutra* near the palace of the Great Bodhisattva Hachiman. This temple has stood ever since the time before Grand Master Dengyō. Thus the Great Bodhisattva must have had opportunities to listen to the teachings of the Buddha. Nonetheless, why did he declare in his divine message that he had not been able to hear the voices of Buddhist sutras? Why did he not donate this robe and sash when many people lectured on the Buddhist scriptures and the *Lotus Sutra*? You should know that those prior to Grand Master Dengyō read only the words without revealing their true meaning.

During the second 10-day period of the 11th month in the 20th year of Enryaku (801), Grand Master Dengyō invited more than 10 high priests of the seven great temples in Nara representing the six schools of Buddhism to his lecture on the *Lotus Sutra* held on Mt. Hiei.

Wake no Hiroyo and his brother Matsuna lamented after listening to him speak: "It is regrettable that this wonderful teaching of the One Vehicle doctrine has not spread widely. It is sad that the perfect harmony of the triple truth has not been revealed." They also sighed: "Both young and old cannot do away with the roundabout way of the provisional teaching to free themselves from the chain of delusion."

Thereafter, on the 19th day of the first month in the 21st year of Enryaku (802), Emperor Kammu visited the Takaodera Temple, where he ordered the high priests of the six Buddhist schools in Nara and Grand Master Dengyō to meet in debate on their respective theologies. None of the 14 scholar-priests of Nara were able to answer questions, and they later offered a letter of submission: "Many sutras and commentaries have been expounded in more than 200 years since the rise of Buddhism through the efforts of Prince Shōtoku. They have been fighting one another for theoretical supremacy without answering with certainty which is the supreme teaching. Besides, the teaching of this most wonderful Tendai-Lotus school has not been spread."

Reflecting on this, I believe that the true teaching of the *Lotus Sutra* had not been revealed before Grand Master Dengyō. What was meant by the Great Bodhisattva Hachiman must have been this when he said in his divine message that "he had never seen or heard of it." There is no question about this.

The *Lotus Sutra*, fascicle four, chapter 10 preaches: "You should know that anyone who expounds even a phrase of the *Lotus Sutra* even to one person even in secret after My extinction is My messenger.... He will be covered by My robe." Contemplating this, I believe that as Maitreya Buddha in the future will inevitably expound the *Lotus Sutra*, Śākyamuni Buddha sent him a robe through Venerable Kāśyapa. Likewise, the Buddha sent one through the Great

Bodhisattva Hachiman to Grand Master Dengyō for expounding the truth of the *Lotus Sutra*.

Reprimanding Hachiman for Not Punishing Slanderers of the True Dharma

Before the time of Grand Master Dengyō, this Great Bodhisattva Hachiman had been fed with the taste of a diluted *Lotus Sutra*, like milk diluted with water. Due to the merit of his virtuous acts in previous lives, the Great Bodhisattva was reborn as Emperor Ōjin and manifested himself as a god to protect the land of Japan. However, Hachiman's merit of good acts in previous lives has been exhausted, the taste of the True Dharma has been lost and for many years slanderers of the True Dharma have filled the country of Japan. Being revered by the people of Japan for many years as their protective deity, Hachiman did not abandon them, but kept the slanderers of the True Dharma under his protection, like aged parents refusing to cast aside unfilial children. Therefore, Hachiman's palace was probably burnt down by heavenly beings as punishment.

Regarding the sash given by Hachiman to Grand Master Dengyō, it should only be worn by those who spread the teaching of the *Lotus Sutra* as supreme. After Grand Master Dengyō, Venerable Gishin, the first Head Priest, *zasu*, of the Enryakuji Temple who preached the *Lotus Sutra* as the supreme teaching, was entitled to wear it. Grand Master Enchō,* the second Head Priest, however, was a disciple of Grand Master Dengyō as well as of Grand Master Kōbō.* Thus he seems to have been a slanderer of the True Dharma, having no qualification for wearing this sash. The third Head Priest Ennin, Grand Master Jikaku, was a disciple of Grand Master Dengyō in name. He was, however, a disciple of Grand Master Kōbō in mind, declaring, "The *Great Sun Buddha Sutra*, the first and the *Lotus Sutra* the second." He had absolutely no right to wear this sash. Simply wearing it does not make him one who practices the *Lotus Sutra*.

Moreover, the Head Priests of the Tendai school today have all been Shingon priests while the heads of the Hachiman Shrine have been either head priests of the Onjōji Temple or lower branches of the Tōji Temple. They are sworn enemies of Śākyamuni Buddha, the Buddha of Many Treasures, Buddhas of all the worlds in the universe in the past, and foes of Grand Master Dengyō today. They are like Devadatta* wearing the sash of Śākyamuni Buddha* or a hunter wearing a Buddhist robe to skin a lion.

The Head Priests of the Enryakuji Temple on Mt. Hiei today are the foremost slanderers of the True Dharma. They wear the sash granted to Grand Master Dengyō by the Great Bodhisattva Hachiman but plunder the fief of the *Lotus Sutra*, converting it to that of Shingon Buddhism. They are like King Ajātaśatru* becoming a disciple of Devadatta, the sworn enemy of Śākyamuni Buddha. Despite this, the Great Bodhisattva Hachiman does not take back the *kesa* sash from them. This is the most serious sin of all.

This Great Bodhisattva Hachiman attended the lecture assembly of the *Lotus Sutra* on Mt. Sacred Eagle and made a written pledge to protect those who practice the *Lotus Sutra* after the passing of the Buddha. It is inexplicable, therefore, that this bodhisattva has done nothing to deal with the sworn enemies of the *Lotus Sutra*, who persecuted me for the past several years. Moreover, upon the appearance of one who practices the *Lotus Sutra*, the bodhisattva, who did not rush to protect him, should at least try to discipline the rulers of Japan who persecute the one who practices. It is regrettable that Hachiman has not done this even once although the rulers persecute the one who practices, like a dog biting a monkey, a snake swallowing a frog, a hawk preying on a pheasant, and a lion killing a rabbit under the nose of the bodhisattva. Even if he seems to have punished them, the punishments inflicted on them must have been purposely mild. As a result, Hachiman probably was scolded by such heavenly beings as the King of the Brahma Heaven, Indra, the sun, the moon, and the Four Heavenly Kings.

For instance, three sovereigns of Japan, Emperors Kimmei, Bidatsu and Yōmei, issued imperial edicts due to the urging of Mononobe Moriya and others that allowed them to burn the gilt bronze statue of the Buddha, set fire to the hall where it was enshrined, and punish Buddhist priests and nuns by death. As a result, fire rained from the sky to burn the imperial palace. Moreover, people from all over Japan who were without any sin suffered from malignant swellings, the majority of whom perished. In the end, beside the three emperors and two ministers, many imperial princes and court nobles died either from the malignant swellings or from fighting. Also, palaces of Japanese gods, 180 in number, were all burnt down. It was due to their grave sin of protecting the enemies of Śākyamuni Buddha.

The Onjōji Temple existed even before the Enryakuji Temple on Mt. Hiei. Ever since Grand Master Chishō, Enchin, transmitted the teaching of Shingon Buddhism to this temple, its head priest is called *chōri*, but there is no question that it is a branch temple of Mt. Hiei, Enryakuji Temple. Nevertheless, the Onjōji Temple plundered Mt. Hiei of its Mahayana precept platform, established it in its own temple, and declared itself independent of Mt. Hiei. This is equivalent to a minor subject opposing a great king or a disobedient child standing against his parents. As Shiragi Daimyōjin, the community deity of Mii, where the Onjōji Temple stands, protected such a rebellious temple as Onjōji, the deity's palace was burnt down often by priests and supporters of Enryakuji Temple. Likewise, the Great Bodhisattva Hachiman lost his palace in a fire showered from the sky because he protected the sworn enemies of the *Lotus Sutra*.

Let me cite another example. An ancestor of the First Emperor of Ch'in, King Hsiang, later became a snake god and protected the emperor. Self-conceited, the emperor burnt the books of the Three Emperors and Five Rulers and the *Classic of Filial Piety* by the Three Sages of ancient China: Confucius, Lao-tzu, and Yen Hui. As a result, a man called the Duke of P'ei, later Han Kao Tsu, used a sword to slaughter a huge snake, which was the protective deity of the First Emperor. Shortly after, the rule of the Ch'in Empire came to an end. The same is true in Japan. A great Shinto god of Itsukushima, Aki Province, was the protective deity of the Taira Clan. For the sin of allowing the Taira Clan to be arrogant, the god of Itsukushima was punished by Goddess Amaterasu of the Ise Shrine and the Great Bodhisattva Hachiman, and soon thereafter the Taira Clan was destroyed. The recent burning of the Hachiman's palace is for the same reason.

Accusing Hachiman of Not Protecting the One Who Practices the Lotus Sutra

The *Lotus Sutra*, fascicle four, chapter 11, Beholding the Stupa of Treasures, preaches: "Anyone who understands the meaning of this sutra after My extinction, will be the eye of the world of gods and men." Now it is I, Nichiren, who spreads the *Odaimoku*, the essence of the *Lotus Sutra*, in Japan. Am I not "the eye of the world of gods and men"?

To begin with, there are five kinds of eyes — human eye, divine eye, wisdom eye, dharma eye and Buddha-eye. These five kinds of eyes* are all born from the *Lotus Sutra*, so it is preached in the *Sutra of Meditation on Universal-Sage Bodhisattva*:* "This Hōdō sutra is the eyes of Buddhas. Buddhas are able to have five kinds of eyes because of this sutra." In this citation, "this Hōdō sutra" refers to a Mahayana sutra that expounds the vast and equal truth of reality, namely the *Lotus Sutra*. The *Sutra of Meditation on Universal-Sage Bodhisattva* also states: "The *Lotus Sutra* is a fertile field where men and gods should sow the seeds of merit. Offerings to the one who practices this sutra are most meritorious."

According to these scriptures, the *Lotus Sutra* is the eye of men and gods, the eye of the Two Vehicles, *śrāvaka* and *pratyekabuddha*, the eye of bodhisattvas, and the eye of the Buddhas in all the worlds throughout the universe in the past, present and future lives. Therefore, those who hate the one who practices the *Lotus Sutra* scoop out the eyes of men and gods, and those protective deities who do not punish such people in effect protect those who gouge out the eyes of men and gods. Nevertheless, it is true that for the past 400 years or so, such Shingon priests as Kōbō, Jikaku and Chishō have slandered the *Lotus Sutra* in their writings:

"Lord Śākyamuni Buddha of the *Lotus Sutra* is in the realm of ignorance. He is not enlightened," "Compared to such sutras preached later as the *Great Sun Buddha Sutra*, the *Lotus Sutra* is a joke," and "Śākyamuni does not amount to a palanquin bearer or sandal carrier." Isn't it inexcusably unfair for the Great Bodhisattva Hachiman both to have allowed all the people in Japan, from the emperor above to the populace below, to slander the *Lotus Sutra* and to have protected those who gouge out the eyes of all the people during all these years?

As for myself who has committed no sin whatsoever, I, Nichiren, was blamed at the discretion of the ruler of Japan for committing the grave sin of chanting *Namu Myōhō Renge-kyō*, and was exiled to Izu Province in the first year of Kōchō (1261). Again on the 12th day of the ninth month in the eighth year of Bun'ei (1271), I was paraded around on horseback as a prisoner in front of the Great Bodhisattva Hachiman and was made a laughing stock by all the slanderers of the True Dharma in Japan. Was this not a mistake of the Great Bodhisattva Hachiman, who did not stop it from happening? It was not that Hachiman did not at all admonish slanderers of the True Dharma, but the only admonition from Hachiman seems to have merely caused domestic quarrel among members of the Hōjō clan.

The Great Bodhisattva Hachiman was once the wise emperor of Japan, Emperor Ōjin. In addition, he is one of the greatest gods in Japan, competing with Goddess Amaterasu of the Ise Shine for supremacy. I do not believe that there is any god superior to Hachiman and that he can ever be unfair. Nevertheless, according to the rules of all the Buddhist scriptures and the *Lotus Sutra*, Hachiman committed a great sin by protecting the slanderers of the True Dharma and refusing to help the one who practices the *Lotus Sutra*.

The 11,037 Buddhist temples in Japan, 66 provinces and two islands, Iki and Tsushima, all enshrine Buddhas consisting of portraits and wooden statues. Some temples existed before the introduction of Shingon Buddhism to Japan while others were established after. At any rate these Buddhas have become Buddhas enlightened by the *Lotus Sutra*, hence their eyes all should be eyes of the *Lotus Sutra* as it is preached in the *Sutra of Meditation on Universal-Sage Bodhisattva* cited above: "This Hōdō, Mahayana sutra is the eyes of Buddhas." Grand Master Miao-lê also states in his *Annotations on the Words and Phrases of the Lotus Sutra*: "This *Lotus Sutra* makes the eternal presence of Buddha-nature the throat, the practice of the One Vehicle teaching the eye, revival of the Two Vehicles the heart, and revealing the eternal life of the True Buddha, the life."

Nonetheless, it is customary in Japan that not only the Shingon school but also all other Buddhist schools in Japan perform the eye-opening ceremony by finger signs, *mudrā*, for the Buddha-eye of the Great Sun Buddha and chant the mantras of the Great Sun Buddha, enabling the attainment of five wisdoms. This is an offering of the Shingon sutras to the Buddhas enlightened by the *Lotus Sutra*. It does not open the spiritual eye. On the contrary, it will kill the Buddhas, gouge out the eyes, extinguish the life and slit the throat. This is an evil act comparable to Devadatta injuring Lord Śākyamuni Buddha and King Ajātaśatru* becoming a disciple of Devadatta and receiving punishment in this life.

The Great Bodhisattva Hachiman is Emperor Ōjin, the emperor of a small country while King Ajātaśatru is the king of the great Kingdom of Magadha in India. Superiority between the two is as clear as between gods and people or a king and his subjects. However, even Ajātaśatru, the great king, received the punishment of having malignant swellings all over his body when he stood against the Buddha. How can Hachiman, emperor of a small country, escape the sin of slighting the Buddha and the one who practices the *Lotus Sutra*?

Actually, when the troops of the Great Mongol Empire invaded Japan in the 11th year of Bun'ei (1274), they not only killed and wounded many Japanese soldiers but also burned down the palace of the Great Bodhisattva Hachiman at the Usa Hachiman Shrine. Why were not those Mongol soldiers punished then? It is clear that the great king of the Great Mongol Empire was superior in power to a Japanese god. The snake god of King Hsiang, most powerful protective deity of the First Emperor of Ch'in, was killed by a sharp sword of the Duke of P'ei, Han Kao Tsu, proving the greater power of the Chinese Emperor over gods.

Likewise, when Priest Dōkyō, intimate friend of Empress Shōtoku, attempted to ascend the throne, Wake no Kiyomaro, under an imperial order said a prayer to the Great Bodhisattva Hachiman at the Usa Hachiman Shrine. The Bodhisattva responded in a divine message: "In the first place, gods can be divided into major and minor ones as well as virtuous and evil ones.... Evil ones are many and virtuous ones are very few. Evil gods are powerful while virtuous gods are feeble. Therefore, aided by the strength of the Buddha, we have to rectify imperial succession." We should know from this that the Great Bodhisattva Hachiman with the strength of the True Dharma protected the imperial government. Nevertheless, in the Jōkyū Incident, the imperial court tried to defeat Hōjō Yoshitoki through the evil prayer services performed by priests of Mt. Hiei, the Tōji Temple and others. This is the reason why Hōjō Yoshitoki won the war, and retired Emperor Gotoba was thoroughly defeated. This is what is meant by the *Lotus Sutra*, chapter 25: "A curse will come back to the very person who starts it."

Again, 11,037 Buddhist temples and 3,132 Shinto shrines throughout Japan are worshipped for the purpose of peace and tranquility of the country. However, head priests of those temples and Shinto priests of those shrines all contradict the mind of the *honzon*, the Most Venerable One, and the gods they worship. Although those Buddhas and gods are different in body, they are one in mind, in that they all are protectors of the *Lotus Sutra*. Yet chief priests of those temples and shrines are Shingon priests, Pure Land believers, Zen Priests and Ritsu priests, who are all enemies of the Great Bodhisattva Hachiman. Hachiman protected those slanderers of the True Dharma unfilial to Buddhas and gods, leaving me, one who practices the True Dharma, to have been exiled and sentenced to death. Thus, his palace was burned to ashes by heavenly beings as punishment. Some disciples of mine, with the residue of slandering the True Dharma, believe that I, Nichiren, am not protected by Hachiman because I contradict him. This is the way of thinking of those who do not know that when a prayer is unanswered even if it is reasonable, we should blame the honzon to whom the prayer was said.

Rationale for Admonition of Hachiman

The *Sutra of Transmission of Buddhist Teaching*, fascicle one, speaks of the previous life of Venerable Kāśyapa:

> "Once upon a time there lived a Brahman named Nyagrodha in the Kingdom of Magadha. Because of the great merit of his good acts for a long time in a previous life ..., he was immensely rich and piled up vast wealth in this life ... which was worth a thousand times more than that of the king of Magadha.... Although he was very wealthy, he was childless, so the Brahman said to himself, 'My days are numbered, but I have nobody to inherit my treasures filled in the warehouse. I wish to have a child.' Thus the Brahman prayed to the forest god in the neighborhood for good luck of having a child. Having prayed for years without any luck, he became furious and said to the forest god: 'I have prayed to you for the last several years to no avail. I am going to pray to you from the bottom of my heart for seven more days. If it does not do any good, I am going to burn down your shrine.' Hearing this, the forest god in agony relayed his problem to the Four Heavenly Kings, who in turn reported the matter to Indra.
>
> "Indra looked around all over the world, but could not find anyone worthy of being Nyagrodha's child, so he went to the King of the Brahma Heaven for help. With his divine eye, the King of the Brahma Heaven then closely observed the whole world, finding a heavenly being in the Brahma Heaven who was about to die. The King told him that if he was to be reborn in the human world, he should be born as a child of Nyagrodha Brahman in the Jambudvīpa. The dying being answered that he did not want to be reborn in a family of a Brahman because Brahman dharma includes many evil and false views. The King of the Brahma Heaven told him again: "Nyagrodha Brahman is such a powerful man of virtue that there is no one in the world worthy to be born as his child. If you are reborn to his family, I will protect you lest you should fall into 'evil view.'

Thereupon the heavenly being in the Brahma Heaven answered, 'I will respectfully follow your words.'

"The King of the Brahma Heaven then reported the turn of events to Indra, who in turn informed the forest god. Elated by the good news, the forest god called upon the Brahman at home saying, 'You should no longer have a grudge against me. Your wish will be fulfilled in seven days.' As expected, the wife of the Brahman became pregnant in seven days and gave birth to a baby boy 10 months later. This is Venerable Kāśyapa today."

It is stated in this sutra that Nyagrodha became furious when his prayers were not answered. Ordinarily, those who get furious at the community deity will destroy themselves in this life and fall into evil realms in the next life. Nevertheless, millionaire Nyagrodha was able to achieve his great wish of having a child as wise as Kāśyapa by getting very angry at the community deity and speaking ill of him. You should know that anger may be both good and evil. My admonition of the Great Bodhisattva Hachiman today is anger for a good cause.

For the past 28 years, since the 28th day of the fourth month in the fifth year of Kenchō (1253), until the 12th month in the third year of Kōan (1280), I have devoted myself to nothing but encouraging all the people in Japan to recite the *Odaimoku*, the five or seven character title of the *Lotus Sutra*. This is exactly like the compassion of a mother trying to breast feed her baby. Now is the time for us to expound the teaching of the *Lotus Sutra* as predicted by the Buddha to be spread in the fifth 500-year period,* the beginning of the Latter Age of Degeneration after His death. The days of Grand Masters T'ien-t'ai and Dengyō were still in the Age of the Semblance Dharma prior to the time for the propagation of the *Lotus Sutra*. Nevertheless, as there were some people whose capacity to understand and believe the *Lotus Sutra* was ripe, the sutra was spread a little. How much more it should be spread today, the Latter Age of Degeneration! How can we not spread the *Lotus Sutra* even if very few people have the capacity for it while most people contradict it like water against fire? When we single-mindedly spread the *Lotus Sutra*, there is no doubt that we will eventually succeed even if we should encounter such great difficulties as those that have befallen Never-Despising Bodhisattva. Nonetheless, due to the false charges made by believers of the Shingon, Zen and Pure Land schools, ignorant rulers of Japan persecute me and interfere with the dissemination of the *Lotus Sutra*. The Great Bodhisattva Hachiman, the community deity who is supposed to chastise these ignorant rulers, does not punish them at all for their grave sin of slandering the True Dharma. Thus, I admonish the deity. Am I acting against reason? My admonition* is exactly like that of millionaire Nyagrodha with the forest god.

The *Sutra on the Act of Perfection* states, "When one's prayer is not answered by the *honzon*, the Most Venerable One, one should punish it as one eradicates evil spirits." It means that when you perform a devotional prayer service according to the sutra for many years in vain in order to fulfill your wishes, you should chastise the honzon by binding or striking it. Venerable Sōō, the founder of the Mudōji Temple on Mt. Hiei, is said to have tied up the Fierce Spirit Immovable, to whom he said prayers. Perhaps it was because he was aware of this statement in the *Sutra on the Act of Perfection*.

Now, my admonition of the Great Bodhisattva Hachiman is not at all the same as that of Nyagrodha or of Venerable Sōō. Virtuous people in Japan all either observe Buddhist precepts, give alms, build temples and stupas as a filial act to their parents and ancestors, or divert the funds of feeding family to the fund to support Buddhist priests for the purpose of attaining Buddhahood and gaining emancipation. However, as those Buddhist priests who accept their alms are slanderers of the True Dharma, the virtuous acts of Japanese people today have no meritorious value. They are like offering shelter to a traitor or sharing a bed with an unfilial man. Such people are bound to encounter various troubles in this life and fall into evil realms such as hells in the next life. Feeling pity for such people, I am trying to save them, but the protective deities in Japan all side with those priests who slander the True Dharma, become enemies of the True Dharma and persecute the one who practices the True Dharma. Therefore, I chastise them in accordance with scriptural statements, which is consistent with reason.

The Necessity of Aggressive Means of Propagation

My ignorant disciples think: "Our master, Nichiren, propagates the *Lotus Sutra*. However, not only is he unsuccessful but also he often encounters great difficulties. This is because he uses the aggressive means of propagation, declaring that Shingon Buddhism is the evil dharma that destroys the country, the *nembutsu* is the teaching that leads people into the Hell of Incessant Suffering, Zen is the teaching of heavenly demons, and Ritsu priests are national traitors. This is like slandering mixed with reasons in a lawsuit."

I will cross-examine such ignorant disciples of mine by asking, "Why don't you try urging all those Shingon priests, Pure Land believers and Zen Buddhists to chant the *Odaimoku, Namu Myōhō Renge-kyō*?" Those Shingon priests would probably say, "Our teacher, Grand Master Kōbō, writes that the *Lotus Sutra* is a joke and Śākyamuni Buddha is in the realm of ignorance, who does not amount to a palanquin bearer or a sandal-carrier. Rather than reading the *Lotus Sutra*, which is useless, it is better to recite our short magic spell just once."

Pure Land Buddhists all would say: "Our Venerable Shan-tao* speaks of the *Lotus Sutra* as leading not even one out of 1,000 to attain Buddhahood. Hōnen

Shōnin* advises us to 'abandon, close, set aside and cast away'* all Buddhas and sutras except those of the *nembutsu*. And Zen Master Tao-ch'o* declares, 'Nobody has ever attained Buddhahood except through the *nembutsu*.' Your *Namu Myōhō Renge-kyō* will be an obstacle to our *nembutsu*, so we will never chant the *Odaimoku* even if it means creating evil karma."

Followers of the Zen school all would maintain: "Zen is the supreme dharma transmitted directly from heart to heart, without being committed to the writings of all the Buddhist scriptures. For instance, Zen is like the moon in the sky while all the Buddhist scriptures are like a finger pointing at the moon. Ignorant masters such as Grand Master T'ien-t'ai regard the expedient finger more important than the moon itself. The *Lotus Sutra* is a finger while Zen is the moon. After finding the moon, what is the use of the finger?"

When believers of other Buddhist schools thus slander the *Lotus Sutra*, how can we induce them to take the excellent medicine of *Namu Myōhō Renge-kyō*? The Buddha thought that it would be better to try to induce the Two Vehicles, *śrāvaka* and *pratyekabuddha*, to the *Lotus Sutra* after preaching the Āgama sutras for a while. When the Two Vehicles, attached to the Āgama sutras, refused to believe in the *Lotus Sutra*, how did the Buddha deal with them? The Buddha explains this in the *Vimalakīrti Sutra*: "Even those who committed the five rebellious sins, or those who supported such sinners can eventually attain Buddhahood. It is also possible that evil sins can become the seed of Buddhahood. Nonetheless, the meritorious acts of those of the Two Vehicles can never be the seed of Buddhahood."

The Hinayana teaching and Mahayana teaching are not the same, but both were preached by the same Buddha. The Mahayana Buddhism that rejects Hinayana Buddhism but tries to convert it to Mahayana Buddhism is the same as the Mahayana Buddhism that rejects provisional Mahayana Buddhism but attempts to lead it to the *Lotus Sutra*. Although these objects of rejection, Hinayana and provisional Mahayana, are not the same, in both cases the purpose is to lead people to the *Lotus Sutra*. Therefore, the *Sutra of Infinite Meaning*, the preface to the *Lotus Sutra*, disregards all the sutras preached before the *Lotus Sutra*, declaring, "The true intention of the Buddha has not been revealed yet."

It is also preached in the *Lotus Sutra*, chapter two, Expedients, "If the *Lotus Sutra* is not expounded after the preaching of other sutras, the Buddha is accused of being stingy with the dharma. This is without doubt impermissible." Namely, the Buddha said to Himself, "Born to this world, if I die after preaching sutras such as the *Flower Garland Sutra* and the *Wisdom Sutra* without expounding the *Lotus Sutra*, it would be as if I am stingy by not turning over My property to My beloved children or leaving the sick to die without giving the best medicine to cure their illness." The Buddha also predicts that He would fall into hell for the sin of not preaching the *Lotus Sutra*. It is stated in the *Lotus Sutra*, "This is impermissible." Here "impermissible" means going to hell. How much more so will it be for those who attach themselves to pre-*Lotus* sutras and refuse to convert themselves to the *Lotus Sutra* after hearing it preached. They are like subjects who refuse to follow the orders of the great king, or children who are disobedient to parents.

Even if one does not slander the *Lotus Sutra*, praising the pre-*Lotus* sutras would be the equivalent to slandering the *Lotus Sutra*. Grand Master Miao-lê, therefore, states in fascicle three of his *Annotations on the Words and Phrases of the Lotus Sutra*, "If one praises the pre-*Lotus* sutras, it means that one slanders the *Lotus Sutra*." Then in fascicle four he states, "Even if one has awakened aspiration for enlightenment, unless one knows the difference between the perfect and imperfect teachings and understands the basic purpose of the Buddha's vow to save all living beings, one will not be able to escape the sin of slandering the True Dharma even if one hears and practices the dharma in the future."

Even if such Shingon priests as Śubhākarasiṃha,* Vajrabodhi, Amoghavajra, Kōbō, Jikaku and Chishō had merely disseminated the *Great Sun Buddha Sutra* without discussing its superiority over the *Lotus Sutra*, they still would have committed the sin of slandering the True Dharma by praising the pre-*Lotus* sutras. As the Grand Master declares, how can these *tripiṭaka* masters, born after the Buddha expounded the *Lotus Sutra* and passed away, escape the sin of slandering the True Dharma without knowing the difference between the perfect and imperfect teachings and understanding the basic purpose of the Buddha's vow? How much more so with Śubhākarasiṃha, Vajrabodhi and Amoghavajra, who equated the *Lotus Sutra* and the *Great Sun Buddha Sutra* as the concise and expanded versions of the one sutra and tricked those who practice the *Lotus Sutra* into believing the *Great Sun Buddha Sutra*! How much more so with Kōbō, Jikaku and Chishō, worst slanderers of the True Dharma, who called the *Lotus Sutra* a joke! As nobody pointed out their grave sin, however, people in the last 400 years have all been slanderers of the True Dharma in Japan.

They are like the four evil priests, such as Kugan, toward the end of Great Adornment Buddha's time in the eternal past, misleading numerous people, six million, 100 million, 100,000 million in number, into the Hell of Incessant Suffering. And Monk Shōi in the Latter Age after Lion-Voice King Buddha, misleading innumerable number of precept-observing Buddhists, both clergy and laity as well as male and female, such as Monk Kikon, into the Hell of Incessant Suffering.

Likewise, following the teaching of the three grand masters Kōbō, Jikaku and Chishō, all the people of Japan numbering 4,900,094,828, or as many as 4,900 million people died and fell into the Hell of Incessant Suffering during the last 400 years, and those of other worlds who were reborn in this world also died and fell into the Hell of Incessant Suffering. The number of those who repeatedly fell into the Hell of Incessant Suffering is larger than the number of dust particles of the great earth. It is entirely due to the sin of those three grand masters.

While seeing this misery, if I, Nichiren, do not speak up as if I knew nothing of it, I will also have to go to hell without any sin and go around the Hells of Incessant Suffering in all the worlds throughout the universe. Considering this, how can I spare my life in this world and keep my mouth closed? The Buddha preached in the *Nirvana Sutra*, "Various sufferings of all the people will all be borne by Me alone." Likewise, I now declare, "All the suffering of all the people going to hell will all be borne by Nichiren alone."

Expecting the Protection of Hachiman

During the reign of Heizei, the 51st Emperor, the Great Bodhisattva Hachiman sent a divine message, "I am the Great Bodhisattva Hachiman, protector of Japan, who has vowed to protect 100 rulers* of the country of Japan." As I contemplate this now, the 81st Emperor, Antoku, 82nd Emperor, Gotoba, 83rd Emperor, Tsuchimikado, 84th Emperor, Juntoku and 85th Emperor, Chūgyō were defeated by their subjects, Minamoto Yoritomo and Hōjō Yoshitoki while the remaining 20 or so emperors have already been abandoned when the Great Bodhisattva Hachiman burned his palace and ascended to heaven. Therefore, Hachiman's vow to protect the 100 rulers of Japan seems to have been broken.

In my opinion, protecting 100 rulers* does not mean protecting all rulers from the first to 100th. It is the vow to protect 100 honest* rulers. This is because Hachiman's vow states, "He will reside in the head of honest persons, not in the heart of evil persons." The moon reflects itself in clear water, but not in muddy water. Also the Great Bodhisattva Hachiman lives in the head of pure and honest men, but not in the heart of impure and dishonest men. The ruler is originally an honest person who does not tell a lie. In this sense, Minamoto Yoritomo and Hōjō Yoshitoki were honest men who did not tell lies. They are among the 100 rulers, in whom the Great Bodhisattva Hachiman resides. That is the reason why they were victorious under the protective wings of Hachiman.

There are two meanings of honesty:* first, honesty in the worldly sense and in the second place, honesty in Buddhism. Speaking of honesty in the worldly sense, the Chinese character for king means running through the heaven, human world and earth. The three horizontal lines stand for heaven, human world and earth, which are run through by a vertical line. That is to say, the king is a person who treads the way of honesty throughout the heaven, human world and earth. The character king also stands for the color yellow. In ancient China, five colors stood for five directions, with the yellow color in the center. As the ruler in the center, the king is also called "yellow emperor." The lord of the heavens, lord of the human world as well as that of the earth are all called king. Ex-Emperor Gotoba, however, was the ruler in name only. He was a liar, wicked and dishonest. On the contrary, Shogunal Regent Hōjō Yoshitoki was a subject in name, but he was worthy of a great ruler without double-talk, in whom the Great Bodhisattva Hachiman vowed to reside.

Next, speaking of honesty in Buddhism, pre-*Lotus* sutras and commentaries and interpretations of the seven schools of Buddhism in Japan based on those pre-*Lotus* sutras are all dishonest, while the *Lotus Sutra* and the teaching of the Tendai (T'ien-t'ai) school based on it are honest. The original substance of the Great Bodhisattva Hachiman is Śākyamuni Buddha who preached the honest sutras and manifested Himself in Japan as the honest Great Bodhisattva Hachiman. The eight petals of the lotus flower surrounding the central platform for Lord Preacher Śākyamuni Buddha are the Great Bodhisattva Hachiman. Śākyamuni Buddha, who was born on the eighth day of the fourth month, passed away on the 15th day of the second month 80 years later. How can it not be that Lord Śākyamuni Buddha was reborn in Japan as the Great Bodhisattva Hachiman! To prove this, it is stated on the stone monument at the Shō Hachiman Shrine of Ōsumi Province, "Expounding the *Lotus Sutra* on Mt. Sacred Eagle in the past, He now manifests Himself as a bodhisattva in the palace of the Shō Hachiman Shrine." The *Lotus Sutra*, chapter three, Expedients, states, "Now this triple world all belongs to Me, and all the people therein are My children." Then in chapter 16, The Duration of the Life of the Tathāgata, He declares, "I always preach and enlighten the people on Mt. Sacred Eagle in the *Sahā* World." Therefore, all sentient beings faraway in the entire universe are children of Śākyamuni Buddha, and the 4,900,094,828 people nearby in Japan are all children of the Great Bodhisattva Hachiman. All living beings in Japan today, nevertheless, worship the Great Bodhisattva Hachiman, who is a manifested trace of Śākyamuni, and ignore Śākyamuni Buddha, the original substance of Hachiman. This is like worshipping a shadow and slighting the substance, or speaking ill of somebody to his children. The original substance of the Great Bodhisattva Hachiman is Śākyamuni Buddha, who was born in India, justly discarded the provisional sutras and expounded the lone true teaching of the *Lotus Sutra*. His manifested trace was born in Japan and resides in the head of an honest person.

Tracing the substance of Buddhas and bodhisattvas appearing in this world as avatars in order to save all living beings, we reach the sole doctrine of ultimate reality, though there are numerous avatars as manifested traces. For example, Venerable Hakura, Handsome Man, a disciple of the Buddha, set an example to observe the precept against killing for past, present and future lives. Aṅgulimāla repeatedly committed evil acts of killing life after life. And Venerable Śāriputra was born in a non-Buddhist family.

The reason why the manifested traces differ from one another is that those Buddhas and bodhisattvas had originally been ignorant and unenlightened. They then awakened the aspiration for enlightenment, practiced the Buddhist way and reached the state of enlightenment. When teaching people, Buddhas and bodhisattvas first show their original ignorant status to the people. Thus, Grand Master Miao-lê states in his *Annotations on the Great Concentration and Insight,* fascicle two, "Speaking of the original substance, a manifested trace, avatar, once committed such sins as killing, and this karma eventually enabled him to attain Buddhahood. Therefore, the avatar preaches and guides people by means of killing as expedients."

Now, the Great Bodhisattva Hachiman's original substance, Śākyamuni Buddha, expounded the sole, true *Lotus Sutra* in India. As He manifested Himself in Japan, He summarized the sutra in two Chinese characters for honesty, and vowed to live in the head of a wise man. If so, even if Hachiman burned his palace and ascended to heaven, whenever he finds one who practices the *Lotus Sutra* in Japan, he will not fail to come down to reside where this person is and protect him.

Therefore, it is preached in the *Lotus Sutra,* fascicle five, chapter 14, Peaceful Practices, "Various gods always protect the one who practices for the sake of the dharma day and night." This means that the great King of the Brahma Heaven,* Indra,* the sun and moon, the Four Heavenly Kings and others will never fail to protect those who say *"Namu Myōhō Renge-kyō."*

This sutra also preaches in the sixth fascicle, chapter 16, The Duration of the Life of the Tathāgata, "Sometimes I speak of Myself, sometimes of others. Sometimes I show Myself, sometimes others. And sometimes I show My deeds, sometimes those of others." Even Bodhisattva Avalokiteśvara manifests himself in 33 traces, and Wonderful Voice Bodhisattva in 34 traces. How can Lord Śākyamuni Buddha not appear as the Great Bodhisattva Hachiman? Grand Master T'ien-t'ai declares in his *Profound Meaning of the Lotus Sutra,* "The Buddha manifests Himself variously in the 10 realms of living beings."

Japanese Buddhism Shining in the Darkness in the Latter Age of Degeneration

India is called the country of the moon, where the Buddha appears shining in the world as brightly as the moon. Japan is called the origin of the sun. How can it be that no sage as bright as the sun appears in Japan? The moon moves from west to east. It is the omen of Buddhism in India spreading to the east. The sun orbits from east to west. This is a lucky omen of Buddhism in Japan returning to India. Moonlight is not as bright as sunlight, therefore the Buddha preached the *Lotus Sutra* for only eight years of His lifetime. Sunlight is brighter than moonlight. This is an auspicious omen of Japanese Buddhism shining through the long darkness of the fifth 500-year period. The Buddha did not save slanderers of the *Lotus Sutra* because there existed no slanderers during His lifetime. In the Latter Age of Degeneration, there will be many formidable enemies of the One Vehicle Lotus teaching everywhere. This is the time when we can reap the harvest of Never-Despising Bodhisattva's aggressive propagation sowing the seed of Buddhahood. Each of my disciples should exert himself to spread the teaching of the Buddha even at the cost of their life.

In the 12th month of the 3rd year of Kōan (1280)
Nichiren (signature)

Notes

1. See "Four kalpa" *(shikō)* in the glossary.
2. Ibid.

Glossary

Note: Included in this glossary are words and phrases marked with asterisks in the text. They were chosen by the authors of the modern Japanese translations of the original writings of Nichiren for the purpose of clarifying the characteristics of his doctrine. Most entries are in English as they appear in the text, except proper nouns (which appear in the language of the country of their origin), and a few special terms for which appropriate English terms are not readily available. Words and phrases within parentheses following each entry are the Japanese terms used by Nichiren which are alphabetically rearranged and attached to the end of the glossary for the convenience of those who are well versed in Japanese.

A moment of true faith *(ichinen shinge)*
A phrase used in the 17th chapter of the *Lotus Sutra*, Variety of Merits. It means to have a true faith, even momentarily, while hearing of the attainment of Buddhahood by Śākyamuni Buddha in the eternal past. It is designated as the initial stage in the practice of the *Lotus Sutra*. The 17th chapter preaches that the merit of having a moment of true faith is a hundred, a thousand, ten thousand, and a hundred million times greater than that of practicing the first five of the six perfections, or *pāramitā*: charity, observing precepts, perseverance, devotion and meditation. This is the scriptural proof for Nichiren Shōnin's insistence that religious practice in the Latter Age of Degeneration should be based on faith.

Abandon, close, set aside and cast away *(sha, hei, kaku, hō)*
The term *shahei kakuhō* was coined by Nichiren to represent the doctrine of Hōnen, who insisted that only the nembutsu is the appropriate teaching for the people in the Latter Age of Degeneration, negating all other doctrines and practices. The four characters are taken from the *Collection of Passages on the Nembutsu* by Hōnen advising the people to put aside the Holy Way teachings, namely all teachings other than those of the Pure Land.

Abrupt teaching *(tongyō)*
Refers to a teaching which enables one to attain Buddhahood very quickly. It is in contrast to the "gradual teaching" which requires a long period of learning

and practicing step by step. The abrupt teaching also means a profound doctrine expounded directly without the explanatory preliminary teachings while the gradual teaching begins with an explanation of preliminary teachings before going into the profound doctrine.

Achieving Buddhahood through a minor act of merit *(shōzen jōbutsu)*
Chapter 2 of the *Lotus Sutra*, Expedients, preaches that such minor acts of merit, such as donations to temples and towers, carving statues and drawing portraits of the Buddha, offering incense and flowers, or calling the name of the Buddha even once, can be a cause of attaining Buddhahood.

Admonition *(kangyō)*
Śākyamuni Buddha urged those who listened to Him to spread the *Lotus Sutra* in the Latter Age of Degeneration at the cost of their lives. Nichiren Shōnin referred to this as the Buddha's admonition and tried to carry this out as His messenger by submitting the *Risshō Ankoku-ron, Treatise on Spreading Peace Throughout the Country by Establishing the True Dharma*, to the Kamakura military government, urging the shogunate as well as the people to put faith in the *Lotus Sutra*. This *Rissho Ankoku* campaign of Nichiren Shōnin is designated as his national admonition.

Āgama sutras *(Agon-gyō)*
Original Buddhist scriptures. As they contain many words which are believed to have been preached by the historical Śākyamuni Buddha, it is believed that they were written earlier than *Kegon-kyō*, the *Flower Garland Sutra*. There are four groups of Chinese Āgama sutras: (1) *Jō-agongyō*, Long Āgama sutras; (2) *Chū-agon-gyō*, Middle-length Āgama sutras; (3) *Zōitsu-agon-gyō*, Increasing-by-One Āgama sutras; and (4) *Zō-agon-gyō*, Miscellaneous Āgama sutras. According to T'ien-t'ai's classification of the Five Periods and Eight Teachings, Nichiren considers the Āgama sutras to be Hinayana teachings preached in the second period, which are several steps below the *Lotus Sutra*.

Ajātaśatru, King *(Ajase-ō)*
A king of Magadha in Central India during Śākyamuni's lifetime, who is said to have been incited by Devadatta to have his father Bimbisāra killed and his mother Vaidehī imprisoned. He also tried to kill Śākyamuni with a drunken elephant. Later however, he converted to Buddhism and supported the first Buddhist Council for the compilation of Śākyamuni's teachings. To Nichiren the salvation of King Ajātaśatru, who had committed the Five Rebellious Sins, represented an example of salvation of evil persons by virtue of the Lotus teaching. Nichiren thus cited the story of the king in his attempt to convert people in the Latter Age of Degeneration.

All the scriptures of Buddhism (*Issaikyō*)

In a narrow sense, this refers to all the sutras which Śākyamuni Buddha preached. In a broader sense it refers to all the Buddhist scriptures including the sutras, *vinaya* or precepts, and *abhidarma* or discourses on Buddhism written by later scholars or propagators after the passing of the Buddha. They are also called the Great Pitaka sutras, *Daizōkyō,* All Pitaka sutras, *Issaizōkyō,* or All sutras, *Issaikyō.* Nichiren considered them all as "The Buddha's Golden Words," and held fast to the affirmative viewpoint of scriptures. Nevertheless, he insisted that the *Lotus Sutra* is supreme of all Buddhist scriptures, and that it alone reveals the true intent of the Buddha.

Ānanda (*Anan*)

One of Śākyamuni's ten great disciples, Ānanda was a cousin of Śākyamuni and also younger brother of Devadatta. As a personal attendant, Ānanda accompanied Śākyamuni for many years, and is known as the foremost in hearing and remembering the Buddha's teachings. He played a central role in compiling the Buddha's teachings at the First Buddhist Council after the death of the Buddha. Describing the history of the *Lotus Sutra,* Nichiren considers him along with Kāśyapa as two pioneering leaders of Buddhism during the Age of the True Dharma after the death of Śākyamuni.

Annen, Venerable (*Annen Wajō*)

841–? CE. A Tendai monk also known as Godai-in. Having studied Tendai and Shingon Buddhism under Henshō and Ennin, also known as Grand Master Jikaku. He is credited with establishing the theological foundation of Tendai esotericism. Nichiren Shōnin, however, criticized him harshly as a man who made the Tendai-Lotus school highly esoteric, contradicting the teaching of the *Lotus Sutra* and Grand Master Dengyō. Nichiren branded Annen, together with Ennin and Genshin, also known as Eshin, one of the three parasites of Tendai-Lotus Buddhism.

Annotation on the Great Concentration and Insight (*Maka Shikan Fugyō-den Guketsu*)

Abbreviated as *Guketsu* or *Gu* in Nichiren's writings. In this writing of ten fascicles, Grand Master Miao-lê annotates on T'ien-t'ai's *Great Concentration and Insight, Mo-ho Chih-kuan,* revealing the profound practices expounded by T'ien-t'ai and refuting misunderstandings which arose after T'ien-t'ai's death. Along with T'ien-t'ai's *Great Concentration and Insight,* this writing of Miao-lê had great influence on the theology of Nichiren Shōnin, who often cited it to prove his points.

Attaining enlightenment in the eternal past *(kuon jitsujō)*
Central theme of the *hommon,* the essential section of the *Lotus Sutra,* especially of the 16th chapter. It insists that Śākyamuni Buddha did not attain Enlightenment for the first time at Buddhagayā in India, but that He has been enlightened since the eternal past. Attainment of Buddhahood by Śākyamuni at Buddhagayā is merely a temporal appearance of the Original True Buddha who has been guiding and saving all the people ever since. Nichiren's claim of the *Lotus Sutra* as the ultimate True Teaching of the Buddha based on the two doctrines: "attaining Enlightenment in the eternal past (by Śākyamuni Buddha)" and "obtaining Buddhahood by Two Vehicles (two groups of Hinayana sages — *śrāvaka* and *pratyekabuddha*)."

Attainment of Buddhahood *(jōbutsu)*
Refers to the fundamental purpose of practicing Buddhism, that is to say reaching enlightenment and becoming a Buddha. After attaining Buddhahood by practicing Buddhism for many years, Śākyamuni Buddha preached various teachings for the purpose of making all people Buddhas. Sutras preached before the *Lotus Sutra* were all expedient and provisional, requiring a long period of practice for one to become a Buddha. These sutras could not save the Two Vehicles or women. The *Lotus Sutra,* with its fine doctrines of "3,000 existences contained in one thought" and "attaining Enlightenment in the eternal past," preaches the salvation of the Two Vehicles, women, as well as evil persons. Nichiren emphasized the attainment of Buddhahood with the present body by chanting the Odaimoku: *Namu Myōhō Renge-kyō*.

Becoming a Buddha with one's present body *(sokushin jōbutsu)*
Attainment of Buddhahood by ordinary people with their present body in this world. The Japanese term *genshin jōbutsu* is also used to mean an ordinary, that is ignorant person becoming a Buddha with his present body. This doctrine is preached by the Tendai and Shingon sects, in contrast to the doctrine of rebirth in the Pure Land of Utmost Bliss, where people can practice Buddhism to become Buddhas. Nichiren Shōnin preaches that Buddhahood is attainable for one who upholds and chants the Odaimoku: Namu Myōhō Renge-kyō.

Beginning and ending of the Buddha's guidance *(kedō no shijū)*
One of the three standards of doctrinal comparison which T'ien-t'ai preached in his commentary, *Profound Meaning of the Lotus Sutra.* T'ien-t'ai asserted the superiority of the *Lotus Sutra* over all sutras from three viewpoints: (1) no sutra other than the *Lotus Sutra* states that all people are capable of attaining Buddhahood; (2) only the *Lotus Sutra* states when Śākyamuni's instruction

to people begins and ends; and (3) in this sutra the relationship between the Buddha and His disciples is eternal. The first and second standards are based on the theoretical section while the last standard was established on the basis of the 16th chapter in the essential section. Nichiren Shōnin regards this third standard as most important, whereas T'ien-t'ai considered the first two more essential. See also "Three standards of doctrinal comparison."

Bodhisattvas appearing from underground *(jiyu no bosatsu)*
The term *jiyu no bosatsu* refers to the numerous bodhisattvas who emerged from the earth as described in the 15th chapter of the *Lotus Sutra*. They are also called *honge no bosatsu* meaning bodhisattvas guided by the Original Buddha in the eternal past. Their emergence revealed that the attainment of enlightenment by Śākyamuni was in the eternal past, and provided Him with the occasion of preaching the True Dharma of the last half of the *Lotus Sutra*. Headed by Bodhisattvas such as Superior Practice, Jōgyō, they were entrusted in the 21st chapter of the *Lotus Sutra* to spread the sutra after the death of Śākyamuni. Realizing himself to be an avatar of Jōgyō Bodhisattva, Nichiren strived to spread the *Lotus Sutra*.

Buddha in the Land of Emerald Light to the East *(Tōhō Nyorai)*
Refers to Medicine Master Buddha, who is believed to have made twelve vows to heal all illnesses of the people and bring happiness to them. Belief in this Buddha is popular in both China and Japan.

Buddha-eye *(butsugen)*
One of the five kinds of eyes or *gogen:* (1) human-eye; (2) divine-eye of gods which can see beyond physical limitations; (3) wisdom-eye of *śrāvaka* and *pratyekabuddha* which can perceive the principle of emptiness; (4) dharma-eye of bodhisattvas penetrating all teachings; and (5) Buddha-eye which can see through the past, present, and future, and which also includes all the other four kinds of eyes.

Buddhas in manifestation *(funjin)*
Funjin Buddhas are various forms the Buddha uses as means of saving different beings. They preach to guide beings in the worlds all over the universe. In the 11th chapter of the *Lotus Sutra,* Beholding the Stupa of Treasures, they gathered to listen to the Lotus assembly in front of the Stupa of Many Treasures; and in the 21st chapter of the sutra, The Supernatural Powers of the Tathāgata, they proved the truth of Śākyamuni's preaching by touching the Brahma Heaven with their long, wide tongues.

Buddhas in ten directions *(jippō no shobutsu)*
Refers to Buddhas who preach in the worlds all over the universe. See "Buddhas in manifestation."

Capacity of people to understand *(kikon)*
Refers to the mental capacity of people to react to the dharma, or to understand and accept a religious teaching. Kikon is sometimes abbreviated as *ki*.

Chances of being born in the human realm as small as the amount of soil on a fingernail *(sōjō no shō)*
A small amount of soil on a fingernail is likened to a rare chance of being born into the human world. It is also likened to a small number of people who put their faith in the *Lotus Sutra*.

Chang-an, Grand Master *(Shōan Daishi)*
561–632 CE. His name was Kuan-ting, but he was known as Grand Master Chang-an after his birthplace. He was a disciple and the successor to Grand Master T'ien-t'ai, founder of the T'ien-t'ai school in China. Chang-an recorded and compiled most of his master's lectures including the three major works: *Profound Meaning of the Lotus Sutra, Words and Phrases of the Lotus Sutra,* and *Great Concentration and Insight.* He deserves credit for making T'ien-t'ai's lectures available today. He himself wrote the *Profound Meaning of Nirvana,* and the *Annotations on the Nirvana Sutra.* Nichiren recognized his relationship to T'ien-t'ai as analogous to that of Ānanda to Śākyamuni, and often quoted from his *Annotations on the Nirvana Sutra,* though comparably less than from T'ien-t'ai and Miao-lê.

Ch'êng-kuan *(Chōkan)*
738–839 CE. Fourth patriarch of the Hua-yen or Kegon school in China. He is credited for the revival of Flower Garland or Kegon theology. Also known as National Master Ch'ing-liang, *Seiryō Kokushi.* Ch'eng-kuan studied various Mahayana schools of Buddhism, including Tendai meditation under Miao-lê. He later concentrated on the study of Flower Garland Buddhism, producing many books such as *Kegon-gyō-sho, Commentary on the Flower Garland Sutra,* in 60 fascicles. Believing firmly in the supremacy of the *Lotus Sutra,* Nichiren harshly criticized Ch'eng-kuan for claiming superiority of the *Flower Garland Sutra* and for "stealing" the "3,000 existences in one thought" doctrine of T'ien-t'ai.

Chi-ts'ang *(Kichizō)*
549–623 CE. Also called Grand Master Chia-hsiang after the temple where he resided. He systematized the *San-lun,* or Three Discourses theology and is

sometimes regarded as the founder of the San-lun sect in China. He lectured not only on the San-lun but also the *Lotus* and *Flower Garland Sutras*, and wrote such commentaries as the *Profound Meaning of the Three Treatises* and *Profound Meaning of the Lotus Sutra*. Nichiren maintained that Chia-hsiang misinterpreted the *Lotus Sutra*, but later repented, becoming a disciple of T'ien-t'ai. Chi-ts'ang is said to have been impressed by T'ien-t'ai so deeply that he offered himself to T'ien-t'ai to use as a stepladder whenever T'ien-t'ai went up to the platform on the stage to preach.

Chien-chên *(Ganjin)*
668–763 CE. Chinese monk who founded the Japanese Ritsu sect. Chien-chên studied the T'ien-t'ai, *Tendai,* and Lü, *Ritsu,* teachings, eventually becoming a famous lecturer on Lü Buddhism. In response to the invitation of the Japanese monks, Yōei and Fushō, he came to Japan in 753 after five unsuccessful attempts. He built the precept-platform, *kaidan,* in the Tōdaiji Temple, making it the center for granting Buddhist precepts. Afterward, he built the Tōshōdaiji Temple in Nara, where he spread the Ritsu teachings. Nichiren Shōnin stated that Chien-chên transmitted the Ritsu and Tendai teachings but propagated only the Ritsu as an expedient means of spreading the *Lotus Sutra*.

Chishō, Grand Master *(Chishō Daishi)*
814–891 CE Also called Enchin, he was a disciple of Gishin, first *zasu,* Chief Minister of the Enryakuji Temple, and became the fifth *zasu*. He studied both Tendai and Shingon teachings in China for six years, and vigorously spread Tendai esotericism in Japan. Nichiren severely criticized him for following the example of Ennin, Grand Master Jikaku, in betraying their founder, Grand Master Dengyō, and slandering the true Dharma.

Collection of Passages on the Nembutsu and the Original Vow *(Senjaku-shū)*
Abbreviation of *Senjaku Hongan Nembutsu-shū, Collection of Passages on the Nembutsu and the Original Vow,* by Hōnen, founder of the Jōdo or Pure Land sect. Citing from the triple Pure Land sutras and Shan-tao's interpretation of them, Hōnen advocates the Pure Land doctrine concentrating on the nembutsu for rebirth in the Pure Land. In *Risshō Ankoku-ron, Shugo Kokka-ron,* and other writings, Nichiren harshly criticized Hōnen and his *Senjaku-shu* for insisting on single-minded devotion to the nembutsu.

Commentator *(ronji)*
Literally commentators on sutras, but Nichiren uses it to refer to high Buddhist priests in India.

Comparative study of Buddhist doctrines *(kyōsō)*
Abbreviation of the *Kyōsō Hanjaku,* classification of Buddhist scriptures from some sectarian points of view such as T'ien-t'ai's "five periods and eight teachings" and "three standards of doctrinal comparison" and Nichiren's "five-fold comparison" and "four sets of the three divisions in teaching." It also refers to the doctrinal aspect as opposed to *kanjin,* practice of meditation or *jisō,* ritual.

Comprehensive Interpretations *(Kōshaku)*
Refers to the *Futsū Koshaku Ju-bosatsu-Kai Kōshaku, Comprehensive Interpretations Concerning the General Ceremony for Conferring the Bodhisattva Precepts*. It was written in three fascicles by Annen, a scholar-priest of Tendai esotericism. The book is also known as the *Futsū Kōshaku*. Early writings of Nichiren Shōnin, such as *Shugo Kokka-ron* and *Sainan Taiji-shō* cite from this writing. Nichiren's emphasis on repayment of kindness may reflect the influence of Annen, who preached in this writing about repayment of four favors.

Concentrated mind and scattered mind *(jōsan)*
The term *jōsan* is the contraction of *jōzen,* meditative good deeds, and *sanzen,* scatterbrained good deeds. The former means meditation on the Buddha of Infinite Life and His Pure Land while the latter designates the act of merit one practices in one's daily life. Shan-tao divided the 16 kinds of meditation for rebirth in the Pure Land, preached in the *Sutra of Meditation on the Buddha of Infinite Life,* into these two categories of good acts, maintaining that the Buddha's real intent was the one act of nembutsu, which Hōnen termed the "correct practice" for rebirth in the Pure Land.

Correct and miscellaneous practices *(shōgyō, zōgyō)*
Meaning literally the correct practice leading to enlightenment, the *shōgyō* in Pure Land Buddhism denotes the practice for one to be reborn in the Pure Land of Utmost Bliss. Shan-tao in his *Commentary on the Sutra of Meditation on the Buddha of Infinite Life* defined it to be the five practices of recitation, observation, worship, nembutsu, and praising the Buddha of Infinite Life for the purpose of rebirth in the Pure Land, and slighted all other practices as "miscellaneous," *zōgyō*. Following this definition from Shan-tao, Hōnen insisted on the sole practice of the nembutsu as the way of rebirth in the Pure Land. Nichiren Shōnin criticized Hōnen for preaching the abandonment of Śākyamuni Buddha, the *Lotus Sutra,* and all other Buddhas and sutras.

Dainichi *(Dainichi)*
?–? CE. Dainichi Nōnin was a self-educated Zen priest in the early Kamakura Period. He founded the Sambōji Temple in Settsu Province, Hyōgo Prefecture, and spread Zen Buddhism of the Southern Sung tradition, which he named the Nihon Daruma-shū, insisting that the essence of Buddhism, Zen, is transmitted by non-literal and non-verbal means. Nichiren was critical of Dainichi for relying on the *Ryōga-kyō*, a provisional sutra preached in the third period, and for insisting on *kyōge betsu-den*, non-literary, non-verbal transmission. Nichiren referred to Dainichi's teachings as "an act of heavenly demons."

Deciding the Meaning of the Pure Land *(Jōdo Ketsugi-shō)*
Written by Kōin, 1145–1216 CE, of the Onjōji Temple in three fascicles, it rebukes the *Collection of Passages on the Nembutsu* by Hōnen. Kōin criticized Hōnen's insistence on the nembutsu alone as the correct practice since the *Lotus Sutra* preaches instant rebirth in the Pure Land of Tranquility and Bliss, and the *Sutra of Meditation on the Buddha of Infinite Life* preaches the reading and recitation of Mahayana sutras as a cause of rebirth in the Pure Land. It is said, however that Kōin later was converted to Hōnen's way of thinking and burned this writing, which does not exist today.

Dengyō, Grand Master *(Dengyō Daishi)*
767–822 CE. Founder of the Tendai sect in Japan, he is also known as Saichō. He was ordained at the Tōdaiji Temple, but later entered Mt. Hiei and studied the teaching of T'ien-t'ai, the patriarch of the T'ien-t'ai school in China. Entering T'ang China in 804, Dengyō mastered the teachings of T'ien-t'ai, Zen, esoteric Buddhism and precepts before returning to Japan. He engaged in heated debates against the Hossō priest Tokuitsu on Buddha-nature and also against the superintendent of Buddhist priests in Nara on the establishment of the Mahayana Precept Platform on Mt. Hiei. His major works include the *Shugo Kokkai-shō, Defense of the Country, Hokke Shūku, Passages of the Lotus Sutra,* and *Kenkai-ron, Treatise on Precepts*. Regarding Saichō as a practicer of the *Lotus Sutra*, Nichiren respected him as an indispensable transmitter of the teaching of the *Lotus Sutra*.

Denouncing the Collection of Passages on the Nembutsu *(Dan Senjaku)*
One-fascicle essay by Jōshō denouncing Hōnen's *Collection of Passages on the Nembutsu*. Its contents are not clearly known because of its early disappearance. Rebuffing Jōshō, Ryūkan of the Jōdo, or Pure Land sect, wrote *Revealing the Collection of Passages on the Nembutsu*. This offended monks on Mt. Hiei, causing Ryūkan to be exiled to northern Honshu in 1227 CE.

Devadatta *(Daibadatta)*

Daibadatta, also called Daiba or Chōdatsu in Japanese, was an elder brother of Ānanda, a cousin and a follower of Śākyamuni. He was extremely intelligent and is said to have memorized all 80,000 scriptures of Buddhism. Nevertheless, attached to worldly gains and fame, he tried to take over the leadership of the Buddhist order and even tried to kill the Buddha. He is said to have fallen into the Hell of Incessant Suffering while yet alive for committing three of the Five Rebellious Sins. Based on the 12th chapter of the *Lotus Sutra*, in which he is guaranteed to be a future Buddha, Nichiren maintained that all evil-doers, even slanderers of the True Dharma, can be saved by the *Lotus Sutra*.

Devadatta Chapter *(Daiba[datta]-hon)*

The 12th chapter of the *Lotus Sutra*. The first half of the chapter preaches that Devadatta, the archenemy of Śākyamuni Buddha, had been His teacher in a past life, and assures Devadatta of his future existence as a Buddha. It shows the strength of the *Lotus Sutra* enabling even evil persons to attain Buddhahood. The second half proved the attainment of Buddhahood by women through the example of a dragon girl attaining Buddhahood immediately with her present body.

Diamond Peak Sutra *(Kongōchō-kyō)*

Two Chinese versions exist. One translated by Amoghavajra in three fascicles. The other by Vajrabodhi in four fascicles. This and the *Dainichi-kyō, Great Sun Buddha Sutra,* are the two basic scriptures of esoteric Buddhism. While the *Great Sun Buddha Sutra* reveals the Womb World, this sutra expounds the teaching of the Diamond World, on which the Diamond World Mandala is based. According to T'ien-t'ai's five-period doctrine, Nichiren Shōnin relegates this sutra as expedient and provisional preached during the third Hōdō period.

Difficult to practice way *(nangyō-dō)*

Based on Nāgārjuna's *Commentary on the Ten Stages*, Pure Land teachers in China and Japan have maintained that all Buddhist practices leading to Buddhahood, except for rebirth in the Pure Land, are difficult to practice requiring a great deal of effort by practicers. According to Hōnen, founder of the Pure Land sect in Japan, the nembutsu is the only easy practice, not requiring self effort, while all other practices are hard.

Direct road to Buddhahood of Lotus-Shingon Buddhism *(Hokke Shingon no jikidō)*

In his initial period of propagation, Nichiren Shōnin accepted the teaching of the Shingon sect, considering both the *Lotus Sutra* and the triple Shingon sutras, i.e. the teachings of the Tendai-Lotus and Shingon sects, as direct ways leading to Buddhahood.

Disciples of Buddhas in manifestation *(shakke)*
The Japanese term *shakke* refers to followers taught and guided by Buddhas of the pre-Lotus sutras and the first half, or *shakumon*, of the *Lotus Sutra*. These Buddhas are manifestations of the Eternal, Original Buddha. They are differentiated from those bodhisattvas who emerged from the earth in the 15th chapter of the *Lotus Sutra*, who are disciples of the Original Buddha and are called *honge*. Disciples of manifestation Buddhas consist of two groups of bodhisattvas: those who had been in this Sahā World and those who came from other worlds in the universe. Nichiren maintained that the duty of *shakke* was to spread the dharma in the Buddha's lifetime, the Age of the True Dharma and that of the Semblance Dharma. It was the duty of the *honge* to spread the teaching of the Buddha in the Latter Age of Degeneration. He believed himself to have been an avatar of Jōgyō, Superior Practice Bodhisattva, and strived to spread the message of the *Lotus Sutra*.

Domestic Disturbance *(jikai hongyaku-nan)*
Refers to domestic power struggles or fighting among comrades, as mentioned in the *Medicine Master Sutra*, as one of the seven disasters predicted to occur if the True Dharma is slandered. Nichiren pointed out in his *Risshō Ankoku-ron* that the troubles of domestic disturbance and invasion of Japan by foreign forces were inevitable so long as Japan stood against the True Dharma of the *Lotus Sutra*. The prediction of civil war became a reality when a power struggle erupted among the Hōjōs in the 2nd month of the 9th year of the Bun'ei Era, 1272 CE, and Hōjō Tokisuke attempted a coup d'etat. Nichiren then likened his *Risshō Ankoku-ron* to the prediction of Śākyamuni Buddha.

Dragon girl *(ryūnyo)*
Dragon girl refers to an eight-year-old daughter of a dragon king, who listened to the preaching of the *Lotus Sutra* on Mt. Sacred Eagle, donated a gem to the Buddha, and attained Buddhahood with her present body. Together with the attainment of Buddhahood by Devadatta expounded in the first half of Chapter 12, Devadatta, the attainment of Buddhahood by a dragon girl proves the superiority of the *Lotus Sutra* by guaranteeing all living beings to be Buddhas, including an evil man and a woman.

Eight kinds of gods and demi-gods who protect Buddhism *(hachibu-shū)*
These are (1) *ten*, gods; (2) *ryū*, dragons; (3) *yasha*, yakṣas; (4) *kendatsuba*, gandharva; (5) *ashura*, asura; (6) *karura*, garuḍa; (7) *kinnara*, kiṃnara; and

(8) *magoraga*, mahoraga, who appear in the first chapter of the *Lotus Sutra*, Introductory. Invisible to the eyes of ordinary beings, they work in the order of Buddhas and bodhisattvas.

Eight streams *(hakke)*
Refer to the eight Buddhist masters who went to T'ang China to study and returned to transmit esotericism to Japan. Five were in Shingon esotericism: Kūkai, Eun, Shūei, Jōgyō and Engyō, Three were in Tendai esotericism: Saichō, Ennin and Enchō.

Eighteen elements of cognition *(jūhachi-kai)*
Refer to *rokkyō*, six realms of perception: color and shape, sound, smell, flavor, touch, and object of thought; *rokkon*, six sense organs: eye, ear, nose, tongue, body, and mind; and *rokushiki*, six consciousness corresponding to the sense organs. Of these 18, the first five realms of perception and the first five sense organs are material elements, six consciousnesses and the mind are spiritual functions, while the object of thought is half material and half spiritual.

Enchō, Grand Master Jakkō *(Enchō Jakkō Daishi)*
771–836 CE. Second Chief Minister, *zasu*, of Enryakuji Temple. Born in Musashi Province, present day Tokyo area, he entered the priesthood at the age of 18 as a disciple of Dōchū and named himself Hōkyō. He then went to Mt. Hiei to become a disciple of Grand Master Dengyō at the age of 27. He studied T'ien-t'ai Buddhism from Dengyō. At the same time he learned Shingon esotericism from Grand Master Kōbō. Nichiren Shōnin, therefore, criticized him as being "half a disciple of Dengyō and half of Kōbō." Nevertheless, according to Nichiren, Mt. Hiei had supported the *Lotus Sutra* up through the time of Chief Minister Enchō.

Eshin, Venerable *(Eshin Sōzu)*
Also named Genshin, 942–1017 CE. A priest of the Tendai sect who studied both exoteric and esoteric teachings on Mt. Hiei under Ryōgen, 18th head of the Enryakuji Temple. He wrote the *Ōjō Yōshū, Essentials of Salvation*, which had a tremendous influence on Pure Land Buddhism in Japan. He later wrote the *Ichijō Yōketsu, Essentials of the One Vehicle Teaching*, stressing the universal existence of Buddha-nature and One Vehicle teaching of the *Lotus Sutra* as opposed to the Hossō doctrine of "five distinctive natures of living beings." Nichiren at first considered Eshin as an outstanding priest of the Tendai sect, but later criticized him harshly as a parasite within the Lotus school.

Essential Collection Concerning Rebirth in the Pure Land *(Ōjō yōshu)*
A work of Genshin, Venerable Eshin, in three fascicles completed in 985 CE. Compiling in one book both passages from various sutras and treatises concerning the subject of rebirth in the Pure Land of Amitābha Buddha, Genshin preached the practice of the nembutsu as the best way to be reborn in the Pure Land of Utmost Bliss. It became extremely popular, motivating Priest Hōnen to start a new school of Buddhism, known as the Pure Land sect in Japan. Nichiren, before being exiled to Sado, regarded this book of Genshin's as leading people to the *Lotus Sutra*. After the Sado exile he harshly criticized Genshin for transforming the Japanese people into Pure Land Buddhists.

Essentials of the One Vehicle Teaching *(Ichijō Yōketsu)*
A treatise written in 1006 CE by Genshin, Eshin Sōzu, based on the One Vehicle teaching of the *Lotus Sutra*. It asserts the possession of Buddha-nature by all people, contradicting the "five mutually distinctive natures" of the Hossō doctrine. Regarding the purpose of Genshin in writing the *Essential Collection Concerning Rebirth in the Pure Land* and *Essentials of the One Vehicle Teaching*, Nichiren Shōnin maintained that Genshin's true intent was to publish the latter by following the example of Śākyamuni Buddha's preaching the expedient first in order to reveal the True Dharma in the end.

Ever-Weeping Bodhisattva *(Jōtai Bosatsu)*
The story of Ever Weeping Bodhisattva, who wept unceasingly in his pursuit of perfect wisdom, is from the *Daibon Hannya-kyō*, one of the Wisdom sutras. Tested by Indra, he is said to have sold part of his own flesh and bone in order to make an offering and to have won wisdom from Bodhisattva T'an Wu-chieh. Nichiren Shōnin cites him as an example of willingness to give his life.

Evil friend *(aku-chishiki)*
Meaning literally "bad knowledge." The term *aku-chishiki* refers to an evil friend or teacher who preaches the evil dharma to lead people astray blocking the right way leading to Buddhahood. It is used as an antonym of *zen-chishiki*, good friend. The third chapter of the *Lotus Sutra*, A Parable, uses it as an antonym of a good friend, *zen'yū*. Nichiren considered Devadatta, who incited King Ajātaśatru, a typical "evil friend." Nichiren also uses the term to mean an "evil teacher" like Hōnen who destroys the virtuous minds of people while leading them by slandering the True Dharma.

Exoteric and esoteric teachings *(kengyō-mikkyō)*
Exoteric teachings are those preached clearly in words and writings according to the ability of listeners. These are contrasted with esoteric teachings preached

by the Great Sun Buddha secretly and beyond the understanding of ordinary people. The Shingon sect maintains that exoteric teachings were preached by the Accommodative-bodied Śākyamuni Buddha while the esoteric teachings by the Dharma-bodied Great Sun Buddha, and that therefore the latter is superior. However, Nichiren insists that Shingon sutras, which preach neither the "attainment of Buddhahood by *śrāvaka* and *pratyekabuddha*" nor the "attainment of Buddhahood by Śākyamuni Buddha in the eternal past," are inferior to the *Lotus Sutra*, which is the true esoteric teaching.

Expedient means of encouraging idlers *(betsuji ishu)*
Meaning literally "the Buddha's intention [of preaching the expedient teaching expecting to gain results not immediately but] some day." The term is explained in the *Collection of Mahayana Essentials*, fascicle 5, translated into Chinese by Hsüan-chuang: "The term *betsuji ishu* means preaching that if one chants the name of the Buddha of Many Treasures, one will attain enlightenment; and if one chants the name of the Buddha of Infinite Life, one will be reborn in the Pure Land of Utmost Bliss. This is an expedient means of inducing people into the Buddhist way, particularly for the purpose of encouraging idlers. The Buddha does not expect such people to attain the goal immediately, but gradually improve themselves and attain it some day."

Expedients Chapter *(Hōben-pon)*
The second chapter of the *Lotus Sutra*. At the beginning of this chapter, Śākyamuni arises from meditation and tells Śāriputra that only Buddhas can realize the true aspect of all phenomena consisting of ten factors. This is the doctrine of *shohō jissō,* all phenomena as the reality of existence, and *jūnyoze,* ten suchnesses. Upon repeated requests by Śāriputra to explain why only Buddhas can understand it, the Buddha revealed the truth: that Buddhas appear in this world in order to lead all people to attain Buddha wisdom, and that teachings for Three Vehicles, *śrāvaka, pratyekabuddha* and bodhisattvas, are merely expedients to lead the people to the One Buddha Vehicle.

Fa-ts'ang *(Hōzō)*
643–712 CE. The third patriarch of the Chinese Hua-yen, Flower Garland sect. He is considered the systematizer of the Flower Garland doctrines. After studying Buddhism on Mt. Tai-po, he became a disciple of Chih-yen. After the death of his master, Fa-ts'ang entered the priesthood, writing many books and spreading the Flower Garland teachings. He was patronized by Empress Wu, *Sokuten Bugō,* and was given the title of Grand Master Hsien-shou, *Genju Daishi.*

Factual proof (*genshō*)
One of the three proofs: scriptural proof, theoretical proof and factual proof, used to verify a given teaching. Scriptural proof means that the given teaching is based on the sutras. Theoretical proof means that it is compatible with reason. Factual proof means that it is borne out by actual results when put into practice. Nichiren Shōnin insisted that these three proofs, especially factual proof, are vital when judging a given teaching to be valid.

Fifteen-altar ritual (*jūgodan no daihō*)
Also called *jūgodan-hō*, it refers to the 15 prayer services ex-Emperor Gotoba ordered the high priests of Tendai and Shingon sects to perform for the defeat of the shogunal forces in the Jōkyū Incident in 1221 CE. Although the term suggests a prayer service in which 15 deities enshrined on the 15 altars were invoked, Nichiren seems to have used the term to denote all the 15 imperially ordered services for the purpose of defeating the Kamakura forces.

Finger signs and mantras (*in-shingon*)
Finger signs in esoteric Buddhism symbolizing the enlightenment attained by Buddhas and bodhisattvas. Fingers represent the five elements of earth, water, fire, wind, and space. Those on the left hand are for meditation and those on the right hand, wisdom. These signs are one of the three secrets of body, mouth, and mind, through which one can attain Buddhahood in this corporal life. The secret of the mouth involves speaking mantras, called *shingon*, true word, or *darani*. spells. The secret of the mind includes meditation upon their *honzon* or object of reverence: the Great Sun Buddha.

Five-altar ritual (*godan no daihō*)
Also known as *godan-hō*. Esoteric prayer services beseeching for good health, good fortune, or pacification of disorder. These were simultaneously performed before the altars of five *myō-ō*, Wisdom Kings such as Fudō. Nichiren Shōnin states in his *Shinkoku-ō Gosho* that this ritual was performed to defeat the Kamakura Shogunate during the Gempei War, 1180–85 CE.

Five defilements (*gojoku*)
Five spiritual, physical and social evils which characterize the Latter Age: (1) defilement of the age including famines, plagues, and wars; (2) defilement of views meaning wrong views; (3) defilement by evil passions of greed, anger and stupidity; (4) defilement of people through their physical and spiritual decline; and (5) defilement of life through shortening life span. In Japanese literature the term "evil world with five defilements" means corruption and pollution of the world.

Five Flavors *(gomi)*

Many teachings were preached during the lifetime of Śākyamuni Buddha. Grand Master T'ien-t'ai divided these into five categories by the periods in which they were preached. He named these periods Flower Garland or *Kegon*, Āgama or *Agon*, Expanded Teachings or *Hōdō*, Wisdom Teachings or *Hannya*, and *Lotus* and *Nirvana Sutras* or *Hokke-Nehan*. The *Kegon* period is the first three weeks after the Buddha attained enlightenment. The *Agon* period covered twelve years of preaching Hinayana sutras. The *Hōdō* Period is the following eight years of preaching Mahayana sutras. The *Hannya* period is twenty-two years of preaching the *Wisdom Sutra*. The *Hokke-Nehan* period is the last eight years preaching the *Lotus* and *Nirvana Sutras*. These five periods of preaching are likened to the five tastes of milk and milk products: *Kegon* to milk, *Agon* to cream, *Hōdō* to curdled milk, *Hannya* to butter, and *Hokke-Nehan* to ghee, a finished product, proclaiming that the *Lotus* and *Nirvana Sutras* reveal the true teaching of the Buddha.

Five kinds of eyesight *(gogen)*

These include: (1) the eyes of ordinary beings; (2) the divine eye; (3) the eye of wisdom; (4) the eye of the Dharma; and (5) the Buddha eye, which also includes the other four kinds. See "Buddha-eye."

Five monks *(go-biku)*

When Śākyamuni left home to enter the priesthood, His father, King Śuddhodana, ordered five men to accompany Him: Ājñāta-kauṇḍinya, Aśvajit, Bhadrika, Mahānāman, and Daśabala-Kāśyapa. When Śākyamuni gave up the practice of asceticism, they left Him to continue the practice at the Deer Park in Bārāṇasī. Later, when Śākyamuni attained Buddhahood, they listened to His first sermon at the Deer Park and were enlightened.

Five mutually distinctive natures *(goshō kakubetsu)*

The Hossō doctrine dividing sentient beings into five groups by their spiritual capabilities: (1) *bosatsu* or *butsu jōshō*, those with the fixed nature of becoming bodhisattvas or Buddhas; (2) *engaku jōshō*, those with the fixed nature of becoming *pratyekabuddha*; (3) *shōmon jōshō*, those with the fixed nature of becoming *śrāvaka*; (4) *fujō-shō*, those with an indeterminate nature — not fixed to be one of the above three; and (5) *musho*, those incapable of becoming any of the three sages. It holds that these natures are inherent and cannot be changed or acquired in the course of a lifetime, and that therefore those in categories 2, 3 and 5 will have no possibility of attaining Buddhahood. The denial of attaining Buddhahood to certain people is diametrically opposed to the Lotus teaching, which strongly insists on attainment of Buddhahood by all people. This is the reason Dengyō, the founder of the Tendai sect in Japan, and Tokuitsu of the Hossō sect were engaged in a spirited debate, and Nichiren harshly criticized this Hossō doctrine.

Five periods (*goji*)

The Tendai doctrine classifying the Buddha's lifetime teaching according to the following five periods: (1) *Kegon* period, first 3 weeks after His enlightenment; (2) *Agon* period, 12 years preaching Hinayana sutras; (3) *Hōdō* period, 8 years preaching Mahayana sutras; (4) *Hannya* period, 22 years preaching the Hannya-kyō; and (5) *Hokke-Nehan* period, last 8 years preaching the *Lotus* and *Nirvana Sutras*. T'ien-t'ai also systematized what was preached during these five periods by the Buddha in Eight Teachings: four methods of teaching and four doctrinal teachings. He insisted that the Buddha's ultimate intent was expressed in the *Lotus Sutra*. Following this T'ien-t'ai doctrine, Nichiren emphasized the supremacy of the Lotus teaching.

Five rebellious sins (*gogyaku*)

Those who committed any of the five rebellious sins are said to fall into the Hell of Incessant Suffering. They are: (1) killing one's own father; (2) killing one's own mother; (3) killing an arhat; (4) injuring the Buddha; and (5) causing disunity in the Buddhist order. Nichiren Shōnin explains that the "five rebellious sins" do not exist because neither the Buddha nor an arhat are in the Latter Age of Degeneration, and he emphasizes the seriousness of the sin of slandering the True Dharma rather than that of the five rebellious sins in the Latter Age. Three of the five, killing an arhat, injuring the Buddha, causing disunity in the Buddhist order, are called the "three rebellious sins."

Five supernatural powers (*gotsū*)

See "Six superhuman powers."

Five Teachings (*gokyō*)

The Kegon sect classifies Buddhist scriptures into five categories: (1) the Hinayana teachings such as the Āgama sutras; (2) the initial Mahayana teachings such as the *Hannya* and *Gejimmitsu* sutras; (3) the later teachings of Mahayana such as *Kishin Ron,* or *Awakening of Faith in Mahayana;* (4) the Sudden-Enlightenment Teachings of Mahayana such as the *Yuima Sutra;* and (5) Perfect One Vehicle Teachings such as the *Flower Garland Sutra* and *Lotus Sutra*. The Perfect Teachings are further divided into two teachings of the distinct and common, considering the *Flower Garland Sutra* as being the unsurpassed doctrine of the One Vehicle teachings with the *Lotus Sutra* being placed in an inferior position, the same as the Three Vehicle teachings.

Fixed nature *(ketsujō-shō)*
This term refers to those whose nature is predetermined to become *śrāvaka*, *pratyekabuddha*, or Buddhas. This is according to the Hossō doctrine of *goshō kakubetsu*, five mutually distinctive natures. This doctrine states that the first two of these, *śrāvaka* and *pratyekabuddha*, also called those of the Two Vehicles, have no chance of becoming Buddhas. However in the *Lotus Sutra*, it is guaranteed that they will become Buddhas in the future.

Flower Garland school *(Kegon-shū)*
Also known as the Kegon sect. One of the thirteen Buddhist schools in China and also one of the six Buddhist schools in Nara, based on the *Kegon-kyō, Flower Garland Sutra*. This school classifies the Buddha's lifetime teachings into five teachings and ten doctrines to show the superiority of the *Flower Garland Sutra*. The school preaches that all phenomena are one and interpenetrate without obstruction: one penetrates all and all are contained in one. This school was introduced to Japan by the Chinese monk Tao-hsüan during the Nara period in 736 CE. Nichiren considered the Kegon school to be one of the better Mahayana schools but still inferior to the *Lotus Sutra*. This is because it does not preach the two important doctrines of the attainment of Buddhahood by the Hinayana sages called the Two Vehicles, and the attainment of Buddhahood by Śākyamuni Buddha in the eternal past. When Nichiren criticized the Flower Garland school, he always spoke of Ch'êng-kuan, who in his view stole the "3,000 existences contained in one thought" doctrine of T'ien-t'ai and put it into the theology of his own school while criticizing the T'ien-t'ai (Tendai) school.

Flower Garland Sutra *(Kegon-kyō)*
This sutra is said to have been preached by the Buddha upon attaining enlightenment under the bodhi tree in Buddhagayā. Saying that the whole world is a manisfestation of Vairocana Buddha, the sutra maintains that one is the whole and the whole is one, insisting that a particle of dust contains the whole world and a moment includes eternity. Based on the T'ien-t'ai concepts of the five periods of preaching and eight kinds of teaching of the Buddha, Nichiren Shōnin insisted that the *Flower Garland Sutra* is inferior to the *Lotus Sutra* because it preaches neither the attainment of Buddhahood by Hinayana sages called the Two Vehicles, *śrāvaka* and *pratyekabuddha*, nor the attainment of Buddhahood by Śākyamuni Buddha in the eternal past.

Foreign invasion *(takoku shimpitsu no nan)*
Refers to the threat of foreign powers preached in the *Medicine Master Sutra* as one of the seven disasters. *The Sutra of the Benevolent King* also warns of bandits approaching from four directions to invade the country. Nichiren issued a warning to the Kamakura Shogunate and predicted in his *Risshō Ankoku-ron* that unless the military regime prohibited slandering of the True Dharma, putting faith in the *Lotus Sutra*, Japan would surely be devastated by civil war and invasion by foreign forces. In the first intercalary month of the fifth year of the Bun'ei Era, 1268 CE, a state letter arrived from the Mongol Empire that indicated its intention to invade Japan if necessary. Mongol forces then actually invaded northwestern Kyushu in 1274 CE and 1281 CE. This verified Nichiren's prediction in the *Risshō Ankoku-ron*.

Forty years or so *(shijū yonen)*
The *Seppō-hon*, Expounding the Dharma chapter of the *Muryōgi-kyō, Sutra of Infinite Meaning*, states, "The truth has not been revealed during forty years or so." It states in Chapter 15 of the *Lotus Sutra, Yūjuppon*, Appearance of Bodhisattvas from Underground, "For the first time in about forty years since attaining enlightenment." It means that the *Lotus Sutra*, revealing the true intent of the Lord Śākyamuni Buddha, was preached during the last eight years of His preaching after having preached expedient sutras in the Kegon, Agon, Hōdō, and Hannya periods. The phrase, forty years or so, is used to divide the expedient teachings and the true teaching of the Buddha's lifetime preachings. See "Truth has not been revealed."

Four Heavenly Kings *(Shiten-nō)*
Also called the Four Great Heavenly Kings, *Shidaiten-nō*. They are kings of the four-king heavens, *shiō-ten,* around Mt. Sumeru. While serving Indra, they control the eight kinds of gods and demi-gods to protect Buddhism and those who put faith in it. As they vowed to protect this world and Buddhism in it, they are also called the Four Heavenly Kings Who Protect the World, *Gose Shiten-nō*. They consist of four guardian kings: *Jikoku-ten*, Sanskrit *Dhṛtarāṣtra* in the east, *Zōchō-ten*, Sanskrit *Virūḍhaka* in the south, *Kōmoku-ten*, Sanskrit *Virūpākṣa* in the west, and *Tamon-ten,* Sanskrit *Vaiśravaṇa* in the north. Nichiren Shōnin highly esteemed the Four Heavenly Kings as protectors of the *Lotus Sutra*, placing large signs for them at the four corners of the great mandala honzon.

Four holy ones *(shishō)*

In dividing all living beings into ten stages of spiritual development, ten realms, the bottom six stages of unenlightenment are called the six realms while the top four stages of enlightenment, realms of *śrāvaka, pratyekabuddha*, bodhisattvas and Buddhas, are termed the four holy realms.

Four kalpa *(shikō)*

According to Buddhist cosmology, the world goes endlessly through four kalpa. These are periods of construction, *jōkō*; continuance, *jūkō*; destruction, *ekō*: and emptiness, *kūkō*. Each period lasts 20 small kalpa. *Kusha-ron*, the *Discourse on the Repository of Abhidharma Discussions*, states that during the period of continuance, human longevity gradually decreases from infinite to 10 years at the rate of one year in a century. It then begins to increase a year in a century until it reaches 84,000 years. This is repeated 10 times.

Four-king Heavens *(shiō-ten)*

One of the six heavens, *rokuten* or *rokuyoku-ten*, in the realm of desire. This is the lower layer of the heaven situated on four hillsides of Mt. Sumeru. Each of the Four Guardian Kings reigns over each of the four heavens, where one day lasts as long as 50 years in the human world. Above these four heavens the Trāyastrimśa, the heaven of the 33 gods, is located on the top of Mt. Sumeru reigned over by Indra, *Taishaku-ten*.

Four Noble Truths *(shitai or shishōtai)*

Teaching for *śrāvaka*, revealing the truth from four aspects. These were *kutai*, the truth of suffering; *jittai*, the truth regarding the cause of suffering; *mettai*, the truth regarding the extinction of suffering; and *dōtai*, the truth regarding the path to Nirvana. *Kutai* reveals that the world of delusion in the cycle of life and death is full of suffering. *Jittai* shows that suffering is caused by evil passions and karma. *Mettai* tells that exclusion of evil passions and karma leads to the extinction of suffering. *Dōtai* is the Eightfold Noble Path to extinguish the suffering. *Kutai* is the result of *jittai*, which is the cause of *kutai*. *Mettai* is the result of *dōtai*, and *dōtai* is the cause of *mettai*. Causal relationship between *kutai* and *jittai* is in the world of suffering, and that between *mettai* and *dōtai* is in the world of Nirvana.

Four Reliances *(shie)*

According to the *Nirvana Sutra*, four standards which Buddhists must follow: (1) to rely on the dharma, not upon persons; (2) to rely on the meaning, not upon words; (3) to rely on wisdom, not upon knowledge; and (4) to rely on the sutra completely revealing the truth, not upon sutras that do not reveal the whole truth. This term also refers to four ranks of Buddhist leaders whom people can rely upon after the death of the Buddha, classified by those leaders' achievements. Nichiren claimed that the dharma on which people should rely is the *Lotus Sutra*. He identified the four ranks of leaders with the Hinayana, Mahayana, theoretical section, and essential section of the *Lotus Sutra*, claiming that those whom people in the Latter Age should depend on are bodhisattvas who emerged from the earth and that he himself was the leader of that bodhisattva group.

Four stages of meditation *(shizenjō)*
The four stages of meditation enabling one to overcome the delusions which one cherishes in the realm of desire and be reborn in the realm of form consisting of only pure matter.

Four ways of preaching Buddhism *(shi-shittan)*
Four ways of preaching the dharma preached in the *Great Wisdom Discourse:* (1) Encouraging people to follow Buddhism by saying it will fulfill their desires, *sekai shittan;* (2) teaching an individual according to his capacity, *i'nin shittan;* (3) helping people to free themselves from their illusions, *taiji shittan;* and (4) preaching the ultimate truth of the Buddha directly, *dai-ichigi shittan.*

Fundamental darkness of mind *(gampon no mumyō)*
Refers to the most fundamental of all illusions and evil passions innate in people. This cannot be extinguished easily but it must occur to advance toward Buddhahood. Nichiren Shōnin preached that fundamental darkness had to be cut off by the sharp sword of the Buddha's secret divine power, namely the *Lotus Sutra*, in order for one to attain Buddhahood.

Genkū *(Genkū)*
See "Hōnen."

Gishin *(Gishin)*
781–833 CE. The first Chief Minister, *zasu*, of Enryakuji Temple on Mt. Hiei. Well versed in Chinese, Gishin accompanied Grand Master Dengyō to T'ang China in 804 as his interpreter. According to the will of Dengyō, he succeeded the Grand Master as the head of the Tendai sect in Japan and established the Mahayana ordination platform, precept platform, on Mt. Hiei, performing ordination ceremonies. His work, *Anthology of the Tendai-Lotus Theology*, does not show all the effects of esotericism. Nichiren Shōnin maintained that the Tendai-Lotus school established by Dengyō in Japan based on the *Lotus Sutra* did not outlast Gishin.

Goddess Amaterasu *(Tenshō Daijin)*
Nichiren often cited Goddess Amaterasu and Great Bodhisattva Hachiman as native deities of Japan.

Gōnin *(Gōnin)*
A Shingon priest living in Fuji, Suruga Province, present-day Shizuoka Prefecture, during the Kamakura Period, 1185–1333 CE. On the 25th of the 10th month in the first year of the Kenji Era, 1275 CE, Gōnin sent a letter to Nichiren Shōnin, condemning Nichiren for his aggressive propagation activities and challenging him to a debate. In response Nichiren wrote a letter known as *Gōnin-jō Gohenji, Response to Gōnin's Letter*. In it he suggested they have a public debate and harshly refuted the fallacy of esoteric Buddhism.

Good friend *(zen-chishiki)*
Meaning literally "good knowledge," the term refers to a reliable friend or teacher who leads one to the Buddha Dharma. Chapter 23 of the *Lotus Sutra* uses it to describe one who causes people to aspire for bodhi-mind, meaning enlightenment. Nichiren said that in the Latter Age of Degeneration we have to take the *Lotus Sutra* as *zen-chishiki* because there is no person worthy of being a "good friend." When Nichiren called Hōjō Tokimune, Shogunal Regent, who persecuted him a "good friend," he meant that Tokimune gave him a chance to prove himself to be one who practices the *Lotus Sutra*.

Good Treasures Bodhisattva *(Zenzai Dōji)*
A bodhisattva mentioned in the *Flower Garland Sutra*. Upon meeting Bodhisattva Mañjuśrī he conceived the desire for enlightenment and then sought out *zen-chishiki*, good friends, to receive their instruction. He met Bodhisattvas Avalokiteśvara as the 28th good friend, Maitreya as the 52nd good friend and Universal-Sage Bodhisattva as the 53rd good friend. Nichiren Shōnin cites this bodhisattva along with Young Ascetic in the Snow Mountains, *Sessen Dōji*, and Bodhisattva Aspiration for Dharma, *Gyōbō Bonji*, as exemplaries of seeking the True Dharma at the cost of one's life.

Gradual teaching *(zengyō)*
See "Abrupt teaching."

Grand Master's Memorial Lecture *(daishi-kō)*
A lecture meeting held on the memorial day of Grand Master T'ien-t'ai, the 24th day of the 11th month. The lecture topics were the *Lotus Sutra* and the *Great Concentration and Insight* by T'ien-t'ai. In Japan the lecture series was initiated by Grand Master Dengyō. Nichiren Shōnin started it around 1268

or 1269 CE, practicing it on a monthly basis until shortly before his death as a means of religious education for his disciples and followers and organizing them into a religious group.

Great collection of sutras *(daizōkyō)*
See "All the scriptures of Buddhism."

Great Comet of the Bun'ei Era *(Bun'ei no chōsei)*
Refers to the great comet that appeared on the fifth day of the seventh month in the first year of the Bun'ei Era, 1264 CE. Motivated by the great earthquake of the Shōka Era, Nichiren wrote the *Risshō Ankoku-ron,* insisting that the spread of an evil teaching was the cause for continuous disasters. The appearance of the great comet of the Bun'ei Era, strengthened his conviction that the reason disasters occurred continuously was the persecution of Nichiren who spread the True Dharma of the *Lotus Sutra.*

Great Concentration and Insight *(Maka Shikan)*
A series of lectures, consisting of ten fascicles, given by Grand Master T'ien-t'ai and recorded by his disciple Grand Master Chang-an. It preaches ten-object, ten-stage meditation to attain the truth of the *Lotus Sutra* expounded in T'ien-t'ai's *Profound Meaning of the Lotus Sutra* and *Words and Phrases of the Lotus Sutra.* Nichiren Shōnin considered the doctrine of "3,000 existences contained in one thought" preached in the seventh chapter, Right Meditation, the ultimate essence of T'ien-t'ai Buddhism and the fundamental truth of the *Lotus Sutra.* Considering the practice of meditation on "3,000 existences contained in one thought" not fully appropriate for the Latter Age of Degeneration, Nichiren maintained that upholding the five-character Odaimoku, *Namu Myōhō Renge-kyō* is the "actual" "3,000 existences contained in one thought" and chanting the Odaimoku the suitable practice in the Latter Age of Degeneration.

Great earthquake of the Shōka Era *(Shōka no dai-jishin)*
On the 23rd of the eighth month in the first year of the Shōka Era, 1257 CE, a severe earthquake shook the Kamakura area. This motivated Nichiren Shōnin to write the *Risshō Ankoku-ron.* Living in Kamakura and experiencing this severe temblor and calamities that followed it, Nichiren studied a collection of all the sacred writings of Buddhism to see what caused these disasters. He then wrote a series of treatises beginning with the *Shugo Kokka-ron, Treatise on National Protection,* followed by the *Sainan Taiji-shō, Eliminating Calamities* and finally *Risshō Ankoku-ron.*

Great Freedom God *(Daijizai-ten)*

Maheśvara in Sanskrit. An alternate name of Siva, the creator of the world who lives in the *Akaniṣṭa*, or Highest Heaven of Brahmanism. Buddhism has accepted this god as one of its protectors.

Great Sun Buddha *(Dainichi Nyorai)*

The indispensable object of worship according to esoteric Buddhism. It is defined as the Buddha in Dharma Body, in which the truth of the whole universe is contained. Esoteric Buddhism claims that this Buddha is the fundamental Buddha from which all other Buddhas emerge. In Tendai esoteric theology, the Great Sun Buddha and Śākyamuni Buddha are identical, while in Shingon esotericism, they are regarded as different Buddhas, Dharma-bodied Great Sun Buddha being superior to Accommodative-bodied Śākyamuni Buddha. Nichiren, from the viewpoint of supremacy of the *Lotus Sutra*, regarded the Shingon doctrine as false, insisting that the Great Sun Buddha is a subordinate of the Original and Eternal Buddha Śākyamuni revealed in the 16th chapter of the *Lotus Sutra*.

Great Sun Buddha Sutra *(Dainichi-kyō)*

Translated in seven fascicles by Śubhākarasiṃha from Sanskrit into Chinese, this is one of the three canons of Shingon Buddhism. The Great Sun Buddha in the Dharma Body preached to Vajrasattva the doctrine of "becoming a Buddha immediately in the present body" through cooperative practices of, body, mouth and mind, of *mudrā* finger signs, mantra and *samādhi*, meditation. On the basis of the "five periods and eight teachings" classification, Nichiren criticized it as being a provisional sutra preached in the Hōdō period. In addition, Nichiren claimed, it is as inferior as Hinayana sutras because it does not reveal the Original and Eternal Buddha.

Great Universal Wisdom Buddha *(Daitsūchi-shō-butsu)*

The story of this Buddha, called *Daitsūchi-shō* or *Daitsū* appears in the seventh chapter of the *Lotus Sutra,* A Parable. According to this chapter, the Buddha preached the *Lotus Sutra* 3,000 dust-particle kalpa ago for a period of 8,000 kalpa. His 16 sons all became Buddhas. The youngest of them was Śākyamuni Buddha, who preached the *Lotus Sutra* in this Sahā World in order to save those who received the seed of Buddhahood by listening to Daitsū Buddha preach the *Lotus Sutra*. Based on this story, T'ien-t'ai divided the process of attaining Buddhahood into three stages: sowing the seed, *shu;* its germination and growing, *juku,* and harvest or enlightenment, *datsu.*

Great Wisdom Discourse *(Daichido-ron)*
This commentary on the *Wisdom Sutra* by Nagarjuna is one of his major writings. He not only annotates each sentence of the sutra, but also discusses numerous theories on various doctrines, especially concerning those of the *Lotus Sutra* and the *Flower Garland Sutra* including the theory of emptiness, Middle path, and ultimate reality.

Guardian Sutra *(Shugo-kyō)*
Abbreviation of the *Shugo Kokkai-kyō, Sutra of Guarding the National Boundaries*. Consisting of ten fascicles in Chinese, it taught that guarding the sovereign of a nation means protecting all the people in the land. Kūkai adopted it as a sutra of praying for national protection. Nichiren Shōnin often cites it and the *Sutra of the Benevolent King* to support his description of why calamities befall on lands after the death of the Buddha.

Gyōki *(Gyōki)*
A priest, 668–749 CE, in the Nara Period. Entering the priesthood at the age of 15, he studied Hossō Buddhism. Later, he travelled around the country to teach. He devoted himself to social works such as building bridges, roads and public lodgings. People revered him as Bodhisattva *Gyōki* or *Gyōgi*. The Imperial Court at first persecuted him for breach of the regulations for priests and nuns, but later changed its policy, appointing Gyōki to be *Daisōjō*: Archbishop. Nichiren Shōnin criticized Gyōki for not propagating the *Lotus Sutra* even though he knew about it. However, we do not know the grounds Nichiren had for this statement.

Hachiman, Great Bodhisattva *(Hachiman Daibosatsu)*
Originally a Shinto god of agriculture worshipped by the Usa clan of Kyushu in southern Japan, Hachiman in association with Buddhism began to be worshipped in the Capital Region during the Nara Period in the eighth century. In the early Heian Period, 894–1185 CE, the Imperial Court granted the title of Great Bodhisattva to Hachiman. In 860, Buddhist Priest Gyōkyō invoked the Shinto god of Hachiman at the Iwashimizu section of Kyoto and worshipped him as the protector of the Imperial Capital. It was around this time that Hachiman began to be regarded as being Emperor Ōjin, 15th Emperor of Japan, in a previous life. The Hachiman Shrine at Iwashimizu was greatly venerated by the Imperial Court as second only to the Ise Shrine for Goddess Amaterasu. In the late 12th century CE, Minamoto Yoritomo, the founder of the first military regime, established the Hachiman Shrine at Kamakura. With the spread of the military government, the worship of Hachiman became nationwide as the guardian deity of local communities. Nichiren Shōnin regarded Hachiman as a

manifested trace of the original substance that is Śākyamuni Buddha. Claiming that Hachiman was a guardian deity of the state of Japan as well as those who practice the *Lotus Sutra,* Nichiren included Hachiman in his mandala honzon.

Hall of Enlightenment *(Jakumetsu Dōjō)*
This refers to two places: (1) where Śākyamuni attained enlightenment located in the vicinity of the Nairañjanā River in Magadha, India; and (2) where Śākyamuni preached the *Flower Garland Sutra* at the foot of a large pipal tree to the south of Gayā in Magadha.

Have the dharma last forever *(ryōbō kujū)*
A phrase in the 11th chapter of the *Lotus Sutra* as the Buddha exerts His followers to spread the teaching forever after His death. Accepting it as the commandment of Śākyamuni Buddha, Nichiren Shōnin risked his life to spread the faith in the *Lotus Sutra* among the people in the Latter Age.

Hell of Incessant Suffering *(mugen jigoku)*
One of the eight hells. The adjectival phrase *mugen* is *avīci* in Sanskrit, meaning to be subjected to incessant suffering. This hell, the worst of all hells, is said to exist under the ground of the *Jambudvīpa:* the world in which we live. Those who have committed the five rebellious sins and slandered the True Dharma will fall into this hell. Those who are in this hell constantly cry out for help from their eternal anguish, so it is also called the Avīci Crying Hell. The hell is also called Avīci Castle because the area is so vast that no one can find the way out easily.

Hinayana *(shōjō)*
See "Mahayana-Hinayana."

Hōdō sutras *(Hōdō-kyō)*
A general term used to mean all Mahayana sutras as a whole. It is also used to mean Mahayana sutras preached during the Hōdō period according to the five period classification of T'ien-t'ai. In the latter use, such sutras as the *Great Sun Buddha Sutra* and the *Pure Land Sutra* are included in the category. Nichiren used the term in the latter sense. Holy teachings preached in Śākyamuni Buddha's lifetime: *ichidai shōgyō*. This included what the Buddha preached between His attainment of enlightenment under the Bodhi tree and His death at the age of 80. Systematizing these teachings into the "five periods" and "eight teachings," Grand Master T'ien-t'ai maintained that the *Lotus Sutra* represented the true intent of the Buddha. Following the T'ien-t'ai doctrines of "five periods" and "eight teachings." Nichiren Shōnin insisted on the supremacy of the *Lotus Sutra* over all Buddhist scriptures.

Holy Way Gate (*shōdō-mon*)
Refers to the teachings of such Buddhist schools as *Hossō*, Dharma Characteristics, *Sanron*, Three Discourses, *Tendai*, T'ien-t'ai, and *Shingon*, True Word, which advocate practicing Buddhism in this Sahā World in order to attain enlightenment and become Buddhas. It is contrasted to the Pure Land Gate, which preaches to be saved by rebirth in the Pure Land of Utmost Bliss instead of in this Sahā World. The Pure Land Gate, in contrast to the Holy Way Gate, was first established in the *Collection of Passages Concerning Rebirth in the Pure Land* by a Chinese monk, Tao-ch'o, and it provided the basic doctrine for Hōnen to establish the *Jōdo-shū*, Pure Land sect, in Japan.

Hōnen Shōnin (*Hōnen Shōnin*)
1133–1212 CE. Founder of the *Jōdo-shu*, Pure Land sect, in Japan. At the age of 13, he went to Mt. Hiei to become a Buddhist priest. At the age of 43, he was converted to Pure Land Buddhism by Shan-tao's *Commentary on the Sutra of Meditation on the Buddha of Infinite Life*. Soon thereafter he left Mt. Hiei to preach the teaching of the *nembutsu*, chanting devotion to Amida Buddha. As the teaching of the nembutsu spread, Buddhists on Mt. Hiei and in Nara appealed to the authorities for suppression and Hōnen was banished to Tosa Province. In writing such essays as the *Shugo Kokka-ron, Treatise on National Protection*, and *Risshō Ankoku-ron, Treatise on Spreading Peace Throughout the Country by Establishing the True Dharma*, Nichiren Shōnin harshly criticized the nembutsu practice and called Hōnen a slanderer of the True Dharma.

Honesty (*shōjiki*)
Nichiren Shōnin maintains that there are two meanings in the Japanese term *shōjiki*: (1) worldly sense, being honest without lying; and (2) in Buddhism, to comply with the true intent of the Buddha, namely the *Lotus Sutra*. Nichiren regards the worldly virtue of honesty highly, and those who believe and practice the *Lotus Sutra* honest people. He also declares himself to be truly honest because he propagates the *Lotus Sutra* in the Latter Age of Degeneration.

Hossō sect (*Hossō-shū*)
One of the six Buddhist schools in the Nara period, the *Hossō*, or Dharma Characteristic school is based on six sutras and eleven treatises such as the *Revealing the Profound and Secret Sutra* and the *Treatise on the Theory of Consciousness-Only*. Transmitted by Hsüan-chuang during the T'ang Dynasty, Grand Master Tz'ŭ-ên established this sect in China. Analyzing and studying the reality of all things from the viewpoint of the Consciousness-Only doctrine, the school is called *Hossō*, meaning "the reality of all things." This school declined in China but flourished in Japan especially at the Gangōji and Kōfukuji

Temples as the core of the six schools in Nara. It insisted on the Three Vehicle doctrine and criticized the One Vehicle doctrine of the T'ien-t'ai or Tendai and San-lun or Sanron schools. Nichiren Shōnin criticized the Three Vehicle doctrine of the Hossō sect from the viewpoint of the supremacy of the *Lotus Sutra*.

Hundred rulers of Japan *(hyaku-ō)*
Refers to 100 generations of emperors in Japan. Originally 100 rulers meant eternal succession of emperors, but a new interpretation appeared toward the end of the Heian Period saying that it means 100, not endless generations. Nichiren also interprets *hyaku-ō* as 100 generations of rulers, saying after the 82nd emperor, rulership of Japan shifted to Kamakura. He also maintained that the vow of the Bodhisattva Hachiman to protect 100 rulers of Japan meant protecting only virtuous rulers.

I-hsing *(Ichigyō)*
683–727 CE. Chinese Shingon priest popularly called I-hsing A-she-li or Zen Master I-hsing. He studied Zen and T'ien-t'ai teachings and also precepts of Buddhism. He was an expert in mathematics, astronomy, and calendars. He studied esoteric Buddhism under Shan-wu-wei, in Sanskrit. Śubhākarasiṃha, assisted him in translating the *Great Sun Buddha Sutra*, and wrote the *Commentary on the Great Sun Buddha Sutra*. Because I-hsing adopted the T'ien-t'ai doctrine of *ichinen-sanzen*, 3000 Existences in one Thought, in writing this commentary, Nichiren criticized him for "stealing" the T'ien-t'ai doctrine.mm-

Icchantika *(issendai)*
Those who are inherently unreceptive to the teaching of the Buddha, and therefore have no possibility of attaining Buddhahood no matter how hard they try. The *Lotus* and *Nirvana Sutras*, however, preach that *icchantika*, too, can attain Buddhahood. Nichiren maintains that even those *icchantika* who slandered the True Dharma, the *Lotus Sutra*, can become Buddhas due to the great compassion of the Original Śākyamuni Buddha. He thus stresses the great power of the *Lotus Sutra* to save all beings.

Immovable Buddha *(Ashuku-butsu)*
The Japanese term *ashuku* is a transliteration of a Sanskrit term *akṣobhya*, meaning immovable. According to the *Sutra of the Land of Ashuku Buddha*, this Buddha resides and preaches in the Land of Joy located in the eastern region of the universe. The seventh chapter of the *Lotus Sutra* states that the first of the sixteen sons of Great Universal Wisdom Buddha attained Buddhahood as Immovable Buddha in the land to the east and preaches the *Lotus Sutra*. According to the *Nirvana Sutra*, King Virtuous who sacrificed his life in

defense of the True Dharma was reborn in the land of the Immovable Buddha. In esoteric Buddhism, Immovable Buddha is one of the five Buddhas of the Diamond World mandala, symbolizing "the great round mirror wisdom" which reflects all things just as they are. These references by Nichiren in such writings as *Risshō Ankoku-ron* are cited from the *Nirvana Sutra*.

Indra *(Taishaku or Shakudaikannin)*
Originally a Hindu god of thunder, he was later incorporated into Buddhism as one of the two main protective deities of Buddhism, together with Bonten, King of the Brahma Heaven. Living in a palace called *Kiken-jō*, Joyful Sight, in the *Tōriten*, Trāyastriṃśa Heaven atop Mt. Sumeru, Indra is the Lord of this heaven who controls the Four Heavenly Kings and 32 other gods of that heaven. While Śākyamuni was practicing the bodhisattva way, Indra is said to have assumed various forms to test His resolution, but protected Him after He attained Buddhahood.

Infinite Life, Buddha of *(Amida-butsu)*
Lord Preacher of the Western Pure Land. According to the *Sutra of Meditation on the Buddha of Infinite Life*, this Buddha originally was a king in the eternal past who entered the priesthood under Sejizaiō Buddha, Sanskrit *Lokeśvararāja*. He was then called Hōzō Biku, Sanskrit *Dharmākara*. Making 48 vows to save people, Hōzō Biku performed bodhisattva practices for aeons of time, finally becoming a Buddha. Since then he has been preaching in the Pure Land of Utmost Bliss in the West. From the viewpoint of the *Lotus Sutra* as the supreme teaching, Nichiren Shōnin claimed that this Buddha is a mere manifestation of the Eternal, Original Buddha Śākyamuni and does not have any relation to us in the Sahā World.

Introductory Chapter *(Johon)*
The first chapter of the *Lotus Sutra*. Those who gathered on Mt. Sacred Eagle to hear Śākyamuni preach witnessed the six kinds of auspicious omens. They learned, through the conversation between Bodhisattvas Maitreya and Mañjuśrī, that the all-important *Lotus Sutra* was about to be preached.

Jambudvīpa *(Embudai)*
Jambu is the name of a tree, and *dvīpa* stands for a continent. According to Buddhist cosmology, four continents exist on four sides of Mt. Sumeru. The one on the south is called *Jambudvīpa*, also *Embudai* or *Nan-embudai*, because it is abundant with jambu trees. It is the world where we people live. It is also called the Sahā World.

Jikaku, Grand Master *(Jikaku Daishi)*
794–864 CE. Also called Ennin. He was the third *zasu*, Chief Minister of Enryakuji Temple. At the age of 15, he entered the priesthood as a disciple of Grand Master Dengyō on Mt. Hiei and studied the Tendai-Shingon teachings in China for more than ten years, 835–847 CE. The record of his travels to China is the *Nittō Guhō Junrei-ki, Record of a Pilgrimage to China in Search of the Dharma*. He wrote many works including the *Kongōchō-kyō-shō, Commentary on the Diamond Peak Sutra*, and the *Soshitsuji-kyō-shō, Commentary on the Act of Perfection Sutra*. He did much to make the Tendai teaching esoteric. For this, Nichiren was harshly critical of Jikaku, branding him a slanderer of the True Dharma.

Jōjitsu sect *(Jōjitsu-shū)*
One of the thirteen sects in China and six schools in Nara. This school focused on the *Treatise on the Establishment of the Truth*. It was studied by many in China until it was judged by Chi-ts'ang as a Hinayana doctrine. This school was introduced to Japan during the Nara period as incidental to the *Sanron*, or Three Discourses school.

Jōkyū Incident *(Jōkyū no kassen)*
Refers to the power struggle between the Kamakura Shogunate and the Imperial Court that erupted in the third year of the Jōkyū Era, 1221 CE. This is commonly called *Jōkyū no hen*. The imperial force, which had been greatly reduced in power by the establishment of the military government at Kamakura, tried to regain power by taking advantage of political instability at Kamakura after the death of Minamoto Yoritomo, the founder of the Shogunate. As the imperial force was badly defeated and three ex-Emperors, Gotoba, Tsuchimikado and Juntoku, were banished, the rule of Japan by the military was greatly strengthened. This motivated Nichiren Shōnin to enter the Buddhist priesthood. Nichiren Shōnin claimed that the defeat of the imperial force proved the falsehood of Shingon esotericism.

Jurui seed and sōtai seed *(jurui-shu, sōtai-shu)*
Two sorts of *kaie*, opening and merging into Buddha vehicle doctrines, in Nichiren Buddhism. The first is *jurui* seed: such acts as listening to sutras and worshipping Buddhas can become a seed of Buddhahood. The second is *sōtai* seed. This claims that three paths of evil: passions, karma and suffering, immediately become three merits of Dharma Body, unsurpassed wisdom and emancipation respectively. With these two doctrines, the *Lotus Sutra* can save both the evil and the virtuous. Nichiren Shōnin preached the *sōtai* seed

as the immediate attainment of Buddhahood with our present body through upholding the *Lotus Sutra*.

Kāśyapa *(Kashō)*
More precisely called Mahā-kāśyapa or *Dai-kashō*. One of the ten senior disciples of the Buddha Śākyamuni, Kāśyapa was known as the most excellent in practicing asceticism. In the *Lotus Sutra* he was assured of enlightenment by Śākyamuni. After the Buddha's demise, Kāśyapa led the Buddhist order and carried out the compilation of Buddhist sutras. For twenty years he propagated the Hinayana teaching as the first of the 24 successors to Śākyamuni. Nichiren pointed out Kāśyapa's future Buddhahood as an example of *nijō sabutsu*, attaining Buddhahood by a person belonging to the Two Vehicle group, stressing the superiority of the *Lotus Sutra* to all other sutras.

Kegon sect *(Kegon-shū)*
See "Flower Garland school."

King of Devils in the Sixth Heaven *(Maō or Dairoku-ten no Maō)*
The king of devils who is said to live in the sixth heaven in, *yoku-kai*, the realm of desire. Also known as *Takejizaiten, Temmahajun*, or *Maō*. Accompanied by many followers, he is said to hinder people doing good to attain Buddhahood.

King of the Brahma Heaven *(Bonten-nō)*
Also called *Daibonten-nō, Bonnō*, or simply *Bonten*. In Indian mythology he was regarded as the supreme god and creator of the universe. In Buddhism, this god is regarded as the lord of the *Shozen-ten*, the first of the four meditation heavens in the realm of *shikikai*. Together with Indra, they are the most supreme protective deities of Buddhism. He requested Śākyamuni Buddha to preach upon His enlightenment, and he also attended preaching assemblies of the *Lotus Sutra*. Nichiren worshipped him and invoked him in his mandala honzon.

Kōbō, Grand Master *(Kōbō Daishi)*
774–835 CE. Founder of the Shingon sect in Japan, he is also known as Kūkai. Entering the priesthood under Gonzō, he went to T'ang China in 804, transmitting Shingon esoteric Buddhism from Hui-kuo or Keika, a disciple of Pu-k'ung. He wrote such treatises as *Jūjūshin-ron, Treatise on Ten Stages of the Mind*, and *Ben-kemmitsu Nikyō-ron, Treatise on Esoteric and Exoteric Teachings*, advocating superiority of the Shingon teaching, insisting attainment of Buddhahood with one's present body, and spreading esoteric teaching. Nichiren harshly criticized him for despising both Śākyamuni Buddha and the *Lotus Sutra*.

Kōjō *(Kōjō)*
A Tendai priest of the early Heian Period known also as Grand Master Bettō 779–858 CE. At the age of 20, he became a disciple of Grand Master Dengyō, studying Tendai Buddhism, but he also studied Shingon esotericism from Kūkai, Grand Master Kōbō. Following the wish of Grand Master Dengyō, Kōjō worked hard to establish the Mahayana Precept Platform, for which imperial permission was granted seven days after Dengyō's death. He is referred to in writings of Nichiren Shōnin as having received esoteric dharma from Kūkai and transmitting it to Enchin. Nichiren, however, had nothing to say about Kōjō's efforts for the establishment of the Mahayana Precept Platform on Mt. Hiei.

Kokālika *(Kugyari, Sonja)*
A member of the Śākya clan, who became the Buddha's disciple by the order of King Śuddhodana. Later he fell under the influence of Devadatta and slandered Śāriputra and Maudgalyāyana. He also, together with a Brahman woman called Chinchamanavika harbored malice toward Śākyamuni Buddha, slandering and persecuting Him in hopes of defeating Him. He is said to have fallen into hell alive. Nichiren Shōnin lists him along with examples of slanderers of the True Dharma falling into hell.

Kumārajīva, Tripiṭaka Master *(Kumarajū)*
344–413 CE. Also known as *Rajū* in a Japanese abbreviation. Coming from Kucha, or Kiji, during the early period of the Northern and Southern dynasties in China, he translated 35 volumes of sutras and commentaries in more than 300 fascicles from Sanskrit to Chinese. These included the *Lotus Sutra, Wisdom Sutra* and *Great Wisdom Discourse*. His disciples are said to have numbered more than 3,000. Nichiren thought of him very highly and respected him for laying the foundation for Lotus Buddhism.

Kusha sect *(Kusha-shū)*
One of the six schools of Buddhism during the Nara Period in Japan. Founded on the teaching of the *Abhidharma-kośa, Kusha-ron, Discourse on the Repository of Abhidharma Discussions,* by Vasubandhu or *Seshin*. It was transmitted into Japan in the seventh century CE and studied by many scholar-monks in the Nara Period as a branch of the Hossō sect, without establishing itself as an independent sect. Nichiren enumerates it, as well as the Ritsu and Jojitsu schools, as a Hinayana school.

Last (fifth) 500-year period *(go-gohyakusai)*
According to *Daijik-kyō,* the *Sutra of the Great Assembly,* the history of Buddhism

after the death of the Buddha is divided into five 500-year periods, each with a characteristic feature: (1) attainment of emancipation; (2) practice of meditation; (3) reading and listening to many Buddhist teachings; (4) building many temples; and (5) doctrinal disputes. Applying these five periods to the theory of gradual decline of Buddhism through three periods, they fit into the 1000 years of the Age of the True Dharma, 1000 years of the Age of the Semblance Dharma, and the beginning of the Latter Age of Degeneration, which Nichiren regarded as the time for the spread of the *Lotus Sutra*. See Nichiren's treatise *Senji-shō, Selecting the Right Time*, for details.

Last in the śāla forest *(sōrin saigo)*
Śāla forest refers to the twin *śāla* trees at Kuśinagara under which the Buddha passed away. Since the Buddha passed away here after preaching the *Nirvana Sutra*, it is referred to as the sutra preached last in the *śāla* forest and the last will of the Buddha. Śākyamuni's death is also referred as the last in the *śāla* forest.

Latter Age of Degeneration *(mappō)*
One of the three periods after the Buddha Śākyamuni's demise: *shōbō, zōbō* and *mappō*. This is the period of degeneration which starts two thousand years after the Buddha Śākyamuni's demise. During this period, it was believed, although the teaching of the Buddha still existed, nobody could achieve enlightenment no matter how hard one studied and practiced it. The period is also called *matsudai* or *masse* in Japanese. The *mappō* idea appeared around the sixth century in India. In China, it appeared during the Sui and T'ang dynasties, 589–907 CE, and in Japan, during the Heian and Kamakura Periods, 794–1333 CE. Hōnen, Shinran, Dōgen and Nichiren were all influenced by this concept. Nichiren tried to save the people in the Latter Age by putting faith in the *Lotus Sutra* and chanting the Odaimoku: *Namu Myōhō Renge-kyō*.

Lay Priest Yadoya *(Yadoya Nyūdō)*
?–? CE. Also called *Yadoya Saemon Nyūdō* or *Yadoya Mitsunori*. His Buddhist name was *Saishin*. He was an official of the Kamakura Shogunate through whom Nichiren Shōnin submitted the *Risshō Ankoku-ron* to Hōjō Tokiyori in 1260 CE. In 1268 CE, when the Mongol state letter arrived, Nichiren asked Lay Priest Yadoya to convey a copy of the *Risshō Ankoku-ron* to Shogunal Regent Tokimune. At first Mitsunori was a follower of Ryōkan of the Gokurakuji Temple upholding the nembutsu and Ritsu teachings, but after the Tatsunokuchi Persecution in 1271 CE, when five of Nichiren's disciples including Nichirō were imprisoned in a dungeon at his residence, it is said that he was converted to the Lotus teaching.

Lives in the past, present and future *(sanze)*

In Buddhism every existence in this world is conceived not as static but as always changing throughout the past, present and future. Applying it to our life, it may be our past life, present life or future life; in reference to Buddhas, they may be Buddhas in the past, present or future. These three are, however, never in separation; they, like the current of a large river flowing into the ocean, are fused in the eternal future. This is why we may call all the Buddhas "the Buddhas from the ten directions throughout the past, present and future lives." The 16th chapter of the *Lotus Sutra* preaches that the Eternal, Original Śākyamuni Buddha continues to save all living beings throughout their past, present and future lives.

Lord of the Land of Bliss to the West *(Saido Kyōshu)*

Refers to the Buddha of Infinite Life (Amida Buddha).

Lord Toki *(Toki-dono)*

See "Toki Jōnin."

Lotus Sutra *(Hokke-kyō)*

Abbreviation of the *Sutra of the Lotus Flower of the Wonderful Dharma*, translated into Chinese by Kumārajīva in eight fascicles, originally seven fascicles. There exist two more Chinese versions: *Shō Hoke-kyō* translated by Dharmarakṣa in ten fascicles and *Tembon Hoke-kyō* by Jñānagupta and Dharmagupta in seven fascicles. According to Grand Master T'ien-t'ai, the first half, 14 chapters, of the *Lotus Sutra*, Kumārajīva version, is called the theoretical section and the latter half, 14 chapters, the essential section. The theoretical section with the second chapter, Expedients, preaches at its core that the Three Vehicle teachings are expedient and that the true intention of the Buddha is to lead all living beings to Buddhahood by the One Vehicle teaching. The essential section, especially the 16th chapter, Duration of the Life of the Tathāgata, preaches that Śākyamuni Buddha has been enlightened since the eternal past saving all living beings ever since. It reveals also that this Sahā World is the eternal, imperishable Pure Land. While Grand Master T'ien-t'ai formulated his doctrine based on the theoretical section, Nichiren formulated his doctrine and faith based on the essential section, and promulgated the Odaimoku, *Namu Myōhō Renge-kyō*.

Magadha Kingdom *(Makada-koku)*

Also called *Makadai-koku* in Japanese. One of the richest and strongest of the 16 large countries in India at the time of the Buddha, located in the southern part of Bihar state today. The Buddha attained enlightenment under the Bodhi tree by the Nirañjanā River in this kingdom, the capital of which, Rājagṛha, was the center of the Buddha's missionary activities. Mt. Sacred Eagle, where the *Lotus Sutra* was preached, is located northeast of Rājagṛha.

Mahayana-Hinayana *(daijō-shōjō)*
Meaning literally a great vehicle and a lesser vehicle, the terms were used to designate two major streams of Buddhism. Vehicles were likened to doctrines leading people to enlightenment. Great Vehicles are large and superior means of transportation in which not only those who themselves practice Buddhism, but many others are also carried to salvation, while lesser vehicles are smaller and inferior in which only self-salvation is attainable. Following T'ien-t'ai's interpretation, Nichiren regarded the Āgama sutras as Hinayana and sutras preached in the Kegon, Hōdō, Hannya, and Hokke-Nehan periods as Mahayana. He also declared that the true Mahayana is the hommon section of the *Lotus Sutra* alone, considering the sutras preached before the *Lotus Sutra* all Hinayana.

Main discourse *(shōshū-bun)*
See "Preface, main discourse and epilogue."

Maitreya Bodhisattva *(Miroku Bosatsu)*
A bodhisattva who is said to be a Buddha in the future replacing Śākyamuni. It is believed that upon death he was reborn in the Tuṣita Heaven, where he will reside for 5,670,000,000 years before being reborn in this Sahā World to save those who had not been saved by Śākyamuni Buddha. In the *Lotus Sutra*, he is a bodhisattva disciple of Buddhas in manifestation, *shakke*, who request the Buddha to preach, *hokki-shū*.

Mañjuśrī Bodhisattva *(Monjushiri Bosatsu)*
Left-hand attendant of Śākyamuni, mounted on a lion, Bodhisattva Mañjuśrī represents the virtue of wisdom and enlightenment. In the first chapter of the *Lotus Sutra* he foretells the preaching of the Lotus by Śākyamuni Buddha, and in Chapter 12 he reveals the attainment of Buddhahood by a dragon girl. Nichiren lists this bodhisattva's name in his mandala honzon as a representative of bodhisattvas in the theoretical section, *shakumon*, of the *Lotus Sutra*.

Many Treasures, the Buddha of *(Tahō-butsu)*
Also known as *Tahō-nyorai*. The Lord of the Treasure Purity World to the east, who vowed to appear wherever the *Lotus Sutra* is preached after death to verify the truthfulness of the sutra. In Chapter 12 of the *Lotus Sutra*, Beholding the Stūpa of Treasures, *Hōtō-hon*, it is preached that this Buddha in the stupa adorned with seven treasures emerged from the great earth attesting to the truth of what was preached by Śākyamuni Buddha. Nichiren Shōnin claims

this as one of the reasons the *Lotus Sutra* is considered supreme of all Buddhist scriptures.

Maudgalyāyana *(Mokuren)*

Also known as *Mokkenren* in Japanese, he was one of the Buddha Śākyamuni's ten senior disciples. He is said to have been foremost in mastering superhuman power. He became a disciple of the Buddha together with Śāriputra, mastering this power and becoming an *arhat* or *arakan*, a holy man. In the *Lotus Sutra* he was assured of becoming a Buddha in the future, but was killed by a non-Buddhist while the Buddha was still alive. Nichiren cites his death as an example of persecutions against Buddhists during the Buddha's lifetime compared to those after His death. It is well known that he saved his mother who was suffering among hungry spirits after her death. Nichiren advocated that it was the teaching of the *Lotus Sutra* that saved Maudgalyāyana's mother from the realm of hungry spirits.

Medicine-King Bodhisattva *(Yakuō Bosatsu)*

One of the 25 bodhisattvas described in the *Lotus Sutra*. The 23rd chapter of the sutra relates that in previous lives he had been a bodhisattva called *Issaishujōkiken*, Gladly Seen by All Beings, who burned his own body as an offering to the Buddha. Because of this, he was reborn in the land of *Nichigatsujōmyōtoku*, Sun Moon Pure Bright Virtue Buddha, and when this Buddha passed away, the bodhisattva burned his elbow as an offering to Him. He appears in the 10th, 13th, and 26th chapters of the *Lotus Sutra* as a man who listened to the preaching, swore to propagate it after the death of the Buddha, and to protect those who uphold it. Nichiren regarded the bodhisattva's burning himself as an exemplary act of upholding the True Dharma. Nichiren also considered both Medicine-King Bodhisattva and Grand Master T'ien-t'ai, regarded an avatar of Medicine-King Bodhisattva, as foretelling the appearance of bodhisattvas from underground, depicted in Chapter 15 of the *Lotus Sutra*. These bodhisattvas were disciples of the of the Original Śākyamuni Buddha. Nichiren considers himself as an avatar of Bodhisattva Superior-Practice, head of the group entrusted to spread the Lotus teaching in the Latter Age of Degeneration.

Medicine Master Sutra *(Yakushi-kyō)*

Revealing the twelve great vows of the Medicine Master Buddha, the lord and teacher of the Pure Emerald World to the East, this sutra teaches the virtues of a person who upholds the name of this Buddha. Nichiren Shōnin quotes phrases from this sutra and also from the *Sutra of the Golden Splendor* concerning the causes of the three calamities and seven disasters that beset the world during the period of mappō, or the Latter Age of Degeneration.

Miao-lê, Grand Master *(Myōraku Daishi)*
(711–782). Known also as Chan-jan or Venerable Ching-shi, Miao-lê is the sixth, or possibly ninth, patriarch of the T'ien-t'ai sect in China. Regarded as the restorer of the T'ien-t'ai sect, he wrote many books including commentaries on T'ien-t'ai's three major works: *Annotations on the Great Concentration and Insight*, *Annotations on the Words and Phrases of the Lotus Sutra*, and *Commentary on the Profound Meaning of the Lotus Sutra*. Nichiren esteemed him highly as the legitimate successor to T'ien-t'ai and quotes him often.

Mutual possession of ten realms *(jikkai gogu)*
According to T'ien-t'ai the world consists of ten realms: hell, realms of hungry spirits, beasts, asura demons, human beings, heavenly beings, *śrāvaka*, *pratyekabuddha*, bodhisattvas and Buddhas. Each of these realms mutually contains characteristics of the nine other realms in itself. This means that human beings have characteristics of the nine other realms from beings in hell up to Buddhas; asura demons have those of the rest of the ten realms; Buddhas also have characteristics of the nine other realms. This idea was set up by Grand Master T'ien-t'ai based on some passages in the *Lotus Sutra* such as "The Buddhas appear in the worlds in order to cause all living beings to open the insight of the Buddha." It meant to him that those beings in the nine realms other than the realm of Buddhas also possessed characteristics of Buddhas. This idea of "Mutual possession" provided the basis for another important T'ien-t'ai doctrine, "3,000 existences contained in one thought." Nichiren Shōnin founded and spread the practice of chanting *Namu Myōhō Renge-kyō* on the foundation of these two inseparable ideas as the ultimate means of attaining Buddhahood by ordinary, meaning unenlightened people.

Namu Myōhō Renge-kyō *(Namu Myōhō Renge-kyō)*
Namu Myōhō Renge-kyō refers to the "Odaimoku of the essential section," one of the Three Great Secret Dharmas of Nichiren Shōnin. Namu means putting absolute faith in or seeking refuge in, so this phrase means to have faith in the teaching of the *Lotus Sutra*. According to Nichiren, the Odaimoku of the *Lotus Sutra* is not a mere title of a sutra but it is charged with all the merits of the *Lotus Sutra* preached by Śākyamuni Buddha. Therefore, by putting faith in it and chanting it we will be given all the merits of the sutra. Thus, he considered chanting the Odaimoku as the basis of practicing the *Lotus Sutra* and the only way leading to Buddhahood for us in the Latter Age of Degeneration.

Never-Despising Bodhisattva *(Fukyō Bosatsu)*
As described in the 20th chapter of the *Lotus Sutra*, this bodhisattva, also called *Jōfukyō Bosatsu* in Japanese, believed that everyone had Buddha nature, and bowed to everyone he met saying, "I respect you deeply because you surely will become a Buddha." Some of those to whom he said these words became angry and threw stones and pebbles at him, but he never stopped bowing and uttering those words to them. The chapter tells us that what Never-Despising Bodhisattva did was identical to what Buddha Śākyamuni had done in his past lives. The chapter also states that those who persecuted this bodhisattva had to endure the Hell of Incessant Suffering. But upon hearing Śākyamuni Buddha's lectures on the *Lotus Sutra*, they were guaranteed to become Buddhas in the future. Nichiren Shōnin exerted himself to follow the example of Never-Despising Bodhisattva as one who practices the *Lotus Sutra* in the Latter Age of Degeneration. Nichiren interpreted the aggressive means of propagation, *shakubuku*, practiced by this bodhisattva as well as by himself, as the way to sow the seed of the *Lotus Sutra* in the heart of those who persecuted them.

Never-Despising Bodhisattva Chapter *(Fukyō-hon)*
The 20th chapter of the *Lotus Sutra*, the full title of which in Japanese is *Jōfukyō Bosatsu-hon*. See "Never-Despising Bodhisattva."

New translation *(shin'yaku)*
See "Old translation."

Nichiren, the Buddha's disciple *(Shakushi Nichiren)*
Part of the full title of the *Senji-shō, Selecting the Right Time, A Tract by Nichiren, the Buddha's Disciple*. This expresses Nichiren's confidence that he is Śākyamuni Buddha's true disciple who spreads the teaching of the Odaimoku, Namu Myōhō Renge-kyō, in the Latter Age of Degeneration.

Nirvana *(nehan)*
The ultimate goal of Buddhist practice, enlightenment or Buddhahood, in which evil passions are all extinguished; the state of mind completely free from the illusions of the three poisons: greed, anger, and stupidity.

Nirvana Sutra *(Nehan-gyō)*
Nehan-gyō, Nirvana Sutra, is an abbreviation of *Daihatsunehan-gyō, Great Nirvana Sutra*. Two versions of the Chinese translation exist: (1) the so-called Northern version translated by Dharmakṣema in 40 fascicles; and (2) the Southern version revised and reorganized by Hui-kuan, Hui-yen and Hsieh Ling-yün of the six-fascicled *Daihatsunaion-gyō* translated by Fa-hsien in 36 fascicles. The

sutra preaches that the death of Śākyamuni Buddha is an expedient, and that actually His life is eternal and imperishable. It preaches also the "existence of Buddha-nature in all living beings." Grand Master T'ien-t'ai regarded this sutra, together with the *Lotus Sutra,* supreme of all the sutras preached by the Buddha during the five periods of His preaching. Following T'ien-t'ai, Nichiren Shōnin considered it to be the teaching to save those who were missed by the *Lotus Sutra.* Nichiren also placed great importance on such doctrines preached in the *Nirvana Sutra* as "Depend on the Dharma, not on people" and "Ruthless chastisement of evil monks is the duty of a Buddhist."

Non-Buddhist scriptures *(geten)*
Literally "outer" scriptures, meaning those of non-Buddhist teachings. See "Non-Buddhist Teaching."

Non-Buddhist teaching *(gedō)*
Meaning literally "an outside way," in contrast to *naidō,* "inner way," meaning Buddhism. The term is used by Buddhists to designate a non-Buddhist teaching or its followers, sometimes as a derogative term to mean an evil or false opinion. In writings of Nichiren the outer scriptures generally refer to writings of Confucianism or Brahmanism. Nichiren Shōnin considered these and such non-Buddhists as "two heavenly beings and three hermits" of India as initial steps leading to Buddhism.

Notional understanding, perception and practicing *(myōji, kangyō)*
The second and third of the six stages, *rokusoku,* in the practice of the *Lotus Sutra* formulated by T'ien-t'ai. The former refers to the stage at which one hears the name and reads the words of the *Lotus Sutra* and begins to believe in it while the latter is the stage at which one practices what he perceives. Nichiren Shōnin, however, insists that one can attain Buddhahood, without going through the six stages, immediately upon believing in the Odaimoku, *Namu Myōhō Renge-kyō,* and chanting it.

Obtaining Buddhahood by Two Vehicles *(nijō sabutsu)*
One of the two great doctrines of the *Lotus Sutra.* Expounded in the theoretical section, *shakumon,* of the *Lotus Sutra,* this doctrine maintains that even the two groups of Hinayana sages called *śrāvaka* and *pratyekabuddha,* Two Vehicles, who are declared incapable of becoming Buddhas in such Mahayana sutras as *Kegon* and *Yuima Sutras,* can attain Buddhahood through the One Vehicle teaching of the *Lotus Sutra.* It shows that salvation through the *Lotus Sutra* is available to all. Along with the *kuon jitsujō* doctrine, attainment of Buddhahood by the Original Buddha in the eternal past, it provided Nichiren with a theoretical

foundation when he claimed the superiority of the *Lotus Sutra* of all the teachings preached by the Buddha.

Ocean-imprint meditation of the Flower Garland Sutra *(Kegon kaikū)*
A kind of meditation preached in the *Flower Garland Sutra*. In this meditation all phenomena appear clearly in the Buddha's wisdom, just as all things are reflected on the surface of the quiet ocean. The Buddha is supposed to have entered this meditation when He preached the *Flower Garland Sutra*.

Old translation *(kuyaku)*
In the history of translating Buddhist scriptures into Chinese, those translated by Hsüan-chuang, 600–664 CE and thereafter, are referred to as "new translations" in contrast to those translated earlier, which are called "old translations." Of the old translations, those translated before Kumārajīva, 344–413 CE, are sometimes referred to as the "antique translations" or *koyaku*.

One hundred realms and 1,000 aspects *(hyakkai sen'nyo)*
T'ien-t'ai doctrine based on the *Lotus Sutra* saying an individual mind has ten realms, from hell up to the Buddha realm, each of which includes in itself characteristics of the other 9 realms, making 100 realms. Each of these 100 realms has 10 factors, such as form, nature, etc., so there are 1,000 aspects of existence. As these 1,000 aspects have three modes, there are 3,000 modes of existence within a mind at any moment.

One Vehicle teaching *(ichijō-kyō)*
The One Vehicle means the only teaching which leads people to Buddhahood. It is stressed in the *Lotus Sutra* which states: "In all the Buddha lands throughout the universe, there exists but the One Vehicle dharma; there is neither a Two Vehicle teaching nor a Three Vehicle teaching." The One Vehicle also means unification, both unification of the teaching and the unification of those who practice the teaching. Thus the *Lotus Sutra* preaches attainment of Buddhahood by those of the Two Vehicles, *śrāvaka* and *pratyekabuddha*. While the Tendai doctrine stresses unification with the term *Kaisan ken'itsu*, outgrowing the Three Vehicles and revealing the One Vehicle, Nichiren maintained that the One Vehicle doctrine shows the superiority of the *Lotus Sutra* over other sutras.

One who practices the Lotus Sutra *(Hokke-kyō no gyōja)*
As it is preached in the *Lotus Sutra* that those who practice the sutra after the death of the Buddha will encounter great difficulties, Nichiren Shōnin believed that he was one who practiced the *Lotus Sutra* because he experienced various persecutions and difficulties as predicted in it.

Ordinary man *(bombu or bompu)*
In contrast to a sage, an ignorant and ordinary man; an unenlightened man. Nichiren considered that the people in the Latter Age of Degeneration are all ignorant and slanderers of the True Dharma, stressing that the boundless compassion of the Original Śākyamuni Buddha is to save these ignorant and ordinary people in the Latter Age.

Parishioner *(ujiko)*
People living in the community under the protection of a community deity, *ujigami*. Nichiren Shōnin regarded Goddess Amaterasu and the Great Bodhisattva Hachiman as the protective deities of Japan and the Japanese people as their parishioners. The term *ujiko* is believed to have been used for the first time in the late Kamakura Period, and in this sense the use of the term in the writings of Nichiren is an important piece of data.

Past seven Buddhas *(kako no shichi-butsu)*
Six Buddhas who are said to have appeared in the world before Śākyamuni Buddha: Vipaśyin, Śikhin, Viśvabhu, Krakucchanda, Kanakamuni, and Kāśyapa, plus Śākyamuni Buddha.

Potent omen of emitting a ray of light *(hō-kōzui)*
Refers to the ray of light emitted from the forehead of the Buddha shining over 18,000 worlds to the east described as one of the six omens in the first chapter, Introductory, of the *Lotus Sutra*.

Pre-Lotus period *(nizen)*
Meaning literally "prior to," the term is used by Nichiren to mean the teachings and sutras preached by the Buddha before the *Lotus Sutra* was expounded. According to Grand Master T'ien-t'ai's five period classification, sutras preached before the *Lotus Sutra* are provisional and expedient. Following T'ien-t'ai's idea, Nichiren Shōnin maintains that no one can attain Buddhahood through the teachings of the pre-Lotus sutras.

Preaching of the Buddha *(tem-bōrin)*
Meaning literally to turn the wheel of the dharma, *tem-bōrin* refers to the preaching of the Buddha. The Buddha's teaching, which eliminates all evil passions of the people, is likened to the wheel treasure, *rinbō*, of the Wheel-Turning Noble King, *Tenrinjōō*, which crushes all the evils of living beings. *Sho tem-bōrin*, the first preaching of the Buddha, refers to His first preaching for the five monks, His former attendants, at Bārāṇasī.

Prediction *(mirai-ki)*
Refers to sutras or other writings foretelling something to occur in the future. Nichiren considered the *Lotus Sutra*, and others such as the *Sutra of the Great Assembly* and *Sutra of the Benevolent King*, which describe the state of the Latter Age of Degeneration, as well as writings of such masters in the past as T'ien-t'ai, Miao-lê and Dengyō as "predictions." The 20-line verse in the 13th chapter and Śākyamuni's wish to spread the Lotus teaching in the Latter Age stated in the 23rd chapter of the *Lotus Sutra* are the "predictions" that supported Nichiren's missionary zeal. In a sense the *Risshō Ankoku-ron* was a "prediction" by Nichiren.

Preface *(jobun)*
See "Preface, main discourse and transmission."

Preface, main discourse and transmission *(jo, shō, rutsū)*
It is customary to explain scriptures in three steps: preface or introductory remarks, main discourse or central theme, and transmission or amplifying the virtue of the sutra for the purpose of dissemination. Likewise, Nichiren organizes the teachings of the Buddha's lifetime into three stages, claiming that the core teaching of the Buddha's 50 years of teaching lies in the 16th chapter of the *Lotus Sutra*, and that the *Nirvana Sutra* is its transmission.

Prince Shōtoku *(Shōtoku Taishi)*
574–622 CE. The third prince of Emperor Yōmei, who served Empress Suiko as her Imperial Regent. He carried out reform programs such as promulgation of the 17 Article Constitution and the adoption of the 12-cap rank system. He was a devout Buddhist who greatly contributed to the rise of Buddhism in Japan by writing commentaries on three Buddhist sutras: *Hokke* or *Lotus*, *Yuima* or *Vimalakīrti*, and *Shōman* or *Lion's Roar of Queen Shrimala*. He also built the Shitennōji Temple. Nichiren stressed the relationship between the prince and the *Lotus Sutra* by claiming that the prince was an avatar of Kannon Bodhisattva.

Profound Meaning of the Lotus Sutra *(Hokke Gengi)*
Fa-hua-hsüan-i in Chinese, consisting of ten fascicles. What T'ien-t'ai lectured on the title of the *Lotus Sutra* was recorded and compiled by his disciple Chang-an. It explains the title in detail and expounds the profound doctrine of this sutra through the five major principles: *ming*, name; *t'i*, entity; *tsung*, quality; *yung*, function; and *chiao*, teaching.

Provisional and true teachings *(gonjitsu)*
See "Provisional teachings."

Provisional teachings (*gongyō*)
The term *gon* means provisional as against what is "true" and "ultimate." Provisional teachings were used by the Buddha or His assistants as the most effective means of helping the people who lacked the capacity to understand the true teachings. Nichiren Shōnin considers that all Buddhist teachings, except the *Lotus Sutra,* are provisional.

Pu-k'ung, Tripiṭaka Master (*Fukū*)
Also known as Amoghavajra, 705–774 CE. The sixth patriarch of the Shingon sect. Born in northern India, Pu-k'ung came to China at the age of thirteen and entered the Buddhist order under the guidance of Vajrabodhi studying esoteric Buddhism. After Vajrabodhi's death, he visited India and returned with twelve hundred fascicles of sutras and discourses. He was trusted by the three reigning Emperors: Hsüan-tsung of the T'ang dynasty and two successors, who established esoteric Buddhism as the state religion. He translated sutras such as *Hannyarishu-kyō, Heart and Perfection of Naya Wisdom Sutra* and *Bodaishin-ron, Treatise on Bhodi-Mind.* Pointing out his mistakes in the *Bodaishin-ron* and failure in praying for rain, Nichiren condemned him for slandering the True Dharma.

Pure Land school (*Jōdo-shū*)
Also called the Nembutsu school, it was founded in Japan by Hōnen, or Genkū Shōnin, who preached that one should put faith in the original vow of the Buddha of Infinite Life, Amida Buddha, and chant the name of this Buddha, *nembutsu,* to be reborn in the Pure Land of Utmost Bliss. The school was founded on the basis of the triple Pure Land sutras, regarded the Buddha of Infinite Life the *honzon,* and divided all of the teachings of Śākyamuni Buddha into pairs: Holy Way and Pure Land, hard and easy practices, or right and miscellaneous practices. According to this classification, this school negates all other Buddhas and sutras and insists on chanting the nembutsu single-mindedly. Nichiren Shōnin harshly criticized this school for neglecting the Original, Eternal Śākyamuni Buddha, and the true teaching of the Buddha, the *Lotus Sutra,* according to the provisional sutras. He said that for this believers of the Pure Land teaching would all fall into the Hell of Incessant Suffering.

Pure Land Sutra (*Amida-kyō*)
One fascicle, translated by Kumārajīva. One of the triple Pure Land sutras, this sutra describes the Pure Land of Utmost Bliss to the West of the Buddha of Infinite Life. It mentions that numerous Buddhas of the six directions appeared to praise the virtue of the Buddha and testify to the truth of this sutra. It then states that one can be reborn in this Pure Land by chanting the name of this Buddha. Based on T'ien-t'ai's "five period teaching" doctrine, Nichiren

maintains that the *Pure Land Sutra* is a provisional teaching preached in the third period and that the Buddha of Infinite Life has nothing to do with and is useless to the people in this world, the Sahā World.

Pūrṇa *(Furuna)*
One of Śākyamuni's ten major disciples, noted as the foremost in preaching the dharma. Originally a non-Buddhist, Pūrṇa was converted to Buddhism, actively assisting the Buddha in propagating the dharma. The eighth chapter of the *Lotus Sutra* predicts him to be a Buddha called *Hōmyō*, Dharma Brightness. Nichiren often cites him as an example of the Two Vehicles obtaining Buddhahood.

Rebirth in the Pure Land *(ōjō)*
Upon death in this Sahā World, to be reborn in other worlds such as the Tuṣita Heaven, the heaven of 33 gods or Trāyastriṃśa Heaven, and Pure Land of Utmost Bliss, etc. In Pure Land Buddhism the term means leaving this Sahā World for the Pure Land of Utmost Bliss. Based on the teaching of the essential section of the *Lotus Sutra*, Nichiren Shōnin preaches that the true Pure Land is this Sahā World where we live, negating the rebirth in the Pure Land of Utmost Bliss preached by Hōnen and his followers.

Rebirth in the Pure Land through miscellaneous practices *(shogyō ōjō)*
Hōnen, the founder of the Pure Land sect in Japan, negated various practices except the nembutsu as a means of rebirth in the Pure Land. However, such Pure Land masters as Kakumyō-bō Chōsai and his disciple Dōa Dōkyō, or Shōkō-bō Benchō and his disciple Nen'a Ryōchū, maintained that various acts of merit other than the nembutsu could be practiced for rebirth in the Pure Land. Nichiren Shōnin was harshly critical of such theological contradictions in Pure Land Buddhism.

Refuting the Evil Dharma *(Sai jarin)*
Three fascicle treatise by Myōe-bō Kōben, 1173–1232 CE. Pointing out 13 shortcomings of Hōnen's *Collection of Passages on the Nembutsu*, such as denial of aspiration for Buddhahood and calling the Holy Way Gate a group of bandits, Kōben rebuffed Hōnen. He later added three more faults in Hōnen's contention. Nevertheless, as his criticism of Hōnen was from a traditional Buddhist viewpoint accommodating rebirth as a means of salvation, Nichiren did not consider Kōben a substantial critic.

Revealing the Profound and Secret Sutra *(Gejimmitsu-kyō)*
This five-fascicled sutra translated into Chinese by Hsüan-chuang is the basic canon of the *Fa-hsiang*, Dharma Characteristics sect. It is regarded as the first

Buddhist scripture to preach the consciousness-only doctrine which insists that all things and phenomena represent the mind. According to the T'ien-t'ai doctrine of the five periods, Nichiren considered it to be a provisional sutra preached in the third period, Hōdō.

Reverend Hōkan-bō *(Hōkan Gobō)*
1268 CE. Some claim that Hei no Saemonnojō Yoritsuna's father, Moritoki, was called Hōkan when he became a lay priest. Others claim, however, that the suffix *bō* indicates Hōkan was a full-fledged monk, not a lay priest, *nyūdō* or *zemmon*. Being the addressee of Nichiren's *Ankoku-ron Gokanyurai*, Hōkan-bō must have been a Buddhist monk close to the Hōjō family and therefore politically influential.

Right time *(toki)*
At the outset of his *Senji-shō, Selecting the Right Time,* Nichiren states, "To study Buddhism, first of all we must know the right time, *toki.*" The right time in this context means proper time to spread the teaching of the *Lotus Sutra* as it does in the second chapter of the *Lotus Sutra,* when the Buddha declares, "The reason why I did not tell this to you is that the right time, *toki,* had not come yet. Now is the very time, *toki,* to say this. I will definitely preach the Great Vehicle." According to Nichiren, the proper time to preach the *Lotus Sutra* was the last eight years of the Buddha's lifetime and during 10,000 years of the Latter Age.

Ritsu sect *(Ritsu-shū)*
One of the six sects of the Nara period in Japan that preached the observance of the Mahayana precepts as the way to attain Buddhahood. It was transmitted to Japan by Chien-chên, in Japanese *Ganjin,* who arrived in 754 CE. Nichiren regarded it as one of the three Hinayana sects, calling it "Ritsu, the national enemy." Especially critical of Ritsu Masters Eison and Ninshō, also called Ryōkan, contemporaries of Nichiren, he insisted that in the Latter Age of Degeneration the observance of the Hinayana precepts was useless and that upholding the *Lotus Sutra* is the true observance of the precepts.

Roundabout ways to Buddhahood *(ryakkō shugyō)*
The term *ryakkō shugyō* literally means practicing various preachings for many *kalpa,* or aeons, in order to attain Buddhahood. Nichiren maintains that the teachings expounded in the pre-Lotus Mahayana sutras are ways requiring inconceivably long periods of time to reach Buddhahood and that only the *Lotus Sutra* preaches the way to attain it with this corporal body.

Rules of frugal living *(zuda)*

Ascetic practice to eliminate evil passions and remove desire for clothing, food and housing. There are altogether 12 rules to observe, two on clothing, four on food and six on dwelling.

Sahā World *(shaba sekai)*

This world in which we live. The Sanskrit term *sahā* means endurance. Unlike the world of Bliss to the west, this world is conceived as being polluted by three poisons and the people in it must endure sufferings. Based on the 16th chapter of the *Lotus Sutra*, Nichiren insists that this Sahā World is the Land of Eternal Tranquil Light, where the Original Śākyamuni Buddha resides, and that we should uphold the *Odaimoku*, sacred title of the *Lotus Sutra*, to purify this Sahā World, polluted with evil passions, in the Latter Age of Degeneration.

Sanron sect *(Sanron-shū)*

See "Three Discourse school."

Śāriputra *(Sharihotsu)*

One of the Buddha's ten senior disciples, he is known as the foremost in wisdom. He had practiced Brahmanism before joining the Buddhist Order together with Maudgalyāyana. He was an *arhat, arakan* or holy monk in Hinayana teachings until he was enlightened by the "Revealing the single path replacing the Three Vehicle teaching" doctrine in the second chapter of the *Lotus Sutra*. The Buddha assured him of becoming a Buddha in the future. He assiduously assisted the Buddha in spreading Buddhism but died before Him. Nichiren took him as an example of attaining Buddhahood by men of the Two Vehicles: *śrāvaka* and *pratyekabuddha*.

Scriptural proof *(monshō)*

One of the three criteria Nichiren Shōnin used to judge the truthfulness or superiority of doctrines: scriptural proof, *monshō*, theoretical proof, *rishō*, and factual proof *genshō*. Nichiren Shōnin insisted on all three proofs to judge a given doctrine to be true.

Sen'yo, King *(Sen'yo-ō)*

Also called King Ṛṣidatta or *Sen'yo Kokuō*. The name of Śākyamuni Buddha in a previous life preached in the *Nirvana Sutra,* Chapter 7 on Holy Behavior. When Śākyamuni Buddha was practicing the Bodhisattva way as King Sen'yo in a previous life, he had the 500 Brahmans who slandered Mahayana Buddhism put to death. Because of this act of protecting Mahayana Buddhism, the sutra says, he was never in danger of falling into hell. Nichiren Shōnin highly esteemed King Sen'yo, as well as King Virtuous for upholding the True Dharma. Supported by the act of King Sen'yo, Nichiren Shōnin insisted also that slanderers of the True Dharma should be strictly dealt with.

Seven Disasters *(shichinan)*
See "Three calamities and seven disasters."

Seven rebellious sins *(shichigyaku)*
The "five rebellious sins" plus killing a Buddhist monk, who is one's own teacher, and killing a Buddhist master ajari. See "Five rebellious sins."

Shan-tao, Venerable *(Zendō Oshō)*
618–681 CE. Third patriarch of the Pure Land school in China. He was popularly known as 'the Master of the Kuang-ming-ssŭ' after the temple where he lived and was also called Grand Master Chungnan. He learned Pure Land Buddhism from Tao-ch'o and wrote such works as the *Commentary on the Sutra of Meditation on the Buddha of Infinite Life*, establishing the theological foundation of Pure Land Buddhism. He considered nembutsu chanting to be the right practice and rejected all other practices as miscellaneous. Hōnen, the founder of the Pure Land sect in Japan, especially respected Shan-tao and depended on him. However, Nichiren Shōnin criticized Shan-tao for not knowing the profundity of the teaching. He said Shan-tao fell into hell alive for slandering the *Lotus Sutra* by saying "not even one out of one thousand" can attain Buddhahood by the teaching of the *Lotus Sutra*. He is said to have committed suicide by jumping from a willow tree at the Kuan-ming-ssŭ Temple.

Shoji and shojū stages *(shoji-shojū)*
According to the *Sutra of the Original Karma of Necklace Bodhisattva*, shoji is the 41st stage and *shojū* is the 11th stage of the 52 stages of bodhisattvas: the ten stages each of faith, security, practice, devotion, development, the stage of approaching Buddhahood and that of Buddhahood. Shoji is the stage of joy, the first of the ten stages of development, in which the bodhisattvas partially master the principle of the middle path and feel joy. In the distinct teaching, shoji is the first stage of the sacred stages in which bodhisattvas can attain Buddhahood. Shojū is the stage of aspiration for Buddhahood, the first of the ten stages of security, in which bodhisattvas of the perfect teaching partially master the principle of the middle path. In the perfect teaching, shojū is the first stage of sacred stages, called the stages of non-retrogression from which bodhisattvas never slide back to the lower stages. Presumably, bodhisattvas extinguish ignorance and enter the sacred stages when they enter the stage of shoji in the distinct teaching; or the stage of shojū in the perfect teaching.

Generally those on the first 40 stages are regarded as unenlightened and those on or above the 41st stage enlightened, but T'ien-t'ai considered those on or above the 11th stage enlightened. Nichiren Shōnin, however, insists that whoever upholds the Odaimoku, *Namu Myōhō Renge-kyō*, can attain Buddhahood without going through the 52 stages of bodhisattva practice.

Six-fascicled Nirvana Sutra *(Hatsunaion-gyō)*
Refers to the *Nirvana Sutra* translated into Chinese by Fa-hsien in six fascicles. These correspond to the first 10 of the 40 fascicles of the sutra translated into Chinese by Dharmakṣema.

Six superhuman powers *(rokutsū or rokujinzū)*
Refers to transcendental faculties of a Buddha, bodhisattva, or arhat: (1) heavenly eyes; (2) heavenly ears; (3) ability to read other people's minds; (4) ability to know former lives; (5) ability to go anywhere; and (6) ability to destroy all evil passions. The first five faculties are referred to as five superhuman powers, *gotsū* or *gojinzū*.

Slandering the True Dharma *(hōbō)*
In general, *hōbō* or *hihō shōbō* means abusing or speaking ill of Buddhism, but Nichiren specifically stated that abusing or condemning the *Lotus Sutra*, the true teachings of the Buddha Śākyamuni, was an act of *hōbō*, the most serious sin of all. He insisted that those who knew the true intent of Śākyamuni and did not try to spread it were committing the sin of *hōbō*. Nichiren tried to secure the tranquility of the country by stopping people from slandering the True Dharma. For this purpose, Nichiren tried to spread the teaching of the *Lotus Sutra* throughout his lifetime at the risk of his own existence.

Southern Capital *(Nanto)*
Alternate name for Nara, located south of Kyoto, the Northern capital. Nara was the Imperial Capital for 75 years, 710–784 CE, during the reigns of seven Emperors from Gemmyō to Kammu. During these years the seven great Buddhist temples, Tōdaiji, Kōfukuji, Gankōji, Daianji, Yakushiji, Saidaiji, and Hōryūji, adorned the skyline of Nara, and scholar-monks of the six sects of Buddhism, Sanron, Hossō, Kegon, Ritsu, Jōjitsu and Kusha, competed in scholarship.

Specific granting of the Mahayana precepts *(daijō betsu jukai)*
Also known as *endon no betsu jukai* or *ryozen no daikai*, it refers to the special ceremony of the Tendai-Lotus school, in which the ten major precepts and

the forty-eight minor precepts preached in the *Brahma-Net Sutra* are received. These precepts are the same for the clergy and laity, and their merits are said to last forever. While trying to establish the true precept platform late in his life, Nichiren Shōnin regarded the Tendai-Lotus precepts to be "theoretical" in contrast to the "actual" precepts which he advocated.

Spotted-Feet, King *(Hansoku-ō)*
According to the *Sutra of the Benevolent King*, King Spotted-Feet, *Hansoku-ō*, was the disciple of a non-Buddhist teacher who suggested that the king take the heads of 1,000 kings and dedicate them to a certain god. After he captured 999 kings, the 1,000th king named Universal Brightness, *Fumyō*, begged for and was allowed to hold a lecture meeting on the *Sutra of the Benevolent King* by 100 Buddhist masters. King Spotted-Feet was also delighted by the lectures and realized that he had been led astray by non-Buddhist teaching. Citing the conversion of King Spotted-Feet, Nichiren Shōnin preaches that King Universal Brightness is the "good friend," *zen-chishiki*, of King Spotted-Feet.

"Sprinkling water on the head" ceremony *(kanjō)*
Performed in esoteric Buddhism on such occasions as conferring a certain mystic dharma and the precepts on a person or promoting the rank of a person performing esoteric practices.

Strange phenomena in the sky, natural calamities on earth *(tempen chiyō)*
The Japanese term *tempen* refers to abnormal phenomena due to unusual conditions in the sky such as severe rains and winds, eclipse of the sun and moon, and droughts. The term *chiyō* means calamities on earth such as earthquakes and floods. These cause such disasters as famines and epidemics. Holding that these disasters were caused by the people who abandoned the True Dharma and put faith in evil dharmas, Nichiren Shōnin insisted that they should promptly eliminate the evil dharmas and seek refuge in the True Dharma.

Śubhākarasiṃha, Tripitaka Master *(Zemmui Sanzō)*
637–735 CE. Śubhakarasiṃha left the throne of Udayana in Central India and learned esoteric Buddhism at Nalanda Monastery. Entering China under the patronage of Emperor Hsüan-tsung of T'ang, he translated sutras and wrote discourses, laying the foundation for Chinese esoteric Buddhism. Nichiren claimed, however, that Śubhakarasiṃha fell into hell upon death due to his slandering of the True Dharma.

Sumeru, Mt. *(Shumisen)*

According to Buddhist cosmology, this is the mountain in the center of the universe. It stands 80,000 yojana high above as well as below sea level. At the top is the palace of Indra. The Four Heavenly Kings dwell half way up the mountain. On the four sides are the Four Continents, the southern of which is the Sahā World of human beings. Nichiren likens the *Lotus Sutra* to this mountain as the prime of all the sutras. The 10th chapter of the *Lotus Sutra* states that of the numerous sutras which had already been preached, Hinayana and Mahayana sutras preached before the *Lotus Sutra*, are now being preached, the triple Lotus sutras, and will be preached, the *Nirvana Sutra*, the *Lotus Sutra* is supreme and most difficult to believe and comprehend. Nichiren considered this statement as proof of the supremacy of the *Lotus Sutra* among all the scriptures.

Superior-Practice Bodhisattva *(Jōgyō Bosatsu)*

One of the four leaders of those who emerged from the earth described in the 15th chapter of the *Lotus Sutra*. They are the *honge no bosatsu*, bodhisattvas guided by the Original Buddha in the eternal past, and entrusted with the task of spreading the *Lotus Sutra* in the Latter Age of Degeneration. After being exiled to Sado, Nichiren was firmly convinced that he was Jōgyō Bodhisattva who was entrusted by the Eternal True Buddha with the task of saving the world of Defilement and evils in the Latter Age of Degeneration.

Supernatural Powers of the Tathāgata Chapter *(Jinriki-hon)*

The 21st chapter of the *Lotus Sutra*, *Nyorai Jinriki-hon* is abbreviated as *Jinriki-hon*. In this chapter, the Buddha displays His superhuman powers, transmitting the essence of the sutra, the five-character Odaimoku, *Namu Myōhō Renge-kyō*, to the bodhisattvas from underground, and entrusting them with the duty of saving the people in the Latter Age of Degeneration. It was based on this chapter that Nichiren Shōnin realized himself to be the avatar of Bodhisattva Superior Practice, head of the bodhisattvas from underground, who was entrusted by the Buddha to save all the people in the Latter Age.

Sutra of Infinite Meaning *(Muryōgi-kyō)*

Translated into Chinese by Dharmajātayaśas in 481 CE, it consists of three chapters: Virtuous Practices, Preaching, and Ten Blessings. From its content, the sutra is regarded as an introductory teaching to the *Lotus Sutra*, or as a part of the *Threefold Lotus Sutra*. It is stated in the Preaching chapter: "The truth has not been revealed for forty years or so," differentiating the *Lotus Sutra* from all the sutras preached before it. Based on this statement, Nichiren claims all the pre-Lotus sutras to be provisional and considers the *Lotus Sutra* the True Dharma.

Sutra of Meditation on the Buddha of Infinite Life *(Kan-muryōju-kyō, Kangyō)*
One of the triple Pure Land sutras, basic scriptures of the Pure Land sect. According to its content, Śākyamuni expounded the Buddha of Infinite Life and His Pure Land of Bliss for the imprisoned Vaidehī at Rājagṛha in Magadha. Shan-tao of T'ang China wrote a commentary on it claiming the nembutsu, chanting the name of the Buddha of Infinite Life, to be the only way of salvation. Based on this, Hōnen Shōnin founded the Pure Land sect of Japan. Based on T'ien-t'ai's "five periods and eight teachings" classification, Nichiren Shōnin relegated the sutra to a provisional teaching preached in the third Hōdō period. Also abbreviated as Kangyō.

Sutra of Meditation on Universal-Sage Bodhisattva *(Kan Fugen Bosatsu Gyōbō-kyō)*
One fascicle sutra translated into Chinese in 442 CE by Dharmamitra, also called *T'en-mo-mi-to* or *Dommamitta*. It is abbreviated as the *Kan Fugen-gyō* in Japanese. Preached shortly before the Buddha passed away, the sutra declares the death of the Buddha in three months and teaches how to repent the evils resulting from six sense organs. Since this sutra is a continuation of the last chapter of the *Lotus Sutra*, T'ien-t'ai considered it as the conclusion of the *Lotus Sutra*.

Sutra of the Benevolent King *(Ninnō-kyō)*
There are two Chinese versions, both in two fascicles, translated by Kumārajīva and by Amoghavajra, Pu-k'ung. Preached to King Prasenajit of Kosala regarding the way to protect the nation, it has been revered both in China and Japan as one of the three state-protecting sutras. Nichiren cites from the Kumārajīva version in explaining "three calamities and seven disasters." The Shingon sect uses the Amoghavajra version.

Sutra of the Golden Splendor *(Konkōmyō-kyō)*
Two Chinese translations of this sutra exist. One translated by Dharmakṣema, *Dommushin*, in four fascicles and another by I-ching, *Gijō*, in ten fascicles. Together with the *Lotus Sutra* and the *Ninnō-kyō*, *Sutra of the Benevolent King*, it has been worshipped as one of the three state-protecting sutras. I-ching's version has been recited and preached in Japan in state-temples and in the Imperial Court since the Nara Period. Nichiren cited a chapter of the sutra translated by I-ching, *Shitennō Gokoku-bon*, *Protection of the Country by the Four Heavenly Deities*, when he gave his account of the reasons for disasters and calamities in the Latter Age.

Sutra of the Great Assembly (*Daijik-kyō or Daishū-kyō*)
Consisting of 60 fascicles, it was translated into Chinese by T'an Wu-chien of Northern Liang and others separately. Nichiren's concept of the Latter Age of Degeneration stems from the descriptions in this and three other sutras about the causes of calamities and the gradual decline of Buddhism through five "500-year periods." Nichiren insists that the Latter Age of Degeneration, when the *Sutra of the Great Assembly* predicts the disappearance of the "pure dharma," virtuous teaching, is the very period when the virtuous teaching of the Lotus would widely spread.

Sutra on the Act of Perfection (*Soshitsuji-kyō*)
Translated by Śubhākarasiṃha in three fascicles. One of the three mystic sutras of esoteric Buddhism, the other two being the *Great Sun Buddha Sutra* and the *Diamond Peak Sutra*. It preaches the way to attain perfect results in all works in both the mundane world and the dharma world. It is regarded specially important by Tendai esotericism, but Nichiren Shōnin slights it as a provisional teaching preached in the Hōdō period according to T'ien-t'ai's five period doctrine.

Sutras now being preached (*konsetsu*)
See "Sutras which had been preached, are being preached, and will be preached."

Sutras thoroughly revealing the truth (*ryōgi-kyō*)
Used in the *Nirvana Sutra*, the term refers to the sutra in which the whole truth of the dharma is clearly revealed. On the other hand, sutras preaching expedient teachings are referred to as the *furyōgi-kyō*. Nichiren Shōnin claims that of all the Buddhist scriptures, the *Lotus Sutra* is the sole sutra thoroughly revealing the True Dharma.

Sutras to be preached (*tō-setsu*)
See "Sutras which had been preached, are being preached, and will be preached."

Sutras which have been preached, are being preached, and will be preached (*i-kon-tō*)
The 10th chapter of the *Lotus Sutra*, The Teacher of the Dharma, states that of the numerous sutras which had already been preached, are now being preached, and will be preached, the *Lotus Sutra* is supreme and most difficult to believe and comprehend. Interpreting this, Grand Master T'ien-t'ai states in his *Words and Phrases of the Lotus Sutra* that the sutras which had already been preached

refer to the pre-Lotus sutras; those which are now being preached mean the *Sutra of Infinite Meaning,* which is the introduction to the *Lotus Sutra,* and that which will be preached is the *Nirvana Sutra.* The *Lotus Sutra* is superior to all these sutras. According to Nichiren, these three categories of sutras are easy to believe and understand because they were provisional teachings preached according to the capacity of the people while the *Lotus Sutra* is difficult to believe and comprehend because it is the true teaching expounding the true intent of the Buddha without compromising. Thus the term *i-kon-tō* is often used by Nichiren to prove the superiority of the *Lotus Sutra,* in the same way as he quotes "The truth has not been revealed during the pre-Lotus period of forty years or so" from the *Sutra of Infinite Meaning* and the Buddha of Many Treasures verifying the words of Śākyamuni Buddha in the 11th chapter of the *Lotus Sutra,* Beholding the Stūpa of Treasures.

T'an-luan *(Donran)*
476–542 CE. Founder of the Chinese Pure Land sect. Ordained on Mt. Wut'ai, he at first studied the four-discourse teaching, but later was converted to Pure Land Buddhism when he met Bodhiruci and received the *Sutra of Meditation on the Buddha of Infinite Life.* Nichiren Shōnin criticized T'an-luan for not knowing the difference in profundity of doctrines and also for slandering the Buddha by defining the Pure Land teaching to be supreme according to his two-way classification: the easy and difficult ways to practice.

Tao-ch'o *(Dōshaku) {757}*
562–645 CE. The second patriarch of Chinese Pure Land Buddhism. He entered the priesthood at the age of 14, studying the *Nirvana Sutra.* At 48, however, he was converted to the Pure Land teaching by T'an-luan. He wrote the two-fascicled *An-lo-chi, Collection of Passages Concerning Rebirth in the Pure Land.* At the beginning of the *Senjaku-shū, Collection of Passages on the Nembutsu,* Hōnen cited from *An-lo-chi,* proclaiming the establishment of the Pure Land sect in Japan by dividing the holy teaching of the Buddha into the Holy Way and the Pure Land. Nichiren criticized the Pure Land masters for disregarding both the profundity of doctrines and the difference between true and provisional dharmas.

Teachers in China and Japan *(ninshi)*
Nichiren used the term *ninshi* to mean Buddhist priests in China and Japan who spread Buddhism guided by commentators and translators.

Ten similies *(Jūyu)*

The ten similes enumerated in the Previous Life of Medicine-King Bodhisattva chapter of the *Lotus Sutra* in order to explain the superiority of the *Lotus Sutra* among all the Buddhist sutras. It claims that the *Lotus Sutra* is the king of all Buddhist sutras just as the ocean is of all the waters, Mt. Sumeru is of all the mountains, the moon is of all the stars, the sun is in brightness, Wheel-turning Noble King is among all kings, Indra is in the heaven of the 33 gods known as Trāyastriṃsa Heaven, the King of the Brahma Heaven is among living beings, a *pratyekabuddha* is among ordinary unenlightened people, a bodhisattva is among the three vehicles, and the Buddha Dharma is of all other teachings. Nichiren Shōnin often cited the passage on the ten similes to prove the supremacy of the *Lotus Sutra*.

Ten supernatural powers *(jūjinriki)*

Refers to the ten kinds of divine powers of the Buddha shown in Chapter 21 of the *Lotus Sutra,* The Supernatural Powers of the Tathāgata, prior to transmitting the Dharma to bodhisattvas emerged from the earth: (1) the broad, long tongue that reached the Brahma Heaven; (2) rays of light emitted from His pores shining over all the worlds in the universe; (3) coughing; (4) snapping fingers; (5) all the worlds in the universe quaking in six ways; (6) all living beings in those worlds seeing the two Buddhas sitting in the stupa of treasures in the sky; (7) gods in the sky telling all living beings in all the worlds in the universe to believe in Śākyamuni Buddha in the Sahā World; (8) all living beings embracing the Buddha and the *Lotus Sutra;* (9) various offerings from all the worlds strewn over the Sahā World; and (10) all the worlds becoming passable through each other as though they were a single Buddha land. T'ien-t'ai said that the first of them was for those in the Buddha's lifetime and the rest were for those after the death of the Buddha, but Nichiren Shōnin claims that they all are for the Latter Age of Degeneration.

Those without Buddha-nature *(mushō)*

The Japanese term *mushō* refers to those who do not have Buddha-nature. According to the Hossō doctrine such people will never become Buddhas. However, the *Lotus* and *Nirvana Sutras* preach that even the *icchantika*, who have no Buddha-nature, can attain Buddhahood. Nichiren stresses the attainment of Buddhahood by *icchantika* without Buddha-nature through the great compassion of the Eternal True Buddha.

Three calamities *(sansai)*

See "Three calamities and seven disasters."

Three calamities and seven disasters *(sansai shichinan)*
According to Buddhist cosmology, the world goes through four periods: kalpa of construction, kalpa of continuance, kalpa of destruction, and kalpa of emptiness. The three calamities of warfare, epidemic, and famine that occur in the kalpa of continuance are called the three minor calamities while fires, floods, and severe winds in the kalpa of destruction constitute the three major calamities. Seven disasters refer to those caused by slandering the True Dharma. According to the *Sutra of the Benevolent King* these are: (1) loss of brilliance of the sun and the moon; (2) loss of brilliance of constellations; (3) fire; (4) flood; (5) strong winds; (6) drought; and (7) bandits. According to the *Medicine Master Sutra* these are: (1) epidemics; (2) foreign invasions; (3) civil wars; (4) changes in constellations; (5) eclipses of the sun and the moon; (6) unusual storms; and (7) unseasonable storms. According to Chapter 25 of the *Lotus Sutra* these are: (1) fire; (2) flood; (3) *rakṣasa* or *rasetsu* demons; (4) the ruler; (5) other demons; (6) imprisonment; and (7) bandits.

Three Discourse school *(Sanron-shū)*
One of the thirteen Buddhist schools in China and also one of the six schools in Nara. It is based on the *Fundamental Verses on the Middle Way* and the *Treatise on the Twelve Gates* by Nāgārjuna, and the *One-hundred Verse Treatise* by Āryadeva, a disciple of Nāgārjuna. The theology of the Sanron school in China was established by Grand Master Chia-hsiang, or Chi-ts'ang, and transmitted to Japan in 625 CE.

Three evil realms *(san'aku-dō)*
Also referred to as *sannakudō, san'aku, sannaku,* or *san'akushu* in Japanese. Hell, realm of hungry souls or *gaki,* and realm of beasts and birds or *chikushō,* where living beings would fall into after death due to their sins, are the bottom three of the ten stages of spiritual development within each individual. Adding the realm of fighting spirits, *shura,* they are called the four evil realms: *shiakushu* or *shiakudō.*

Three kinds of enemies *(sanrui no tekinin)*
Also called *sanrui no gōteki* or *sanrui no onteki,* the term refers to three kinds of enemies who try to persecute propagators of the *Lotus Sutra* in various ways. The first group is lay followers who believe in and support the second and third groups. The second group is self-conceited priests and priestesses who mislead suffering people. The third group is those priests, male or female, who are highly respected by people but are strongly attached to worldly matters. Encountering all these enemies as predicted in the 13th chapter of the *Lotus Sutra,* Nichiren strengthened his belief that he was the practicer of the *Lotus Sutra.*

Three meetings at two places *(nisho san'e)*
Refers to where Śākyamuni Buddha preached the *Lotus Sutra*. The *Lotus Sutra* was expounded on Mt. Sacred Eagle and up in the sky above it in three lecture meetings. From Chapter 1 to the first half of Chapter 11 the *Lotus Sutra* was expounded on Mt. Sacred Eagle. From the last half of Chapter 11 through Chapter 22 it was expounded up in the sky. Then from Chapters 23 to 28 it was expounded on the mountain again.

Three-period teaching *(sanji-kyō)*
Classification of the Buddhist scriptures by the *Hossō* or Dharma Characteristics sect into three categories: (1) the teaching of existence, *ukyō*, preached first in sutras such as the Āgama sutras; (2) the teaching of the void, *kūkyō*, expounded next in sutras such as the *Wisdom Sutra*; and finally (3) the teaching of the Middle Way preached in sutras such as the *Flower Garland Sutra* and the *Revealing the Profound and Secret Sutra*. The teaching of the Middle Way insists that reality lies beyond existence and non-existence and is considered supreme.

Three robes and one alms-bowl *(sanne ippatsu)*
Three robes and one alms-bowl were what priests were allowed to own. They wore one big robe and two kinds of kesa made of nine or five pieces of cloth. They also used a bowl for begging for food. Besides these, ordained monks were also allowed to have a cushion to sit on and a water filter. Nichiren Shōnin criticized Zen and Ritsu priests as deceivers who broke the "three robes and one bowl" rule as they approached those in power in order to curry favor and special treatment.

Three Southern and seven Northern masters *(Nansan Hokushichi)*
This term was first used by T'ien-t'ai in his *Profound Meaning of the Lotus Sutra* to describe the state of Buddhist studies in China during the Period of Northern and Southern Dynasties centering to the south of the Yangtze River and north of the Yellow River. Though their systems of comparative studies of Buddhist doctrines varied, they all held that either the *Nirvana Sutra* or the *Flower Garland Sutra* to be supreme of all sutras. T'ien-t'ai rearranged and integrated them into his Five Period and Eight Teaching classification asserting the supremacy of the *Lotus Sutra*. Highly esteeming this classification, Nichiren praised T'ien-t'ai in the highest terms for completely refuting the false doctrines of the three Southern and seven Northern masters and establishing the new classification centering on the *Lotus Sutra* for the first time in the history of Buddhism.

Three standards of doctrinal comparison *(sanshu no kyōsō)*
To prove the superiority of the *Lotus Sutra*, Grand Master T'ien-t'ai examined it against all other sutras through three standards explained in his *Profound Meaning of the Lotus Sutra*. The first standard is to see whether the sutra is provisional or true by looking at the capacity of the people to understand the Dharma. This is shown in the fourth chapter of the *Lotus Sutra*, Understanding by Faith. While the pre-Lotus sutras preached expedient teachings according to the inferior capacity of the people, the *Lotus Sutra* revealed the True Dharma because the people were able to understand and accept it. The second standard was to see whether a sutra mentioned when the Buddha began and finished expounding the way to enlightenment. No other sutra besides the *Lotus Sutra* mentions this. The seventh chapter, A Parable, shows that at the time of the Great Universal Wisdom Buddha, the seed of Buddhahood was sown in the people, and guidance continued until they were assured of future Buddhahood. The third was to see if the relationships established between the Buddha and His people were eternal. This is shown in the 16th chapter, Duration of the Life of the Tathāgata, which reveals that the life of the Buddha is eternal and that various Buddhas and bodhisattvas residing in the worlds throughout the universe in the past, present, and future are manifestations disciples of the Buddha.

Three thousand existences contained in one thought *(ichinen sanzen)*
The doctrine preached in the *Great Concentration and Insight* by Grand Master T'ien-t'ai maintaining that 3,000 modes of existence are contained in the mind of an ordinary person at any given moment. It is based on the teaching of the ten aspects of all phenomena preached in the second chapter of the *Lotus Sutra*. 3,000 modes of existence, conditions under which all things exist and phenomena take place, are arrived at by multiplying 10 realms, stages of spiritual development, by 10 because each of the 10 realms is said to be equipped also with characteristics of the other nine realms. The resulting 100 realms are further multiplied by the 10 aspects of all phenomena and also by the 3 factors of existences: living beings, environment, and the five constituent elements of living beings. As it is proved that 3,000 modes of existence are included in an individual's mind, it is logically possible that those who practice Buddhism known as the Two Vehicles, *śrāvaka* and *pratyekabuddha*, who have been denied attaining Buddhahood in the pre-Lotus sutras, as well as we, ordinary persons, enter the world of enlightenment attained by the Buddha. Based on the T'ien-t'ai doctrine of "3,000 existences contained in one thought," Nichiren advocated that chanting the Odaimoku of Namu Myōhō Renge-kyō is the only practical way for ordinary people in the Latter Age of

Degeneration to attain Buddhahood. A related concept is "3,000 existences in 100 realms," *hyakkai sanzen*. This refers to all things in the universe expressed in terms of ten realms, ten reality aspects and the three categories of realm. The 100 realms are the world in which each of the ten realms: hell, hungry spirits, animals, asura, men, heavenly beings, *śrāvaka, pratyekabuddha*, bodhisattvas, and Buddhas, contains the characteristics of the other nine realms. Each of the 100 realms contains 10 reality aspects: form, nature, substance, function, action, cause, condition, effect, reward, and ultimate non-differentiation of the above nine aspects, and each of these 1,000 reality aspects contains the three categories of realm: realms of sentient beings, non-sentient beings and the five elements of all existences. The resulting figure 3,000 refers to the whole universe. The doctrine that the 3,000 existences are contained in the thought of a person, "3,000 existences contained in one thought," is the ultimate teaching which Grand Master T'ien-t'ai expounded in the fifth fascicle of the *Great Concentration and Insight*.

Three treasures in Buddhism *(sambō)*

Refers to the Buddha, who attained enlightenment, the dharma preached by the Buddha, and disciples of the Buddha, who practice the teachings preached by the Buddha. The three treasures are basic elements of Buddhist doctrine, and putting faith in them is a prerequisite for Buddhists. In Nichiren Buddhism, the Buddha is the Eternal Śākyamuni Buddha revealed in the 16th chapter of the *Lotus Sutra*, the dharma is the Odaimoku, *Namu Myōhō Renge-kyō*, representing the gist of the *Lotus Sutra*, and the disciples of the Buddha are Nichiren Shōnin, leading master in the Latter Age of Degeneration, and those who follow his lead.

Three vehicles *(sanjō)*

Three kinds of vehicles or teachings leading three categories of people, *śrāvaka, pratyekabuddha* and bodhisattvas, to Buddhahood. Teachings for *śrāvaka* and *pratyekabuddha* are Hinayana while the teaching for bodhisattvas is Mahayana. *Śrāvaka* are said to attain enlightenment through the doctrine of Four Noble Truths, *pratyekabuddha* through that of the twelve links of cause and effect, and bodhisattvas with the practice of the six perfections or *pāramitā*. The Buddha preached various expedients according to the capacity of people to understand. The *Lotus Sutra* declares that preaching the three different teachings for three different categories of people is merely an expedient and that they all should be led by the one teaching: the Buddha vehicle. The *Hossō* or Dharma Characteristics doctrine contradicts this, insisting the opposite. Calling the *Hossō* doctrine of the three vehicles slandering of the True Dharma, Nichiren Shōnin emphasized the doctrine of attaining Buddhahood by Two Vehicles, *śrāvaka* and *pratyekabuddha*, preached in the *Lotus Sutra* as revealing the true intent of the Buddha.

T'ien-t'ai, Grand Master *(Tendai Daishi)*
Also named Chih-i, 538–597 CE, he founded the T'ien-t'ai sect of China, which presided over most of the Buddhist orders during the dynasties of Liang, Ch'ên and Sui in China. With the *Lotus Sutra* as his basis, T'ien-t'ai wrote *Fa-hua hsüan-i*, the *Profound Meaning of the Lotus Sutra*, *Fa-hua wên-chü, Words and Phrases of the Lotus Sutra*, and *Mo-ho chih-kuan, Great Concentation and Insight*, which are known as the three major works constituting the core of his theology. Nichiren's theology was much influenced by that of T'ien-t'ai. Nichiren developed and expanded T'ien-t'ai's concept of "3,000 existences in one thought" making it applicable to the Latter Age of Degeneration. In his writings, Nichiren depended heavily on the three major works of T'ien-t'ai as well as the *Lotus* and *Nirvana Sutras*.

Toki Jōnin *(Toki-dono; Jōnin Shōnin)*
1216–1299 CE. One of the earliest lay followers of Nichiren Shōnin. A vassal of the Chiba family, Protector of Shimofusa Province, Jōnin lived in Wakamiya in Shimofusa Province, present-day Nakayama section of Ichikawa City in Chiba Prefecture. He was highly esteemed by Nichiren Shōnin, who entrusted him with a number of important works written in classic Chinese such as *Kanjin Honzon-shō, Spiritual Contemplation and the Most Venerable One*. He understood Nichiren's doctrine and spread the words of Nichiren among Nichiren's lay followers. After the death of Nichiren, Jōnin entered the priesthood calling himself Nichijō, converted his family temple Hokke-dō, Lotus Hall, into the Hokkeji Temple, which is regarded as the origin of the present-day Nakayama Hokekyōji Temple.

Too exquisite *(rijin gemi)*
Criticizing the Holy Way teachings such as the *Lotus* and *Nirvana Sutras*, Hōnen in his *Senjaku-shū*, Collection of Passages on the Nembutsu, says that they are too profound in doctrine for inferior people in the Latter Age to understand and too difficult to put into practice.

Tranquility of mind at the moment of death *(rinjū shōnen)*
To face one's own death with peace of mind, without doubt about attaining Buddhahood. The Pure Land sect preaches to maintain proper manners and wait for the arrival of the Buddha of Infinite Life to escort one to the Pure Land. Nichiren Shōnin preaches that one can have tranquility of mind by upholding the Odaimoku, Namu Myōhō Renge-kyō.

Tripiṭaka masters *(sanzō)*
Meaning literally "three baskets," the Sanskrit term *tripiṭaka* refers to three divisions of the Buddhist scriptures: sutras, precepts, and commentaries. It also refers to one who is well-versed in all the three divisions of the Buddhist teachings, in Japanese *sanzō hosshi*.

Triple Pure Land sutras *(Jōdo Sambu-kyō)*
Refers to the three canons of Pure Land Buddhism: *Muryōju-kyō*, the *Sutra of the Buddha of Infinite Life*; *Kammuryōju-kyō*, the *Sutra of Meditation on the Buddhia of Infinite Life*; and *Amida-kyō*, the *Pure Land Sutra*. Each of these preaches rebirth in the Pure Land of Utmost Bliss, *gokuraku jōdo*, the land of the Buddha of Infinite Life, Amida Buddha.

Triple truth *(santai)*
The term applied by T'ien-t'ai to explain reality in three aspects: (1) *kūtai* or *shintai*, the truth of voidness, i.e. all existences are void and nonsubstantial in essence; (2) *ketai* or *zokutai*, the truth of temporariness, i.e. all existences are temporary manifestations produced by causes and conditions; and (3) *chūtai*, the truth of the middle, i.e. the absolute reality of all existences cannot be explained in either negative or affirmative terms. This term is interpreted differently in the distinctive teaching and the perfect teaching: in the former the three truths are perceived independent of each other while the latter considers them perfectly fused together in one.

Triple world *(sangai)*
The triple world refers to the three regions of the world of illusion: (1) the region of desires, *yoku-kai*, consisting of hell, realms of hungry spirits, beasts and birds, fighting spirits, men, and part of heaven; beings of which have sexual desire and other appetites; (2) the region of form, *shiki-kai*, consisting of part of heaven, where inhabitants have material form but no desires; and (3) region of non-form, *mushiki-kai*, consisting of part of heaven where inhabitants are free from both desires and restrictions of material existence. Unenlightened beings transmigrate between these three regions. The third chapter of the *Lotus Sutra*, A Parable, likens this world of illusion and suffering to a house on fire.

True sutra *(jikkyō)*
Refers to the sutra in which the Buddha revealed His true intent, the True Dharma, without adapting to the time and capacity of people to understand. Nichiren Shōnin regarded the *Lotus Sutra* alone as the sole true sutra and all others as provisional.

True Word school *(Shingon-shū)*
One of the esoteric schools of Buddhism in Japan founded by Grand Master Kōbō, also named Kūkai. The Great Sun Buddha is worshipped as the Most Venerable One: *honzon*. Its basic scriptures are the *Great Sun Buddha Sutra*, *Diamond Peak Sutra*, and *Sutra on the Act of Perfection*. It insists on the supremacy of esotericism to exotericism and attainment of Buddhahood in one's present body. Entering China, Grand Master Kōbō received the teaching of esoteric Buddhism from Master Hui-kuo, or *Keika*. Returning to Japan in the first year of the Daidō Era, 806 CE, he propagated its teaching at the Kongōbuji Temple on Mt. Kōya and the Tōji Temple in Kyoto. Nichiren called both the esotericism of the Tōji Temple and Tendai esotericism the "Shingon sect," severely criticizing them for their insisting on the superiority of the Shingon teaching over the *Lotus Sutra* by their doctrines of the "ten stages of mind" and "superiority of esotericism to exotericism."

Twelve kinds of scriptures *(Jūnibu-kyō)*
Scriptures divided into twelve groups according to the style of exposition such as sutras (prose), verses, allegories, and narratives of past lives.

Two storehouses *(nizō)*
Sanron doctrine categorizes Buddhist scriptures into the storehouse of *śrāvaka*, Hinayana preaching the way of the Two Vehicles *śrāvaka* and *pratyekabuddha*; and the storehouse of bodhisattvas, Mahayana preaching of the way of bodhisattvas. It differentiates the Mahayana from the Hinayana scriptures but does not explain the differences among Mahayana scriptures.

Two Vehicles *(nijō)*
Two kinds of Hinayana sages called *śrāvaka* and *pratyekabuddha* are referred to as the Two Vehicles. They are arhats who are completely rid of evil passions, but Mahayana Buddhists consider them as selfish because they are concerned with self-salvation, neglecting to help others. Most Mahayana sutras regard them as unable to attain Buddhahood, but the *Lotus Sutra* preaches the possibility of attaining Buddhahood by the Two Vehicles. Nichiren Shōnin placed great importance on the doctrine of Buddhahood by the Two Vehicles, considering it one of the two reasons for the superiority of the *Lotus Sutra* to all other sutras.

Two-fascicle Sutra *(Sōkan-gyō)*
Refers to the *Sutra of the Buddha of Infinite Life*, which consists of two fascicles.

Tz'ŭ-ên, Grand Master *(Jion Daishi)*
632–682 CE. Also known as K'uei-chi, he founded the Fa-hsing, or *Hossō* school in China. He was one of the disciples of Hsüan-chuang, or Hsüantsang, and translated Buddhist scriptures including the *Cheng-wei-shih-lun*, in Japanese *Jōyuishikiron*, and in English *Perfection of Consciousness-Only*. He also wrote commentaries such as the *Fa-hua-hsüan-lun*, in Japanese *Hokke-genron*, and in English *Treatise on the Profundity of the Lotus Sutra*, and *Fa-yüan-i-lin*, in Japanese *Hō'on-girin*, and in English *Forest of Meanings in the Garden of the Law*. Nichiren criticized him for admiring the *Lotus Sutra* superficially by insisting that the One Vehicle teaching was expedient. Nichiren also said that T'zŭ-ên subjected himself to T'ien-t'ai in mind though not outwardly.

Universal-Sage Bodhisattva *(Fugen Bosatsu)*
Right-hand attendant of Śākyamuni Buddha, representing the virtue of principle, *ri*, meditation, *jō*, and practice, *gyō*. Universal-Sage Bodhisattva leads other bodhisattvas to assist the Buddha's missionary endeavor. In Chapter 28 of the *Lotus Sutra*, he appears riding on a white elephant to protect those who practice the *Lotus Sutra*. Nichiren's Great Mandala Honzon includes the name of Fugen representing bodhisattva disciples of Lord Śākyamuni in the theoretical section of the *Lotus Sutra*.

Upholders of the Lotus Sutra *(jikyō-sha)*
The Japanese term *jikyō-sha* refers to believers of the *Lotus Sutra* who devoted themselves to such practices as reading, reciting and copying the sutra during the Heian and Kamakura Periods. Without the purpose of saving others, they merely tried to gain divine favors through the power of the sutra. By establishing and practicing the logically sound principle of upholding the *Lotus Sutra*, Nichiren Shōnin called himself one who practices the *Lotus Sutra* differentiating himself from those upholders of the sutra without sound purpose.

Vaiśravana *(Bishamon-tennō)*
One of the Four Heavenly Kings, this god resides halfway up Mt. Sumeru and protects people living in the northern part of the world. Together with some guardian gods and demigods under his control, he also protects the preaching place of the Buddha and hears Him preach, thus he is also known as *Tamon-ten*, Much Hearing God. He and his followers attended the Lotus assemblies and he vowed to protect those who practice the *Lotus Sutra* in the 26th chapter, so he is included in Nichiren's Great Mandala as one of the Four Heavenly Kings who protects the *Lotus Sutra*.

Vajrabodhi *(Kongōchi)*
671–741 CE. Regarded as the fifth patriarch of the Shingon sect. Born in Central India as a prince, he studied esoteric Buddhism from Nāgābodhi, a disciple of Nāgārjuna, in the Nālanda Monastery. Entering China by sea in 720 CE, Vajrabodhi founded a temple in China, where Buddhist ordination ceremonies for transmitting teachings were performed. In criticizing Shingon Buddhism, Nichiren pointed out Vajrabodhi's failure in prayers for rain-making.

Various gods of the realms of desire and form *(nikai hachiban)*
Refers to one of the three groups of listeners in the assembly of the *Lotus Sutra*, namely the miscellaneous group. The other two groups being bodhisattvas and *śrāvaka*. The Japanese term nikai means the realms of desire and form in the triple world, while *hachiban* refers to eight groups of gods and demi-gods.

Vasubandhu Bodhisattva *(Tenjin Bosatsu)*
A Buddhist scholar known also as *Seshin* in Japanese, he is believed to have lived around the 5th century CE in Gandhara in northern India. At first he studied Hinayana Buddhism, but was converted to Mahayana by his older brother, Asaṅga, becoming a great promoter of the Consciousness-Only school of Mahayana Buddhism. He wrote many works such as *Kusha-ron*, the *Discourse on the Repository of Abhidharma Discussion,* and *Hokke-ron*, the *Discourse on the Lotus Sutra*. Nichiren says of him that living in the Age of the True Dharma, Vasubandhu spread the provisional Mahayana teachings although he grasped the true meaning of the *Lotus Sutra* in his heart because he knew that neither the time nor the capacity of the people to understand were ripe for the True Dharma.

Vimalamitra *(Muku Ronji)*
Buddhist commentator of Kashmir, who is said to have fallen into the Hell of Incessant Suffering with his tongue split into five pieces as he strongly believed in Hinayana and vehemently slandered Mahayana Buddhism. Nichiren cites him as an example of slandering the True Dharma.

Virtue Consciousness, Monk *(Kakutoku Biku)*
As preached in the second chapter of the *Nirvana Sutra,* Monk *Kakutoku,* Virtue Consciousness, in a past life strove to uphold the True Dharma and was attacked by heretics. He was rescued by King *Utoku,* Virtuous, who died from a wound he sustained. Nichiren often cites this tradition of Monk Virtue Consciousness and King Virtuous who helped him, likening himself to the monk. Nichiren also uses this story to justify his own aggressiveness in propagation.

Virtuous, King *(Utoku-ō)*

The name of Śākyamuni in a previous lifetime preached in the *Kongoshin*, Unbreakable Body chapter of the *Nirvana Sutra*. He sacrificed his life in defending Monk Virtue Consciousness, Kakutoku, who spread the True Dharma. Nichiren Shōnin highly esteemed the king as a model of upholding the True Dharma and chastising those who slandered it.

Wheel-turning Noble King *(Tenrinjōō)*

Cakravartin in Sanskrit, and *Tenrinjōō, Tenrinnō* or *Rinnō* in Japanese. The term refers to an ideal king who rules by the True Dharma, not by force, and is believed to have the 32 physical excellences of a Buddha and seven treasures including a wheel, or *cakra*. There are four kinds of kings according to the qualities of the wheel: One with a golden wheel, *konrin-ō*, rules all the four continents of the world; one with a silver wheel, *ginrin-ō*, rules three continents; one with a copper wheel, *dōrin-ō*, rules two; and one with an iron wheel, *tetsurin-ō*, rules only one.

Wisdom Sutra *(Hannya-kyō)*

Abbreviation of the *Hannya haramitta-kyō, Mahāprajñapāramitā-sutra*, a general term covering various sutras which claim to have the power of leading upholders to enlightenment through the power of wisdom or prājñā. There are many Chinese translations of the *Wisdom Sutra* including those by Kumārajīva and Hsüan-chuang. According to Grand Master T'ien-t'ai's classification, Nichiren Shōnin criticized the *Wisdom Sutra* as provisional, stressing the supremacy of the *Lotus Sutra* of all Buddhist scriptures.

Wish-fulfilling gem *(nyoi hōju)*

A gem which is said to have supernatural powers of fulfilling all wishes. It is likened to the virtue and teaching of the Buddha. Nichiren Shōnin likened the doctrine of "3,000 existences contained in one thought" to this wonderful gem when he said, "A wish-fulfilling gem of 3,000 existences contained in one thought."

Wonderful-Adornment, King *(Myōshōgon-ō)*

As described in the 27th chapter of the *Lotus Sutra*, King Wonderful-Adornment was originally a believer in non-Buddhist teaching, but at the urging of his wife, Lady Pure-Virtue, and his two sons, Pure-Store and Pure-Eyes, he went to see the Buddha and was converted by Him. Eventually the king was guaranteed by the Buddha to become a Buddha in the future. Nichiren Shōnin cites this King Wonderful-Adornment together with King Ajātaśatru as the exemplary of attainining of Buddhahood by "evil" persons through the teaching of the *Lotus*

Sutra. He also preaches that the king's wife and two sons are "good friends" who led the king to the faith in the True Dharma.

Written opinion *(kammon)*
In pre-modern Japan, specialists on religions and divination were often consulted by the Imperial Court or the shogunate on such matters as dates, year names, ancient practices, and unusual natural phenomena. Their opinions and findings were submitted to the government in a written form, called *kammon* or *kamon*. Although Nichiren Shōnin considered his *Risshō Ankoku-ron* to be a *kammon*, strictly speaking the term *kammon* refers only to official documents. As Nichiren's *Risshō Ankoku-ron* proposes how to prevent natural disasters, it is a document of admonition rather than written opinion.

Yōkan *(Yōkan)*
1032–1111 CE. Also called *Eikan*, he was a minister of the *Sanron*, or Three Treatises sect in the last years of the Heian Period. He was ordained at the age of 11 and began his studies of Sanron. He also studied with other sects such as *Kegon*, Flower Garland, and *Hossō*. He practiced nembutsu and devoted himself to the spread of the Pure Land teaching by writing the *Ōjō-jūin* and *Ōjō-kōshiki*, etc. Nichiren Shōnin recognized him, along with Genshin and Hōnen, as an important figure in the history of Pure Land Buddhism and criticized him severely.

Young Ascetic in the Snow Mountains *(Sessen Dōji)*
The name of Śākyamuni Buddha in a previous life expounded in the *Shōgyō* or Holy Practice chapter of the *Nirvana Sutra*. When Śākyamuni Buddha was practicing austerities in the Snow Mountains in pursuit of enlightenment, a hungry demon appeared reciting half of a verse from a Buddhist teaching: "All things and phenomena are changeable, this is the law of life and death." The Young Ascetic begged the demon to tell him the second half, and was told that the demon was too hungry to tell. Promising his own flesh and blood, Young Ascetic was able to hear the last half of the verse: "Extinguishing the cycle of birth and death, one enters the joy of nirvana." Following the example of Young Ascetic's willingness to give his life to the True Dharma, Nichiren Shōnin risked his life for the spread of the *Lotus Sutra*.

Zen school *(Zen-shū)*
School of Buddhism which claims to attain Buddhahood by way of sitting meditation, *zazen*. In Japan the term generally refers to three schools of Zen: Rinzai, Sōtō and Ōbaku. They maintain that the True Dharma is transmitted directly from a master to disciples without writing or preaching. Therefore, it

can be attained not through studies of doctrines but by meditation. Nichiren Shōnin criticized them saying that abandoning all Buddhist scriptures is an act of heavenly devils.

Zentoku, Buddha *(Zentoku-butsu)*
Among the numerous Buddha lands throughout the universe, Zentoku Buddha is the Lord Preacher of the world to the east known as *Muu,* Without Worry.

Japanese Equivalents

Japanese Entry	English Entry
Agon-gyō	Āgama sutras
Ajase-ō	Ajātaśatru, King
aku-chishiki	Evil friend
Amida-butsu	Infinite Life, Buddha of
Amida-kyō	Pure Land Sutra
Anan	Ānanda
Annen Wajō	Annen, Venerable
Ashuku-butsu	Immovable Buddha
betsuji ishu	Expedient means of encouraging idlers
Bishamon-tennō	Vaiśravana
bombu	Ordinary man
bompu	Ordinary man
Bonten-nō	King of the Brahma Heaven
Bun'ei no chōsei	Great Comet of the Bun'ei Era
butsugen	Buddha-eye
Chishō Daishi	Chishō, Grand Master
Chōkan	Ch'êng-kuan
Daibadatta	Devadatta
Daiba[datta]-hon	Devadatta chapter
Daichido-ron	Great Wisdom Discourse
Daijik-kyō or Daishū-kyō	Sutra of the Great Assembly
Daijizai-ten	Great Freedom God
daijō betsu jukai	Specific granting of the Mahayana precepts
daijō-shojō	Mahayana-Hinayana
Dainichi	Dainichi
Dainichi Nyorai	Great Sun Buddha
Dainichi-kyō	Great Sun Buddha Sutra
daishi-kō	Grand Master's Memorial Lecture
Daitsūchi-shō-butsu	Great Universal Wisdom Buddha
daizōkyō	Great collection of sutras
Dan Senjaku	Denouncing the Collection of Passages on the Nembutsu

Dengyō Daishi	Dengyō, Grand Master
Donran	T'an-luan
Dōshaku	Tao-ch'o
Embudai	Jambudvīpa
Enchō Jakkō Daishi	Enchō, Grand Master Jakkō
Eshin Sōzu	Eshin, Venerable
Fugen Bosatsu	Universal-Sage Bodhisattva
Fukū	Pu-k'ung, Tripiṭaka Master, Amoghavajra
Fukyō Bosatsu	Never-Despising Bodhisattva
Fukyō-hon	Never-Despising Bodhisattva chapter
funjin	Buddhas in manifestation
Furuna	Pūrṇa
gampon no mumyō	Fundamental darkness of mind
Ganjin	Chien-chên
gedō	Non-Buddhist teaching
Gejimmitsu-kyō	Revealing the Profound and Secret Sutra
Genkū	Genkū
genshō	Factual proof
geten	Non-Buddhist scriptures
Gishin	Gishin
go-biku	Five monks
go-gohyakusai	Last (fifth) 500-year period
godan no daihō	Five-altar ritual
gogen	Five kinds of eyesight
gogyaku	Five rebellious sins
goji	Five periods
gojoku	Five defilements
gokyō	Five Teachings
gomi	Five Flavors
gongyō	Provisional teachings
Gōnin	Gōnin
gonjitsu	Provisional and true teachings
goshō kakubetsu	Five mutually distinctive natures
gotsū	Five supernatural powers
Gyōki	Gyōki
hachibu-shū	Eight kinds of gods and demi-gods who protect Buddhism
Hachiman Daibosatsu	Hachiman, Great Bodhisattva
hakke	Eight streams
Hannya-kyō	Wisdom Sutra

Hansoku-ō	Spotted-Feet, King
Hatsunaion-gyō	Six-fascicled Nirvana Sutra
hō-kōzui	Potent omen of emitting a ray of light
Hōben-pon	Expedients chapter
hōbō	Slandering the True Dharma
Hōdō-kyō	Hōdō sutras
Hōkan Gobō	Reverend Hōkan-bō
Hokke Gengi	Profound Meaning of the Lotus Sutra
Hokke-kyō	Lotus Sutra
Hokke-kyō no gyōja	One who practices the Lotus Sutra
Hokke Shingon no jikidō	Direct road to Buddhahood of Lotus-Shingon Buddhism
Hōnen Shōnin	Hōnen Shōnin
Hossō-shū	Hossō sect
Hōzō	Fa-ts'ang
hyakkai sen'nyo	One hundred realms and 1,000 aspects
hyaku-ō	Hundred rulers of Japan
i-kon-tō	Sutras which have been preached, are being preached, and will be preached
Ichigyō	I-hsing
ichijō-kyō	One Vehicle teaching
Ichijō Yōketsu	Essentials of the One Vehicle Teaching
ichinen sanzen	Three thousand existences contained in one thought
ichinen shinge	A moment of true faith
in-shingon	Finger signs and mantras
Ishikawa Hyōe Nyūdō-dono no hime gozen	Princess of Lay Priest Ishikawa Hyōe
Issaikyō	All the scriptures of Buddhism
issendai	Icchantika
Jakumetsu Dōjō	Hall of Enlightenment
jikai hongyaku-nan	Domestic Disturbance
Jikaku Daishi	Jikaku, Grand Master
jikkai gogu	Mutual possession of ten realms
jikkyō	True sutra
jikyō-sha	Upholders of the Lotus Sutra
Jinriki-hon	Divine Powers of the Buddha chapter
Jion Daishi	Tz'ŭ-ên, Grand Master
jippō no shobutsu	Buddhas in ten directions
jiyu no bosatsu	Bodhisattvas appearing from underground

jo, shō, rutsū	Preface, main discourse and transmission
jobun	Preface
jōbutsu	Attainment of Buddhahood
Jōdo Ketsugi-shō	Deciding the Meaning of the Pure Land
Jōdo Sambu-kyō	Triple Pure Land sutras
Jōdo-shū	Pure Land school
Jōgyō Bosatsu	Superior Practice, Bodhisattva
Johon	Introductory chapter
Jōjitsu-shū	Jōjitsu sect
Jōkyū no kassen	Jōkyū Incident
Jōnin Shōnin	Toki Jōnin
jōsan	Concentrated mind and scattered mind
Jōtai Bosatsu	Ever Weeping Bodhisattva
jūgodan no daihō	Fifteen-altar ritual
jūhachi-kai	Eighteen elements of cognition
jūjinriki	Ten supernatural powers
Jūnibu-kyō	Twelve kinds of scriptures
jurui-shu, sōtai-shu	Jurui seed and sōtai seed
Jūyu	Ten similes
kako no shichi-butsu	Past seven Buddhas
Kakutoku Biku	Virtue Consciousness, Monk
kammon	Written opinion
Kan Fugen Bosatsu Gyōbō-kyō	Sutra of Meditation on Universal Sage Bodhisattva
Kan-muryōju-kyō, Kangyō	Sutra of Meditation on the Buddha of Infinite Life
kangyō	Admonition
kanjō	"Sprinkling water on the head" ceremony
Kashō	Kāśyapa
kedō no shijū	Beginning and ending of the Buddha's guidance
Kegon kaikū	Ocean-imprint meditation of the Flower Garland Sutra
Kegon-kyō	Flower Garland Sutra
Kegon-shū	Flower Garland school
kengyō-mikkyō	Exoteric and esoteric teachings
ketsujō-shō	Fixed nature
Kichizō	Chi-ts'ang
kikon	Capacity of people to understand
Kōbō Daishi	Kōbō, Grand Master

Kōjō	Kōjō
Kongōchi	Vajrabodhi
Kongōchō-kyō	Diamond Peak Sutra
Konkōmyō-kyō	Sutra of the Golden Splendor
konsetsu	Sutras now being preached
Kōshaku	Comprehensive Interpretations
Kugyari, Sonja	Kokālika
Kumarajū	Kumārajīva, Tripiṭaka Master
kuon jitsujō	Attaining Enlightenment in the eternal past
Kusha-shū	Kusha sect
kuyaku	Old translation
kyōsō	Comparative study of Buddhist doctrines
Maka Shikan	Great Concentration and Insight
Maka Shikan Fugyō-den Guketsu	Annotation on the Great Concentration and Insight
Makada-koku	Magadha Kingdom
Maō or Dairoku-ten no Maō	King of Devils in the Sixth Heaven
mappō	Latter Age of Degeneration
mirai-ki	Prediction
Miroku Bosatsu	Maitreya, Bodhisattva
Mokuren	Maudgalyāyana
Monjushiri Bosatsu	Mañjuśrī Bodhisattva
monshō	Scriptural proof
mugen jigoku	Hell of Incessant Suffering
Muku Ronji	Vimalamitra
Muryōgi-kyō	Sutra of Infinite Meaning
mushō	Those without Buddha-nature
myōji, kangyō	Notional understanding, perception and practicing
Myōraku Daishi	Miao-lê, Grand Master
Myōshōgon-ō	King Wonderful-Adornment
Namu Myōhō Renge-kyō	Namu Myōhō Renge-kyō
nangyō-dō	Difficult to practice way
Nansan Hokushichi	Three Southern and seven Northern masters
Nanto	Southern Capital
nehan	Nirvana
Nehan-gyō	Nirvana Sutra
nijō	Two Vehicles
nijō sabutsu	Obtaining Buddhahood by Two Vehicles

nikai hachiban	Various gods of the realms of desire and form
Ninnō-kyō	Sutra of the Benevolent King
ninshi	Teachers in China and Japan
nisho san'e	Three meetings at two places
nizen	Pre-Lotus period
nizō	Two storehouses
nyoi hōju	Wish-fulfilling gem
ōjō	Rebirth in the Pure Land
Ōjō yōshu	Essential Collection Concerning Rebirth in the Pure Land
rijin gemi	Too exquisite
rinjū shōnen	Tranquility of mind at the moment of death
Ritsu-shū	Ritsu sect
rokujinzū	Six superhuman powers
rokutsū	Six superhuman powers
ronji	Commentator
ryakkō shugyō	Roundabout way to Buddhahood
ryōbō kujū	Have the dharma last forever
ryōgi-kyō	Sutras thoroughly revealing the truth
ryūnyo	Dragon girl
Sai jarin	Refuting the Evil Dharma
Saido Kyōshu	Lord of the Land of Bliss to the West
sambō	Three treasures in Buddhism
san'aku-dō	Three evil realms
sangai	Triple world
sanji-kyō	Three-period teaching
sanjō	Three vehicles
sanne ippatsu	Three robes and one alms-bowl
sannō	Three Kings
Sanron-shū	Three Discourse school
sanrui no tekinin	Three kinds of enemies
sansai	Three calamities
sansai shichinan	Three calamities and seven disasters
sanshu no kyōsō	Three standards of doctrinal comparison
santai	Triple truth
sanze	Lives in the past, present and future
sanzō	Tripiṭaka masters
Senjaku-shū	Collection of Passages on the Nembutsu and the Original Vow

Sen'yo-ō	Sen'yo, King
Sessen Dōji	Young Ascetic in the Snow Mountains
sha, hei, kaku, hō	Abandon, close, set aside and cast away
shaba sekai	Sahā World
shakke	Disciples of Buddhas in manifestation
Sharihotsu	Śāriputra
shi-shittan	Four ways of preaching Buddhism
shichigyaku	Seven rebellious sins
shichinan	Seven disasters
shie	Four Reliances
shijū yonen	Forty years or so
shikō	Four kalpa
Shingon-shū	True Word school
shin'yaku	New translation
shiō-ten	Four-king Heavens
shishō	Four holy ones
shishōtai	Four Noble Truths
shitai	Four Noble Truths
Shiten-nō	Four Heavenly Kings
shizenjō	Four stages of meditation
shō-zō-matsu	Ages of the True, Semblance and Latter Dharmas
Shōan Daishi	Chang-an, Grand Master
shōdō-mon	Holy Way Gate
shōgyō, zōgyō	Correct and miscellaneous practices
shogyō ōjō	Rebirth in the Pure Land through miscellaneous practices
shoji-shojū	Shoji and shojū stages
shōjiki	Honesty
shōjō	Hinayana
Shōka no dai-jishin	Great earthquake of the Shōka Era
shōshū-bun	Main discourse
Shōtoku Taishi	Prince Shōtoku
shōzen jōbutsu	Achieving Buddhahood through a minor act of merit
Shugo-kyō	Guardian Sutra
Shumisen	Sumeru, Mt.
sōjō no shō	Chances of being born in the human realm as small as the amount of soil on a fingernail

Sōkan-gyō	Two-fascicle Sutra
sokushin jōbutsu	Becoming a Buddha with one's present body
sōrin saigo	Last in the śāla forest
Soshitsuji-kyō	Sutra on the Act of Perfection
Tahō-butsu	Many Treasures, the Buddha of
Taishaku or Shakudaikannin	Indra
takoku shimpitsu no nan	Foreign invasion
tem-bōrin	Preaching of the Buddha
tempen chiyō	Strange phenomena in the sky, natural calamities on earth
Tendai Daishi	T'ien-t'ai, Grand Master
Tenrinjōō	Wheel-turning Noble King
Tenshō Daijin	Goddess Amaterasu
tō-setsu	Sutras to be preached
toki	Right time
Toki-dono	Toki Jōnin
tongyō	Abrupt teaching
ujiko	Parishioner
Utoku-ō	Virtuous, King
Yadoya Nyūdō	Lay Priest Yadoya
Yakushi-kyō	Medicine Master Sutra
Yakuō Bosatsu	Medicine King Bodhisattva
Yōkan	Yōkan
Zemmui Sanzō	Śubhākarasiṃha, Tripitaka Master
zen-chishiki	Good friend
Zen-shū	Zen school
Zendō Oshō	Shan-tao, Venerable
zengyō	Gradual teaching
Zenzai Dōji	Good Treasures, Bodhisattva
zuda	Rules of frugal living

Index

A moment of true faith,* 26, 33
"Abandon, close, set aside and cast-away,"* 47, 90, 111, 114, 117, 125, 247
Abrupt teaching,* 17
Accommodative-bodied Śākyamuni Buddha, 67, 74(n15), 228(n16), 266
Account of Pilgrimage in China, 115
Achieving Buddhahood through a minor act of merit,* 28
Act (work) of a heavenly devil, 143, 220
Admonition,* 169, 214, 245
Admonition of Hachiman, 245
Āgama sutras,* 7, 15, 33
Age of the Semblance Dharma, 1, 20, 51, 59, 107, 130, 178-198, 208, 245
Age of the True Dharma, 1, 20, 59, 107, 120, 130, 178-195, 208
Ages of the True, Semblance and Latter Dharmas,* 4, 222, 236
Agon period, 12, see Five periods*
Ajātaśatru, King,* 53, 164, 173, 213, 239, 243
All the scriptures of Buddhism,* 135, 183, 192, 234
Amaterasu, Goddess,* 125, 136, 155, 159, 167, 213, 241
Amplification, 14, 57, 65, 66, see Preface, main discourse and transmission*
Ānanda,* 17, 18, 40, 180, 198, 218
Aṅgulimāla, 250

Annen, Venerable,* 77, 92, 171, 199, 209, 219
Annotations on the Great Concentration and Insight, 36, 50, 51, 55, 77, 92, 115, 157, 251
Annotations on the Nirvana Sutra, 174, 187
Annotations on the Words and Phrases of the Lotus Sutra, 28, 37, 63, 79, 178, 195, 242, 248
Antoku, Emperor, 158-160, 166, 169, 170, 249
Arhat, 40, 47, 55, 84, 101, 106-108, 118, 119, 130, 151, 162, 223, 226
Asaṅga, 19, 182, 189, 198
Aspiration Dharma Bodhisattva, 153
Aspiration for enlightenment, 179, 248, 251
Aśvaghoṣa, 180, 189, 198, 223
Attaining Enlightenment by Śākyamuni Buddha in the eternal past,* 10, 11, 16, 65, 66, 172, 180
Attaining enlightenment, 5
Attainment of Buddhahood,* 22, 26
Attainment of Buddhahood by all people, 181
Avalokiteśvara, Bodhisattva, 53, 67, 68, 70, 216, 251
Avatar, 48, 51, 55, 64, 70, 71, 113, 250, 251
Avatar of Bodhisattva Gainer of Great Strength, 113

Banished twice, 187
Bārāṇasī Kingdom,* 7
Becoming a Buddha with one's present body,* 165, 172, 191
Beginning and ending of the Buddha's guidance,* 181
Benevolent governing, 98
Bhadraruci, Commentator, 208, 227
Biographies of Buddhist Patriarchs of Sung, 194
Bodhidharma, Grand Master, 69
Bodhiruchi, 66
Bodhisattva in the highest rank (stage), 175, 236
Bodhisattvas appearing from underground,* 177
Bodhisattvas who will take the Buddha's place in the next life, 160
Books of the Three Emperors and Five Rulers, 241
Brahma Heaven, King of,* 2, 6, 73(n3), 117, 123, 158, 161-177, 214-227, 236-251
Brahman the Boaster, 207, 108, 222, 227
Brahma-net Sutra, 43, 47, 48, 185
Brahmans, 47, 80, 87, 107, 119, 124, 127
Buddha in the Land of Emerald Light to the East*, 98, 112, 122
Buddha of Infinite Life,* 3, 56, 70, 112, 114, 129, 156, 176, 200; avatar of, 70; calling the name of, 26-33, 45, 50, 98, 110, 113, 175, 176, 200, 201, 215; finger sign of, 122
Buddha of Infinite Life and His two attendants, 111
Buddha of Joy, 120
Buddha Repository Sutra, 51
Buddha-eye,* 84, 101, 175, 241
Buddha-nature, 34, 53, 55, 64, 65, 108, 117, 119, 226, 242
Buddhas in manifestation,* 23, 62, 65, 86, 152, 169, 180, 227

Buddhas in ten directions (throughout the universe),* 167, 172, 177
Buddhas in the worlds in six directions, 71
Buddha's purpose of appearing in this world, 11
Capacity of people to understand,* 25, 173, 175, 182
Chances of being born in the human realm as small as the amount of soil on a fingernail,* 2
Chang-an, Grand Master,* 174, 187
Chanting the name of the Buddha, 26, 29, 98
Chao, King, 77, 78, 137
Ch'êng-kuan,* 164
Chia-hsiang (Chi-tsang),* 64, 70, 164, 194, 198, 206
Chieh, King, 75, 76, 92, 213
Chien-chên, Venerable,* 135, 156, 164, 184, 195
Chih-i, Monk, 182
Chih-yen, 64, 70
Chin-kang-chui, 67, 183
Chishō, Grand Master,* 97, 11, 154,157, 158, 166, 226, 234, 240, 241, 248
Chou Hsin, King, 75, 76, 92
Chu Fa-lan, 181
Collection of Mahayana Essentials, 19
Collection of Passages Concerning Rebirth in the Pure Land, 26, 30, 31, 89, 108, 176, 188
Collection of Passages on the Nembutsu,* 1, 3, 4, 28-35, 44-66, 76-79, 88-93, 108-125, 188, 215
Commentary on the Diamond Peak Sutra, 157, 210
Commentary on the Discourse on the Pure Land, 26, 89, 109, 176
Commentary on the Lotus Sutra, 19, 66, 189, 206

Commentary on the Profound Meaning of the Lotus Sutra, 191
Commentary on the Sutra of Meditation on the Buddha of Infinite Life, 89, 109, 110
Commentary on the Ten Stages, 26, 29, 33, 34, 38-40, 53, 89, 109, 176, 190, 200, 212
Commentators,* 3, 18, 25, 39-41, 55, 64, 180, 190, 193-196, 206, 207, 234
Community deity, 240, 245
Comparative study of Buddhist doctrines, 34
Comparison of exoteric and esoteric Buddhism, 205
Comprehensive interpretations,* 77, 92
Concentrated mind and scattered mind,* 45, 90, 110
Concise Chronicle of Japan, 237
Confucius, 75-78, 92, 195, 207, 241
Congregation, 67
Correct and miscellaneous practices,* 29-45, 89, 109, 111, 200
Country of the moon, 251
Cream flavor, 234, see Five flavors*
Curdled milk (*shōso*), 73(n6), 233, 234, see Five flavors*
Curse will come back, 213, 243
Daily life, 35, 36
Dainichi,* 136, 156
Dairymaid, 14, 15
Debate on the Teaching and Time, 209
Debt of gratitude to the native land, 222
*Deciding the Meaning of the Pure Land,** 4
Deer Park, 7, 174
Dengyō, Grand Master,* 20, 111, 112, 135, 138, 154, 156, 157, 167, 178-180, 184, 185, 188, 189, 192-199, 204-226, 230, 237-239, 245

*Denouncing the Collection of Passages on the Nembutsu,** 4
Destruction of the pure dharma, 175-177
Devadatta,* 51, 124, 168, 173, 179, 187, 219, 222, 239, 240, 243; empty words of, 225
*Diamond Peak Sutra,** 165, 183, 202, 207, 211
Diamond Realm Mandala, 210
Difficult to believe and understand, 11, 17, 23, 69, 116, 152
Difficult-to-practice way,* 29-33, 51, 53, 200
Direct road to Buddhahood of Lotus-Shingon Buddhism, 3
Disciples of Buddhas in manifestation,* 180
Divine message, 237, 238, 243, 249
Divine mirror, 163, 199
Dōkyō, Priest, 243
Domestic disturbance,* 97, 102, 126, 145, 150-152, 230
Dragon girl,* 173
Dragon King, 155, 169
Dream of a golden man, 103
Duke of Chou, 207
Earth Repository, Bodhisattva, 111
Easy to practice way, 29-38, 200
Effects of T'ien-t'ai on Buddhist Schools, 205
Eight kinds of supernatural beings,* 23
Eight streams,* 158
Eighteen elements of cognition,* 8
Eighty thousand Buddhist teachings, 122
Eighty thousand holy teachings, 20,
Eleven-faced Avalokiteśvara, 70
Enchin, Venerable, 157, 158, 171, 240, see Grand Master Chishō*
Enchō, Grand Master,* 150, 210, 239

Enlightenment in the present life, 21, 225
Enlightenment of Śākyamuni, 65
Enlightenment through pre-*Lotus* sutras, 56
Ennin, Venerable Priest, 157, see Grand Master Jikaku*
Enryakuji Temple,, 113, 136, 145, 160, 166, 176
Entrusting the dharma, 42, 180, 197
Eshin (Genshin), Venerable,* 21, 24, 26, 32-38, 62, 112, 209, 215, 219
Esoteric doctrine with rituals, 211
Esoteric Rites Based on the Lotus Sutra, 191
Esoteric teaching only in doctrine, 211
Esoteric teachings, 98, 211
Essential Collection Concerning Rebirth in the Pure Land,* 21, 26, 32, 34, 38, 112, 201, 209; preface, 32, 201, 209
Essentials of the One Vehicle Teaching, 27, 34, 35, 62
Eternal presence of Buddha-nature, 64, 65, 242
Eternal relationship between the Buddha and His disciples, 181
Ever-Weeping, Bodhisattva,* 46, 53, 55
"Evil friend,"* 51-53, 106
Ex-Emperor in Buddhist Robes on Oki Island (ex-Emperor Gotoba), 158
Exoteric teaching,* 211
Exoteric and Esoteric teachings,* 21, 27, 31-34, 89, 113, 162, 181, 201, 207, 210
Expedient Buddha, 71
Expedient means of encouraging idlers,* 19, 28, 41
Factual proof, 168, 191, 213
Fa-hui, 67
False Dharmas for true Buddhism, 217
False teachings destroying the country, 87, 88, 162

False teachings destroying the teaching of Buddhism, 87, 88, 108, 162, 230, 235
Fa-tao, *Tripiṭaka* Master, 187
Fa-tsang,* 183, 194, 196, 206, 223
Fa-yün, 64, 114
Fierce Spirit Immovable, 246
Fifteen-altar ritual,* 161
Fiftieth person who with joy hears the *Lotus Sutra* transmitted from one person to the next, 33
Finger sign, 122, 199, see Finger sign and mantra*
Finger signs for the Buddha-eye, 242
First among those who practice the *Lotus Sutra* in Japan , 216
First Emperor of Ch'in, 241
First enlightenment, 174
First year of Shōka, 44, 46, 132, 135, 150, 230
Five-altar ritual,* 160
Five central provinces and seven circuits, 104, 155
Five defilements,* 21, 24
Five flavors,* 64, 65, 233
Five great protective deities, 199
Five hundred dust-particle *kalpa*, 38, 73(n8)
Five kinds of eyes,* 241
Five mighty bodhisattvas, 98
Five monks,* 7, 51
Five mutually distinctive natures,* 16, 74(n14), 197
Five periods,* 5
Five periods and eight teachings, 193
Five planets, 98
Five precepts,
Five rebellious sins,* 33, 34, 43, 57, 88, 111, 118, 121, 163, 199, 201, 247
Five stages, 237
Five teachings,* 16, 136, 197
Five virtues, 75-78, 91-93

Index

Five wisdoms, 242
Fixed nature,* 19, 34, 44, 173
*Flower Garland Sutra,** 5-73, 114, 163-165, 172-223, 234, 247
Flower Light Buddha, 151
Foreign invasion,* 102, 126, 132, 137, 147, 151, 217, 221, 222, 230
Former bodhisattvas, 237
Formidable enemies of the One Vehicle teaching, 252
Forty years or so,* 8-72, 114, 135, 164, 203
Four categories of Buddhists, 42, 47, 48, 120, 129
Four evil realms, 43, 83, 100
Four great śrāvaka, 68
Four Heavenly Kings,* 5, 43, 83, 99
Four holy ones,* 3
Four-king Heavens,* 17
Four major sins, 33, 43, 88, 118
Four modes of birth, 204, 227(n4)
Four Noble Truths, 6, 7, 9
Four Reliances,* 3, 16, 18, 25, 33, 91
Four stages of meditation,* 52
Four ways of preaching Buddhism,* 153
Fundamental darkness of mind,* 216
General commentary, 38, 39
General Sutra, 208
Ghee *(daigo)*, 64, 73(n6), 234, 235, see Five flavors*
Gishin, Venerable, 111, 158, 210, 239
Gleaning, 64, 65
Go-between, 199
Golden words of the Buddha, 17, 229
Gōnin, Priest, 229, 231
"Good friends," 48, 53-55
Good karma accumulated in the past, 38
Good Treasures, Bodhisattva,* 53
Gotoba, ex-Emperor, 108, 116, 136, 158,159, 166, 200, 213, 243, 259, 250

Gradual teaching,* 17
Grand Master's Memorial Lecture, 144
Grandfather's shoes, 24, 46
Great Adornment Buddha, 51, 248
Great Buddha of the Tōdaiji Temple, 184
Great Cloud Sutra, 10
Great collection of sutras,* 230
Great comet of the Bun'ei Era,* 141, 188, 216, 217
Great Commentary on the Abidharma, 19
*Great Concentration and Insight,** 36-55, 77-79, 92, 115, 130(n12), 144, 165, 189-195, 251
Great earthquake of the Shōka Era,* 141, 150, 188, 216, 217, 230
Great Forest Monastery, 9
Great harvest, 11, 65
Great Mongol Empire, 137, 142, 219, 243
Great Sun Buddha,* 165, 199, 207, 210
Great Sun Buddha sect, 156
*Great Sun Buddha Sutra,** 15, 29, 39, 156, 165, 166, 176, 183, 184, 188, 190, 200-224, 230, 233-248; Annotations on, 157; commentary to, 210
Great Universal Wisdom Buddha,* 38, 50, 61, 73(n9), 172
*Great Wisdom Discourse,** 25, 39, 40, 130(n11), 190, 206
Greatest man in Japan, 222
Groups of bandits, 25-29, 47,111
Guarantee of future Buddhahood, 65
*Guardian Sutra,** 104, 105, 162, 206, 218
Guṇaprabha, Commentator, 222
Gyōki, Bodhisattva,* 164
Hachiman, Great Bodhisattva,* 99, 125, 155-167, 232-251
Hall of Enlightenment,* 5, 163, 164, 172
Han-kuang, Priest, 194, 195
Have the dharma of the *Lotus Sutra* last forever,* 23

Heavenly deity (god), 135, 155
Heavenly King Buddha, 173
Hei no Saemonnojō, 152, 220
Hell of Incessant Suffering,* 3, 27, 38, 46-61, 79, 80, 88-94, 111-129, 143, 153, 163-170, 179-227, 231, 236-249
Heretics, 25, 27, 29, 47, 80, 87,105, 226
Hermit Asita, 179
Heterodox History of the Chou Dynasty, 77, 78
Hiei, Mt., 21, 26, 27, 32, 104-122, 136, 145, 157-167, 184-223, 230, 237-246
Hinayana precept platform, 184
Hinayana teaching, 7, 66, 228(n10), 247, see Mahayana-Hinayana*
Hōdō sutras,* 6-63, 73(n6), 174, 190, 233, 234
Hōjō, Yoshitoki, 158, 161, 213, 243, 249, 250
Hōkan-bō,* 138
Holy teachings preached in His lifetime,* 20, 21, 69, 108
Holy Way Gate,* 3, 26, 27, 89, 90
Homage to Śākyamuni Buddha, 178
Hōnen (Genkū), Shōnin,* 24-51, 88-94, 108-125, 136, 166, 171-215, 246
Honesty in Buddhism, 249, 250
Honesty in the worldly sense, 249
Hossō sect,* 15-70, 89, 109, 135, 136, 156, 182-207, 234, 237
Hsin-hsing, Zen Master, 208
Hsüan-chuang, 19, 159, 182-224
Hsüan-tsung, Emperor, 124, 166, 183, 202, 224
Huai-kan, 41
Hui-kuan, 64
Hui-kuo, 205, 224
Hui-tsung, Emperor, 168, 186, 187
Hundred rulers of Japan,* 160, 249
*Icchantika,** 19-66, 79, 80, 94, 107-125, 199-226

I-hsing, Zen Master,* 203, 204
Immovable Buddha,* 57, 120, 121
Inattentively, 36
Indra,* 4, 5, 105, 158-170, 172-227, 236-251
Initial ten ranks of bodhisattvas, 175, 236
Inner chamber of the Tuṣita Heaven, 172
Intestinal parasite in a lion, 59
Jambudvīpa,* 14, 84, 102, 244
Jewel Key to the Store of Mysteries, 205
Jie, Grand Master, 26
Jien, 160, 161
Jikaku, Grand Master,* 97-115, 157-166, 199-227, 230, 234-248; biography of, 211
Jingūji Temple, 237, 238
Jiron (Ti-lun) sect, 41, 89, 109
Jīvaka, Minister, 53, 213
Jōjitsu sect* (school), 135, 156, 184, 219, 234, 237
Jōkaku, 117
Joke, 114, 188, 242, 246, 248
Jōkyū Incident,* 116, 158-167, 213, 214, 243
Jukuso (butter), 64, 73, 234, see Five flavors*
Jun-gengō, 78, 93
Jun-gogō, 78, 93
Junji shōgō, 78, 93
Jurui seed,* 37
Kalpa of practice, 22
Kalpa of construction, 233, see Four kalpa*
Kalpa of continuance, 179, see Four kalpa*
Kammu, Emperor, 135, 136, 156-167, 184-212, 238
Karmic powers, 78, 93
Kāśyapa (Mahā-kāśyapa),* 18, 47, 52, 57, 69, 104, 151, 174, 180, 198, 202

Kāśyapa Bodhisattva, 11, 18, 47, 49, 64, 65, 120, 121
Kāśyapa Buddha, 121, 122
Kegon (Flower Garland) sect,* 15, 67, 89, 109, 135, 136, 156, 184, 202, 207, 234, 237
Kenshin, Gonsōjō, 166, 201
Kimmei, Emperor, 135, 155, 156, 184, 195, 215, 237, 240
King of Devils in the Sixth Heaven,* 158, 221, 236
King Puṣyamitra, 230
King Spotted Feet,* 53, 55
Kōbō (Kūkai), Grand Master,* 111, 114, 158, 166, 188-227, 230, 234-248
Kōfukuji Temple, 117, 135, 160, 168
Kōjō (Grand Master Bettō),* 158
Kokālika,* 168, 122, 125
Kuang-hsiu, 210
Kumārajīva, *Tripiṭaka* Master,* 19, 39, 40, 62, 192, 203, 234
Kung-te-lin, 67
Kutoku, 52, 151, 152
Lao-tzu, 76, 78, 172, 241
Last (fifth) 500-year period,* 14, 24, 149, 168, 175-198, 245, 252
Last in the *śāla* forest,* 18, 86, 163
Last year's calendar, 46
Late Lay Priest Hōjō Tokiyori, 133, 135, 143
Latter Age of Degeneration,* 3-59, 79, 80, 106, 114, 130(n8), 149, 162-170, 175-224, 233-252
Lawsuit, 105, 246
Leaders, 129
Letter of submission, 197, 238
Light Buddha, 151
Liturgy for the Ceremony Dedicated to the Buddha's Relics, 207
Lives in the past, present and future,* 84, 101, 186

Living Buddha, 208
Lord of the Land of Bliss to the West,* 98, 112, 122
Lord (preacher) Śākyamuni Buddha, 10, 112, 125, 167, 169, 172, 208, 225, 227, 242, 243, 250
Lotus and *Nirvana Sutras*, 16-25, 34-72, 122, 146, 234
Lotus Flower Mask Sutra, 218
Lotus sect, 157
Lotus-Shingon teachings, 24-28, 45-47, 59, 79, 93
Lotus-Shingon True Dharma, 59
Lotus Sutra,* 8, 16, 117, 129, 180, 189, 206, 240; "Esoteric Rites Based on," 191; one who practices,* 62, 129, 167-170, 188, 227, 236-251; ranked first, 182; ranked second, 183; ranked third, 182; title (*daimoku*) of, 54, 57
Magadha Kingdom,* 5, 244
Maha-kāśyapa, 151
Mahādeva, 223
Mahayana,* 12, 89
Mahayana precept platform, 204, 240
Mahayana Ritsu sects, 157
Main discourse,* 17
Maitreya Buddha, 238
Maitreya, Bodhisattva,* 5, 63, 172, 203, 216, 222
Manifested trace, 250, 251
Mañjuśrī,* 5, 8, 18, 24, 53, 60, 67, 70, 116, 174, 216
Mantra, 165, 202-212, 242, see Finger sign and mantra*
Many Treasures, Buddha,* 11-72, 86, 152, 164-169, 177-227, 236, 239
Maudgalyāyana,* 70, 124, 152
Māyā Sutra, 174, 189
Medicine-King, Bodhisattva, 146, 153, 169, 216, 226

Medicine Master Buddha, 70, 111, 112, 122,
*Medicine Master Sutra,** 96, 98, 102, 103, 126, 150
Meditating on the ultimate reality of all phenomena, 9
Meditation and wisdom of the *Lotus Sutra*, 195
Meditation on the Buddha Sutra, 34, 174, 189
Meditation on the Mind-base Sutra, 19
Mental mystic practice, 204
Miao-lê, Grand Master,* 13, 22, 28, 35-38, 41, 51, 55, 63, 77-79, 92, 115, 130, 178-195, 221, 226, 242, 248, 251
Middle Doctrine, 190
Middle Way, 7, 16, 67, 68
Mihirakula, King , 218, 219
Miidera Temple, 27, 158
Minamoto, Yoritomo, 136, 158-169, 249
Ming, Emperor, 103
Miscellaneous practice in worship, 89, 109
Miscellaneous practice of reciting sutras, 89, 109
Miscellaneous practices, 24-47, 89-92, 109-112, 200, see Correct and miscellaneous practices*
Mixture of true and provisional sutras, 25
Mo-t'eng (Mātaṅga), 181
Mongol state letter, 134, 145
Mononobe, Moriya, 103, 168, 240
Mt. Sacred Eagle, 9, 65, 71, 104, 185, 194, 222, 240, 150; preaching of the *Lotus Sutra* on, 173; Pure Land of, 227
Mt. Sumeru, 84, 102, 105, 116, 162, 196, 218-227
Mutual possession of the ten realms,* 16, 35, 55, 56, 66, 72

*Myōji-kangyō,** 55
Myōun, Chief Priest of Engyakuji, 160, 166
Nāgārjuna, Bodhisattva, 22-41, 53, 71, 89, 109, 130, 176-224
Namu, 219
Namu-bō, 25
*Namu Myōhō Renge-kyō,** 170, 176-188, 215-225, 242-251
Nan-yüeh, 53, 64, 194, 196
Nembutsu is the teaching that leads people into the Hell of Incessant Suffering, 246
Nembutsu, 3-71, 76-79, 88-93, 97-125, 143, 198-215, 246, 247
Never-Despising Bodhisattva,* 38, 88, 152, 168, 174, 190, 214, 227, 252
New translation,* 16, 192
Nichiren, 56, 58, 94,135-138, 145, 158-170, 176-225, 241-249
Nichiren, Buddhist Monk, 98
Nichiren, the Buddha's disciple,* 172
Nine realms and realm of Buddhas are one, 173
Nirvana,* 6, 9, 151
*Nirvana Sutra,** 5-72, 73(n4), 76-80, 85-94, 106-129, 162-168, 174-226, 234-235,
Non-Buddhist scripture,* 40, 76, 92, 118, 181, 207, 213, 220
Non-Buddhist teaching,* 22, 80
Not one out of 1,000, 26, 27, 29, 90, 109, 176, 188, 200, 208, 246
Notional understanding , 238, see *Myōji-kangyō**
Numerous bodhisattvas from underground, 177, 227
Nyagrodha, 244-246
Oath from Śākyamuni, 14
Obtaining Buddhahood by Two Vehicles,* 10, 172, 180

Ocean-imprint meditation of the *Flower Garland Sutra*,* 9, 10
Odaimoku, 36, 60, 241, 245-247
Ōjin, Emperor, 155, 237-243
Old translation,* 16, 192
One hundred out of one hundred, 29, 44, 90, 109, 176, 201
One hundred realms and 1000 aspects, 181
One vehicle,* 125, 145, 178-210, 238, 242, 252
One Vehicle teaching of the Lotus Sutra, 145, 178, 188, 197, 198
Onjōji Temple, 104, 159, 160, 176-214, 239, 240
Order of Service for Rebirth in the Pure Land, 215
Ordinary man* , 2, 178, 216, 222, 223
Original *"Risshō Ankoku-ron,"* 147
Original substance, 250, 251
Original vow, 54
Outstanding Principles of the Lotus Sutra, 178, 196, 212, 223, 224
Pacification (tranquility and safety) of the country, 91, 118-130, 136, 184, 210-217, 243
Paramārtha, *Tripiṭaka* Master, 19, 189
Parishioner,* 235, 236
Past seven Buddhas,* 17
Peace in the country and security of the emperor, 160
People who slighted Never-Despising Bodhisattva, 38, 61, 152, 219
People without Buddha-nature,* 19, 34, 41, 50
Perception and practice, 236, see *Myōji-kangyō**
Perfect and sudden Mahayana precept platform, 195, 198, 204
Perfect and sudden specific granting-the-precepts ceremony, 185

Perfect and sudden teaching, 50
Perfect Buddha, 72
Perfect Tendai school, 136
Period of quarrels, 168, 175, 177, 186, 187
Period of solid liberation, 180
Period of solid meditation,, 175, 181
Period of solid temple construction, 176, 185
Period of wide reading and discussion, 182, 195
Pillar of Japan, 220
Postscript to *Translating the Lotus Sutra*, 62
Potent omen of emitting a ray of light,* 5
Practice of copying the *Lotus Sutra*, 122
Practice of the One Vehicle teaching,, 242
Praise of Rebirth in the Pure Land, 176, 188
Prajñā, *Tripiṭaka* Master, 206
Prasenajit, King, 42, 84, 102, 119
Prayer for defeat of the enemy, 166, 213
Preach as fluently as Pūrṇa,* 152
Preaching of the Buddha,* 5, 9
Preaching the expedient dharma according to the caliber of those who listened to Him , 45
Preaching the True Dharma in accordance with His true intent , 45
Prediction,* 51, 58, 94, 145, 151, 152, 175-222
Prediction of Prince Shōtoku, 137
Preface,* 8, 17
Pre-Lotus period,* 10, 22; sutras of 20-71, 223, 248, 250
Profound Meaning of the Lotus Sutra,* 36, 37, 64, 130, 189-212, 251
Profundity of the teaching, 33

Protective deities, 46, 86, 91, 99, 136, 145, 164, 199, 235, 241, 246
Provisional (expedient) and true teachings,* 3, 4, 25, 31, 41, 51, 88, 89, 108, 114, 181
Provisional (Expedient) Mahayana, 12, 31, 89, 164, 193, 215, 230, 233, 247
Provisional sutras,* 3, 175
Pu-k'ung, *Tripiṭaka* Master, (Amoghavajra), 165, 183, 191, 192, 194, 198, 202, 224, 227, 248
Pure doctrine, 203
Pure Land of Bliss, 21, 63, 112, 176
Pure Land of Tranquil Light, 63
Pure Land sect,* 68, 70, 89, 97
Pure Land Sutra, 71, 72, 215, 234
Pure Land way, 108, 109, 111, 200
Pure Lands all over the universe, 21, 63
Queen Māyā, 189, 213
Reading and reciting Mahayana scriptures, 110
Real (True) Mahayana, 12, 51, 55, 87, 215
Realm of Peace and Sustenance, 63
Realm of spiritual darkness (ignorance), 83, 205, 206, 242, 246
Rebirth in the Pure Land,* 21, 22, 26
Rebirth in the Pure Land through miscellaneous practice,* 46
Receiving a real reward in this life, 225
Receiving the seed of Buddhahood in the eternal past, 38
Record of the Western Regions, 159
Refuting the Evil Dharma, 4
Rely on the dharma, not on persons, 55, 64, 70
Renouncement of family, 9
Repentance, 164
Revealing the Profound and Secret Sutra, 16, 67, 68, 182, 206, 207, 223, 234

Revival of the Two Vehicles, 242
Reward-bodied Buddha, 67, 74(n15)
Right time,* 172, 173
Ritsu sect (Lü school),* 156, 157, 176, 184, 185, 219, 230, 234, 237
Ritualism, 205, 211
River of birth and death, 100
Roundabout practices, 31
Roundabout Ways to Buddhahood,* 9
Rule of Fu-hsi, and Shen-nung, 125
Rules of frugal living,* 13
Ryūkan, 117
Sages, 86, 99
Sahā World,* 2, 21, 26, 36, 47, 62, 63, 68, 172, 178, 236, 250
Saichō, 135, 136, 156, 184, 185, 196, 223
Śākyamuni Buddha's lifetime preachings in five periods, 112, 114, 122
San-chiai, Zen Master, 208, 219
Sanron sect,* 15, 16, 135, 136, 156, 182, 184, 197, 201, 207, 234, 237
Śāriputra,* 70, 71, 104, 151, 174, 203, 251
Scriptural proofs,* 12, 135,178
Seed of Buddhahood, 27, 38, 121, 128, 173, 219, 221, 247, 252
Seng-chao, 62
Sen'yo, King,* 47, 119, 124, 146
Seven calamities,* 68, 81-94, 97, 101, 102, 126, 130(n3), 150, 159, 162, 233
Seven fierce gods, 98
Seven great temples in Nara, 136, 167, 176, 185, 196-201, 230, 238
Seven Rebellious Sins,* 33, 34
Shan-tao, Venerable, 3, 21-72, 89, 109-122, 130(n2), 176-219, 246
She-lun masters, 26, 41
She-lun sect, 19
Shikan-in, 210
Shingon sect,* 156, 157, 165, 166, 199, 202

Shiragi Daimyōjin, 240
Shitennōji Temple, 103
Shōgakubō, 207
Shōgishō, Bodhisattva, 67, 224
Shō-Hachiman, Bodhisattva, 125
Shō-Hachiman Shrine, 136
Shoji and *shojū* stages,* 37
Shōkō-bō (Shōkō), 25, 117
Shōtoku, Prince, 103, 137, 156, 184, 197, 238, 243
Śīlāditya, King, 124
Siṃha, Venerable, 187
Six base realms, 186, 227(n5); seeds of Buddhahood in, 28
Six-character title, 68
*Six-fascicled Nirvana Sutra,** 107, 226
Six *pāramitā,* 33
Six Pāramitā Sutra, 128, 206
Six schools of Buddhism, 135, 184, 238
Six-stage practice of the *Lotus Sutra*, 236
Six superhuman powers,* 55, 106, 162, 226
Six unenlightened realms, 12, 56
Six worms, 219
Sky-Repository, Bodhisattva, 111
Slandering the (True) Dharma, 3, 4, 10, 28-35, 40, 47-55, 78-80, 93, 94, 103, 114, 121, 124, 129, 154, 165, 168, 207, 227, 235, 244-248
Small dharma, 13
Sōji-in, 210
Sông-myông, King, 155
Sōō, Venerable, 246
Sōtai seed, 37, see *shurui* seed and *sōtai* seed*
Southern Capital,* 104, 136
Specific granting of Hinayana precepts, 185
Specific granting of Mahayana precepts,* 185, 295

Spoiled seeds, 40
Spread the sutra widely, 24, 61, 70, 176, 189, 195
Sprinkling Water on the Head Ceremony,* 157, 207
Stage of non-regression, 122
Strange phenomena in the sky, natural calamities on earth,* 98, 156, 177, 202, 214, 217, 231
Subhadra, 213
Śubhākarasiṃha,* 165, 166, 183-227, 248
Śuddhodana, King, 174, 189
Suiko, Emperor, 156
Sunakṣatra (Zenshō Biku), 47, 48, 51, 52
Sun-Moon-Light Buddha, 8
Superior-Practice, Bodhisattva,* 186, 198, 216
*Sutra of Infinite Meaning,** 6-22, 33, 34, 65-72, 164, 203, 223, 247
*Sutra of Meditation on the Buddha of Infinite Life,** 18-63, 89, 90, 109-112, 215
*Sutra of Meditation on Universal-Sage Bodhisattva,** 9, 76, 92, 151, 241, 242
*Sutra of the Benevolent King,** 8-81, 84-94, 96-127, 162, 210, 217
Sutra of the Buddha of Infinite Life, 20-22, 33, 215
*Sutra of the Golden Splendor,** 10, 43, 46, 76-79, 83-93, 96-126, 150, 162, 210, 217
*Sutra of the Great Assembly,** 20-42, 81, 84-94, 96-127, 149, 150, 175-221, 234
Sutra of the Pure Land of Mystic Glorification, 10
Sutra of Transmission of the Buddhist Teaching, 190, 244
*Sutra on the Act of Perfection,** 165, 183, 201, 210, 211, 246

Sutras for the tranquility of the nation, 210
Sutras not thoroughly revealing the truth, 15, 72
Sutras now being preached,* 10, 65, 69
Sutras thoroughly revealing the truth,* 15, 72, 182
Sutras to be preached,* 11
Sutras which have been preached, are being preached, and will be preached,* 11, 17, 23, 24, 65, 69, 164, 169, 203, 204, 224
Taira no Kiyomori, 158, 168
Takaozan (Takaodera) Temple, 136, 196, 238
T'an-luan,* 3, 24-31, 89, 109-114, 176, 200
Tao-ch'o, Zen Master,* 3, 21-31, 89, 108-114, 175-200, 247
Tao-hsüan, Precept Master, 194
Taoism, 181
Teachers in China and Japan,* 2, 178
Teaching of heavenly demons, 246
Temple of the Imperial Guardian Star, 136
Ten factors of existence, 221, 228(n18)
Ten out of ten, 100 out of 100, 29, 44, 176, 201
Ten realms, 12
Ten Reasons for Rebirth in the Pure Land, 201, 215
Ten similes,* 24
Ten supernatural powers,* 177
Ten virtuous acts, 38, 73(n7), 76, 81(n1)
Tendai-Lotus school (sect), 145, 156, 157, 166, 185, 209, 223, 224, 238
Tendai school, 136, 179, 185, 199, 204, 205, 210, 211
Terrestrial deities (gods), 135, 155, 202, 214, 219
Thinking nine times before uttering a word, 207

Thirty-four traces, 251
Thirty-three traces, 251
Three (Buddhist) robes, 162, 218
Three calamities,* 42, 44, 46, 126, 150, 159, 199, 233
Three evil realms,* 2, 43-61, 88, 101, 106, 122, 167, 184
Three great (major) works of T'ien-t'ai, 37, 165, 191
Three kinds of enemies,* 226
Three meetings at two places,* 169
Three minds, 110
Three misfortunes, 84, 86, 94, 103
Three mystic practices, 165, 183, 204
Three outstanding predictions, 220
Three-period teaching,* 16, 136, 197, 206
Three poisons, 50
Three robes and one alms bowl,* 199
Three sages, 76, 78, 241
Three Southern and seven Northern masters,* 164, 167, 199
Three thousand dust-particle *kalpa*, 38, 61, 73(n8)
Three thousand existences contained in one thought,* 36, 172, 173, 181, 204, 211, 221, 237
Three treasures,* 21, 42, 58, 80, 87, 99, 104
Three vehicles,* 21, 63, 114, 159, 182, 210
Three virtuous realms, 167
Three wisdoms, 236
Three worms, 219
Threefold body of Śākyamuni Buddha, 207, 228(n16)
T'ien-t'ai, Grand Master,* 14, 22, 28, 35-64, 77-79, 92, 139, 164, 167, 174-228, 245, 247, 250, 251; memorial lecture-meeting, 144; prediction of, 137

Time and capacity of people, 3, 18, 29, 30, 59, 175
Tōji Temple, 27, 104, 157-159, 176-214, 239, 243
Toki, Lord,* 147
Tokuitsu, Monk, 206
Too exquisite to understand,* 18
Tranquility in this life and rebirth to a better world, 144
Tranquility of mind at the moment of death,* 37
Translators, 3, 40
Transmission of the dharma outside of the sutras, 202, 247
Trāyastriṃśa Heaven, 174
Treasure Purity World, 164
Treatise on the Aspiration for Buddhahood, 191, 205
Treatise on Buddha-nature, 25
Treatise on the Light for the Latter Age of Degeneration, 20
Treatise on the Nirvana Sutra, 19, 64, 66
Treatise on the Protection of the Nation, 178
Treatise on the Ten Stages of Mind, 188, 205
Treatise on the Theory of Consciousness Only, 25
Tripiṭaka masters,* 3, 248
Triple Pure Land sutras,* 3, 20-45, 72, 76, 90, 92, 109-114, 122, 129, 176
Triple Pure Land sutras in four fascicles, 112
Triple truth,* 10
Triple works of the Shingon sect, 157
Triple world,* 127, 129, 158, 161, 222, 223, 250
True and sole teaching, 129
True Dharma, 57, 217
True sutra,* 3
Truth has not been revealed, 9, 12, 22, 69, 72, 164, 238

Ts'ung-i, 191
Tuṣita Heaven, 63, 172
Twelve kinds of scriptures,* 6, 182, 218, 234
Twenty profound doctrines in the theoretical and essential sections, 180
Twenty-eight constellations,* 84, 101
Twenty-four successors to the Buddha's teaching, 164
Two Fascicle Sutra, 20
Two kinds of faith, 70
Two storehouses,* 16, 136, 197
Two Vehicles,* 15
Tz'ŭ-ên, Grand Master,* 21, 70, 114, 164, 193, 196
Universal-Sage Bodhisattva, 14, 36, 53, 54, 70
Upholder of the *Lotus Sutra*,* 27, 36
Upholders of precepts, 13
Utpalavarṇā, Nun , 124
Vaiśravaṇa,* 5, 85
Vajrabodhi,* 165, 166, 183, 202, 224, 227, 248
Vajrasattva, 204, 224
Various gods of the realms of desire and form, 169
Vasubandhu, 19-71, 180-207
Verification of truth with tongues, 23
Verses on the Treasury of Abhidharma, 25
Vimalamitra,* 114, 164, 223
Violate the Buddha's commandments, 87
Virtue Consciousness, Monk,* 57, 120-122, 168, 189, 214
Virtuous, King,* 57, 120-121
Vow of saving all people, 56
Wake no Kiyomaro, 243
Wars and disorder, 85, 103, 115, 150
Wei Yüan-sung, 76, 81(n3)
Wei-chüan, 210

Wheel-turning Noble King,* 10, 158, 159, 173, 224
Wild elephant, 53, 106
*Wisdom Sutra,** 6-40, 63, 64, 127, 165, 190-224, 234, 247
Wiser among ordinary men, 172
Wish-fulfilling gem,* 50, 173
Wonderful-Adornment, King,* 53
Wonderful Voice Bodhisattva, 251
Words and Phrases of the Lotus Sutra, 28, 37, 130(n12), 139, 174, 178, 189, 193, 195
Written challenge, 142
Written opinion,* 132, 135, 142, 145
Written pledge, 160, 240
Wu-tsung, Emperor, 115, 181, 218, 230
Yadoya, Lay Priest,* 96, 133, 135, 139, 141, 220
Yama, King, 166
Yao and Shun, 125
Yellow Emperor, 75-77
Yōkan, Precept Master,* 113, 201, 215
Young Ascetic in the Snow Mountains,* 46, 145, 153, 169, 226
Yu, King, 75, 76, 93, 217
Yüan-chi, 76, 81(n2), 115
Zen sect (school, Buddhism), 68, 132, 135, 136, 145, 156, 157, 171-220, 230, 234-247